SHAKESPEARE'S THEATER

THE MACMILLAN COMPANY
NEW YORK · BOSTON · CHICAGO · DALLAS
ATLANTA · SAN FRANCISCO

MACMILLAN & CO., LIMITED
LONDON · BOMBAY · CALCUTTA
MELBOURNE

THE MACMILLAN CO. OF CANADA, LTD.
TORONTO

Swan   Hope   Globe

THREE BANKSIDE THEATERS

From Vischer's Panorama of 1616.

SHAKESPEARE'S
THEATER

BY

ASHLEY H. THORNDIKE, Ph.D., L.H.D

PROFESSOR OF ENGLISH IN COLUMBIA UNIVERSITY

WITH ILLUSTRATIONS

New York
THE MACMILLAN COMPANY
1916

BRANDER · MATTHEWS
LITTERARVM · IVDICI · CANDIDISSIMO
CVM · DE · RE · SCAENICA · TVM · DE · AMICIS · SVIS
IAM · DIV · OPTIME · MERENTI

PREFACE

In this book I have tried to survey all the information that we possess in regard to the theater of Shakespeare's time. On matters offering difficulty I have endeavored to indicate the evidence and to arrive at some conclusion, in the hope of presenting within the compass of a single volume a synthesis of the subject that will be of service both to the student and the general reader.

Although sometimes the material is of a sort better suited for reference than for reading, it is hoped that other chapters may not wholly lack that wider interest belonging to a history of the stage, and so finely justified in the words of Burke:

> "A history of the Stage is no trivial thing to those who wish to study human nature in all shapes and positions. It is of all things the most instructive, to see not only the reflections of manners and characters at several periods, but the modes of making their reflection, and the manner of adapting it at those periods to the taste and disposition of mankind. The Stage indeed may be considered as the republic of active literature, and its history as the history of that state."

The study of Shakespeare's theater virtually began with the researches of Edmund Malone, which were embodied in his Historical Account of the English Stage, included in his 1790 edition of Shakespeare's works. Although valuable additions in this field were made by the publications of Collier, Halliwell, Fleay, and others, it could still be said, a century after Malone's essay, that our knowledge of the theater of Shakespeare was much less than our knowledge of the theater of Sophocles. The last twenty-five years have changed that. Many investigators have been at work, important documents have been discovered, and the existing evidence has been given new significance. With this large and rapid growth of information and discussion, the general subject has passed into the hands of many specialists. But in hardly any part of the subject have the specialists come to a conclusion. Unfortunately, from the days of Steevens and Malone down to the present time, opposing interpretations have often resulted in prolonged and personal controversies. The time would seem ripe for an amicable approximation toward agreement on essentials. Perhaps this book may be a first step in this direction and prepare the way for a more thorough synthesis.

In undertaking a more comprehensive survey than has hitherto been attempted, I have been at every step indebted to preceding writers, yet often obliged to rely mainly on my own study or judgment. My plan has been to avoid detailed consideration of the arguments pro and con on disputed questions. Nor have I usually been able to take the space to state precisely my points of difference or agreement with the various disputants. In the Bibliographical Notes at the end of the volume, however, I have tried to indicate my obligations to preceding investigators and to furnish the student with directions for more specialized inquiries.

I must also express my indebtedness to the investigations carried on by students under my direction at Columbia University. Some of them have been published, as the monographs of Dr. Albright and Dean Gildersleeve, on which I have leaned very heavily in certain chapters. Others, which have not been published or perhaps even completed, have been of much assistance. My students, indeed, have been my collaborators.

Documents on the theater have been reprinted with so much care and are now so readily accessible that I have rarely reprinted them or even quoted from them at length. In quotations, I have often retained the old spelling, but have not hesitated to adopt a modernized version if demanded by clearness or convenience. Through the great kindness of Mr. W. A. White, I have had access to his large collection of Elizabethan quartos. I am also indebted to Mr. Henry Huntingdon for use of his copy of Messallina; to Miss Henrietta C. Bartlett for bibliographical assistance, and to several of my colleagues, who have read or criticized the manuscript or proofs.

ASHLEY H. THORNDIKE.

February 15, 1916.

CONTENTS

ILLUSTRATIONS

SHAKESPEARE'S THEATER

SHAKESPEARE'S THEATER

CHAPTER I

THE PLACE OF SHAKESPEARE'S THEATER IN THE HISTORY OF THE ENGLISH STAGE

In 1576 James Burbage leased a plot of land to the north of London, just outside Bishopsgate, and built there a wooden building which he called "The Theater." A new epoch had begun in the modern stage; for this was the first permanent London playhouse. Indeed, it was one of the earliest theaters in Europe to be planned and built as a commercial venture. Burbage, a carpenter by trade who had turned actor, had been for some time a member of a theatrical company under the patronage of the Earl of Leicester, and now foresaw that a permanent playhouse might afford larger profits than the innyards and rooms where the professionals had hitherto acted. His enterprise was not accomplished without financial and managerial difficulties, but in the end his shrewd foresight in meeting the public demand for plays brought ample reward to himself and his family.

For more than twenty years the Theater continued in constant use; here Shakespeare acted, here many of his plays were performed, and when, in 1599, the materials of the building were transferred to the south bank of the Thames and rebuilt into the Globe, the great traditions of the Elizabethan drama and stage had been well established. The elder Burbage was succeeded by his two sons, one of whom, Richard, became the most famous actor of his time and the first interpreter of the leading parts in Shakespeare's plays. Through the brothers the family interests were carried on into the Globe and the Blackfriars theaters; so that from 1576 until the Puritan revolution in 1642, the Burbages were leading managers or stockholders in London playhouses. The importance of Burbage's original venture extends, indeed, beyond the lives of his descendants and through the entire course of the English drama. The Theater was the direct ancestor of all English theaters. The careers of its immediate successors were ended temporarily by the Revolution; but some reopened later; and, as we shall see, gave place to the houses of the Restoration, to Drury Lane and Covent Garden, which in turn became the parents of all modern theaters in England and America. From Burbage's Theater we have received, through a direct line of descent, the traditions and practices of the stage, actors, and management.

Our interest in the playhouses which Burbage and others established in Elizabethan London arises primarily from their connection with Shakespeare. He belonged to their companies, and for their stages, actors, and audiences he designed his plays. Such ancient and mutilated records as survive of their methods and activities become precious memorials of his genius, and the imagination is ever vivifying these relics in terms of "Twelfth Night" and "Hamlet." This interest, however, gains a new scope from the discovery that this theater for which Shakespeare wrote was in many ways peculiar, temporary, and transitional. The theatrical conditions were not only very different from those of to-day, they were also different from those which had obtained fifty years before his birth or from those which characterized the stage fifty years after his death. It happens that our greatest dramatist was intimately associated with theatrical affairs at this era of greatest change. His stage is a transitional stage, halfway between the medieval and modern, partaking in some respects of the characteristics of each, but partaking also of the imperfections that come with the breaking from the old and beginning with the new. Even apart from Shakespeare's plays, his era is still one of extraordinary interest in the history of the stage.

It becomes necessary, therefore, at the beginning of this study of Shakespeare's theater to recall its inheritance from the practices of the medieval stage and to note its place in the great changes which characterize the theatrical history of Europe in the sixteenth century. For the sixteenth century stage is everywhere transitional. The new developments in comedy and tragedy that followed the new knowledge of classical drama and theater found the medieval methods of acting and staging already changing. A new class, that of the professional actors, was making itself indispensable; and in each nation of western Europe the modern theater comes into existence as the home of the professionals. The transition from the medieval miracles and moralities is made through various experiments in staging and acting, and often under the direction of school or court; but it ends by placing the modern drama in the hands of professional actors. In different nations, however, this process has its own peculiarities and goes its own gait. In the transitional period national peculiarities become strengthened, and so the stage of Shakespeare offers more points of difference from the stages of the professional actors of France, Italy, or Spain than would be true of the English theater at any later date. It is with the English popular stage that I am to deal in this volume and at a time of unusual national independence. The scope of this book is defined by the activities of the professional companies in this transitional period. It must include the organization of these companies, the relations between management, actors, and dramatists, the governmental regulation of the theaters, the methods of acting, and the habits of audiences, as well as the physical characteristics of stage and theater, and the principles and practice of stage presentation.

It will not be sufficient, however, to view this transitional era as solely an affair of the professionals. The new drama owed much to the courts and schools, and the new stage owed scarcely less. Even in the *Commedia dell' Arte* in Italy and in the popular dramas of Spain and England, the relations of professionals to court are constant and important. Moreover, there is a certain unity in the court theaters of Europe that is lacking in the popular. A representation at Ferrara might be copied almost with exactness for a special performance in Paris or London. An innovation, however expensive, might be immediately adopted in the courts of Europe, and yet remain an impossibility for the public theaters. In England the court stage is sometimes, as in the pageants of Henry VIII, or again in the masques of James I and Charles I, far removed from the simplicities of the public theater, yet there is never a moment that there are not intimate relations and communication between the two. The task of separating their characteristics and defining their interrelations is one of the most difficult that confronts the investigator. So far as the physical stage is concerned, the general differences are, I think, clear. The court stage retained the multiple setting of the medieval stage long after the professionals had discarded this because it was so expensive and cumbersome. On the other hand, the extravagant courts of James and Charles adopted from Italy, in the court masques, moving scenery and some other striking features of the modern stage, while these were prohibited to the professionals because of their cost and elaboration. The peculiar nature of the physical stage of Shakespeare's time is the result of the development in the professional theaters, and little affected by court practice. But these generalizations, whose accuracy must be tested later in this volume, concern only the physical stage. There are many other matters in which a study of the professionals must be supplemented by a trip to court. In the very year that Burbage built his Theater, a certain official of the court made over some rooms in the dismantled Blackfriars monastery, in order that the Queen's choir boys might give plays there before the public. This combination of court and public theater is peculiar to England and indicates one of many fields in which a study of the theatrical doings of the court will be necessary to supplement and correct our main investigation of the professionals.

In this introductory chapter I wish to glance first at the characteristics of the medieval stage, and then at the changes which, working in court, school or

professional company from 1500 on, had already transformed theatrical conditions by the year 1576, when
Burbage raised the flag over the Theater. We may
then better understand why this one item in a long
line of theatrical history is a fit starting point for our
further discussion of the Shakespearian stage.

The long line of theatrical evolution goes back to a
time when the drama was a part of the church service,
when the church was the theater, the nave the stage,
and the clergy the actors. This development, up to
the accession of Elizabeth, has been treated with
great care in Mr. E. K. Chambers' brilliant work,
the "Medieval Stage," and only its main features
need be recalled here, and those chiefly as they affect
our period.

The religious drama of the Middle Ages, which had
no connection whatever with classical drama or stage,[1]
took its origin in the church service; the modern
theater, therefore, has its origin in the church. At
first the choir seems to have been the stage; but as
the drama lost direct connection with the service, it
required more room, and spread from the choir to the
nave, while the audience was crowded into the aisles.
This stage was undecorated; but from the first, certain properties, as the sepulcher, the altar, the cross,
or the manger, were centers of dramatic interest.
After the clergy actors had entered — perhaps in procession — each took his place at some position assigned
to him and often indicated by some property, or by a
chair, or a simple platform against one of the pillars.
When required by the action, he moved from one

---

[1] The survival through the mimes of a theatrical tradition and its effect
on the liturgical drama are, at all events, controversial matters of no importance to our hasty survey.

place to another, but when not taking part in the play he remained quiescent at his appointed station. The essentials of this stage arrangement, then, were fixed places called *loca*, *sedes*, *domus*, or *maisons*, occupied by different actors and specifically designated and localized; and a neutral space, or *plateæ*, without localization or properties. Heaven, Hell, Paradise, the Manger at Bethlehem, the Sepulcher, and other places might all be indicated with more or less elaborate structures, and the actors might speak and act either from their respective stations or on the intervening neutral territory. The essentials of the presentation, so far as they differed from modern or classical practices, were, first, that the actors all remained in sight of the audience throughout the performance; second, that various places could be represented at the same time; third, that the neutral unpropertied *platea* might be used to represent any place whatsoever.

When, by processes that were similar and nearly contemporaneous throughout western Europe, the drama was transferred from Latin to the vernaculars, from clerical to lay actors, and from the church to the market place, it carried with it these essential traditions of stage and staging. More elaborate decoration, more realistic properties, are the natural accompaniments of a growing dramatic art but do not change the methods of presentation. The great out-of-doors religious plays, although varying much in other particulars, maintained fixed and propertied stations for individual actors, and an unpropertied and unlocalized neutral zone. This may be illustrated by one typical stage of which a diagram has been preserved in the manuscript of a fifteenth century morality play, the "Castle of Perseverance."

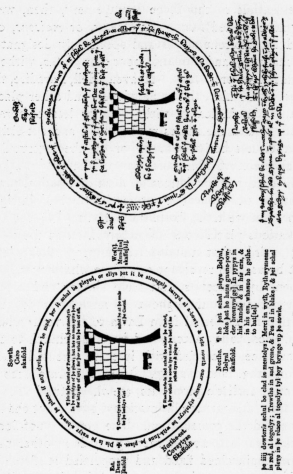

STAGE PLAN OF THE CASTLE OF PERSEVERANCE

In this morality play the various stations are for
actors; in other plays the stations represent specific
places; thus, in another fifteenth century morality
play, there are stations for Heaven, Hell, the Holy
Land, Marseilles and various other places.

While these performances are typical of the principles of staging, there were, of course, many variations. In France, the great provincial mysteries were
usually staged on a platform or a series of platforms
of different levels, erected alongside of the city square.
Here the number of *maisons* might be many and the
arrangement of the stage most elaborate. In England, a distinct development arose through the performance of Biblical plays by the town guilds in
connection with the Corpus Christi festival; and the
York and the Chester plays are familiar examples.
Each manuscript contains a number of plays representing a cycle, which originally contained a larger
number. These short plays, acted in succession, made
up a fairly continuous survey of Biblical history from
creation to doomsday. Each little play was mounted
on a wagon and places for performance were fixed in
the city, where each pageant stopped and its play was
performed. The long procession started early in the
morning and advanced slowly through the city. A
spectator at a given place saw one play after another,
and so, in the course of one day or sometimes two or
three days, witnessed the entire cycle. This method
of performance is called processional, in distinction
from the stationary performance, as illustrated by the
"Castle of Perseverance."

The difference between the two methods was not
so great as these two illustrations may seem to indicate.
Sometimes the wagons were not dragged through the

town, but remained stationary, as apparently was the case with the Towneley series and the *Ludus Coventriæ*. In the processional play, the different pageants seem sometimes to have been regarded as so many *domus* or *sedes* mounted on wheels, while the ground or street provided the neutral place. Thus Noah's ark, or the place of crucifixion, or some other propertied and localized place, was indicated by a particular pageant; and a change of place was apparently indicated by passing from one pageant to another, or even to a subsidiary scaffold erected to represent some other locality. In other cases, however, it is clear that the pageant was a stage by itself carrying both a *platea* and certain structures or *loca*.[1] In any case multiple setting was maintained, although the number of different places that could be represented at once was necessarily limited if the area was small.

In addition to the long cyclical dramas and the early moralities intended for out-of-door performance, there were shorter plays from the Bible, or plays dealing with miracles of the saints, or even plays from secular story, requiring less time, fewer properties, and a simpler stage setting. In France, it is clear that many of these shorter plays, as the Miracles acted indoors by the Puy de Notre Dame, or the later plays by the Con-fréries, had a far simpler stage setting than the great out-of-door plays. Though they might retain a multi-ple setting, the *maisons* would be few; and moralities and farces might be accommodated on a bare stage.[2]

---

[1] For elaboration of this view and criticism of the opinions of Chambers, Albright, *et al.*, see M. Lyle Spencer, *Corpus Christi Pageants in England*, New York, 1911.

[2] For discussion of variety of staging, see D. C. Stuart, *Stage Decoration in France in the Middle Ages*, New York, 1910.

In England we have few records of brief indoor performances before the sixteenth century; but the many performances outside of the Corpus Christi cycles must have afforded some confined and simple stages. The tendency toward a simpler stage may also have been encouraged by the folk plays of the mummers and by the entertainments of wandering acrobats, clowns, and other performers.

During the Middle Ages, however, there is little to indicate any marked departure from the principles of the liturgical performance. We do hear occasionally of one property that was to be of great service later, the curtain. In the eleventh century "Adam," the lower part of Paradise was curtained, so that Adam and Eve could retire from view by stooping behind it. In the Chester pageants the lower story was curtained off as the retiring-room, and in the *Ludus Coventriæ* curtains were sometimes used to discover actors to the audience. Some attempts were being made to discriminate between on and off the stage, and some use was made of curtains. But in general the medieval performance exhibited all its actors before the audience, represented different places at the same time by means of properties, and used the neutral unpropertied space to represent all other places.

In many other respects besides that of staging, the medieval stage handed its traditions down to the sixteenth century. Its drama was in the hands of amateurs, it developed no strictly professional class of actors; but it developed methods and traditions of acting. It undertook the representation of all kinds of scenes and events in the open air, without the aid of a roof, walls, scenery, or artificial light. Its stage was exposed to spectators on all sides. Not only in these general respects, but in the nature of situations, types of character, and methods of acting, it created traditions that influenced Shakespeare's stage. In the matter of costume, for example, this influence can be traced. On costume, medieval plays largely depended for spectacular effects. Certain plays were assigned to certain guilds in order to secure the most attractive exhibition possible of dress and properties. The play of the "Magi" was given to the jewelers, the play of "Noah" to the ship-builders, the play of the "Harrowing of Hell" to the bakers; and the various guilds vied with each other in costly, elaborate costumes, as well as in effective acting. Entertainments, processions, and various celebrations of the court also served to foster public taste for expensive dress and machinery. Costume on the Elizabethan stage was likewise elaborate and anachronistic, and contributed largely to the stage spectacle. However strange and conventional the medieval stage may seem to us, it was often as realistic as its limitations would permit. A practicable ark was provided for the play of "Noah," a lake or sea was represented by an actual ditch, when possible; and a palace, at least by a throne. Compared with modern realistic effects, this stage may well be called symbolic; but it strove to make its mimic world approach as near to the real world as possible, though it cheerfully accepted inadequate means and refused to permit any necessary incongruities to destroy the enjoyment of illusion.

So much for the methods of presenting plays that prevailed in England as late as 1500. All such performances were occasional, given by men ordinarily engaged in other occupations than acting. The medieval theater had neither theaters, nor professional

actors, nor dramatists. It was essentially amateur
and it remained subject to occasion and circumstance,
without attaining self-support, independence, or the
power of free development.

By 1500 the European stage had started on its transitional era. Knowledge of the classical theater as
well as of the classical drama was revived. In Italy
Latin plays were given elaborate presentation, and
humanistic imitations were now acted and not merely
recited. In England neither the classical theater
nor drama was to exercise much direct influence for
another fifty years, and Mr. Chambers is quite right
in including the reigns of Henry VIII, Edward VI, and
Mary in his volumes on the Medieval Stage. But
if both stage and drama were still medieval, both
were changing and multiform. The old miracles and
moralities continued, but farces, secular stories, and
educational and controversial matters competed with
Biblical and moral subjects. The older forms were
giving way to a short morality, usually mixed with
farce, a kind of play that took the name Interlude.

The medieval methods of performance could still
be found, not only in the surviving guild plays, but in
the performance of such new plays as Lindsay's "Three
Estates" and Skelton's "Magnificence," and indeed
in the many other plays given at court, or at some
place where an elaborate presentation could be provided. But this kind of play was gradually disappear-
ing. Instead of out-of-door performances once a year,
the public was coming to desire frequent short plays.
The schools and universities became the chief centers of
dramatic activities, and a class of professional actors
was growing rapidly in importance. The so-called
interludes represent the new method of performance:

very short plays, requiring only an hour or so to
act, and suitable for performance either indoors or
outdoors, by a few actors, on an extemporized stage.
The main difference between this performance and
that of the Middle Ages was the recognition of the
distinction between off and on the stage. Actors no
longer remained in view, unless they were taking part
in the play. Another difference is found in the small
importance given to the *domus* or *loca*. In these
simple performances it was difficult to provide elaborate properties; the stage was generally a small platform, and may be said to represent the medieval
platea. When, however, special places were represented, they seem to have been as carefully propertied
as were the *maisons* and *domus*. In the Interlude,
the drama was brought indoors, given a platform
stage, rendered portable and suited to performances
by the traveling professional companies.

Though the main movement was toward a simplification of the stage to suit the exigencies of the shorter
plays and the traveling companies, there were tendencies in the opposite direction. The court of
Henry VIII in its early years was much given to
entertainments and spectacles. These shows involved
extravagant expenditure on machines, costumes, and
properties. Huge pageants were wheeled into the
halls, laden with imposing castles, bowers, mountains,
or other structures, on which gentlemen of the court
represented some allegorical or mythological device.
These shows with their tableaux and pantomimes and
their accompanying music and dancing, required only
scanty dialogue and bore little resemblance to regular
drama; but they unquestionably encouraged elaboration and not simplicity in dramatic representation. In

the main they offered no marked departures from similar tableaux and spectacles of preceding reigns, though they adopted new devices and amusements from abroad, as notably the Italian Masque. But they tended to preserve the multiple setting of the medieval stage and to elaborate it. In the presentation of a play or any kind of spectacle at court or university, the opportunity was seized for building castles, mountains, and clouds, and for preparing realistic hunting scenes, rainstorms, battles, and so on. Such performances were, of course, by amateurs, gentlemen of the court or university; but they might also be shared in by the professional players of interludes. Indeed, the professionals gained their only status in society as servitors of king or noble, and might earn their living partly by performing at court and partly by traveling from town to town. Further, a special class of actors was created by the employment of choir boys in acting plays. The children of the Royal Chapel gained an especial prominence through their skill in dancing, singing, and acting, and both under Henry VIII and in the early years of Elizabeth's reign surpassed the adult professionals in court favor. The court stage thus tended to create a special set of theatrical practices different from, though not unconnected with, the practices of the professionals.

By the middle of the century another tendency in theatrical matters was created by the acquired knowledge of the classical stage. Definite knowledge of the Greek and Roman theaters first came to the modern world through the researches of the architect Vitruvius, and was disseminated by means of revivals of classical plays, and soon exercised its effect on the different vernacular dramas.   The passage in Vitruvius on stage decoration is not of the clearest, but it was accepted as authoritative.

The "scaena" itself displays the following scheme.   In the center are double doors decorated like those of a royal palace.   At the right and left are the doors of the guest chambers.   Beyond are spaces provided for decoration-places that the Greeks call περίακτοι, because in these places are triangular pieces of machinery (△△) which revolve, each having three decorated faces.   When the play is to be changed, or when gods enter to the accompaniment of sudden claps of thunder, these may be revolved and present a face differently decorated.   Beyond these places are the projecting wings which afford entrances to the stage, one from the forum, the other from abroad.

There are three kinds of scenes, one called the tragic, second, the comic, third, the satyric.   Their decorations are different and unlike each other in scheme.   Tragic scenes are delineated with columns, pediments, statues, and other objects, suited to kings; comic scenes exhibit private dwell-ings, with balconies and views representing rows of windows, after the manner of ordinary dwellings; satyric scenes are decorated with trees, caverns, mountains, and other rustic objects delineated in landscape style.[1]

Italian attempts to reproduce these decorations were doubtless imitated at the English universities and court, but this notion of the classical stage also had a more pervasive effect.   Simplified, it was only an elevated platform with a background through which doors were cut, and this was readily assimilated with the simple stage of the interlude.   In Plautus or Terence, the doors in the back represented houses, but

[1] Vitruvius, *Ten Books on Architecture*, trans. M. H. Morgan, 1914, Book V. Chap. 6.

all the action took place in front of the houses, and this convention was readily enough adopted into English comedy. The Plautian representation of a specified place was readily adapted to the medieval representation of neutral *platea;* in place of the *domus,* doors, in place of the *platea,* a neutral place, not always a particular street, but any street or any place where people can come together to talk. The suggestion of Vitruvius for the Greek satyr play was adopted by the Humanists as suitable to the pastoral.[1] This provided a decoration similar from one view to the medieval simultaneous set, since mountain, cave, and forest might be considered as separate places. It will be observed, however, that this pastoral or satyr decoration was really conceived as a single decorated background for a stage governed by the unity of place. The influence of the classical stage, so far as it can be traced, is away from the multiple set and toward the use of the platform as representing a single place. The provision of several doors in the background manifestly limited the utility of practicable structures or mansions. From the periaktoi seem to have come the first hints for a shifting background and moving scenes.

This classical influence must also be extended to include all its derivatives developed in Italy, France, and Holland. The Terentian Neo-Latin drama had a marked influence on England, and there is some reason to suppose that England also looked to Holland and Flanders for instruction in staging. Professor Creizenach has reproduced a picture of a stage in Antwerp,[2] which bears a very striking resemblance

---

[1] G. Lanson, "Note sur un Passage de Vitruve," *Revue de la Renaissance,* 1904, v. 72.   [2] Vol. IV. 424.

C

to the peculiar form that the stage finally took in England. On the whole, however, the influence of the classic theater on the court or the public stage in England is indeterminate and indecisive. Whatever the variety of theaters or methods of staging, it was not until 1576 that the drama had a permanent and influential abiding place, and not until then do we have any stage or playhouse which can certainly serve as a model for the future.

If the places and methods of presenting plays varied during the first half of the sixteenth century, the characters of the performers varied no less. The schools, perhaps, held the lead as purveyors of the drama, but there were all sorts of amateur performers, and the professional companies were constantly increasing in numbers and popularity. The children, from the choir boys of the Queen's Chapel and St. Paul's, as well as from the public schools, were trained to act before the court, and were in some measure under royal patronage. If you had been a courtier in the early years of Elizabeth's reign, you might have gone to Oxford to see an elaborate performance of a Latin play; or you might have seen an amateur production of an English tragedy on Senecan models by the gentlemen of the Inns of Court; or you might have seen the children of Westminster school or the boys of the Royal Chapel perform a romance at court; or, following the Queen on her progresses, you might have witnessed a splendid pageant at Kenilworth, or have seen some village Holofernes or Bottom marshal his troop in an amateur performance not much less absurd than that given before Theseus and Hippolyta. Had you been a student at the university, or an idle apprentice in London, your range of entertainment would have been hardly less, and you would have had greater opportunity than the Queen herself to witness the performance of the adult professional companies that were now swarming about the country and requiring legal restriction and restraint. These companies, often composed of only five men and a boy, obtained a license from some gentleman or nobleman, and were thus exempt from the statute against beggars and masterless men. They wandered about England, acting where they might, in moot-hall, school, private house, church, or on the village green. Records of their performance are scanty, and few plays of this period that can certainly be attributed to them have been preserved; but by the first twenty years of Elizabeth's reign, in quantity, not in quality, of dramatic entertainments, the professionals doubtless surpassed the amateurs.

Through these different classes of entertainers the drama had come to have a greater importance in the life of the people than ever before. At school or court it might be subordinate to particular purposes of education or entertainment; but in the country at large and in London in particular it had become a popular and almost a universal means of amusement and culture. If the conditions of its control were still varied and tentative, there was no question of its importance in the daily life of Englishmen. Puritans and sober-minded citizens might protest, but the stage had made its way into both palace and tavern, and its actors had found a daily occupation in ministering to the public. The moralists found difficulty in rescuing even Sunday from the drama's conquests.

Amid all these varied theatrical conditions, one fact stands out as of first importance: the steady

and rapid progress of the professional companies. In
1572, the statute compelling them to obtain a license
from some nobleman reduced the number of adult
companies, but strengthened those that remained,
which henceforth were known as Lord Leicester's
men, Lord Howard's men, etc. The stronger of these
companies now established themselves in London,
with the support of the court and against the opposition of the city authorities and the protests of the
moralists. They acted at various places, usually at
innyards, until the regular theaters were built. The
building of Burbage's theater, 1576, was followed immediately by another, and in 1583 a company of
selected players was licensed under the Queen's direct
patronage. The date 1576, therefore, marks not only
the erection of a permanent theater, but the establishment of professionals rather than amateurs as the
chief purveyors of the drama.

In later chapters we shall have a glance at court
performances, pastorals, and masques which departed
from the practice of the public stage, and we must
remember that various kinds of performers long continued as rivals of the professionals. For a time, indeed, the child actors at court affected the course of
the literary drama as decisively as did the adult companies. But the year 1576 also marks a change in
their career. In that year a company of these children
was established in an indoor theater in Blackfriars and
gave plays to the public. Somewhat intermittently
for the next thirty years the child actors were rivals
of the adults. But, although they still retained some
special connections with the court, they were henceforth semi-professionals and their rivalry was for the
favor of London audiences. Their careers are no

longer important at court; they rather form a part of the record of the public stage. They constitute a modifying but not a determining factor in the future development of the theater. From 1576 on, the professional companies took charge of the drama, and they kept it in their hands until the Puritan revolution; the traditions and methods, the stage, and the principles of staging which they inherited from three centuries of dramatic history remained henceforth in their custody. Of the nature of their plays before 1576 we have little direct information, and we shall have to rely mainly on inference; but it must be clear that they adopted simple and flexible arrangements as far as possible. As soon, however, as they became established with some degree of permanency as organized companies in regular places of entertainment, with an established repertory, their practices unquestionably became more fixed. The English stage was henceforth in a position to determine its own organization and methods.

The changing conditions that I have summarized for England find a general parallel throughout western Europe in the rivalry between amateurs and professionals, and in the transition from the medieval to the modern method of staging. The court performances, always indulging in elaborate decorations, were similar in the capitals of Europe, and underwent the same process, their expensive spectacles changing from the multiple setting to successive scenes. In this process the influence of the classical stage played a considerable part. The professionals, while developing along parallel lines from extreme simplicity to some kind of established method, yet present many national variations. In Paris, for example, a simplified multiple set was maintained by the comedians of the Hôtel de Bourgogne until well into the seventeenth century, and provided the means for staging the plays of Hardy. In Italy, the forty plays in Scala's scenarios, 1611, all require street scenes after the fashion of Roman comedy, and the public performances by his company, the Gelosi, in the sixteenth century were clearly given on a very simple stage.[1] In Spain, the wandering actors established themselves in permanent theaters in the cities at just the time when Burbage was building in London, and developed a stage very similar to that in England, except that their stage was a recess and not a projection. Later, Lope de Vega accepts the triple decoration proposed by Vitruvius.[2] Everywhere there was a confusion of old and new methods of staging, and a condition of theatrical management tentative and changing. The use of the curtain, for example, is everywhere experimental and uncertain with various peculiarities; and there is some confusion between the principles of the simultaneous set, of the classical stage, and of successive sets concealed and discovered by curtains. Contemporary conditions on the continent must always be kept in mind and are often valuable in confirming or correcting an interpretation of English circumstances. But in our period the stage history of the professionals is a national affair and rests on the examination of detailed evidence that will not often take us outside of England.

Our survey of the medieval stage and of the changes at work in the sixteenth century has brought us back again to Burbage's theater as a starting point for our further discussion. It is, however, manifestly

[1] *The Commedia dell' Arte*, Winfred Smith, 116 ff.
[2] *L'Arte Nuevo de hazer comedias en este tiempo*, vv. 350–351.

impossible to set the beginning of the transitional epoch in the English theater absolutely at this point. I shall often return to the period 1500 to 1576 to examine the changes which were then taking place and establishing practices that later prevailed. The end of our period is definitely marked by the closing of the theaters in 1642 on account of the Civil War. The later years of the period have, however, little that is significant for my discussion, although they are of interest in the signs they offer of the changes that were postponed to the Restoration; women actors, footlights, moving scenes, and a theatrical monopoly. To the reign of Charles I and to the Restoration itself I shall turn from time to time for evidences of conditions preserved from Shakespeare's day. My main interest, however, is with the Shakespearian period, or more exactly, the period from 1576, twelve years after Shakespeare's birth, when Burbage built the Theater, until 1625, nine years after Shakespeare's death, the year when Fletcher died and Charles I came to the throne. The chronology within this limited period often becomes a matter of moment, for it is essential to view the conditions which we are studying as never static, but as always changing. Nevertheless, the stage history of this Shakespearian period has a very striking unity, fixed, as has been observed, by the existence and interrelation of permanent theaters and by the growth and continuity of the leading companies of professional actors, and still more by the amazing wealth of dramatic literature which gives to those two generations of theaters and actors a preëminence over their predecessors and followers.

CHAPTER II

THE theater belongs to the city. In the country it always has had to eke out a spasmodic or itinerant existence; amid the many activities of a large and crowded population, it has found its abiding place. Its actors and playwrights have ever catered to the tastes and pleasures of the citizens and have been wont to regard the countryman as something of an outsider. In the city they have found not only the support and patronage of audiences, but the incentives of a stirring and complex life for their inventions and impersonations. There that form of literature which concerns itself most directly with the contrasts and conflicts of human motives and passions finds its material and its inspiration. Its great periods in the past are associated with Athens, Paris, and London; and in modern times the theater's allegiance to city life seems to be growing more and more intense.

During the Middle Ages, London does not appear to have been an important dramatic center. Just as in France the great open air mysteries are found in the provincial towns rather than in Paris; so in England, York, Chester, and Coventry, rather than London, are the homes of the great religious plays. In the Elizabethan era, however, all dramatic interests focus in the metropolis. Local organizations of actors disappear, and the provincial towns have to rely on the visits of traveling companies. Some of these wanderers never acquire a home in the city, but all such remain of secondary importance to the leading London companies. No other city, except Dublin for a few years in the reign of Charles I, supports a regular theater; but London usually has five or six. Ever since, it has continued the dictator of the drama in Great Britain and, at least until recent years, in the United States as well. In its theaters play acting first became a flourishing and prosperous profession. There the traditions of the English stage were formed and fostered, and thither came Marlowe, Greene, Shakespeare, and the rest to write plays. There were the great actors and writers, the new plays, and the new fashions. The country might have an abundance of dramatic entertainment; but London was the head and fount of it all.

The London to which Shakespeare came was still in many respects a medieval town; it was bounded by a defensive wall, guarded by the Tower, and its center was the great cathedral church of St. Paul's. Its shops and residences were mostly small and mean, huddled along narrow alleys, almost impassable for traffic, and broadening here and there into market places. In contrast to the private dwellings were the great palaces and castles along the river; and the multitude of churches made the city appear from a distance like a grove of spires clustering about the great central tower of St. Paul's. The buildings of the religious orders, dispersed within the memory of many, were also numerous and extensive both without and within the walls, and were now given over to philanthropic or private purposes. Within the precincts

HOLLAR'S VIEW OF LONDON, 1657

This shows four theaters on the Bankside in the foreground.

of the old monasteries of Blackfriars and Whitefriars, theaters were later to find a place.

The city was still practically bounded by the river and the wall, although just without, the suburbs were growing rapidly. Beginning with the Tower on the east, the wall described an arc, of which the river was the chord, and which extended to the Fleet on the west, a distance of over two miles in circumference. This wall was pierced by some nine gates, from which highways ran into the country. Two of these, Bishopsgate and Cripplegate on the north, are of special interest, because in the fields just beyond them were built some of the earliest playhouses. West of the Fleet, the jurisdiction of the city extended only to the Temple, where that of Westminster began. Along the riverside were the palaces of Savoy, Whitehall, and others, and building was practically continuous as far as Westminster Hall. From the south, the only approach was by the London Bridge, which, with its twenty arches and its handsome rows of houses, crossed the Thames to Southwark. Here there was a considerable town with the Tabard Inn, much as Chaucer had known it two hundred years before; and west of the bridge along the Bankside was the future site for Shakespeare's theater, the Globe. From the landing place one looked north across the river to the roofs and towers of the city beyond and the hills stretching to the horizon. Often, indeed, Shakespeare's thoughts as he gazed must have passed from the motives and manners of the crowd which he observed so intently, to their mimicry which was his daily calling; from the city of church and market and palace, to the playhouse that had inscribed over its door *Totus Mundus agit histrionem.*

Of the daily life of the Londoners in Elizabeth's reign we are well informed through the plays; they give a brilliant panorama of city and country, of court and street. They seem, however, to the modern reader to devote a disproportionately large space to the affairs of courts and kings, to insurrections, conspiracies, and palace intrigues, to councils, coronations, and embassies. But the affairs of the court played certainly a much larger part than they do to-day; they were important, not only in the imaginations of the poets, but in the daily affairs of every citizen. Every one, everywhere, had to give way to the Queen's pleasure or interest; every cargo of fish brought to London wharves must wait a certain time in order that the court might have the first choice, and so with every load of fruit or vegetables brought from the country. A multitude of men obtained employment in various services under the direct control of the great officials, or in the retinues of the great nobles. A large proportion of the population was directly dependent in some way on the court. On the other hand, the public relied on the court in part for its entertainments, its spectacles, processions and pageants; and various royal palaces and the homes of nobles were the chief embellishments of the city. The expenditure of court and courtiers was on a scale of lavish extravagance, whether for banquets, buildings, masques, or processions. Even parsimonious Elizabeth left a wardrobe of three thousand dresses; and under James I the reckless expenditure and display ran to the limits of extravagance. The interest of every one was attracted also by the affairs of the court or dynasty. These occupied the share of man's attention which political interests do to-day. Upon the affairs of the Queen and the great nobles the interest of all was centered. The careers of Mary Stuart, of Leicester, of Essex, — in whose rebellion the theaters became directly concerned, — of Bacon and Raleigh, were the subjects of daily talk. The average citizen might be an official at court, or derive from it some monopoly, or be dependent on its patronage for the success of his trade. At all events, he witnessed its pageants, found it interfering with his occupations; and as his interest and affairs extended beyond his daily trade, he was especially attracted by the ambitions and achievements and scandals of princes and dynasties.

Between the nobility and the common people in the nation at large there was a wide gulf, not yet filled by a large and prosperous middle class. In London, however, the middle class had already risen to prosperity and influence. The citizens of wealth, — bankers, promoters, and great merchants, — were all-powerful in municipal matters, and there was a still larger class of prosperous traders and manufacturers. Of the professional classes, lawyers were perhaps the most important, and certainly the most closely connected with the theaters. There were hundreds of gentlemen, mostly younger sons, who came from all parts of England to reside for a time in the Inns of Court. They had leisure and culture and exercised an influence not altogether unlike that of a university. In dramatic entertainments they took an active part, performing in plays or masques for the entertainment of the queen, and they seem to have been among the most active patrons of the public playhouses.

The mass of inhabitants were, during Elizabeth's reign, only emerging from the condition of filth, disease,

and slavery which during the Middle Ages had characterized even so wealthy and independent a city as
London. The population as a whole was still unclean,
ill-fed, and poorly housed; though in these, as in
other respects, there was during Elizabeth's reign constant improvement. In London there were probably
few who did not have at least enough to eat. The
city would seem to us very unsanitary; the sewers
were open, and there were many complaints of the
stench in the markets and along Fleet Ditch; but it
must be admitted that the Thames was still unpolluted,
famous for its pure water and its swarms of fish. The
water supply, however, was inadequate; it had out-
grown the old wells and depended in part on water
raised by mills from the river, and on small supplies
brought from a distance. Relief was finally supplied
in 1614, with the completion of the New River system
erected through the enterprise of Sir Hugh Middleton.
Public benefactions became numerous and were manifest in the erection of splendid buildings and in the
foundation of hospitals. There was, however, little
scientific attention as yet paid to the prevention or
cure of disease. The plague continued its terrible
devastation; in fact, England was hardly free from
it at any time; year after year there would be some
deaths, and the great visitations of 1593, 1603, and
1625, taken together, resulted in one hundred thousand
deaths in London alone. Under such risks the span
of life was much shorter than to-day. Elizabeth, in
fact, was the first English sovereign to live to be over
seventy, and the chances of such length of life were
very small. Still, after the Spanish Armada, the
nation had peace, and in spite of the plague the population of the city increased rapidly. Including the

suburbs and Westminster, it must have numbered two
hundred thousand by the end of Elizabeth's reign, probably double what it had been at the beginning, and by
the outbreak of the Civil War it had increased at least
fifty per cent more.

The time when the drama flourished was a time of
great commercial prosperity. Like other eras remembered chiefly for their intellectual and artistic ideas,
for their contributions to politics or literature, this era
doubtless seemed to its own men chiefly distinguished
for peace and material prosperity. Life was rapidly
growing more comfortable; houses were better, windows were becoming common, and the ordinary necessi-
ties were within the means of most. The increase of
luxury was notable, and it brought the same sort of
condemnation that we hear to-day. Men of wealth
and also poor scholars traveled on the continent for
education and pleasure, and brought back new tastes,
new vices, and new fashions. The fashions in clothing,
both for men and women, were indeed variable and
extraordinary. Legal enactments were resorted to in
order to limit the width of the ruff and the farthingale.
Forks were introduced from the continent and also
toothpicks, which were used ostentatiously. Within a
decade after the introduction of tobacco, London had
become a city of smokers. Coaches came into general
use, and caused the same protests of extravagance and
danger that the automobiles do to-day. They must
also have resulted in some improvement in the streets;
for by the reign of James I their use was general and a
great crowd of them waited outside the Blackfriars
theater.

It was a time of increase of wealth, the amassing of
great fortunes, and also a time of extravagance, luxury,

and idleness. The reaction from all this came in the steady growth of Puritanism, of the insistence on a stern and restrictive morality. By the beginning of the reign of James I, tendencies toward a corrupt society and toward a moral reform were both marked, and are frequently the subjects of the drama. The plays satirized, on the one hand, the Puritans with their dislike of plays and amusements; and, on the other hand, the various classes of the newly rich, the new knights who would purchase their honor at the expense of their estates, the city wives who must ride in coaches and go to court to masques, and the city men who strove to imitate the fashions and manners of the courtiers. If there had been no commercial prosperity, there would perhaps have been no Puritans; certainly there would have been but few theaters. The theater itself is a luxury; it must depend in large part on the rich, on those who have an excess of time and money. But in Tudor England it was not by any means altogether dependent on the noble and wealthy; it attracted all idlers, and there were many in London who could afford a holiday.

The life of the average citizen, while closer to death and disease than to-day, was not without a good deal of recreation. London was a part of Merry England and lived outdoors as much as possible. The houses and shops opened on streets, and shopping, marketing, bargaining, and visiting were all carried on largely in the public thoroughfares. Holidays were spent in the fields beyond the walls, in ball playing, running, and jumping, or in archery and military drill. There were also cockfights and bull and bear baiting.

The favorite places for these amusements and for outdoor sports were in the fields to the north and

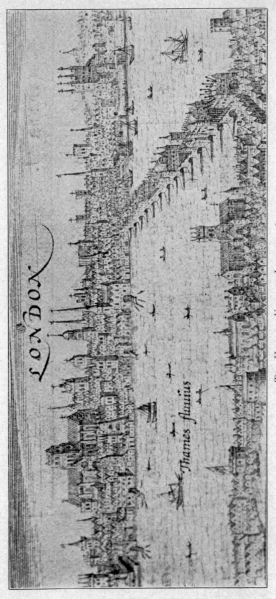

LONDON

Thames fluuius

THE HONDIUS VIEW OF LONDON, 1611

across the river to the south. When, as we shall see, the theaters were forced outside of the city limits by the magistrates, they were naturally located in places long used by amusement seekers, at Newington Butts, a place for archery to the south of the Bankside, or in the fields to the north. The amusements, however, with which the playhouses became rivals were not all of an innocent kind. Close by the Globe on the Bankside were the Stews, houses of ill fame which were driven out from the city and maintained themselves in the Clink under the sovereignty of the Bishop of Winchester. Hard by the theater was the bear garden, where bears fought with dogs. One interesting variation was afforded by a fierce blind bear, Old Hunks, who was assaulted by men who lashed him with whips, while he struggled to the limit of his chain in his efforts to reach his tormentors. In looking back at a past period, one is always struck both by the resemblances to the present and also by the differences. Nearly everything about Elizabethan London has some parallel to-day; but perhaps the most obvious contrast with our more sophisticated civilization is in the incongruity with which the Elizabethans mingled jewels and filth, pageantry and disease, brutality and poetry. "Midsummer Night's Dream" competed with the attractions of the Stews, and Hamlet contended with Blind Hunks for the patronage of the crowd.

The government of the city was under virtual control of the twelve great Livery companies, the successors of the medieval Trade Guilds. These, by one method or another, elected the mayor, sheriffs, aldermen, and councilmen. Although these companies bore the names of the various trades — grocers, goldsmiths, drapers, fishmongers, etc. — they were all really

D

managed by the merchants, capitalists, and employers.
They represented the conservative interests of property
and business, exercised, on the one hand, against the
encroachments of the court and centralized administration, and, on the other, against the revolutionary
instincts of the mob. The jurisdiction of the magistrates was confined to the city proper, substantially
the territory bounded by the wall. Over certain outside wards, and over the borough of Southwark to the
south, the jurisdiction was in dispute; and other Liberties were outside of the control of the city corporation.
These, later, were the refuge of players and of various
other persons who feared authority. Of these Liberties, Holywell, Finsbury, on the north, Blackfriars
and Whitefriars within the city limits, and the Clink
and Paris Garden across the river, furnished sites for
the playhouses. From the first, the erection of theaters
or, indeed, the acting of plays was vigorously opposed
by the city authorities. Naturally, therefore, the
players repaired to the Liberties where they had a
direct appeal from local objectors to the Court, represented by the Lord Chamberlain and the Privy Council.

In the matter of playhouses and regulation of the
drama, as in various other questions of government,
the city and the court found themselves in pretty
constant opposition. If the amount of patronage
furnished the players by the court was limited, they
were at least sure of a certain amount of protection
and support. Naturally, the arguments offered by
the court in defense of the theater show a certain
sympathy with this form of "honest recreation" and
also urge that, as the players are to provide entertainments for the Queen, they should be allowed a chance
to practice and should be supported in order that

they might adequately provide for the Queen's pleasure. Moreover, the court was always asserting the principles of central administration and of paternal government, against the local independence of the city. In the end, the players were taken under the direct patronage of King James and other members of the royal family and under the direct management of his court officers. The city corporation, after a long struggle, had to rest content with keeping the public playhouses outside of the city and with preventing performances on Sunday. The opposition to the theater by the city was doubtless in part due to moral and religious grounds, but perhaps in larger part to direct social causes, — to the dangers that the theaters offered for rioting, fire, and the spread of the plague.

These three dangers were among those most constantly feared and guarded against by the corporation. London was already a city of crowded buildings and a swarming population, presenting in some measure most of the problems that engage modern municipal governments. The danger of rebellion and sedition was prominent in the minds of all Tudor and Stuart monarchs, and the danger of rioting was equally prominent in the mind of every property holder. The force of constables, 240 in number, though much admired by the chronicler Stow, seems to have been active chiefly at night and to have been asleep or inefficient by day. At all events, rioting was constant during all of Elizabeth's reign, and frequently broke out at the theaters. The assembling of crowds and the excitement of plays, sometimes of an incendiary order, were naturally viewed as dangerous. Within the city these would have added to the crowded conditions and led to extensive outbreaks, a danger that was not avoided even by building the theaters in the fields outside. The danger from fire was not less feared than that from rioting. Already strict building laws were being enacted to limit the erection of wooden buildings and to encourage buildings of stone. The erection of wooden theaters lighted by torches and introducing fireworks on the stage was an obvious danger within the city. Still more to be feared was the dissemination of the plague through the crowds gathered for a theatrical performance. An attempt was made at an early date to prohibit play acting during the plague season, and an extended correspondence between the city and court authorities, in 1582–84, shows an active discussion of the proper measures to be employed both within the city proper and in the localities outside its jurisdiction. After the theaters came directly under royal control, their patents sometimes forbade acting when the deaths from the plague exceeded a certain number weekly. During most of the reigns of James and Charles this number was fixed by ordinance at forty. For these reasons the city corporation may well seem justified in its continuous hostility to the theaters. The opposition, both for these social causes and also for moral and religious reasons, increased among the soberer class of citizens up to the triumph of Puritanism and the final overthrow of the playhouses.

It is not easy, however, to fix the exact legal limitations which were at any time enforced against the theaters. Even if we have record of definite enactments, we usually have also indications that they were not rigidly enforced. The public playhouses were driven outside of the city limits, but some acting in innyards continued, and after a while some private theaters established themselves within the city proper. Playing on Sunday was frequently forbidden, but apparently was never absolutely prevented. In spite of the care taken against riotous assemblages, rioting frequently broke out in connection with theatrical performances, and even led to the demolition of the playhouses themselves. Ordinances for the suppression of performances during the plague did not work with a mechanical regularity, and the players were eager to avoid them whenever public opinion or the support of the court gave them a chance. Although the actors met with constant opposition on the part of the city authorities and the upper middle classes, they could usually rely not only on support from the court, but on the enthusiastic approval of a large body of the citizens.

Shakespeare's theater was a democratic institution, and the public seems to have been very fond of plays. The city of 200,000 inhabitants often had six theaters giving regular drama at one time, and they were kept open summer and winter, when the government did not interfere. When it is remembered that a considerable portion of the citizens opposed the theaters on moral grounds, the patronage of the public must seem astonishing. It seems safe to say that a larger portion of the public frequently attended plays than at any subsequent period. The regular drama had a popularity like that of the movies to-day. And certainly this London public was composed of a most diversified and appealing set of individuals. We know them through the men and women of the plays, and how many varieties of human nature and what intense individualities are there represented! It would not be safe to believe that the London average was quite equal to that of the thousand characters of Shakespeare's plays; yet we cannot doubt that he drew his thousand from the varied pageant that this little city afforded. The Elizabethan drama, in its *dramatis personæ*, has a still larger and more diversified population; but, after all, its astounding multitude is only the dramatic reflection of the inhabitants of Elizabethan London.

CHAPTER III

THE PLAYHOUSES

THE professional companies, as we have seen, for a time played wherever opportunity offered, and especially in the innyards of the city. They were accustomed to large rooms, small rooms, or to the open air. In the provinces they acted in moot hall, or inn, or church, and at court they performed in spacious halls. In the city, however, when the audiences were large, the problem of a sufficiently ample and inexpensive acting place was first solved by the innyards.[1] The London inns were numerous and of much importance in both the business and recreation of the day. They served the purpose of modern hotels, restaurants, and clubs, and they were the natural resorts of all kinds of amusement makers and seekers. They were generally built in the form of a hollow square, with a narrow entrance leading to an interior courtyard, around which ran galleries connecting with the rooms in the upper stories. Here was a place most convenient for the players, who

[1] References to innyards are not uncommon, as in the following passage from the city ordinance of Dec. 6, 1574: "greate Innes, havinge chambers and secrete places adjoyninge to their open stagies and gallyries." See also reference to the Bell Savage and Paris Garden on p. 41. Often, however, it cannot be determined whether a reference is to an inn or an innyard. It seems likely that interior rooms may have been sometimes used. On this point, see T. S. Graves, *The Court and the London Theatres during the Reign of Elizabeth*, Menasha, Wisconsin, 1913.

could set up a platform in the yard against one side of the building, and act their plays any afternoon when the weather was pleasant. A curtain hung from the gallery in the rear might provide a dressing room or conceal needed properties, as in the later playhouses; and the gallery itself might be used for an upper stage if desired. The audience must pay at the gateway, and could then stand in the yard or find seats in the galleries. Naturally, when the players built their first theater, they followed the general plan and arrangement of the innyard. One other kind of building also had some influence as a model, the rings or amphitheaters for baiting bears and bulls. These were rude circular structures with scaffolds or galleries encircling the ring. Since the first playhouses were used for acrobatic performances, it was doubtless felt that the innyard arrangement might well be given a circular form, affording every one a good view of the performers, as at the bull rings. But in the main the outdoor theaters were modeled on the innyard.

This development from the innyards to the roofless playhouses is strikingly paralleled in Spain.[1] In Madrid and Seville permanent places were first provided for the professional actors in yards or *corrales*, a name which has since continued to be used for playhouse. The *corral* was a yard or square surrounded by the walls of houses, the windows of which served as boxes or galleries. The stage was erected at one side and most of the audience stood on the ground. In the seventies, these yards gave place to partially roofed wooden buildings very much like the Theater and Curtain which were built at the same time in London.

[1] Rennert, *The Spanish Stage in the Time of Lope de Vega*, 1909.

For many years, however, after permanent theaters
had been erected in London, plays continued to be
given in the places for bear baiting and in the innyards. As late as 1614 we find the Hope theater
designed for both plays and bears; and after a few
years of divided allegiance it was given over wholly
to bear-baiting. Innyards seem to have been used
for plays, at least to some extent, until the outbreak
of the Civil War. Of the playing places within the
city which were closed shortly after the building of
the Theater, at least three were innyards;[1] but these,
the Cross Keys in Gracechurch Street, the Bell Savage
on Ludgate hill, and the Bull in Bishopsgate Street
within,[2] must have been shortly reopened, for they
long continued to be the homes of the drama. In
1582 the Earl of Warwick wrote to the Lord Mayor
requesting that his servant "play his provest prizes
in his science and profession of defence at the Bull
in Bishopsgate street, or some other convenient place."[3]
In the 1596 edition of Lambarde's "Perambulation of
Kent," we find the Paris Garden, the Bell Savage, and
the Theater spoken of as places where pleasant spectacles may be had for "one pannie at the gate, another
at the entrie of the scaffold, and the thirde for a quiet
standing."[4] In 1589 Lord Strange's company, to

---

[1] See a passage in Richard Rawlidge's *A Monster Lately Found-Out*, 1628,
quoted by Prynne, *Histrio-Mastix*, 1633, p. 492. The two other playhouses
mentioned as closed about 1580 are "that nigh Paul's" and "the Whitefriars." Pauls and Whitefriars may have been inns, as Fleay suggests, but
Paul's was probably a room in connection with the singing school. See p. 62.

[2] The Bull and the Bell Savage are mentioned in Gosson's *School of Abuse*,
1579. From Keysar's lawsuit we learn that the elder Burbage was arrested
in 1579 on his way to a play at Cross Keys. C. W. Wallace, "The First
London Theater," *Univ. of Nebraska Studies*, 1913, p. 90.

[3] *Remembrancia, Index*, 351, reprinted *Malone Soc. Coll.*, I. i. 55.

[4] Halliwell-Phillipps, *Outlines* (7th ed.), I. 373.

which Shakespeare perhaps already belonged, was
playing at the Cross Keys.[1] Another important innyard was the Boar's Head in Eastcheap, where the
Queen's men were playing regularly as late as 1603.[2]
We occasionally hear of other inns as playhouses, as
of the Bell in Gracechurch Street, which furnished a
"well counterfeit" for a court performance in 1577;[3]
and doubtless there were many frequently resorted to
by minor companies. Howes mentions five that were
converted into playhouses, and Flecknoe in 1664[4]
declares that some remains of the theatrical apparatus
were still to be seen in the innyards of the Cross
Keys and the Bull in Bishopsgate.

The passage just referred to in Howes' continuation
of Stow's "Survey," 1632, gives us our most authentic
information of the number of regular playhouses
between 1576 and 1642. "This (Salisbury Court) is
the 17th stage or common playhouse which hath been
new made within the space of three score years within
London and the suburbs; viz., 5 inns or common
hostelries turned to playhouses, one cockpit, St.
Pauls singing school, one in the Blackfriars, and one
in the Whitefriars, which was built last of all in the
year 1629. All the rest not named were erected only
for common playhouses, besides the new-built bear
garden, which was built as well for plays and fencers'

---

[1] Collier, *H. E. D. P.*, I. 272.   See also reference to their playing at Cross
Keys in a letter of 1594.   *Remembrancia*, 353 ; *Malone Soc. Coll.*, I. i. 74.

[2] Fleay's errors about this innyard, *Stage*, 145 ff, have been corrected by
Miss Gildersleeve, *Governmental Regulation*, 232, and by W. W. Greg, *H. D.*,
ii. 107.   See also *Remembrancia*, 355 ; *Malone Soc. Coll.*, I. i. 86, which shows
that Oxford's and Worcester's companies were acting there in 1602.

[3] Feuillerat, *Revels Accounts of Queen Elizabeth*, 277.

[4] *A Short Discourse of the English Stage*, 1664, reprinted by Spingarn,
Critical Essays of the Seventeenth Century, II. 92.

prizes as bull baiting; besides one in former times in Newington Butts." The five hostelries turned to playhouses and the bear garden, or Hope theater, have already been noticed. The playhouse at Newington Butts was probably one of the earliest. It was about a mile south of the Globe, and was used by Lord Strange's actors in 1592, and by Strange's and the Admiral's in 1594; but we know nothing more about it. The other theaters I have rearranged and numbered for convenience of reference. The eight public playhouses, including the Hope, were in the order of erection: (1) the Theater, (2) the Curtain, (3) the Rose, (4) the Swan, (5) the Globe, (6) the Hope, (7) the Fortune, (8) the Red Bull. The private houses are all mentioned by Howes, if we understand by one title the several houses which at different times answered to that name. They were: (9) Paul's Singing School, (10) (11) the Farrant and Burbage Blackfriars, (12) Salisbury Court, rebuilt Whitefriars, (13) the Cockpit or Phœnix.

In the remainder of this chapter I shall note the principal facts known about the erection and subsequent history of each building, beginning with the public theaters. Facts concerning the external appearance, construction, and the general arrangement of the interior will be examined; but all matters pertaining to the stage itself and details of the interiors connected with that will be reserved for the next chapter. From our summary here we may hope to arrive at some conclusions on the characteristics of the two classes, public and private playhouses, on the similarities and dissimilarities among the particular theaters, and also on the general course of theatrical activity.

(1) THE THEATER[1] was built in 1576 in the fields in St. Leonard's parish, in the liberty of Holywell in Shoreditch, on a plot which had formerly been a part of the site of Holywell Priory.[2] Access was to be had either by the main road from Bishopsgate to Shoreditch church, or across Finsbury Fields, then the great playground of London. The property was leased on April 13, 1576, by Giles Allen to James Burbage of the Earl of Leicester's company, who spent, according to a statement made in legal papers, six hundred pounds in constructing a playhouse. It was built of wood and was probably round in form with galleries about the pit in the center, like the other public playhouses,[3] but no picture of it survives. Stockwood in his sermon at Paul's Cross, August, 1578, calls it "the gorgeous playing-place erected in the fields."[4] It was used for other "activities" than plays, for fencing, and doubtless for tumbling, ropedancing, etc.; and possibly it had a movable stage. When the lease expired in 1597 a dispute arose between Allen and Cuthbert and Richard, the sons of John Burbage, over its renewal. During the dispute, 1597–98, the Burbages still remained as tenants, but they finally

[1] For full information and documents on the Theater, see Halliwell-Phillipps, *Outlines*, I. 345-375, and C. W. Wallace's "The First London Theater," *Univ. of Nebraska Studies*, 1913.

[2] "The church being pulled down, many houses have been their builded for the lodgings of noblemen, of straungers born, and other; and neare thereunto are builded two publique houses for the acting and shewe of comedies, tragedies, and histories for recreation, where of the one is called The Courtein and the other The Theatre, both standing on the south-west side towards the Field." Stow, *Survey*, ed. 1598, p. 349. For the exact site see W. W. Baines, "Holywell Priory and the Site of the Theatre, Shoreditch," London County Council — *Indication of Houses of Historical Interest in London*. Part xliii. 1915.

[3] It must have been one of the "four amphitheaters" of wood mentioned by De Witt as existing about 1596.   [4] Halliwell-Phillipps, *Outlines*, I. 351.

took advantage of their rights in the lease, and in December–January, 1598–99, they pulled down the Theater and carried the timbers to the Bankside, where they used this material in erecting the Globe.

(2) Within a few months of the building of the Theater in 1576, THE CURTAIN was built close by, probably on the south side of Holywell Lane. It is shown in Ryther's view of London, 1604, and in one in Hughson's London.[1] In both the playhouse is very small, but clearly round in shape; and it was doubtless very like the Theater, and the later Swan and Globe. The name, curiously enough, has nothing to do with a theatrical curtain, but had long been applied to the land on which the Curtain was built. It was in control of Henry Laneman in 1585, when he entered into an arrangement with Burbage of the Theater to share equally the profits of the two playhouses for seven years.[2] Various companies occupied the playhouse during Elizabeth's reign, and at the accession of James it became the home of the Queen's men. It is referred to as late as 1627, and probably was in existence at the closing of the theaters.[3]

From the neighborhood of Bishopsgate we must now journey across the city, over the bridge, to the borough of Southwark. Turning west from the bridge, we come first to the great church of St. Saviour's, and then to Winchester House, the London seat of the bishop of Winchester. Continuing west along the river, we pass without the jurisdiction of the borough of Southwark into the liberty of the Clink and are in the famous Bankside, a strip running along the

---

[1] I have been unable to discover the source and authenticity of this map.
[2] C. W. Wallace, "First London Theater," *Univ. of Nebraska Studies*, 1913, p. 149.   [3] Middlesex County Records, quoted by Ordish, 107.

bank to the liberty of Paris Garden. The total distance from the bridge to the Paris Garden landing, opposite Blackfriars, was about three-fourths of a mile. The portion of this included by the Bankside contained many dwellings, taverns, and the notorious stews. A few hundred feet back from the river, and we are in open fields crossed by brooks and open sewers — a bad district to get about in during the winter, so the old theatergoers thought.

From time immemorial this district had been devoted to the keeping of dogs, bulls, and bears for baiting, and thither butchers had long been permitted to bring offal from the city. About midway between the bridge and the Paris Garden landing, and a few hundred feet from the river, there had been for many years two amphitheaters, one for bull baiting and one for bear baiting, with surrounding kennels and stables. These appear in several of the early maps. They were in the liberty of the Clink, but were apparently generally known under the name of Paris Garden, which was strictly applicable only to the adjoining liberty on the west. It was probably the destruction of one of these amphitheaters that was known as the Paris Garden disaster of 1583. Of the playhouses, the Swan, built directly south of the Paris Garden landing, was the farthest west.

The Hope, a few hundred yards to the east of the Swan and not much over two hundred feet from the river, was on the site of the western amphitheater (at first used for bull baiting and later for bear baiting). A few hundred feet to the east was the Globe, nearly on the site of the eastern amphitheater. Somewhat to the south of these theaters and between them was the Rose. These last three made a triangle which if fenced could not have included much more than an acre of ground. Although many contemporary views of the Bankside show one or more of these buildings, only one shows all four theaters. This is the engraving of London by Hollar, first published in the "Londinopolis" of James Howell, 1657, but representing the

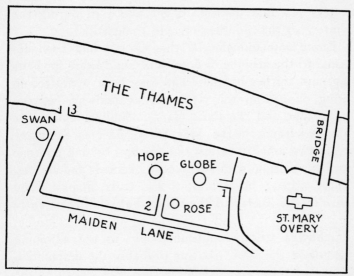

THE BANKSIDE

¹GLOBE ALLEY   ²ROSE ALLEY   ³PARIS GARDEN LANDING

actual conditions of 1614–20. In this, however, the locations do not correspond exactly with those determined upon by antiquarians. Vischer's View of 1616 shows three theaters, the Swan, the Hope, and the Globe, in correct positions.[1]

[1] The locations indicated in the text are somewhat different from those assigned by such authorities as Halliwell, Ordish, and Rendle; and are the results of the discovery by Professor C. W. Wallace of a document in the Coram Rege Roll, 1616, described by him in letters contributed to the

It must be added, however, that several early views oppose the locations stated in the text. Merian's, 1638, and Hollar's, 1647, show a theater to the north of the Hope and the Globe, and the edition of the Porter-Ryther map in the Crace collection (see Morton, Surrey Arch. Col.) shows a theater to the south of Maiden Lane. But of course these Views cannot be relied upon for accuracy.

(3) THE ROSE is the first theater known to have been built on the Bankside, but the exact date is not certain. In 1585 the lease of the property known as the Little Rose, north of Maiden Lane on the corner of Rose alley, was assigned to Philip Henslowe,[1] and on January 10, 1587, he formed a partnership with a John Cholmley looking toward the erection of a play-house on a parcel of this, ninety-five feet square and already containing a small tenement. Probably the playhouse was built immediately;[2] at all events the

London Times on October 2 and October 4, 1909. The document deals with a lawsuit brought by Thomasina Osteler, a daughter of John Hemmings, in regard to shares in the Globe and the Blackfriars; and it recounts the particulars of the lease of the land on which the Globe was erected to the Burbages and their associates. The plot of land, 200 by 156 feet, is described as adjoining Maiden Lane on the South. Hitherto the Globe had been located by antiquarians on the south of Maiden Lane, due mainly to confusion because a second Globe Alley existed there. The location of the Rose north of the Hope was in accord with Hollar's Views, but Henslowe's lease clearly puts it close to Maiden Lane, and therefore south instead of north of the Bear Garden. For a full discussion of the evidence, see C. W. Wallace, London Times, April 30, May 1, 1910; William Martin, Surrey Archæological Collections, XXIII, 1910 (examining early views and summarizing evidence against Mr. Wallace's document), and Arthur Bonner, Trans. London and Middlesex Archæological Society, 1912, II. iii. 334–355, which seems final in its conclusions.

[1] These and following details about the Rose are taken from Greg, H. D., II. 43–55.

[2] It is referred to as "new" in the Sewer Records of April, 1588, according to Prof. Wallace, London Times, April 30, 1914.

Lord Strange's men were acting there on February 19, 1592, when Henslowe opened his account with them in his Diary, a book destined to be one of our main sources for the stage history of its period. There are building accounts in the Diary dated 1592, but in the opinion of Mr. Greg, these refer to extensive repairs rather than to the original building. From them we get only slight information about the house, which was of wood, round, and open to the sky in the middle, but with a thatched roof over the galleries. In addition to the galleries, there was a tiring room in the rear of the stage, a ceiled room over the tiring room (probably the balcony at the rear of the stage but possibly a Hut like those of the Swan and Globe), a lord's room or box also ceiled, and a mast for the flag. Later repairs in 1595 include "making the throne in the heavens, £7 2s.," and seem to imply considerable alterations above the ceiled room. The Rose is represented clearly in Norden's map, prepared by Van der Keere in 1593, which shows its relative position to the Bear garden. It cannot be identified with any likelihood with any of the theaters in other maps.[1] Henslowe's Diary gives an extensive, though not complete, account of plays and companies at the Rose until 1603. In 1605 Henslowe's lease expired, and we do not know what arrangement was made in regard to the theater. Henslowe's son-in-law, Alleyn, paid tithes on the property in 1622,[2] and it was used for prize fights after 1620.

---

[1] Not in the views of Ryther, Vischer, or Hondius; and its identity with any of the playhouses in Hollar's Views is doubtful.

[2] Herbert's Office Book, quoted by Malone, 1821 *Var.*, iii. 56. Rendle, *Bankside*, xv, says it was burned.

E

(4) THE SWAN was built about 1594 by Francis Langley, a well-to-do property holder.[1] From Vischer's view and the map published by Rendle it appears to have been a twelve-sided building similar in external appearance to the other theaters on the Surrey side. It was doubtless used for plays, 1595–97, and was occupied during parts of 1597–98 by the Lord Pembroke's men.[2] After 1598 it was the scene of several non-theatrical exhibitions,[3] but was not used regularly for plays until 1611. Then for four years it was occupied, and again in 1621. After that, it was given over to prize fighters. We know of only one play certainly acted there, Middleton's "A Chaste Maid in Cheapside," about 1611–14. In 1614 the Hope was built for both plays and bear baiting, and, except for a few specified differences, was "made in all things and in such form and fashion as the Swan." It is probable that the Swan, like the Hope, was not long used for plays; and it seems a fair inference that the two houses were less well adapted to acting than were the other public theaters.

The picture of the interior of the Swan reproduced on page 51 has played a larger part in recent discussions of the Elizabethan stage than it deserves. It was first discovered, together with a written description in manuscript, in the university library of Utrecht,

[1] On Nov. 3, 1594, the Mayor prayed that Mr. Langley's new stage or theater on the Bankside may be prevented. Rendle, *Bankside*, xxvi n. On May 1, 1598, the Swan is spoken of as new.

[2] See C. W. Wallace, "The Swan Theater and the Earl of Pembroke's Servants," *Englische Studien*, 1911. The new documents presented by Professor Wallace entirely supplant previous attempts to write the history of Pembroke's men.

[3] Wilson's extempore, 1598, noted in Meres's *Palladis Tamia;* Ordish, 271. Acrobats, 1600. See license, *Acts of Privy Council*, Nov. 6, 1612. Vennar's *England's Joy*, Nov. 6, 1602, announced but not played.

testum

Porticus

sedilia

orchestra

ingressus

mimorum ædes.

proscænium

planities siue arena.

THE SWAN THEATER.

and was published in 1888 by Gaedertz. It was reproduced more accurately in the "Transactions of the New Shakespeare Society" for 1888, with an accompanying article by H. B. Wheatley, F.S.A. Both drawing and description were apparently copied into the commonplace book of one Arend van Buchell from an account, oral or written, of John de Witt, who visited London, probably about 1596. The description, which includes the Theater, Curtain, and Rose, as well as the Swan, is in Latin and may be given in Archer's translation:

There are in London four theaters [amphitheatra] of noteworthy beauty, which bear diverse names according to their diverse signs. In them a different action [varia scæna] is daily presented to the people. The two finest of these are situated to the southward beyond the Thames, named, from the signs they display, the Rose and the Swan. Two others are outside the city towards the north, and are approached "per Episcopalem portem"; in the vernacular, "Bishopgate." There is also a fifth, of dissimilar structure, devoted to beast-baiting, wherein many bears, bulls, and dogs of stupendous size are kept in separate dens and cages, which, being pitted against each other, afford men a most delightful [jucundissimum] spectacle. Of all the theaters, however, the largest and most distinguished is that whereof the sign is a swan (commonly called the Swan theater), since it contains three thousand persons, and is built of a concrete of flintstones (which greatly abound in Britain) and supported by wooden columns, painted in such excellent imitation of marble that it might deceive even the most cunning [nasutissimos]. Since its form seems to approach that of a Roman structure, I have depicted it above.[1]

This description is probably wrong in the two most important of its few particulars. Hentzner, another

[1] *The Universal Review*, June, 1888; quoted in Ordish, 268.

traveler, declared in 1598 that all the theaters were of wood, which agrees with our other information.[1] Again, it seems impossible that the Swan could have held three thousand persons; one half that number would have been the maximum.[2] If the description is inaccurate, how about the picture?[3] That rests on no very authentic evidence. It is of uncertain date, based on hearsay evidence, drawn from description and not from any direct observation. The drawing, indeed, represents things which could not be seen at the same time from any single point of view. It is, moreover, self-contradictory, for, while the stage is evidently removable, it sustains the pillars which support the heavy superstructure. Further, there is no sign of curtains such as appear in other pictures of Elizabethan stages, and such as are known to have existed in most, if not all of the theaters. The drawing does, however, present the leading features common to Elizabethan theaters. The circular interior, the three tiers of galleries, the stage extending into the pit, the balcony in the rear, the two doors, the hut overhead, the flag and the trumpeter, the heavens or shadow supported by pillars — were all the usual accessories of the public theaters. As to the curtains or arras, common on other stages, for which no place appears in this picture, the omission may be another mistake on the part of de Witt or van Buchell. The

[1] Mr. G. P. Baker thinks De Witt may have been misled because the exterior was plastered.

[2] Mr. John Corbin in an article in the *Atlantic Monthly*, March, 1906, argues that the Swan may have held 2500.

[3] For full discussions of this picture, see Albright, *Shakespearian Stage*, 39, 40, and W. J. Lawrence, "Some Characteristics of the Elizabethan-Stuart Stage," *Englische Studien*, xxxii. 44-48, and for a defence of its value, Neuendorff, *Die Englische Volksbühne im Zeitalter Shakespeares*, Berlin, 18 ff.

"hangings, curtains" of the Swan are alluded to in a letter of 1602,[1] but it is possible that there were no curtains in 1596.[2] The movable stage confirms other evidence that the playhouse was used mainly for non-dramatic entertainments, and lessens the importance of the Swan as a representative theater. A discussion of other pictures of interiors will be postponed to the next chapter, when all the evidence in respect to the arrangement of the stage can be considered. The picture of the Swan, the only contemporary drawing of a specified theater, has detained us here : first, because it is the best picture we have of the interior of an Elizabethan theater, and therefore illustrative of the matter of this chapter; and, second, because it has small value in determining questions of the normal Elizabethan stage, and therefore figures little in the detailed discussions of staging in the two following chapters. It should be adjudged as a hasty and self-contradictory drawing on hearsay evidence of the interior of a playhouse that was virtually abandoned for plays within a few years after it was built.

⌐ (5) Directly east of the Hope and on the north side of Maiden Lane, THE GLOBE was built in 1599 by the Burbages, in part from the timbers of the Theater. It was round, with a thatched roof over the galleries ; and its general construction is known to us, because the Fortune, built in the succeeding year, was, according to its contract, in most respects modeled

---

[1] Chamberlain's *Letters*, Camden Soc., 163. See T. S. Graves, "A Note on the Swan Theatre," *Mod. Phil.*, Jan. 1912.

[2] The only play which we know to have been acted at the Swan, Middleton's *A Chaste Maid in Cheapside*, contains this stage direction (III. 2): "A bed thrust out upon the stage: Allwit's wife in it." But such directions sometimes imply a discovery by curtains.

after the Globe. In 1613, during a performance of a new play, "All is True" (Shakespeare's "Henry VIII"), "set forth with many extraordinary circumstances of pomp and majesty, even to the matting on the stage," it caught fire and burned to the ground, the actors and audience escaping with difficulty through its two narrow doors. It was at once rebuilt, octagonal in form, with a tiled roof, more substantial construction, and a more ornamental interior.[1] The first Globe, the home of Shakespeare's company, had been at the time it was built the finest public theater in London, and the new Globe reasserted this primacy. Though the King's men now used the Blackfriars as their winter theater, they continued to act in the Globe during the summers until the Civil War. It remained the home of the drama long after the other playhouses on the Bankside had been given up to other purposes. In 1632 Donna Hollandia, looking forth from her fortress — one of the stews — beheld the "dying Swanne, hanging down her head, seeming to say her own dirge" and the Hope, which "wild beasts and gladiators did most possess"; but the Globe "was still the Continent of the World, because half the year a World of Beauties, and brave Spirits resorted unto it."[2] The house was pulled to the ground on April 15, 1644.[3]

(6) THE HOPE,[4] built in 1614 for Philip Henslowe, was according to Vischer's view an octagonal structure. The building contract required that it should

[1] The first Globe is shown in the view by Hondius, and the second in the view of Vischer. The second theater is also represented in Hollar's Views and others, but not in correct locality.

[2] N. Goodman, *Holland's Leaguer*, 1632.

[3] Collier, *Life of Shakespeare*, ccxiii. C. W. Wallace, *London Times*, April 30, May 1, 1914.

[4] W. W. Greg, *H. D.*, ii. 66–68. For contract, *Henslowe Papers*, Mun. 49.

be closely modeled on the Swan. It had external staircases leading to the galleries, a removable stage supported on trestles, a heaven over the stage, but supported by the main structure and not by pillars as in the Swan, foundations of brick, and a tile roof. It was designed for bear baiting as well as the drama. The Lady Elizabeth's men acted there certain days of the week for a year or two; but no plays, so far as we know, were given there after 1616. It was standing in 1632,[1] and was used for prize fights and bull baiting as late as 1682.[2]

In order to visit the other public theaters, we must now leave the Bankside, take boat across the river, and pass through the city again to the north. A few minutes' walk beyond Cripplegate brings us to Golden Lane, where, in 1599, Edward Alleyn, the famous actor, bought the assignment to a lease of a considerable property. By 1610 he had become sole owner. Here, in 1600, the Fortune was erected under control of Alleyn and Henslowe.

(7) The building contract for THE FORTUNE [3] gives us the fullest details which we possess in regard to the construction of any Elizabethan theater.[4] It was square, measuring 80 feet each way on the outside, and 55 feet on the inside, the difference allowing for large galleries. The framework was of wood, the foundation of brick, the three stories 12, 11, and 9 feet in height, the two upper stories overhanging ten

---

[1] See quotation above from *Holland's Leaguer*.

[2] Rendle, *Playhouses at Bankside*, 18.

[3] For the contract see *Henslowe Papers*, ed. W. W. Greg, Mun. 22; and for the information in regard to the theater, *Henslowe's Diary*, ed. W. W. Greg, II. 56–66.

[4] It is found in Ryther's and Hughson's views; but they are on too small a scale to be exact.

inches, and the galleries were 12 feet 6 inches in depth.
Four divisions were made for the gentlemen's rooms
and others for the twopenny rooms, but the locations
are not specified. The galleries and rooms were provided with seats; the rooms had ceilings; and the
framework of the whole interior was lathed and plastered. The galleries and stage were roofed with tiles,
paled with oak, and floored with deal. A shadow or
heaven over the stage is not described, so we cannot
tell whether it was supported by pillars or not. A
tiring room was provided in the rear of the stage,
taking the place of the gallery, and perhaps built
out in the rear. The width of the stage is specified
as 43 feet, and it extended to the middle of the yard
— $27\frac{1}{2}$ feet deep to the gallery, 40 feet to the rear
wall. This gave a space in the pit of six feet between
the stage and the gallery on either side. In all points
unspecified the building was to be like the Globe,
except that all the chief supports were to be square,
"wrought pilaster-wise" with "carved proporcons
called Satiers," referring, probably, to the pillars
supporting the galleries. Alleyn's memorandum book
states the expenses of the property as £240 for the
lease, £520 for building the playhouse, £440 for obtaining a freehold of the land, £120 for other buildings,
making a total of £1320. The Fortune was occupied
immediately after its erection by the Lord Admiral's
men, who became the Prince's men at the accession
of James I, and long continued one of the chief companies. On December 9, 1621, the Fortune was
burned. The new theater, completed in 1623, was
round and of brick. Wilkinson reported that the
building was still standing in the first years of the
nineteenth century; and published in his "Londina

Illustrata" a picture that has often been reproduced.[1]
But this cannot have any resemblance to the round
Fortune of 1623, though it is barely possible, as Wilkinson asserted, that portions of the galleries of the
old playhouse were still recognizable in the interior
of the building of 1811. In 1650 the people of St.
Giles petitioned for permission to use the dismantled
theater as a place of worship, with what result we
do not know. In 1661 the whole property was ad-
vertised for sale.

(8) THE RED BULL theater was located in Clerken-
well on the upper end of St. John's Street, but the
exact date of its building is not known. There was a
performance of a puppet show in St. John's Street
(on August 23, 1599), during which the house fell and
two persons were killed;[2] and there was some sort of a
building, perhaps an inn, known as the Red Bull,
prior to the building of the playhouse. By 1605 the
playhouse had been built, for in that year it was leased
by the builder, Aaron Holland, to shareholders, including some of the Queen's men.[3] The patent to the
Queen's men, dated April 15, 1609, authorizes them
to act "at their usual houses of the Curtain and the
Red Bull." As the preceding patent of 1603 mentions
the Boar's Head innyard as the second house,[4] it is
probable that the Red Bull was built between 1603
and 1605, and first occupied by the Queen's company,
which long continued there. In 1633 it had, according to Prynne, been lately "reëdified and enlarged."
The picture published in Kirkman's "Wits" (1672)

---

[1] Vol. II. The plate was printed in 1811; the books in 1825.

[2] *Shak. Soc. Papers*, IV. 45–6.

[3] See documents published by C. W. Wallace, "Three London Theatres,"
University of Nebraska Studies, 1909, Woodford *v.* Holland, p. 304.

[4] See draft in Collier, *H. E. D. P.*, i. 336–7. *Malone Soc. Coll.*, I. 3.

and often republished as "the interior of the Red Bull theater," has no authenticity.[1] We learn from Howes that the Red Bull was a public theater; hence it was probably like the Globe and the Fortune in general construction. It sought patronage of more vulgar audiences than the Globe, Fortune, or the private theaters, and was the constant object of girds at the vulgar and sensational character of its plays and acting. During the Protectorate there were various attempts, in 1648, '49, '54, and '55, to reopen this house. In spite of orders commanding the officers to "pull down and demolish all Stage galleries, Seats, and Boxes, erected and used for the acting or playing, or seeing acted or played such Stage plays," it survived until after the Restoration. According to Wright's "Historia Histrionica," the King's players acted publicly at the Red Bull after 1660; but by 1663, according to Davenant, "the house was standing open for fencing, no tenants but old spiders."

From these brief summaries of our information and from the contemporary views, it is evident that the public playhouses were very much alike. The Curtain, built in 1577, was still used at the time of Shakespeare's death. The Hope, in 1614, was modeled on the Swan, built twenty years before. All except the square Fortune were round or nearly round in form. All probably had galleries, pit, stage, and tiring room, after the general fashion indicated roughly in the drawing of the Swan, and more exactly in the contract for the Fortune. Perhaps the chief distinction to be noted is that the Hope and probably the Swan were designed to be used as bear gardens, and were provided with movable stages. Other stages may also

---

[1] Albright, *Shakespearian Stage*, 40–42.

have been movable, but certainly not those of the
Globe and Fortune. These two long continued the
largest and most important of the theaters. Though
they gave way to the increasing importance of the
private houses, they were still used as summer theaters, and together with the Red Bull were occupied
by leading companies until the closing of the playhouses. The Red Bull alone carried the traditions of
the open air public theaters into the period after the
Restoration.

We come now to the so-called "private playhouses."
The origin of the name is doubtful. It is used as applied to the Blackfriars theater in connection with the
efforts of the city government to close that and other
theaters.[1] In this controversy, extending from 1596
to 1608, the actors and their patrons are careful to
describe the Blackfriars as a private house, attempting
thereby to remove from it the opprobrium which the
authorities attached to "common or public theaters."
The city authorities and the inhabitants of Blackfriars, nevertheless, persisted in applying this oppro-
brious term to the Blackfriars theater. From this
time, however, the name "private" is commonly used,
and gained a quasi legal recognition in the patents of
1619 and 1623. The term, however, does not cor-
rectly indicate the distinction from the public theaters,
for the private theaters were managed like the public;
the professional companies used them, admission was
charged, and they were open to any one who would
pay. They were also, like the public theaters, sometimes rented for special performances. They differed
from the public houses in that they were roofed and
artificially lighted; that their performances were in-

[1] Gildersleeve, *Government Regulation of the Elizabethan Drama*, p. 184.

doors by candle light, there were seats in the pit; and that a higher admission was charged than at the public theaters, and apparently the audience was from a more select class. The private houses were also smaller than the Globe or Fortune, and seem to have permitted the gallants to sit on the stage more freely than did the public theaters.[1]

In their origin the private theaters were closely associated with the children's companies. By 1576, and possibly earlier in Elizabeth's reign, the child actors gave plays in public as well as at court. These public performances may have been on private premises and were presumably indoors, in rooms smaller than the Theater or the Curtain, in order to suit the voices of the children. "Campaspe" and "Sapho and Phao," two of Lyly's earliest published comedies (1584), were acted at Blackfriars, and other of his plays at Paul's. Rawlidge's "A Monster Lately Found Out" (1628) alludes to the closing of a place for plays in White-friars and another "nigh Paul's." Fleay thought that these were innyards, but they were more probably interior rooms. At all events, we know that there were regular playing places at Paul's, Blackfriars, and Whitefriars, at an early date.

(9) Of the playing place "nigh PAUL'S," we know that the Paul's boys gave plays in public regularly for a time in the eighties and again, after a suppression for some years, from 1599 on.[2] About 1606 this playing place, then described as "neere St. Paul's church," was discontinued, according to the statement

---

[1] Baskerville, "The Custom of Sitting on the Elizabethan Stage," *Mod. Phil.*, April, 1911.

[2] On December 24, 1578, a letter from the Privy Council to the Lord Mayor mentions the Paul's boys as allowed to play "within the city." Malone, *Variorum*, III. 432.

in Keysar's lawsuit.[1]   It was most likely a room in the singing-school as mentioned by Flecknoe and Howes.[2] It was within the city walls, but may have escaped the prohibition of the city authorities because it was in the private school buildings, or it may have had special protection from the court.

(10) Concerning the FIRST BLACKFRIARS theater, new light has come from recently discovered documents.[3] On December 20, 1576, Richard Farrant, master of the children of the chapel at Windsor, leased from Sir William More six upper chambers within the late dissolved priory of Blackfriars, 146 feet in total length, and from 22 to 25 feet in breadth. Just what the location and size of the theater were, is not clear; but the six rooms included part of the Frater, or refectory, of the old Priory later leased by the Burbages, and so Farrant's theater may have included a portion of the floor space occupied by Burbage's later theater.[4] In any case it must have been a small room not over 25 feet in width. For some years this theater was occupied by various companies of children, and

[1] Documents, publ. by C. W. Wallace. *Univ. of Nebraska Studies*, 1910, p. 355.

[2] Professor G. P. Baker, *Endymion*, cxiv–cxvi, and *The Development of Shakespeare as a Dramatist*, p. 46, suggests that the playing place was in the courtyard of St. Paul's cathedral, and Murray, *English Dramatic Companies*, I. 325, agrees. But it would seem certain that this theater, like that of the Children of the Chapel, was indoors.

[3] From the Loseley Mss. Those pertaining either to Farrant's or to Burbage's theater are published by A. Feuillerat in the *Malone Society Collections*, II. i, 1913. See also "The Origin of Shakespeare's Blackfriars Theatre," A. Feuillerat, *Jahrbuch*, 1912, and the "Evolution of the English Drama," C. W. Wallace, Berlin, 1912.

[4] This seems indicated by the documents and is, as I understand it, the opinion of Feuillerat. But I confess I cannot see any sure indications for the exact location of the theater. Wallace thinks it occupied only the two north rooms, 46 by 25 ft.

was for a time, in 1583–84, under control of John Lyly. In May, 1584, Sir William More regained possession of the premises.

(11) The second Blackfriars theater was made out of buildings purchased by James Burbage from Sir William More, the deed dating February 4, 1596.[1] At this time Burbage seemed likely to lose his lease on the Theater and apparently desired to secure a new playhouse in Blackfriars. Apparently there were no plays there for several years, but on September 2, 1600, Richard Burbage let the building to Henry Evans, who was financing a company of the chapel children,[2] for twenty-one years.[3] The premises deeded by Sir William More included "All those seaven greate upper Romes as they are now devided, being all upon one flower and sometyme being one greate and entire rome." Later, after the building was remodeled, the theater is spoken of as "the great Hall or Roome." [4] It would seem to correspond with the Frater of the old Blackfriars, a room 52 by 107 feet, containing only a sixth less floor space than the Fortune. On the basis of an unpublished document, Professor Wallace fixes the dimensions as 66 by 46 feet, occupying only the south part of Burbage's seven great rooms.[5] It was probably provided with galleries. In the new theater, the Children of the Queen's Chapel, or of Blackfriars,

[1] Halliwell-Phillipps, *Outlines*, I, 299–300. *Malone Soc. Coll.*, II, i, 60 ff.

[2] Fleay, *Stage*, 127 ff.

[3] *Ibid.*, 230. Where the children had been acting from 1584–1600 is unknown. They were doubtless suppressed for most of the time. Fleay's (*Stage*, 125) conjecture that they occupied Blackfriars, 1597–1600, has been shown to be unfounded by E. K. Chambers, *Mod. Lang. Review*, Jan., 1909.

[4] *Ibid.*, 211.

[5] C. W. Wallace, "The Children of the Chapel at the Blackfriars Theater," *Century Magazine*, September, 1910, and "The Evolution of the English Drama," 195, 196.

as they now came to be called, won an immediate popularity. The building of the theater was opposed by the citizens of the neighborhood and by the authorities of the city;[1] but as Blackfriars, though within the walls, was a liberty not under the jurisdiction of the Lord Mayor, these protests did not avail against the direct support of the court and the Queen. Later on, Evans got into difficulty, owing to his high-handed practices in seizing boys for his company; but the theater continued. In 1608[2] it was taken by the Burbages, and was henceforth used in connection with the Globe by the King's men. From 1619 on, and perhaps from an earlier date, it was used during the winter months, the Globe being reserved for the summer season. Until the closing of the theaters, the Blackfriars continued to be the most fashionable and one of the most profitable of the London playhouses. Here were produced the plays of Shakespeare, Jonson, Beaumont and Fletcher, Massinger, and Shirley. The theater was destroyed in 1655.

Another Blackfriars theater was probably built 1615–17, and perhaps used once or twice, but promptly suppressed.[3]

(12) WHITEFRIARS was a notoriously disreputable district, until 1608 without the jurisdiction of the Lord Mayor, and before and long after that date the resort of criminal classes who claimed the right of sanctuary that belonged to the old monastery. The district, also called Alsatia, is well known from Scott's description in his "Fortunes of Nigel." As we have

---

[1] Gildersleeve, 184 ff.

[2] Fleay and Murray (I. 153, and II. Appendix E) think the theater was not opened by the King's men until December, 1609, or later. See note p.241.

[3] Fleay, *Stage*, 264. Gildersleeve, *Governmental Regulation*, 198.

seen, it had long been a place for plays; but of a theater there before 1590 nothing is known beyond the mention by Rawlidge. Keysar's suit against Burbage [1] refers to a well established company acting there in 1608–10; and Keysar received payments for performances at court in the Christmas season of 1609–10 by the Children of the Whitefriars.[2] Rossiter's company of Revels, which was organized by 1610, acted presumably in the same theater until 1613,[3] when they received a patent to build a theater. This playhouse, which may have been the third in Whitefriars, lasted until 1629, when it was supplanted by "a fair new playhouse" in SALISBURY COURT near by; and this continued to be used until after the Restoration, when it in turn gave way, about 1670, to a new theater close by, known as the Dorset Garden.

(13) THE PHŒNIX, also known as the COCKPIT, probably because of its former use, was also in the Whitefriars region on Drury Lane. It was built in 1616, and though greatly damaged by the rioting apprentices on Shrove Tuesday of the following year, remained one of the leading theaters until the Civil War. It was the scene of Davenant's opera in 1658, and it continued in use after the Restoration until a new theater was erected close by, the direct predecessor of many famous Drury Lane theaters.

The private theaters from our summary appear for a time connected with the children's companies. In the last few years of Elizabeth's reign, one of these

---

[1] *Univ. of Nebraska Studies*, 1910.

[2] E. K. Chambers. *Mod. Lang. Review*, January, 1909.

[3] Malone, 1821, *Variorum*, iii. 52 n. Gildersleeve, 64. Rossiter's patent of 1610 refers to acting "within the Whitefriars," *Malone Soc. Coll.*, I. 3. See also Keyser *vs.* Richard Burbage *et al.*, Publ. *Univ. of Nebraska Studies*, 1910, p. 355.

companies at the Blackfriars gained a special importance as a rival of the adult companies. From 1608 on, this theater became the home of Shakespeare's company, and henceforth the private houses seem to have increased rapidly in importance. The later theaters, Salisbury Court and the Cockpit, were in size and form, as we learn from the "Historia Histrionica," exactly the same as the Blackfriars; and these two continued to be used after the Restoration. They thus carried the Elizabethan theatrical tradition over the suppression of twenty years, and they, rather than the public houses, doubtless served as models for Restoration theaters. What changes, if any, the private theaters introduced in the staging of Elizabethan plays, will be considered in a later chapter; but it may be noted that the same plays were regularly performed by the same companies at both the public and private playhouses.

I have now run over the principal items of information which we possess in regard to the seventeen playhouses enumerated by Howes. These comprise several classes: innyards, private and public theaters. The innyards and the private houses were generally within the city proper, although the latter were built in Blackfriars and Whitefriars, precincts which remained outside of the jurisdiction of the city until 1608. The public theaters were all outside of the city, some to the north, and some closely grouped on the Bankside. The differences that existed among these theaters seem on the whole less marked than their general similarity; for, whenever a new theater was built it seems to have been modeled on one existing, and the Curtain was regularly used from its erection in 1577 through the reigns of Elizabeth and James I and well into that of Charles I. During most of this period there were at any one time five or six houses where licensed companies regularly acted. There were doubtless generally more places where plays were occasionally given, and a considerable number where exhibitions of one sort or another — fencing, puppets, cock fighting, bull baiting — sometimes gave place to more dramatic entertainments. But the number of places where the Londoner could regularly see a play, seems rarely to have exceeded six.

The number of performances given weekly varied with the theaters and companies. The innyards and public theaters were dependent upon the weather; and the flags on top of the Bankside houses were necessary in order to inform the public when a play was to be given. The children's companies seem to have acted only one or two days a week;[1] and there was a similar limitation on performances at theaters which gave non-dramatic exhibitions a part of the time. In the private houses the performances seem to have been daily, and in the public theaters, daily when the weather permitted. Concerning the prices of admission, which ranged as widely as to-day, varying from a penny to a half-crown, and concerning many other details of staging, acting, audience, and management, there will be much to say later. Here, however, a word may be added as to the owners. The ownership of a theater or of a long lease was entirely distinct from a share in a company. A theater might be rented to a company or to a group of companies for a fixed sum or on shares; but in any case the profits

---

[1] The Diary of the Duke of Stettin, Pomerania, who visited London in 1602, says the Blackfriars children are required "to act a play every week." *Trans. Royal Soc.*, 1892, IV. 26 ff., quoted by Wallace.

made by a shareholder in the company would be on a different basis from those made by a housekeeper or owner of the theater. However, the theaters were generally owned or controlled by men interested in the companies; and, indeed, they eventually came largely into the control either of the Burbages or of the Henslowe-Alleyn partnership.

The Burbages gave members of their company shares in their theaters, and hence Shakespeare became a part owner of both the Globe and Blackfriars. The Burbages, however, controlled the Theater, Globe, and Blackfriars; and Henslowe and Alleyn controlled the Rose, the Fortune, the Hope, and possibly at times the Swan.

A brief chronological summary will indicate the general course of the theatrical history. Before 1576 the place of the theater was mainly supplied by innyards, and perhaps inside rooms where the children's companies acted. From 1576 to 1590 there were only two regular theaters, the Theater and the Curtain, but some of the innyards still continued to supply performances in spite of prohibitions, and the two children's companies had regular places, probably within doors, one of which in Blackfriars has been identified. On the Bankside two amphitheaters provided for bull baiting and bear baiting, and plays may have been given in some of the innyards; but as yet there were no theaters. Possibly there were plays, and even a playhouse to the south, at Newington Butts.

From 1590 to 1603, *i.e.* from Shakespeare's first play to "Othello," was a time of great activity. Henslowe first appears on the scene with the Rose, where various companies acted, and where by 1596 the Lord

Admiral's men were firmly established. The Swan shortly followed the Rose on the Bankside, but the companies using it are unknown, except the Earl of Pembroke's in 1597–98. The Burbages, when threatened in 1596 with the loss of the Theater, secured a new house in Blackfriars, but leased it to the Children of the Chapel, and in 1598–99 transferred the Theater bodily to the Bankside, where they rebuilt it as the Globe. Here Shakespeare's company, then known as the Lord Chamberlain's men, was established. Immediately after the advent of the Burbages on the Bankside, Henslowe and Alleyn built the Fortune beyond Cripplegate, a theater as large as the Globe, and thither the Admiral's men were moved, the Earl of Worcester's men going to the Rose. Meanwhile, the Paul's Boys at their singing school and the Children of the Queen's Chapel at the new Blackfriars were proving dangerous rivals to the adult companies.

At the accession of James I, a virtual monopoly was given to a few companies. The Chamberlain's men became the King's men and acted at the Globe and (after 1608) at the Blackfriars, under the management of the Burbages. The Admiral's men became the Prince's men and acted regularly at the Fortune under the management of Alleyn and Henslowe. Worcester's company became the Queen's men and acted at the Curtain and the Boar's Head inn, and after a few years at the new Red Bull. What became of the other adult companies and of the Rose and Swan theaters, is not clear. These playhouses seem to have been used less and less for acting, and the minor companies were fairly forced out of London. The two children's companies continued for a time, and another children's company appeared, taking the new theater in Whitefriars. But the supremacy of the adult companies was soon reëstablished; and they took possession of the private as well as of the public theaters. In 1614 the Hope, another venture of Henslowe's, was built on the Bankside, but was soon given over entirely to the bears. The King's men now, not only had the best playwrights, Shakespeare, and such successors as Fletcher and Massinger; they also had the best patronage. / The Globe seems to have maintained its reputation as the chief of the public theaters, while the Curtain and Red Bull, and even the Fortune, were known rather for their efforts to please the vulgar./ The Blackfriars was from the start the most fashionable theater, and it seems to have maintained its reputation to the end, and became the model for the private theaters, the Salisbury Court and Cockpit, and hence, through their descendants in the Restoration period, the direct ancestor of all modern English theaters.

FRONTISPIECE OF "MESSALLINA"

CHAPTER IV

THE PHYSICAL STAGE

THE sources of our information in regard to the physical stage of the Elizabethan theater are uncertain and baffling. Four pictures of theater interiors have been preserved from the seventeenth century, but these are at best of slight assistance in re-creating a detailed view of the stage. The picture of the Swan theater has already been discussed in Chapter III, and has been found manifestly inaccurate in details. The so-called picture of the Red Bull theater, which was first published in Kirkman's "Wits," in 1672, has probably nothing to do with the Bull or any other specific theater; it represents an imaginary stage of a crude type.[1] Two other pictures are taken from title pages of plays — "Roxana," 1632, and "Messallina," 1640. These agree in showing a curtain stretching across the rear of the stage; but they are too small to supply us with any details. In spite of these drawbacks, the Swan picture (p. 51) gives a general view of the interior of a public theater, and the "Messallina" picture opposite gives the best representation we have of a typical stage.[2] In addition to these pictures we have some valuable documentary

[1] Albright, 40–42. The title 'Red Bull' was apparently not attached to this plate until 1809. See W. J. Lawrence, *Elizabethan Playhouse*, 32.

[2] Attention should also be called to the very interesting drawings for a theater by Inigo Jones, preserved in Worcester College, Oxford, and reproduced by Mr. Hamilton Bell in the *Architectural* Record for 1913, pp. 262–

information from travelers' reports and Henslowe's Diary; but even the most important document — Henslowe's contract for the Fortune theater — gives no description of the stage itself.

The stage directions of all the plays printed from 1550 to 1642 furnish additional information, but they do not supply an open book. In general, Elizabethan plays print very few stage directions beyond the necessary entrances and exits. There is never anything like the elaborate description of setting and furniture that modern dramatists use. Rarely, indeed, are there references to properties, furniture, doors, windows, etc. In many cases it is doubtful whether we have directions designed to govern the actual presentation of a play; some are manifestly mere suggestions by the author, and others are not intended for the actors, but for readers of the play.[1] In a few cases, however, we have manuscripts that were apparently used by the companies, and in other cases directions intended solely for the theater have crept into the printed text. Further, in plays where there is a good deal of spectacle, the directions are naturally fuller and more descriptive than usual; and in plays issued piratically from shorthand notes taken at a performance, there are usually somewhat detailed descriptions of the stage business. It is, however, very difficult to classify or evaluate the different kinds of evidence afforded, or to come to a sure decision in the many cases of contradictions. Stage directions are at best scanty and uncertain, though they are one of our main sources of information.

267. They show an octagonal theater, with a stage and background after the fashion of Italian imitations of the classical theater. No clue exists as to their purpose, but they were presumably designed for a court or university theater.   [1] On these and other difficulties, see Neuendorff, Chap. I.

More important still in supplying knowledge of the physical stage and the methods of presentation is a careful study of the plays themselves. The text itself furnished the key to the action, business, properties, and the stage for which these were designed. But the text of a play often fails to give any sure indications of the stage performance. It can be made to fit two very different conceptions of the stage, and it rarely affords decisive evidence if considered singly. One must rely not on this play or that, but on the cumulative evidence offered by all the plays.

Another means of information arises from the fact that the stage, like everything else connected with Elizabethan drama, was part of an evolution; it is the offspring of the medieval stage; although influenced by conditions that did not arise until the sixteenth century, it is still in many respects medieval rather than modern. On the other hand, it is the ancestor of the modern stage, and we can trace, step by step, the successive changes that have gradually transformed the stage of Shakespeare into that of to-day. On all questions where direct contemporary information is lacking, we must attempt to reconstruct the Elizabethan stage and its practices from our knowledge either of earlier or later times. Since our knowledge of the Restoration stage is based on abundant information, we are able to apply this with great advantage in our effort to reconstruct the Elizabethan stage.

A TYPICAL STAGE

In preceding chapters I have hastily traversed the changes in the English stage up to the time that the theaters were erected, and have examined with care the history of playhouses in London from 1576 to 1642.

Certain considerations bearing on the physical stage are important. From 1576, although there was still a medley of traditions in regard to the stage and the staging of plays, yet henceforth these were all subordinated to the practical demands of the professional companies. Variations continued, but the permanent theater created permanent arrangements and unquestionably tended toward agreement in essentials. We must assume differences which are now impossible to determine, but we can also safely assume a typical stage. The result was a platform extending into the body of the theater and exposed on three sides to the view of the spectators. This is, in fact, the chief essential of the Elizabethan stage, as shown in all pictures and in the contract for the Fortune, and this projecting platform stage remained characteristic of the English theater long after the Restoration.

What were the other characteristics? In the upper part of the rear side there was a balcony, represented in all the pictures and alluded to again and again in the plays. Further, in all of the pictures except that of the Swan there is a rear curtain, and in the earliest extant plays acted in London theaters, there is mention of a curtain used when persons or properties were suddenly discovered or concealed. The references to this curtain in later drama are various and numerous; and it is clear that from an early date the curtain became a frequent and finally an invariable feature of the stage. The most obvious use of the inner stage, behind the curtain, was as a recess, a cave, study, bedroom, or an arbor, which needed special properties and concealment until a specified time. It is so used in many plays throughout our period. The most common uses of the upper stage of the balcony were as an upper room, the walls of the town, or any place requiring elevation. The front of the stage must have been used for the main action and dialogue. The exits on a temporary stage might be through the curtain; but in the permanent theaters

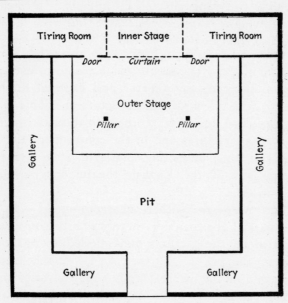

DIAGRAM A.   GROUND PLAN OF THE FORTUNE THEATER

doors were provided, and it was possible to enter or exit through these without passing through the inner stage. One other feature of minor importance seems to have been early adopted by the open-air theaters; the hut, a small building on the roof, whence gods and goddesses descended to the stage below.

A typical stage is represented in Diagram A, conforming to the dimensions of the contract for the Fortune theater.

It must be confessed, however, that the subject cannot be dismissed as simply as this diagram would indicate. The main difficulty is with the curtain and its position in reference to the balcony, the doors, and the front stage. It is possible that some theaters had no regular curtain, though it would have been easy to arrange for one even on the Swan stage. The drawing is manifestly inexact; but over the large door, a curtain might be placed that would correspond roughly to the one in our diagram. The stage directions give no manifest indication of the exact position of the curtains, and these, as well as the Swan drawing, have been differently interpreted by students. A number of scholars have made the inner stage project into the front stage, so that it would form a sort of central room, with the curtains on three sides.[1] This is contrary to the Messallina picture; but is based on the Swan picture, with a curtain placed between the two pillars, and side curtains from the pillars to the rear wall. It has been observed that the pillars on the stage were an evil probably abandoned in the later playhouses, and also that the Swan picture furnishes no basis for the reconstruction of a typical stage. The objections to this central curtained room, however, are manifest; it is an impracticable, unnecessary, and complicated arrangement. That something of the sort might have temporarily been arranged is possible, but there is no evidence that such an arrangement was the general practice of the Elizabethan theater.

[1] See Brodmeier, Wegener, and pictures of reproductions by the Elizabethan Stage Society and Harvard University, in G. P. Baker's *Development of Shakespeare as a Dramatist*. Neuendorff thinks the Swan type of stage was without a curtain.

If the balcony and curtained space be considered to project only a little from the rear wall, there is of course less objection to the three-sided structure. Such a slightly projecting inner stage has some support,[1] but at best it would have been an awkward arrangement and likely to give way to the simpler and more convenient plan of my diagram.

Convincing evidence that the general practice was in accord with Diagram A has been educed by Dr. Albright,[2] who has shown that the theaters of the Restoration period were manifestly modeled on the Elizabethan, and that they presented precisely the features indicated in our diagram: first, a projecting front stage entered by proscenium doors, and, second, an inner stage shut off by curtains across the rear. With the introduction of scenery, the inner stage was used for scenes and properties, and gradually became more important than the front stage. The projection on the front was cut down at various intervals, until it disappeared; but the proscenium doors on either side of the curtain (and opening on the front, not on the inner stage) continued long after they had ceased to be used for entrances and exits, and may be still seen in some theaters to-day. The front stage grew shallower, and the inner stage expanded in depth and size until it has become the picture-frame stage of to-day. We can reverse the process of evolution and reconstruct the Elizabethan stage from the

[1] Creizenach, IV. 430.   T. S. Graves, *op. cit.* 88 ff.   See also Graves's able argument against Neuendorff's theory that on stages like the Swan, the central portion behind the pillars was used as a sort of uncurtained inner stage.   What little evidence there is for such an arrangement by no means suggests any such extensive application as Neuendorff proposes.

[2] See also William Archer, "The Elizabethan Stage," *Quarterly Review*, April, 1908.

arrangement and methods of the Restoration theaters. In fact, in the case of the doors, the strongest evidence of their position comes from their existence in the Restoration and later periods. On the other hand, as we have seen, the Elizabethan stage diagram is the natural outgrowth of the medieval stage, with its neutral ground, and its special propertied places. The projecting platform is the *platea*, and the inner stage and gallery are the successors of the *loca* and *domus* of the church drama. The performances by the professional companies had resulted in this simplification.

Now, Diagram A is manifestly too simple to serve for seventeen theaters and during seventy years. It must have been modified to conform to the needs as shown by experience. The space behind the curtain may have been at first a mere passage, like that behind the arras covering a wall. Later, the pillars on the stage required to support the heavens would be done away with, if possible, as was the case in building the Hope. The balcony would be provided with curtains when needed. Since the square stage would leave narrow and inconvenient aisles for spectators, it might be rounded or cut off on the front corners. There would also be an obvious gain in putting the doors on the bias (or on the side in indoor theaters), instead of at the rear. Then windows or balconies could be placed over the doors and used conveniently to designate the upper rooms of houses. Moreover, if the doors were on the bias, there would be room for a wider inner stage and curtain. We have evidence that these and other changes actually took place; and a considerable variation must have been caused by the change from public to private theaters, that is, from unroofed buildings where the performance was by natural light, to indoor rooms where the light was artificial. The inner stage would be better lighted, more visible, and, consequently, probably enlarged and more frequently used than in the public theaters. The front stage would also presumably become relatively wider and less projecting, though the spectators sitting on the sides of the stage would still leave the actors decidedly in the midst of the audience.

The changes in the arrangement of the inner stage and the use of the curtain cannot be traced chronologically with exactness. The evidence is ample to indicate the general arrangement and the resulting principles of staging, but it is not sufficiently exact to forbid exceptions and variations. So far as the stage directions are concerned, it may be worth while to summarize the evidence in order to indicate the general usage as to the curtains, and the possible departures from that usage.

EVIDENCE OF THE STAGE DIRECTIONS

Reference has already been made to the various terms used to describe the curtain. No exact discrimination can be found in these terms, which are often curiously applied. The 'hangings' of the stage are often mentioned. They must have been occasionally changed, for they were black in the case of tragedy. Usually they seem to have been of arras cloth with pictures, and in the later private theaters were sometimes of silk. They could have hung only on the rear wall, *i.e.* where the doors, curtain, and balcony appear in my diagram. Some cases, however, indicate that the inner stage was hung with arras, disclosed when the curtains proper were opened. The term 'hangings' in a few unmistakable cases and the term 'arras' in many are used as referring to the main curtains.[1] 'Canopy,' another term sometimes used as an equivalent of curtain or of the inner stage, may denote a canopy over the throne or some arrangement different from the regular curtain, which, however, seems always intended by still another word 'traverse.' 'Scene,' a common equivalent for curtain at that period, is so used in the stage directions of only two plays,[2] though it is used occasionally for the inner curtained stage. The words "discover" and "display" require the drawing of a curtain, though not in all cases the main stage curtains. The word "curtain" itself is frequently employed, singular or plural, with definite or indefinite or no articles, but only once does the full expression "the stage curtains" occur.[3] These parted in the middle and were drawn to the sides. Presumably they were of the same material as the other hangings. They were black in the "Warning for Fair Women," and were quite likely referred to by the Grocer's Wife in the "Knight of the Burning Pestle" when she inquires, "What story is that painted upon the cloth?"

It is also necessary to distinguish the main curtains from certain special curtains, as those about a bed, or concealing some other object.[4] That the curtains belong to the bed is clearly indicated in some directions, as the following from Heywood's "Iron Age," IV. i. "Enter Egisthus with his sword drawne, hideth himselfe in the chamber behind the Bed-curtaines." In other cases, however, it is not easy to say

---

[1] Neuendorff, *op. cit.*, 31 ff.

[2] *If this be not a good play. Jovial Crew.* See Graves, *op. cit.*, 15, 16, for other uses of "scene."   [3] *Parson's Wedding*, V. ii.

[4] See Albright, 58 ff. for further examples and discussion.

whether the main curtains or only those of the bed effect the discovery. Small curtains are also used to conceal jewels or small objects. Curtains might also be drawn at right angles to the main curtain, separating the inner stage into compartments.[1]

Further difficulty arises because of the ambiguous language of the directions. 'Enter' is often used in a conventional way, when the actors were manifestly discovered, as in the following direction from "Bon-duca," V. i.

"Enter Caratach upon a rock, and Hengo by him sleeping."

The terms 'set forth,' 'thrust in,' 'set out,' applied to beds and other properties, are sometimes used merely referring to the placing of properties on the inner stage to be disclosed by the opening of the curtains, as in another direction from the "Devil's Law Case."

"A Table set forth with two tapers, a death's head, a book. Iolentha in mourning. Romelio sits by her."

In other cases, however, these conventionalized terms, 'Enter,' 'set out,' 'set forth,' etc., clearly imply definite motion to the front stage. This may have been made from the inner stage, whence the beds or persons were brought down front, but the directions are often open to various interpretations. Take, for example, the following directions which offer somewhat typical difficulties.

Hector of Germany, I. i. "A bed thrust out, the Palsgrave lying sick on it, the King of Bohemia, the Duke of Savoy, the Marquis Brandenburg entering with him." This seems a discovery.

[1] See *Wise Woman of Hogsdon*, V. *Bartholomew Fair*, II. i.

G

Sir John Oldcastle, V. i. "Enter Cambridge, Scroope, and Gray as in a chamber, and set downe at a table, consulting about their treason : King Harry and Suffolke, listning at the door." This may have been a discovery, or may have taken place on the balcony or on the front stage, so far as the stage direction shows.

Woman's Prize, V. i. "Livia brought in on a bed ; Moroso by her." The context indicates that the bed was actually brought on.

The City Night Cap, II. i. "A bed thrust out. Lodovico sleeping in his clothes; Dorothea in bed. Enter clown leading in Francisco." This appears to have been a discovery.

The Lost Lady, V. i. "Enter the Moor on her bed, Hermione, Phillida, and Irene. The bed thrust out." Here there is first a discovery and then the bed is drawn to the front. But do the following more laconic directions indicate discoveries or not?

A Chaste Maid in Cheapside, III. ii. "A bed thrust out upon the stage; Allwit's wife in it."

The Maid's Tragedy, V. i. 12. "King abed."

Efforts have been made to derive from these inconsistencies reconstructions of different stages,[1] especially of two types, one with and one without a curtain ; but contradictory stage directions occur for plays given at the same theater and even in the same play. Dramatists, like Shakespeare and Fletcher, writing during long periods for the same company and the same theater, seem sometimes to plan for a curtain and again to avoid it. In many cases, however, the representation could be managed either way, according as it was desirable or not to have the actors down front. A particular stage direction, 'bed discovered' or 'bed pushed

[1] Neuendorff, *op. cit.*, Chaps. II and III. For disproof of the curtainless stage see T. S. Graves, *op. cit.*, 4–31, where there is a good discussion of the curtain in court and public theaters.

out,' may merely indicate the practice of a single stage manager. Manifestly such stage directions must be interpreted by the context and by our knowledge of the theater. A few have been quoted here to suggest that the inner stage was often used even when there is no mention of curtains and when words in the directions, such as 'Enter,' 'thrust out,' etc., seem at first sight to testify against the use of curtains.

Further, curtains may be assumed in cases where there are no stage directions whatever. In these cases our evidence is furnished by the context. For example, in Tourneur's "Revenger's Tragedy" the stage directions in three scenes imply curtains — I. iv. "Enter Antonio . . . discovering her dead body to Hippolito, Piero and Lords." II. iv. "The Duke and Duchess in bed." V. i. "The Duke's corpse, dressed in Vendice's disguise lying on a bed." The presence of a curtain in these scenes may be also taken as corroborative evidence of its use in other scenes in the play where the context indicates its desirability. In general, clear evidence of the curtained inner stage in one scene of a play must be taken as a presumptive evidence that it was used in others. One other difficulty must be noted. It is not always clear whether the curtain mentioned was on the main stage or the balcony. When a chamber or interior room is indicated it is sometimes in one place and sometimes in the other; both places being curtained, concealment and discovery are possible.

THE CURTAINED INNER STAGE

In spite of these deficiencies and ambiguities, the evidence from the stage directions alone is overwhelming for the use of the curtain. Although there is no question that, at least before 1600, the inner stage was of small importance in comparison with the front stage; yet careful study of the old texts has greatly increased the number of unmistakable references to the curtain. In some one hundred and fifty plays the evidence of the stage directions for its existence seems to me certain; and in many more probable.[1] These plays cover the entire extent of our period and were performed at various theaters.

Further, the evidence of these stage directions is ample to establish the existence of a considerable space closed by the curtain. Dr. Albright[2] instanced nineteen plays giving typical directions to prove this point, and my list includes as many more. A few illustrations will suffice.

II Tamburlaine, II. 3. "The arras is drawen, and Zenocrate lies in her bed of state, Tamburlaine sitting by her, three Phisitians about her bed tempering potions. Theridamas, Techelles, Vsumcasane and the three sons."

Lust's Dominion, I. iii. "The curtain being drawn, there appears in his bed King Philip with his Lords, the Princess Isabella at the feet, Mendoza, Alvero, Hortenzo, Fernando, Roderigo; and to them enter the Queen in haste."

Hoffman, IV. i. "Enter Ferdinand and Sarlois, open a curtain. Kneel Saxony, the hermit, and Mathias; tapers burning."

Faithful Shepherdess, V. v. "The Curtayne is drawne. Clorin appeares sitting in the Cabin. Amoret sitting on the one side of her, Allexis and Cloe on the other. The Satyre standing by."

What You Will, II. ii. "Enter a schole-maister, draws the curtains behind, with Battus, Nows, Slip, Nathaniell, and Holofernes Pippo, schole-boyes, sitting, with bookes in their hands."

---

[1] See Appendix I. [2] *Shaksperian Stage*, 51 ff.

The stage directions alone are also sufficient to establish that the outer stage was entered by two proscenium doors without traversing the inner stage, which was at the rear concealed by a curtain. In many cases, actors enter by the two doors and the outer stage is used independently of the inner, which is not disclosed until the action has progressed for some time on the outer. One example will suffice.

The White Devil, V. iv. "Enter Flam and Gasp at one dore, another way, Giovanni, attended." After other entries and seventy lines of dialogue. Flamineo, who is told of Cornelia's grief, says,

> "I will see them
> They are behind the travers. Ile discover
> Their superstitious howling."

Whereupon the curtains are drawn and "Cornelia, the Moore and 3 other Ladies discovered winding Marcello's coarse. A song."

Occasionally the actors enter the front stage from the inner stage through the curtains.

The English Traveller, III. ii. "Enter at one doore an Usurer and his Man; at the other, old Lionell with his servant. In the midst Reignald."

Another class of directions shows the inner stage arranged as a shop which is discovered, and actors also enter at the doors and pass by.[1] A similar arrangement sometimes occurs with a temple, altar, tavern, or other setting disclosed by the curtains.

The Renegado, I. iii. "A shop discovered. Gazet in it. Francisco and Vitelli walking by."

[1] Albright, 57, 58.

A shop or bed might be discovered at one of the doors, and some stage directions suggest this, *e.g.*,

Shoemaker's Holiday. "Enter Jane in a Sempster's shop working, and Hammon muffled at another doore."
Woman is a Weather-Cock, III. ii. "Scudmore passeth one door, and entereth the other, where Bellafront sits asleep in a chair, under a taffeta canopy."

The word 'door' was, however, sometimes applied to the central opening concealed by the curtains[1]; and that may have been the case in these examples.

The inner stage could, of course, be entered from either side, so that properties could be placed there while the curtains were closed and the action proceeding on the front stage. All discovered scenes are direct proof of this; and in a few cases stage directions specifically direct the placing of properties behind the curtains to serve as settings which are later to be discovered.[2] The clearest case is in one quarto of "Bussy D'Ambois," I. i. In the midst of the scene occurs the stage direction, "Table, Chesbord, & Tapers behind the Arras." These properties are manifestly intended for scene ii, which does not open until thirty lines after the stage direction. Such a direction is so exclusively the affair of the stage manager that we need not be surprised that it has few parallels. Indeed the many printed descriptions of properties at the beginning of scenes may really indicate that those properties were arranged on the inner stage during the preceding scene. So, for example, we may interpret two directions in Davenant's "Platonick Lovers,"

[1] See Albright, 125 ff.
[2] *Ibid.*, 106–108, instances *Cruel Brothers*, III. ii; V. i; *Rape of Lucrece*, V. 3; *Guardian*, III. 7; *Satiromastix*, I. i.

II. ii. "Enter [Phylomont], Ariola, Rosella, with tapers. A Table with Night linnen set out."

Act IV. "Enter Theander, Eurithea, a table, stools, and lights set out."

although there is no mention of the curtains, as there is in a third direction in the same play.

II. iii. "Draws a canopy. Eurithea is found sleeping on a couch, a vaile on, with her lute."

On the other hand, some directions seem clearly to indicate the placing of properties on the front stage. That chairs and banquets and beds were brought forward is clear, but there is little if any evidence that heavy properties remained in view when incongruous with the action.[1] I shall return to this question in the next chapter.

Even the few plays that have been quoted represent widely differing dates and various theaters. The total evidence of the stage directions alone indicates that the arrangement described was in general use in important theaters, public or private, though doubtless its adoption was gradual and subject to variation. We may suppose that the size and visibility of the inner stage varied in different theaters, and that the extent to which the curtain was used changed from decade to decade, or playwright to playwright, or manager to manager, or even according to the state of the weather and light.

On page 88 are given Dr. Albright's plans for a stage drawn to fit the specifications of the Fortune, but placed in a theater nearly circular. His descriptions follow:

---

[1] See Neuendorff. In his best case for incongruity, the alternative fifth act of *Aglaura*, the stage directions seem to me very dubious. The play is supposed to have been acted on the public stage with scenery.

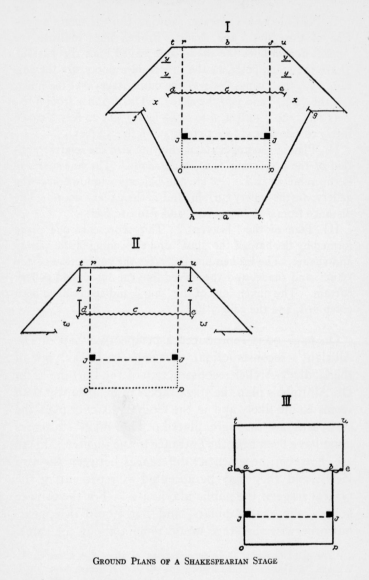

GROUND PLANS OF A SHAKESPEARIAN STAGE

From Albright's "Shaksperian Stage."

I. Plan of the lower stage, showing also the relative position of the "hut" and shade. Broken lines indicate the "hut," dotted lines the shade, and waved lines the curtain. jj are the stage posts, xx the proscenium doors, dce the curtain, $yyyy$ the "wings," $higedf$ the outer stage, $deut$ the inner, $rjjs$ the "hut," and $jopj$ the shade. The distance from h to i is 15 feet, f to g 39 feet, a to c $26\frac{5}{6}$ feet, j to j 20 feet, j to o 6 feet, j to r 20 feet, d to e 25 feet, and b to c 10 feet.

II. Plan of the upper stage, showing also the relative position of the projecting "hut" and shade. The line marking is the same as in I. ww are the balcony windows, $deut$ the gallery, dce the gallery curtain, and zz the gallery doors. The distance from d to e is 25 feet, and d to t 10 feet.

III. Plan of the "heavens." This represents one plane formed by the base of the "hut" and the ceiling of the gallery and shade. The broken line indicates the connection of the "hut" and shade, and the waved line the suspended gallery curtain. The dimensions of the "hut" and shade have been given in I, and the gallery in II.

On page 90 is reproduced a perspective view of Dr. Albright's reconstruction. On page 96 is the view of the Godfrey-Archer reconstruction of the Fortune.[1] In Dr. Albright's plan the stage tapers more abruptly than seems to me likely and in the Godfrey-Archer plan the staircases are wrongly placed. The main staircases must have been near the entrance to the theater. There are, however, no essential differences between the two views, and they may be accepted as representing the typical stage of the public playhouses. For the private houses, the shade, pillars, and hut would disappear, but otherwise the stage would remain about the same.

[1] For plans involving slight modifications of these views, see C. W. Wallace, "Shakspere and the Blackfriars," *Century Magazine*, Sept., 1910; and J. Corbin, "Shakspere His own Stage Manager," *Century Magazine*, Dec., 1911.

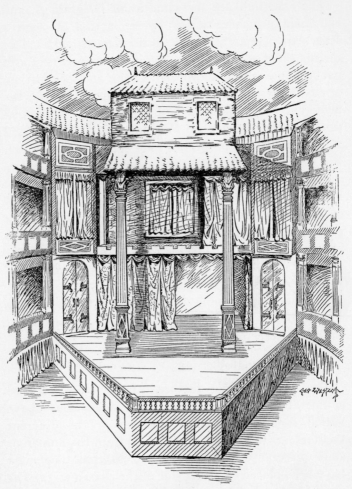

A TYPICAL SHAKESPEARIAN STAGE

From Albright's "Shaksperian Stage."

The essentials are the same as in Diagram A, and the main principles which govern acting on such a stage are apparent. The action must take place mainly on the front stage; the inner stage serves as a background to provide special setting and localization, or to represent special interior places. As in the medieval stage, the Elizabethan can make a distinction between the neutral and unlocalized ground and a place used for properties and specific localization. But the inner stage can represent different localities successively, and it is separated from the front stage merely by a curtain. Just as to-day the rear part of the stage may be shut off in the front by a painted drop, and just as it was shut off by flat scenes in the Restoration, so in the Elizabethan theater, the separation between the front and the back stages was accomplished quickly and readily by the curtains. The inner stage, while still a means for indicating special locality, had become in fact an integral part of the front stage.

MINOR FEATURES OF THE STAGE

The various minor features of the stage may be enumerated. (1) The proscenium doors must have varied somewhat in their position in the different theaters; their existence is inferred from the numerous stage directions, which make it clear that they must have been placed on either side of the curtain. (2) The windows and balconies over the doors are not shown in any picture, but their existence is suggested by many scenes, especially in seventeenth-century plays. A person in one of these balconies could see the inner stage, or be seen from it. Moreover, the persons so located would be clearly visible to the spectators in

the theater. These windows over the doors consequently proved more serviceable than the rear balcony.
(3) The balcony at the rear, over the inner stage,
seems to have been less used in later than in earlier
plays, and it disappears in the Restoration. In the
earlier plays it appears frequently as the wall of the
city, or a tower; but when not required by the action
of the play it seems to have been used for spectators,
or perhaps musicians. (4) The hut shown in the
drawings of the exteriors of the public theaters must
have been replaced by an upper room in the private
theaters. In all spectacular plays there is a good deal
of ascending and descending, and the upper room or
hut would be frequently employed. (5) Trapdoors
seem to have been located in several places on the
front stage, on the inner stage, and in the balcony.
(6) Besides the main curtains, others were employed
for specific purposes; the gallery was curtained and
used as a place of concealment; beds were provided
with curtains, and the opening of these might serve
the purpose of discovery. Sometimes a special object
might be provided with curtains; finally, there were
occasionally traverses, or curtains running at right
angles with the rear of the stage. The evidence for
these has proved puzzling to students, and some
investigators have supposed that traverses were regularly employed. Their use seems to have been rare.
They could be placed in the inner stage serving to
divide that into compartments, but it is doubtful if
they ever extended on the front stage. (7) Of the
dressing or tiring room, little is known. Small space
was required in comparison with a modern theater;
but it seems probable that in the later private houses
more room was provided than is indicated in our

diagram. From the terms of the contracts, one might suspect an addition in the rear of the stage of the Fortune and Hope. (8) The Music Room is another place somewhat difficult to locate exactly. Apparently the musicians were sometimes placed in a box, sometimes in the balcony, and sometimes on the stage itself. The stage directions in Killigrew's "Parson's Wedding" indicate the flexibility of arrangement. A bedroom scene (I. ii) is placed "above in the music-room." In another more elaborate bedroom scene (IV. vi), "The tiring-room, curtains drawn, and they discourse. . . . All above if the scene can be so ordered." In another (V. ii) "The Fiddlers play in the tiring-room; and the stage curtains are drawn, and discover a chamber," etc. The musicians were apparently to be ousted from their usual place in the balcony and placed in the tiring-room, so that the balcony might be used as a bedchamber.

A few other details may complete the picture. The pit was without seats in the public theaters, but was provided with benches in Blackfriars and the later indoor theaters. The floor was not built on an incline, so far as we know, although possibly the later theaters may have had sloping stages, as did some of the Masques. The private as well as the public theaters had galleries. Footlights were not used; but in the private theaters the artificial lighting was then considered brilliant; and we are told that the candles were of wax.

The use of the adjective typical as applied to our reconstruction of the Shakespearian stage implies variety and change. These changes probably took the form of an evolution, which it would be interesting to trace if our evidence was sufficiently exact. Doubtless our

reconstruction is nearer to the stage of Shakespeare's
last years than to that of his youth; but after 1610
there were apparently few changes of importance in
the stage itself. In still another way, our typical
reconstruction is limited; for it applies only to the
professional playhouses and disregards the court stage.
This will be discussed in a later chapter, when we shall
find the court theater presenting important differences
from its popular rival, and after 1605 introducing
innovations of importance in the general evolution of
the modern stage. But in Shakespeare's time, it is
clearly the professional stage that counts, and it is
this stage of our reconstruction that marks a step
from the medieval to the modern. The differences
between Shakespeare's stage and ours are striking,
but we should not forget that these differences
have been of gradual growth. They were far less
advanced a hundred years ago, as may be seen
from the print of the "School for Scandal" at Drury
Lane in Sheridan's day, reproduced at page 128.
That long, narrow, and projecting stage, with its
properties (and scenery) far in the rear, and with its
boxes on the sides, so that the actors when down front
were on a peninsula almost entirely surrounded by
audience, has nearly as many points of likeness to the
Shakespearian as to the modern picture-frame stage.
The illustration (p. 110) from the "Empress of Morocco" shows that the Duke's theater in 1673 was still
closer to the Elizabethan stage. As we go on to consider the methods of Elizabethan stage presentation, we
may be prepared to find them different from ours, but
less different from Sheridan's, and still less different
from Congreve's.

CHAPTER V

STAGE PRESENTATION

We are now prepared to consider the methods of the stage presentation of an Elizabethan play, how far they were governed by fixed principles, in what respect they differ from methods in use to-day, to what extent they conditioned the structure and planning of the plays. It must be remembered that we are considering a period of some seventy years, during which both drama and theater underwent many changes. In the beginning theatrical methods were certainly confused and uncertain rather than precise and established. Traditions of the medieval stage mingled with those of the classical, and amateurs were still almost as much concerned with establishing new models as were professionals. The seventy years of performances at regular London theaters undoubtedly served to develop methods and fix traditions. But even at the closing of the theaters, there was much variety. The actors could still adapt themselves to the simplest conditions and perform on the dismantled stage of the Red Bull or on some improvised platform in the country, as well as in the elaborately equipped private theaters. We shall look for established methods and principles that were generally applicable, but we shall not expect to find these either very rigid or very complex.

The characteristics of the physical stage have been sufficiently discussed, and the various uses of its

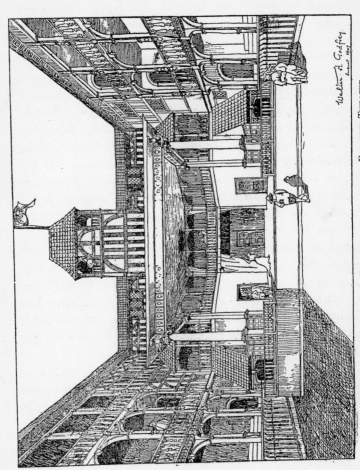

MR. WALTER H. GODFREY'S RECONSTRUCTION OF THE FORTUNE THEATER

different parts have been roughly indicated. The outer stage, with the curtains closed, was without scenery, settings, or properties, and was used for unlocalized scenes. Not only scenes in a street, open place, or before a house could be represented here, but any kind of place in which there were no properties required, or else where they were so few and simple that they could be easily brought on and off. The inner stage, shut off by the rear curtain, was used for definitely localized scenes requiring heavy properties. When the curtains were drawn, the setting, *e.g.* for temple, shop, bedroom, or forest, was disclosed at the rear. If the inner stage represented a temple or shop, the outer stage became a place before the temple or shop ; if the inner stage was occupied by a bench with judges or a throne for the king, the outer stage became courtroom or presence chamber. If the inner was a bedroom, the outer became a hall or anteroom. Indeed, any exact separation of the two stages became impossible, when the curtains were once opened. The inner stage then became an integral part of the outer stage, or rather the outer stage now embraced the inner.

Action was by no means necessarily confined to the inner stage, and might readily overrun its boundaries, inevitably seeking the front of the stage. If the scene was a bedroom, the whole stage might be regarded as the bedroom ; if a forest, the trees and banks set in the rear stage served to convert the whole inner-outer stage into a forest. The inner stage, while it might serve for a specific and limited space, as a cave, shop, cell, might also serve as a sort of background for the outer stage. Doors to right and left of the inner stage served for entrances and exits to the

H

outer stage, and could be regarded as entrances to houses, cities, prisons, or whatever places might be imagined within. There were also entrances to the inner stage, so that persons or properties might be brought on and off without traversing the outer platform. Over the inner stage was a balcony — in some cases hung with curtains, and serving to indicate any localized place above the level of the main stage, — tower, city walls, upper room, etc. Over the doors there were windows or balconies, and these served, more frequently than the balcony, as windows of houses. The hut above and various trapdoors in the floors of the main stage, inner stage, and balcony, were chiefly used in spectacular plays requiring gods, devils, and transformations.

THE PROBLEM OF THE INNER-OUTER STAGE

The chief problem in understanding Elizabethan staging is that of the outer-inner stage. It is here that the English professional stage developed a procedure different from those on the continent. In Paris, when the professional actors came to succeed the confrères at the Hôtel Bourgogne, they continued the methods and even some of the sets of that stage, thus adopting a simplified form of the simultaneous setting. Curtains might be used to conceal or discover properties, but the stage would usually provide for a number of different localities, as *e.g.* a bedchamber, a fortress by the sea, a cemetery, a shop, and a wood, as in the frontispiece of "Agarite," reproduced on page 154.[1] In Spain the simultaneous set did not continue in the public theaters, which presented a bare stage. Curtains were here employed to conceal and discover

[1] Rigal, *Le Théatre Français*, 248 *et passim.*

properties in the rear[1]; but the fact that the stages of Madrid and Seville were recesses and not projections would seem to have prevented such a development of the inner stage for a background as took place on the projecting platforms in London.

No one now thinks that the English stage had a system of multiple setting like that of the Hôtel de Bourgogne, although students differ as to the extent to which multiple sets were used on the London stage. On the other hand, no one now believes that the stage was merely a bare platform; every one admits the existence of a curtained inner stage. On the issue, however, of the use of this inner stage, scholars have differed diametrically, and even now, after years of investigation and discussion, little has been done to harmonize the two opposing theories. Each of these theories is based on unquestioned facts of stage presentation and can be supported by much evidence and argument, and both in their extreme form are demonstrably wrong and inconsistent with general practice. One group of scholars has emphasized the importance of the bare outer stage and minimized the employment of the inner stage. They have insisted on the rapid changing of scene, the absence of properties, the incongruity of setting. They have found plays where the scene changes with actors on the stage, where Faustus before the eyes of the audience passes at once from his study to a pleasant green; and others where several places seem represented at once. They have found other plays where the scene changes from forest to palace and then to street, and then back to

[1] Rennert, the *Spanish Stage*, Chap. V. For the use of curtains to indicate a change of scene, see p. 90; also Schack's *Geschichte der dram. Lit. u. Kunst in Spanien*, II. 723.

forest, and have inferred that trees and other necessary properties of the forest remained before the spectators' eyes all of the time.   They have in consequence
called Shakespeare's stage medieval, plastic, symbolic,
incongruous, and they have elevated its occasional
incongruity into a sort of principle of procedure.   Thus
one of the most thorough and acute of recent investigators declares: "This convention allowed the
presence upon the stage of a property or furnishing
which was incongruous to the scene in progress, and
which during the scene was thought of as absent,
though standing in plain sight.   This incongruity took
two forms: either the close juxtaposition upon the
stage of two properties which in reality should have
been a much greater distance apart, or the presence
of a property in a scene where it never could naturally
have been; as a tree, for example, in the midst of a
room scene." [1]

The evidence that such a convention became established is, however, entirely insufficient.   Whatever
occasional incongruities of this sort the Elizabethan
stage may have presented, these were not usual or
essential.   It might sometimes be necessary to leave
a tree on the stage while the actors were presumably
in a room, but this would not be done if avoidable.
Even on the medieval stage, the tree usually would
have been confined to its particular station, and on
the Elizabethan, it would have been concealed by the
curtain.   There were incongruities then, as on all
stages, but not incongruities that could be readily
avoided.   Again, while the public theaters sometimes,
after the fashion of court or pastoral stages, presented

[1] G. R. Reynolds, "Some Principles of Elizabethan Staging," *Modern Philology*, June, 1905.

two places at once, this was not a usual or characteristic feature of their staging. On the other hand, I find myself in agreement with this theory in so far as it stresses the importance of the outer stage and insists that the Elizabethan indicated locality far less precisely than moderns.

The opposing theory or attitude has rightly made much of the inner stage as a place for setting properties and indicating a change of scene by drawing and closing the curtains; but it has tended to exaggerate the usefulness of this part of the stage and its properties. In the extreme presentation of this theory its followers have exalted the change or alternation of scenes from outer to inner stage into a fixed procedure of staging. They have indeed made it a principle of dramatic composition and imagined the dramatists constructing their plays as series of alternating inner and outer scenes. The use of the inner stage must be discussed at length in this chapter, but it may be remarked at the start, that the alternation theory is not only without sufficient evidence, but rests on the misconception that a large minority of scenes in Elizabethan drama were definitely localized either on the stage or in the minds of their authors.

THE EVIDENCE FOR METHODS OF STAGING

If we turn to the plays themselves, we find few obvious indications as to staging. The plays are rarely divided into acts, and still more rarely into scenes, except by an "exeunt omnes." On the modern stage, the fall of the curtain makes plain the division between scenes and marks an interval for an imaginary change of place or time. On the Elizabethan stage, this break is indicated merely by an empty stage. Yet the scene is a manifest unit in the construction. In the early days, a single scene sometimes covers a long lapse of time and moves from place to place. But as the technic grows more certain, a scene is confined to one place and an interval of time not much longer than the action. Lapses of time and changes of place are to be imagined in the intervals between the scenes. Indeed if a lapse of time is indicated, the persons who exeunt at the close of the scene rarely return immediately to the stage on the beginning of the next scene. A speech or even a scene intervenes before their reëntry. This practice, which has been formulated by Prölss into a law,[1] has various exceptions, but is a natural result of an effort for clarity in construction. There is, however, no tendency to limit the number of scenes. Sometimes a scene occupies an entire act, and in authors seeking to approximate to the unities of time and place, the number of scenes is reduced; but in general a single play includes many scenes. And there is no running on of scenes, except in so far as this is accomplished by use of the inner stage.

In the plays themselves, we find neither place-headings for scenes, nor usually any indications of locality. The majority of scenes give no indication in stage directions or text of the place where they were acted. Nothing is better known to the reader of old quartos, who often finds it difficult or impossible to imagine just where the scene may be. But even a reader familiar with the early editions is likely to be misled by the scene-headings with which modern editors have supplied the plays of Shakespeare. The scene

---

[1] *Von den ältesten Drucken der Dramen Shakespeares*, Leipzig, 1905, p. 307 ff.   See also Neuendorff, p. 192 ff.

is announced as "a room in the palace" or "the sea-shore," and one accepts the designation in spite of oneself. A great number of scenes are not localized in any way whatever. There is no indication where the actors are, how they came, or in what way they will depart. They may be indoors or outdoors, on a ship or in the air, for anything that the text discloses.

A second class of scenes is only vaguely localized. They require no properties, offer no business that will give us a clue, but we infer by the conversation or action that they are in the neighborhood of the palace, or else within it, or that they are on a street, or that they are within doors. The distinction between out-door and indoor scenes is rarely certain unless some properties are introduced. As in Roman comedy, 'before a house' is viewed as virtually the same as within the house. If the actors are invited within, we know that they have been outside; if they sit down to a banquet or cards, we may suppose them within; but in many cases there are no such indications, nothing to show whether the dramatists definitely conceived the scene under roof or sky. Even if the scene is out of doors, in camp, or street, or square, the indications of locality are usually of the slightest; a specific place is rarely conceived.

In comparison with these two classes, the third class of definitely localized scenes is comparatively small. Of course, many scenes where there is no in-dication of locality may have been definitely located in the minds of actors and author, and this may have been indicated by changes in costume, if not in stage setting. But the same costume is apparently often kept through scenes imaginably in very different places; and the indications of locality seem to be frank and distinct enough whenever special locality is intended. "This is the forest of Arden," says Rosalind as soon as she gets there; and nearly every drama has some such specifications for the benefit of the audience. Of the localized scenes, again, only a minority have properties. Caves, shops, trees, beds, candles, etc., are mentioned, but the number of such mentionings is surprisingly small when we consider the total number of plays and scenes.

The main stage was conceived as unlocalized territory. This is the fundamental principle of Elizabethan staging, and this links it with the medieval methods rather than with the modern. The dramatist had the bare open platform in his view and he planned his play for that. Certain places were, of course, furnished by the story he was dramatizing; but he did not visualize for himself or plan for the stage the exact details of room or road, as a modern dramatist would do. If he localized the place at all, he did it vaguely, as, in Venice, on a street, in front of a house, within the palace, or in the hall of a house, places with few or no properties that could be represented on any platform. Take, for example, the second scene of the first act of "Macbeth." Duncan receives the bloody sergeant who brings news of the battle. Where is the scene placed? The modern stage direction, following the historical narrative, says "A camp near Forres," but Shakespeare gives no indication where the scene may be; he planned it for the outer stage of the Globe. Or, take the fourth scene of the same act, where Duncan receives Macbeth and Banquo; the modern editions give "Forres, the Palace," but the scene hints at neither palace nor camp; again it was designed for the bare stage. In the fifth scene, Lady Macbeth enters, reading a letter from her husband, who presently enters. The scene is at Macbeth's castle, and presumably indoors, but there is no sure indication of that, still less of the character of the room and nature of the furnishings. In the first and third scenes, the witches appear. Here Shakespeare's conception is clear and indicated to readers. The scene is out of doors, it thunders and there is lightning, but nothing further of locality is suggested. Take another play, "Twelfth Night," where the action is mostly about the Duke's Palace, and Olivia's house. Twelve scenes take place within or just without Olivia's house, it is hard to determine which; and, except for the box tree used by the merry conspirators and the prison where they confine Malvolio, there is no hint of the appearance or furnishings of the lady's dwelling. All the scenes in an Elizabethan play can, to be sure, by some imaginative ingenuity, be provided with a locality and scenery; but the fact that they are so wanting in properties or indications of place, is evidence that the majority were planned for a bare stage and a presentation without setting of any kind.

The second principle of Elizabethan staging, however, provides for the localization of scenes by the use of the curtain and inner stage. Just as the medieval stage had its *platea* and its *domus*, so the Elizabethan had its neutral unlocalized main stage, and its places for localization and properties, in the upper and inner stage. But as we have seen, during the first three quarters of the fifteenth century — the time of Interludes — the stage was passing through a transformation that may be described as losing its *domus* and becoming reduced to the *platea*. When the inner stage with its curtain became a fixture we do

not know exactly, but the earliest plays extant after
the construction of permanent London theaters bear
evidence that it was frequently used. And its use
unquestionably expanded down to the Restoration.

THE EMPLOYMENT OF THE INNER STAGE

It was early utilized for scenes requiring a small
interior, — cave, arbor, studio, shop, bedroom; and
its use for such localities continued to the closing
of the theaters. In this case it clearly takes the place
of the *domus* or *mansion* of the medieval or multiple
stage.

A further use very early suggested itself in scenes
requiring discovery or disclosure. Since the main
stage extended into the auditorium, with its only
entrance from the rear, actors had something of a
journey on and off between the door and the front.
No disclosures and no tableaux were possible. This
lack was supplied in part by the use of the curtain.
So, to take only three early plays : in "David and Bethsabe," the Prologue speaker, before going out, "draws
a curtain and discovers Bethsabe with her maid,
bathing over a spring: She sings, and David sits above
viewing her"; in "Friar Bacon and Friar Bungay"
(Act IV, Scene i), "Enter Friar Bacon drawing the
curtains, with a white stick, a book in his hand,
and a lamp lighted beside him; and the Brazen Head,
and Miles with weapons by him "; in the "Old Wives'
Tale," the Ghost of Jack "draweth a curtain, and
there Delia sitteth asleep." [1]   Numerous other instances might be given; it is clear that in general
wherever there is a discovery the curtains were used.
Such discoveries might be made by the curtains in the

[1] Cf. *Dido*, I. i; *Looking Glass for England*, II. i.

balcony, or more rarely by curtains concealing one of the doors; but in the great majority of cases the discovery revealed the inner stage.

In two of the cases cited, heavy properties are concealed behind the curtain, and the use of the inner stage was early extended to provide for scenes requiring heavy properties. Examples have been given in Chapter IV. Whenever a propertied scene was required, — and these scenes were largely bedroom scenes, shop scenes, and forest scenes, — the properties were placed on the inner stage while action was going on before the closed curtains. When the curtains were drawn, the inner stage, now an integral part of the whole, supplied the needed localization for the scenes. This would make it necessary or advisable that the preceding scene should be played on the outer stage. When there was a succession of scenes requiring properties, the curtains closed before the end of a scene to permit a shift, or there may have been a pause between the scenes.

These uses of the inner stage are not very extensive, but together with the gallery and windows over the doors, and the doors themselves, they provide considerable variety in stage procedure and afford various means of indicating locality. They denote a decided departure from the medieval scheme of multiple setting. Moreover, the use of the inner and outer stages, if carried no further than described, would affect dramatic structure to an appreciable degree. In "As You Like It," for example, Shakespeare localized much of the action in the Forest of Arden. This could be done by means of the inner stage, where trees, rocks, and other properties for a forest might be placed. And the spectators could be transferred from forest to court

merely by the closing of the curtains and the entrance
of the Duke and courtiers on the front stage.   During
the last four acts the scene is generally the Forest of
Arden, and there are frequent mentions of woods and
trees, and a tree is used to receive Orlando's verses.
The curtains were opened, the inner stage disclosed a
background of trees; perhaps a tree or two or a grassy
mound may have been pushed forward.   Different
parts of a forest may be imagined, but one setting was
enough to aid the illusion of the greenwood.   This
was furthered by properties as well as by costumes of
foresters and shepherds, and by songs and hunting
horns.   But twice the scene changes suddenly to court,
or to an unlocalized place — once for two short scenes
(II. ii. 21 l.) Duke and lords, (II. iii. 76 l.) Adam and
Orlando; and again for a single scene, (III. i. 18 l.)
Duke and Lord.[1]   These short scenes, for purposes of
exposition and supplying connecting links of the plot,
are common in Elizabethan drama, and they seem to
have been used only when either there was no setting
or when the setting could be easily and quickly changed.
Here the curtains were closed, the Duke and lords
entered on the outer stage, announced their plans,
departed; and the curtains were drawn, again reveal-
ing the Forest of Arden.   The curtained inner stage
thus permitted the free and rapid shifting of place
and at the same time encouraged the representation
of certain propertied scenes, as forests, rooms, etc.
The evidence of the stage directions, which we have
glanced at in Chapter IV, seems sufficient in itself
to prove the general adoption of the inner stage for

[1] This play affords a favorite illustration for extreme exponents of incongruity, who think trees remained on stage during these three scenes.   But
with a curtained back stage there is no necessity for this whatever.

these uses : (1) an inner locality, (2) a discovery, (3) scenes with heavy properties.

THE PRINCIPLE OF ALTERNATION

A further extension in the use of the inner stage led to its employment for the representation of scenes where the specification of locality by properties was desirable rather than essential. Almost any scene might thus be prepared with a background and the change of place would come to be regularly indicated by the closing or opening of the curtains. To this extensive use of the curtain we may apply for convenience the name, the *Principle of Alternation*, although we must understand that several outer scenes might follow one another without any use of the curtain, and that the same setting might be employed for different places, as a forest setting for different parts of the forest, or a palace setting for different rooms in the palace.

This principle of alternation can best be illustrated by its use to-day, in the employment of drop scenes. On the modern stage, in the revival of Shakespearian or eighteenth-century plays, or in the modern melodrama which retains so many old customs, frequent changes of scene are managed by the use of drops. If the scene is to change from the Rocky Mountains to the interior of a heroine's room, a drop painted to represent one wall of a room cuts off the mountain scenery. The actors appear in front. In front of the drop are no properties except a few that may be brought on. When the scene is finished, the drop rises and discloses the mountain scene again or a new one which has meantime been prepared. In this fashion many scenes are presented without delay. Here is the exact counterpart of the inner-outer stage.

The rear stage with scenery and properties is an enlargement of the old inner stage. The drop has taken the place of the curtains. The front stage before the drop is the remnant of the old outer stage. This method of representation goes back to the eighteenth-century conditions, when the front stage extended farther into the auditorium and was entered by proscenium doors, and still farther back to the Restoration stage, when the front stage or apron extended far into the theater, and when the curtain or flat scene was used instead of the drop, and the rear stage was employed largely for scenery and setting. In the Restoration plays, the alternation of front and back scenes was a common practice, sometimes, indeed, the flats being opened or closed and the scene changing while some actor remained on the front. Now, the Restoration theaters were direct successors of the Elizabethan private theaters, and we can trace back the employment of inner-outer stage and of alternation of scenes, from the modern melodrama with drop to the comedies and tragedies of Blackfriars.

Innumerable examples from the Restoration drama might be quoted. A few instances must suffice from the plays of Otway, but they are typical of many others. In the fifth act of "Venice Preserved," after several front scenes we come upon this stage direction: "SCENE opening discovers a scaffold and a wheel prepared for the executing of *Pierre*. Then enter officers, *Pierre*, and guards, a Friar, Executioner, and a great Rabble." Many similar stage directions, *Scene opening*, *Scene changing*, or simply *Scene*, indicate the sudden opening of scenes or flats disclosing the propertied inner stage. The other examples illustrate the alternation of scenes to preserve the continuous act.

THE DUKE'S THEATER IN 1673
From Settle's "Empress of Morocco."

CAIUS MARIUS (Alteration of *Romeo* and *Juliet*), ACT V.
1. "Scene, Cinna's Camp before the Walls of Rome." Full
setting, entire stage. 2. "Metellus's House." Front scene,
flats closed. Metellus and Nurse enter and converse.
Metellus bids nurse to "Go, wake Lavinia." — "Scene
draws and discovers Lavinia on a couch," *i.e.* flats draw
and the scene now occupies the entire stage. 3. "Scene
changes to The Forum, where is placed the Consul's tribunal."
The flats closed either before the end of the preceding scene,
or else the Tribunal was not disclosed until after the first
few lines of this scene. Two citizens pass across the stage,
exeunt; and a senator and his grandson enter, converse and
exeunt, thus providing two short front scenes before the
Tribunal is used. 4. "A Church Yard." Front scene with
flats in rear. Marius Junior (Romeo) enters; later, the
apothecary who provides the poison; then Marius declares,
"now for the monument of the Metelli." *Exit.* "Scene
draws off, and shows the Temple and Monument." Re-
enters. "It should be here : The Door is open too." Marius
leaves the stage to go to the Monument, and immediately
reënters. The scene has drawn and he is before the monument. This scene is especially interesting, as it probably
preserves the tradition of the Shakespearian "Romeo and
Juliet," which Otway's play displaced on the English stage
for some fifty years.

THE ATHEIST : or, the second Part of the "Soldier's
Fortune," ACT III. 1. No stage directions. Full stage,
set for a room ; Beaugard's lodgings. Table, chairs, drinking, and dicing. Beaugard is summoned to the corner of
the street. 2. "Scene changes to street." Front, closed
flats. Enter Beaugard. He is carried off by ruffians.
3. Same. Enter Theodont and Gratian. 4. Same, or perhaps a front scene with different flats showing a painting of a
house. Enter Sylvia and Lucretia. 5. Same as 4. Enter
Theodont, Gratian, and Lucretia. 6. "Scene changes to
the inside of a very fair House adorn'd with rich Furniture
and Lights."

Scenes 1 and 6 require the full stage and show properties. Scenes 2, 3, 4, and 5 are unpropertied and played on the front stage before flats shutting off the rear stage.

These examples illustrate a use of inner-outer stage separated by flat scenes or a drop, instead of curtains, by means of which continuous action can be provided in spite of changes of scene during an act, and by which easy and immediate change of scene is always possible from a propertied to an unpropertied scene, or *vice versa*. To what extent was this method, in full use at the Restoration and familiar ever since, employed on the Elizabethan stage? The question is a difficult one, and probably can never be answered with exactness. As has been noted, properties are rarely mentioned, stage directions are few, and we consequently lack decisive evidence for this larger use of the inner stage. When we seek for evidence of its use in a play, the scenes fall into three well-marked classes: first, those in which there are no indications whatever of locality and no properties, and which are clearly acted on the outer stage; second, those in which a curtain or discovery is mentioned, or in which properties are considerable, and which clearly require the inner stage. The third class is the largest. In this there are only vague indications of locality or properties, and no clear evidence whether the scene was on the outer or the full stage. The very fact, however, that there are so many of these scenes without any precise indications of locality must be taken as *prima facie* evidence that the majority of them did not use the inner stage. They must have been written by dramatists without regard to special localization or setting; and these must have been provided only as necessary or convenient.

Now and then a play, as the "Merchant of Venice," seems to suggest frequent alternation, I. ii; II. i; II. iii; II. vii; III. ii; III. iv; IV. i; V. i, utilizing the inner stage. But in another, as "Twelfth Night," the indications are very slight. Take the first act:

Scene i. "Enter Duke Orsino," etc. The scene may be indoors or out; outer or inner stage.

Scene ii. "Enter Viola, a Captain, and Sailors." Outdoors and near the Duke's dominions; outer stage.

Scene iii. "Enter Sir Toby and Maria." Presumably indoors, in the house of Countess Olivia; but there are no properties, unless chairs and tables, and it could be played on outer stage.

Scene iv. "Enter Valentine and Viola in man's attire." Somewhere about the Duke's palace; but no properties; outer stage.

Scene v. "Enter Maria and Clown." Viola is announced "at the gate." On entering, she asks for "the honorable lady of the house." So the scene may be considered within the house; but there are no properties and it could be acted on the outer stage. At the close Olivia sends Malvolio in pursuit of Viola.

Scenes ii and iv are clearly outer scenes; Scenes i, iii and v might have been played with sets on the inner stage; but there is no evidence of this and no real need for it. Indeed, in this case, there is evidence that Scene v was *not* played with an inner stage. If that had been used and the curtain closed at the end, the scene in which Malvolio overtakes Viola could have followed immediately. (See p. 114 ff. for other cases of this.) But this scene (II. ii) does not occur until after an act interval and one other front scene. Apparently Shakespeare wished to avoid the incongruity of making the stage appear in successive scenes as the

I

inside and outside of the house, and yet did not use the curtain to avoid this incongruity. We must be cautious in imagining settings for scenes vaguely localized and entirely free from any dependence on setting or properties.

At the same time it must be remembered that the inner stage and its curtains were there, and it must be granted that they would be used whenever there was special need. The instance just cited from "Twelfth Night," where a curtain was not used, illustrates a difficulty which seems often to have been avoided by using the curtain. The difficulty arises when actors are outside a house, seeking admission, and in the next scene they appear within the house; or, when in one scene they are within a room and start to go out doors, and in the next scene appear on the street. In these cases it seems most likely that the curtain was generally used. One instance has already been mentioned; in the "Merchant of Venice," II. iii, Jessica, who is parting with Launcelot, gives him a letter for Lorenzo — a room setting on inner stage. In Scene iv, Launcelot gives the letter to Lorenzo — a street, front stage. Rapid changes corresponding to these have already been noted in Restoration plays, when the change was made from outer to inner stage by drawing flat scenes. One other striking case instanced by Dr. Albright may be cited, as here the change of scene is accomplished while characters are on the front stage.

AN EVENING'S LOVE, ACT IV, SCENE i, presumably on a street, outer stage with flats closed. Wildblood and others pass, all passing off except Wildblood. "The scene opens and discovers Aurelia and Camilla; behind them a table and lights set on it. The scene is a Garden with an Arbour in it. The Garden door opens." Wildblood passes out, and Melchor enters. After varied action, "The Scene shuts." Melchor is now left alone in front of the flats. Others enter and the scene proceeds as on a street or some public place.[1]

In Elizabethan plays there are a considerable number of similar scenes, though few showing as striking a use of the inner stage, with the scene shifting while some person remains on the stage. An interesting parallel is offered by "A Yorkshire Tragedy," which was acted by Shakespeare's company about 1605. It is a short play, "one of the foure plaies in one," and is divided by modern editors into ten scenes. The first four scenes are apparently all within the house, — but there are no indications of any use of the inner stage. In Scene iv, the Husband enters with the Master of the college, who has come seeking money for the Husband's brother. After some conversation and wine, the Husband says:

> Now, Sir, if you so please
> To spend but a few minutes in a walke
> About my grounds below, my man heere shall
> Attend you, etc.

The Master goes out to wait there for the Husband. The scene continues and the Husband murders his little boy and " Exit with his Sonne."

Immediately following this, comes the stage direction "Enter a maide with a child in her armes, the mother by her a sleepe" (Scene v). Manifestly this is a discovery scene requiring curtains, which are opened disclosing the inner stage. In a moment, "Enter husband with the boie bleeding." He

---

[1] Albright, *The Shakesperian Stage*, p. 98. He gives other instances of a change of scenes with characters on the stage.

struggles with the nurse and throws her down; the mother wakes and seizes the youngest child; the Husband stabs her and the child and, after a struggle with a "lusty servant" who comes to the rescue, makes his escape.

> My horse stands reddy saddled. Away, away;
> Now to my brat at nursse, my sucking begger.
> Fates, Ile not leave you one to trample on.

Immediately following this speech, we have the stage direction "The Master meets him." Apparently the struggle and murders have taken place on the inner stage, often employed for scenes of violent horror that could hardly be enacted in the full light of the front stage, and the Husband has rushed down front. There is no direction for his exit, and the curtains must have closed behind him while he was on the front stage. There enters the Master, who has been awaiting him outdoors.

The action (Scene vi) is now clearly conceived as outside the house, for the Husband at once says, "Please you walke in, Sir," and excuses himself for a moment. Both *exeunt*. The curtains must have been opened again at this point (Scene vii) disclosing the inner stage just as when the Husband had left it, the servant, wife, and others wounded and groaning. Then "Enter Master, and two servants," but they immediately go out to pursue the murderer. The persons remaining soon *exeunt* to seek surgeons. The curtains must have been closed, and the scene is outdoors again, for (Scene viii) "Enter Husband as being thrown off his horse, and falls."

In this rapid action the curtains have been used (1) to discover an interior room, (2) to change from indoors to outdoors with one of the actors remaining on the stage, (3) to change from outdoors back to the same interior, and (4) to change again from interior to outside. Scene ix, it may be added, is an interior again, the house of the magistrate, before whom the Husband is brought for trial, and Scene x is outdoors before the house. The Husband is on his way to execution and the wife is "brought in a chaire" from the house, now probably represented by one of the doors, or possibly by the curtains.[1]

It is possible that in Scenes v and vii, the action was in the balcony, for the Husband cries,

"Ile brake your clamor with your neck: down staires!
Tumble, tumble, headlong!"

Even in this case, the evidence for the use of the curtains is the same; it is often difficult to be sure whether discoveries of rooms were made on the inner stage or the balcony.

In addition to the use of the curtain to mark these abrupt changes, when the same persons are shown first within and then without a specified house, it would be natural to extend the use of the inner stage for all alternations from outdoors to indoors. Evidence for this is to be found in the numerous instances of a shift from a street to a house or *vice versa*. Dr. Albright has cited many acts which seem to have been constructed with the curtained stage in mind, so that a continuity is often maintained through the act.

---

[1] The preceding paragraph and some others in this chapter have appeared in substance in an article, "From Outdoors to Indoors on the Elizabethan Stage," *Kittredge Anniversary Papers*, 1913. See also Albright, *Shakespearian Stage*, pp. 122–5, where a number of instances are given of scenes changing with characters on the stage.

One example may be added to his list for the sake of illustration.[1]

THE COXCOMB, ACT I. *Scene i.* Out-doors, in the street, before Antonio's house, into which several persons *exeunt*. Outer. *Scene ii.* A room in Antonio's house; musicians and a dance. Curtains are opened, possibly discovering musicians as well as properties. After a few lines, enter those who left the stage at the end of Scene i. Inner-outer. *Scene iii.* A street. Curtains close at end of Scene ii. Outer. *Scene iv.* "Enter Viola from a house with a key and a little casket," — a street, as in Scene iii. Outer. *Scene v.* "Enter Ricardo *et al* and a Drawer with a candle." They sit and the drawer brings wine — within a tavern. Curtains open disclosing properties. Inner. *Scene vi.* "Enter Viola." The curtains have closed at the end of Scene vi, and we are back with Viola on the street as in Scene iv, but now arrived at the corner where she is to meet her lover. There is singing within (in the tavern) and then enter the drunken youths and the drawer. Outer.

FURTHER EVOLUTION IN THE USE OF THE INNER STAGE

One other play must be outlined in full, because it illustrates several changes from outdoors to indoors, with persons remaining on the front while the curtains open or close, and because its stage directions happen to be particularly full and convincing on the use

---

[1] D. G. Stuart, "Stage Decoration and Unity of Place in France," *Mod. Phil.*, January, 1913, cites an interesting case of the use of curtains for alternations on the French stage, thus modifying the simultaneous set and perhaps introducing, as he suggests, "the new method of changing the scene." In "Les Galanteries du duc d'Ossone" by Mairet, in Act II, "Comme il est entré, la toile se tire qui represente la façade d'une maison, et le dedans du cabinet paroist." Later, "Icy la seconde toile se tire, et Flavie paroist sur son lict." In the next act the action changes to the street, "Icy les deux toiles se ferment et Emilie paroist dans la rue."

of the inner stage. The play is Marston's "What You Will," probably acted in 1601 by the Paul's boys.[1] Although the entrances and exits are not marked, or the scenes distinguished, the few elaborate directions at the beginning of II. i, II. ii, and V. i, are sufficient to explain the alternation of scenes.

Induction:
Prologue.
I. i. Apparently on the street or a square. Front stage.
I. ii. There is probably a change of scene to the Duke's palace, accomplished by opening the curtains, when the cornets sound, and the Duke *et al.* enter. But the evidence for this must be drawn from a similar change in Act V, *q.v.*
II. i. "One knocks: Laverdure draws the curtains, sitting on his bed, apparrelling himself; his trunk of apparel standing by him." Others enter, and after talk, dance, and song, they go out "to give a notice to an odd pedant as we pass, of my nuptials." Inner stage discovered at beginning. Curtains close during the scene, as the action comes down front.
II. ii. "Enter a schoolmaster, draws the curtains behind, with Battus, Nous, Slip, Nathaniel, and Holofernes Pippo, schoolboys, sitting, with books in their hands." After a time enter the gentlemen of II. i. Evidently the curtains are closed long before the end of the scene, though no *exeunt* is marked. Inner-outer stage.
III. i. "Enter Francisco, half-dressed, in his black doublet and round cap, the rest rich; Jacomo bearing his hat and feather, Andrea his doublet and band; Randolfo his cloak and staff. They clothe Francisco whilst Bidet creeps in and observes them. Much of this is done while the Act is playing." Inner stage.
III. ii. A street scene. Outer stage.
III. iii. The pages enter, possibly in a tavern, but the scene is neutral and may be on inner or outer stage.

[1] R. A. Small. *The Stage Quarrel between Ben Jonson and the so-called Poetasters*, Breslau, 1899; pp. 101–114.

IV. i. Enter the ladies and maids: indoors; Albano's house; curtains open with properties for a room. At the end all exeunt to dinner; curtains close. Inner-outer.

V. i. "The curtains are drawn by a Page, and Celia and Laverdure, Quadratus and Lyzabetta, Lampatho and Meletza, Simplicius and Lucia, displayed, sitting at dinner. The song is sung, during which a Page whispers with Simplicius." In Albano's house. Simplicius announces that he must go out. No *exeunt* is marked, but apparently the curtains close, leaving Simplicius (and Quadratus?) alone on the front stage. Inner, with change to outer, persons remaining on stage.

V. ii. To Simplicius, enter the pages; neutral scene, outdoors. After a time, Enter Quadratus and the other persons discovered at the opening of V. i. They enter on the outer stage (or possibly the curtains are opened disclosing them on the inner). Outer stage.

V. iii. "Enter as many Pages with torches as you can; Randolfo, Andrea, Jacomo bare-headed; the Duke with Attendants." This must be at the palace, the "revels and a play at court" alluded to in IV. i. 368–9. The ladies and gentlemen on the stage at the end of V. ii are not marked for exeunt or entrance. Apparently the curtains opened disclosing the 'state,' and the scene changed from street to presence chamber while eight persons remained on front. Inner-outer.

It should be observed that the convincing proof which this play offers of changes from the outer to inner stage and the reverse, even while actors remain on the stage, depends on the accident that in two important cases the directions include the words "draws the curtains" and "the curtains were drawn." If these words, so obvious to a stage manager and so unnecessary for the reader, had been omitted from the printed text, the method of stage presentation of the play would remain a matter of dispute.

It must not be thought, however, that all indoor scenes required the inner stage. Scenes presumably indoors but not requiring heavy properties could be played on the outer stage; and in plays with forest scenes, as "As You Like It," or "Cymbeline," the forest properties would take the inner stage, and the presumably indoor scenes would of necessity be relegated to the outer stage. "Cymbeline," one of the first plays written by Shakespeare for the Blackfriars, illustrates this form of alternation and several other uses of the inner stage.

Act I. The six scenes afford few references to properties or localities. Scene i appears to be in a garden (l. 81), and in Scene v the Queen sends her ladies to gather flowers (off the stage). Scene iv seems to be indoors, and is later described by Iachimo (V. v. 155) as a feast in a mansion. As it marks a shift from Britain to Rome, it may well have been marked by the curtains. The other scenes are unlocalized, all somewhere about the palace. The arrangement may have been:

Scene i. Garden background on inner stage; inner-outer.

Scene ii. Conversation; outer.

Scene iii. Conversation; outer.

Scene iv. Change of scene to Rome, marked by curtains opening; properties for a room; inner-outer.

Scene v. Change of scene to Britain, marked by curtains closing; outer.

Scene vi. Outer.

Act II. In Scene ii, the stage direction "Imogen in bed; a Lady" indicates that the curtains opening discovered Imogen reading in bed on the inner stage. The trunk, containing Iachimo, had also been placed there. Scene iv transfers to Rome, presumably in Philario's house, as I. iv. The arrangement of this act appears fairly certain:

Scene i. Conversation; outer.

Scene ii. "Imogen in bed"; the curtains open; properties, bed, trunk, candles; inner.

Scene iii. A room near the bedchamber; knocking several times; outer.

Scene iv. Curtains open, marking the change to Rome; inner stage set as in I. iv, for Philario's house; inner-outer.

Scene v. Same as Scene iv; inner-outer.

Act III. The directions and properties for Scenes iii and vi before the cave of Belarius mark the use of the inner stage and indicate the arrangement for the act.

Scene i. "Enter in state, Cymbeline, Queen, Cloten, and Lords, at one door, and at another, Caius Lucius and Attendants." Probably the "state," or throne on a dais, was set on the inner stage, as often in embassy scenes; inner-outer.

Scene ii. Conversation; outer.

Scene iii. "Enter Belarius; Guiderius and Arvigarus"; the text indicates that they enter from the cave; rocks mentioned; the curtains opening disclose the cave-setting on inner stage; inner-outer.

Scene iv. Pisanio and Imogen in the country near Milford-Haven; outer.

Scene v. At court; outer.

Scene vi. Before the cave which Imogen enters; curtains open and disclose setting as in Scene iii; inner-outer.

Scene vii. Rome; curtains closing mark the change of place; expository 16 lines; outer.

Act IV. *Scene i.* Cloten soliloquizes near the cave, which may or may not be disclosed; outer.

Scene ii. "Enter Belarius, Guiderius, Arvigarus, and Imogen from the cave"; curtains disclose setting as in III. iii and vi; inner-outer.

Scene iii. At court; outer.

Scene iv. Before the cave, curtains opening; inner-outer.

Act V. Scenes i, ii, and iii, showing camp and battle are all on the outer stage. Scene iv shows Posthumus in jail, probably on the inner stage; he sleeps; the ghosts enter and "they circle Posthumus round," as he is sleeping; "Jupiter descends in thunder and lightning, sitting upon an eagle," from the hut in an open air theater or from the ceiling in a private theater. The ghosts are commanded by Jupiter to "fade" and their *exeunt* is marked by the stage directions "vanish." They probably kept pretty close to the inner stage, where their enchantments would not be injured by too close examination. The curtains close, and Scene v is on outer stage.

"Cymbeline" illustrates several special considerations in the use of the inner stage in addition to those we have discussed. The possible use of the "state" in III. i is in accord with the usual method of representing the presence chamber in court scenes. The scenes with the ghosts and with Iachimo in Imogen's bedchamber illustrate a rather large variety of scenes which would be more effective in the partial concealment of the inner stage than in the full light of the front. Deeds of horror or of great improbability, as well as supernatural scenes, would fall into this class. This consideration may also explain the different methods used for bed scenes. In the case of sick persons, as in "Lear" (IV. vii, "Enter Lear in a chair carried by servants"), manifestly the action must be down front; in other bedroom scenes, as this one of Iachimo, the action will hardly bear full light and was confined mostly to the inner stage.

In "Cymbeline," moreover, the employment of the inner stage appears to go beyond the special uses we have enumerated and suggests a freer adoption of the principle of alternation, *i.e.* the use of the curtains to denote change of place. The division of an act into a large number of scenes and the frequent shifting from one place to another would then be managed without confusion. Take, for example, "Antony and

Cleopatra," with its forty-two scenes in Europe, Asia, and Africa, perhaps the most difficult of Shakespeare's plays for us to imagine as designed for a theater. The third and fourth acts include twenty-eight scenes; but if we imagine all the parts of the stage in use, the performance would have a panoramic continuity and rapidity without any possible confusion.

ACT III. *Scene i.* Ventidius in triumph in Syria; curtains closed, doors opened; outer.

Scene ii. Cæsar parting from Antony and Octavia; in Cæsar's house; curtains open, showing properties for a room, and marking abrupt change from Scene i; inner-outer, changing perhaps to outer before the end of the act.

Scene iii. "Enter Cleopatra, Charmian, Iras, and Alexas"; in Cleopatra's palace; either at the end, or earlier, of Scene ii, the curtains closed and new properties were substituted to indicate Cleopatra's palace; curtains open, door closed; inner-outer.

Scene iv. "Enter Antony and Octavia"; no reference to properties or place, although from other passages in the play, the scene was at Athens; 38 ll.; outer.

Scene v. Place evidently near that of Scene iv; outer.

Scene vi. In Cæsar's house at Rome; curtains opening mark the change of place from Athens to Rome, and disclose the properties of Scene ii; inner-outer.

Scene vii. In Antony's camp near Actium; curtains close; outer.

Scenes viii, ix, x. Battle scenes, on the plains of Actium, as Scene vi; and all on outer stage.

Scene xi. In Cleopatra's palace; the curtains open and disclose the properties of Scene iii; inner-outer.

Scene xii. Cæsar's camp in Egypt; outer.

Scene xiii. Cleopatra's palace; curtains open, disclose setting as in Scenes iii and xi.

ACT IV. *Scene i.* Cæsar and army; outer.

Scene ii. Antony and Cleopatra; Cleopatra's palace as in III. iii. xi. xiii; inner-outer.

Scene iii. "Enter soldiers," on guard; outer.

Scene iv. In the palace; setting as in Scene ii; inner-outer.

Scene v. "Trumpets sound. Enter Antony and Eros," who had retired four lines before the end of Scene iv; they are now outdoors and are met by a soldier, possibly before one of the open doors, which may symbolize Antony's camp; outer.

Scene vi. Cæsar's camp; entries possibly from the other door; outer.

Scene vii. "Alarum. Drums and trumpets", etc.; the battle field; outer.

Scene viii. "Alarum. Enter Antony, in a march; Scarus with others." Antony, who is victorious for the moment, commands his soldiers to "Enter the city," so he is presumably before the walls, which might be indicated by citizens on the balcony; thus marking the change of place from Scenes vi and vii. Outer stage with balcony.

Scene ix. "Enter sentry and his company"; near Cæsar's camp; outer.

Scenes x, xi, xii represent the battle and are all outer.

Scene xiii. Cleopatra's palace, curtains opened, doors closed, as in Scenes ii and iv; inner-outer.

Scene xiv. Probably the same as Scene xiii; inner-outer.

Scene xv. "Enter Cleopatra and her maids aloft, with Charmian and Iras"; the scene is on the monument (balcony); outer stage with balcony.

In this scheme, the inner stage is used only to supply properties and as a background for two interiors, Cæsar's palace in Rome and Cleopatra's in Alexandria; yet the closing and opening of the curtains serve effectively to indicate the important changes of place. It is impossible to prove that Shakespeare had this arrangement in view, but so many shifting scenes in a play as late as 1608 certainly suggest the utility of the curtains. The same may be said of many other plays with less difficult scenarios than "Antony and Cleopatra," and it is not easy to believe that the later dramatists were unmindful of the advantage afforded them by the inner stage.

A word may be interpolated in regard to the presentation of a succession of different indoor scenes. In the later years of our period such successions are very common. Sometimes all of the scenes are indoors, as in Shirley's "Lady of Pleasure," where the scenes are in four distinct houses. Properties are often mentioned, and the different rooms may have distinctive features. The regular method seems to have regarded the outer stage as a sort of neutral hall or anteroom, and to have indicated specially furnished apartments by means of the inner stage, a method recently used in Mr. Shaw's "Fanny's First Play." It seems possible, however, that in some cases the curtains were drawn after each scene, and the setting altered sufficiently to indicate the change, as from a richly to a poorly furnished room. The procedure in such cases would mark a step in advance from Elizabethan methods and in the direction of modern staging. For, if all the scenes were in rooms, there would be no unlocalized places; each scene would have a distinct locality indicated by its background setting on the inner stage. A play would then be written around a few different settings, ten or twelve scenes being fitted to four or five rooms. Substitute scenery for setting, and you have completed the change from the medieval to the modern scheme. Since this particular development seems to have taken place only after

Shakespeare's death, it needs no special attention here, except as a suggestion of that continuing evolution which we have noted as characterizing the entire period from 1576 to 1642.

SUMMARY OF THE EVOLUTION OF THE INNER STAGE

That evolution, so far as it concerns the inner stage, I have now traced in a number of special uses. These are: (1) for caves, arbors, studios, shops, settings in which the inner stage is a localized part of the outer stage; (2) discoveries of persons or localities, after the discovery the action often moving to the front; (3) various scenes requiring heavy properties, the inner stage providing a background, as in forest scenes, or in temple, church, palace, or other elaborate interiors; (4) in sudden alternations, when actors pass immediately from outside of a house to the inside, or the reverse; (5) any change from an outdoor to an indoor scene, or the reverse; (6) scenes when the action will hardly bear the full light of the front stage; (7) usually in connection with (3) (4) and (5), to mark any notable change of place. The exact chronology or stages of this development cannot be traced; but the uses (1) and (2) probably preceded (3) and (4), and all were practiced by the time Shakespeare came to London. The use of (6) obviously varied with different theaters and (5) and (7) were gradual developments from the earlier practices and not much in evidence before 1600–1610. By the later date, the inner stage had become an important adjunct in the increasing practice of indicating locality, and the curtains facilitated the shift of scenes, after a method carried over to the Restoration stage, and in constant use down to the present day. The front stage was any place (unpropertied); open the curtains, and the inner stage gave the setting for a special locality.

Changes in the use of the inner-outer theater did not, however, mean a break with past practices. Some scenes formerly acted on the outer stage, or even in 1620 still acted on the outer stage at the public theaters, were very possibly provided with a background on the inner stage at the private houses, Salisbury Court or Blackfriars. The first act of "Twelfth Night," which may have been written and acted originally without any use of the inner stage, might conceivably have been produced later at Blackfriars with setting and properties for the interior scenes, as it certainly would have been produced after the Restoration.

After Shakespeare's death, the general progress continued in the direction of more localization, less incongruity, and more alternation. If we compare plays acted from 1620 to 1630 with those acted from 1590 to 1600, there are fewer scenes without any localization whatever, more that are specially localized, and more requiring or suggesting properties. There is an increase in the number of scenes clearly designed for the use of an inner stage, and there is an increase in the number of those that indicate locality sufficiently to suggest its use. This development in the employment of the inner stage seems to be connected with the growing importance of the private theaters. With their greater facilities for lighting, the inner stage must have been given a better display, and with their more fashionable audiences, used to court performances and masques, there must have been a demand for more properties. Moreover, the very fact that the stage was now indoors, without a special heaven and without pillars, made it approximate much more closely

The "School for Scandal" at Drury Lane, 1778.

to the Restoration stage and invited attempts to simulate interiors. What other changes in the arrangement of curtains may have aided, we cannot tell; but the relatively increased breadth of the inner stage, less projection, and the placing of the proscenium doors on the bias, all seem to me likely to have characterized the private theaters, though they may all have been found in the later public theaters.

MINOR QUESTIONS OF STAGING

There remain for consideration in this chapter some matters concerning various parts of the stage that require attention by themselves, although they also afford additional illustration of the general principles of staging.

First, it should be observed that there were sporadic efforts throughout our period to secure unity of place, and consequently a method of staging something like the classical. These efforts for unity of place did not attain the success which they finally won in the theater of Corneille, but there was no great difficulty in trying them on the professional stage. A play as late as the "Covent Garden" of Nabbes observes strictly the unity of place and marks both entrances and exits by specified doors; yet it was acted by the Queen's men at the Cockpit in 1632. I do not think that these classical imitations had much effect on the general practices in staging.

We have discussed the use of the inner stage for heavy properties, but manifestly properties of various kinds might also be brought on the front stage. Many readers of this volume have seen chairs or other properties brought on and off the stage in full view of the spectator. In particular, when the drop scene is used,

K

chairs or other properties are brought on from the wings. This practice, infrequent in the best theaters to-day, was common enough in earlier times and on the Elizabethan stage. Sometimes, doubtless, these properties were brought in through the doors, but usually they appear to have been carried on and off through the rear curtains. Directions in regard to chairs are rare and apparently were not considered necessary, but there are many indicating that banquets are to be brought on and off, tables set up or removed, or a bed moved to the front or the rear. "Set out," "brought in," and even "enter" and "exit" may, however, as we have noted in Chapter IV, merely denote what is to be done before the curtains are drawn and the inner stage revealed. Often, indeed, after the curtains were opened, and the inner stage revealed, properties, as chairs, couches, or even beds were pushed forward so as to be within better view of the audience. But, whether from the inner recess or not, properties would have been brought forward without hesitation, whenever it was important to have the action well to the front. So, we have "Lear in a chair carried by Servants" (IV. vii. 20) in order that the wonderful scene of his recovery may be in full view. And so in Heywood's "Silver Age," "Enter Semele drawne out in her bed," because shortly afterwards, as Jupiter, with burning thunderbolt, "toucheth the bed, it fires, and all flyes up."

Were properties placed on the outer stage left there during the progress of an incongruous action, as trees and rocks during a room scene, or beds during an outdoor scene? In the early period, or in theaters where there was no curtain, or where the inner stage was small, occasional incongruities of this sort may have been necessary. Stage directions for placing properties prior to their use may, however, usually be interpreted as indicating that they were put behind the curtains. What clear cases exist of incongruity are rather to be considered as examples of multiple setting.

Did the stage ever represent two widely separated places at once? We know that in court plays in the early part of Elizabeth's reign, the stage had a multiple setting representing several distinct places at once. We should expect that some plays with such settings were also produced on the public stage, especially by the children's companies and in musical or spectacular plays. I shall discuss these cases in detail in the next chapter, when I consider the influence of the court stage upon the public theaters. Our study of the inner-outer stage has already indicated that the multiple setting never became generally established.

In the popular drama, in general, there are very few scenes in which a multiple setting is required, and these are mostly of the simplest sort with little incongruity. In "Richard III," for example, the two camps of Richard and Richmond appear on opposite sides of the stage. In other plays, two or more different houses are represented, or different places in a forest; but in each of these cases the incongruity of the multiple setting is hardly greater than that which is practiced on the modern stage. The places are not at all remote and it is easy for the mind to admit of their being brought together on one stage. Asia and Africa were not both represented at once on the public stage very long after 1576.

Were signs used to indicate places? In Hieronymo's order in the "Spanish Tragedy" (IV. 3),

> hang up the title
> Our scene is Rhodes,

the sign indicates the general locality. In other cases, as in the prologue to "Wily Beguiled," the "Knight of the Burning Pestle," and the "City Wit," a sign seems to have announced the title of the play. In masques and court plays the titles were often made part of the stage decoration. In the professional theaters, the title and general locality of a play were often announced by the speaker of the Prologue, and also by signs. In Percy's two plays in manuscript, signs were suggested to mark specific localities, and in the First Part of the "Contention," V. ii, a direction reads, "under the signe of the Castle in Saint Albones." Apart from these cases and Sir Philip Sidney's reference to "Thebes written in great Letters upon an olde doore," there are no indications of signs for special localities. As Mr. W. J. Lawrence has noted,[1] evidence that such signs were not used is supplied by the remarks of the persons in the choruses of "Every Man Out of his Humour," which carefully announce to the audience the locality of each scene. Many cases could be cited where a marked change of place is carefully announced by the chorus or in the text. But the proof that such signs were not in general use is to be found in the plays themselves. Not only is there no mention of signs, but no possibility that the exits and entrances could be managed through doors so designated. Manifestly such signs would have been out of place except in plays attempting a multiple setting. In one instance, "Eastward Hoe," IV. i, the direction "Enter Slitgut with a paire of oxe hornes,

---

[1] *The Elizabethan Playhouses and Other Studies*, 62.

discovering Cuckolds Haven above" shows a sign for a special locality disclosed at the proper moment in a play. But business of this sort might be employed occasionally in any theater.

The use of a balcony over the inner stage has been often mentioned and formed an important accessory to the main stage. In principle it served the same purpose as the inner stage, for the presentation of special localities; and, since in many theaters it was provided with curtains, it could also be used for discoveries. It might represent any place above the level of the stage, and when an interior room is presented, one is occasionally in doubt whether the balcony or the inner stage is intended. In the early plays, and especially in the historical ones, it was employed very frequently to represent the walls of a city, or tower, or other fortification. By its use the mimicry of war was made more varied and bustling. The balcony was also utilized for a mimic audience, as in the "Spanish Tragedy," IV. 3; but in the presentation of a play within a play, the arrangement would vary according as it was more important to have the mock play or the mock audience at the front. The use of the balcony was restricted because of its small size and detachment from the main stage; so that in later plays it is often given over to musicians or possibly to auditors. In some cases the musicians occupy it during a part of a play and then remove to some other place in order that it may be used for a particular scene.

In the reign of James I, when historical plays were rare, the windows over the doors seem to have been used more frequently than the balcony to denote upper rooms of houses. Fletcher, in his liking for

movement and bustle, often sends his persons up-
stairs, sometimes to appear on the balcony, but more
frequently at a window. One scene (I. iii) in the
"Maid of the Mill" may serve as an illustration. In
the preceding scene (I. ii) Antonio has received a letter
from Ismenia inviting him to her house.

> If you please to look me
> In the West-street, and find a fair stone window
> Carved with cupids, there I'll entertain you.

Antonio. with his friend Martine at once start out to
find the house. Then a new scene begins, marked
apparently by closing of curtains on the interior scene.
Enter Ismenia and Aminta, who presently see the two
men approaching, and retreat through one of the doors.
"Up to th' chamber, cousin; Get you up." Antonio
and Martine enter, declare "This is the street," look
about in the darkness for the houses, "a merchant's,
a 'pothecary's," and at length discover "a goodly
window, too, carved fair above!" "'Tis dark" and
"grows vengeance black." Then "Ismenia and Aminta
appear at the window with a taper." Then follows a
long conversation; finally the men *exeunt*, and Ismenia
bids Aminta "Pluck-to the windows." Here a practicable window is used decorated by carving; and it
is clearly over one of the doors. The window is used
again in IV. iii of the same play.

From the hut in the public, and from an upper loft
in the private theaters, gods and goddesses could be
lowered and raised to the stage, and apparatus provided for suns, moons, clouds, and other celestial
effects. On the outer and inner stage and in the
gallery, trapdoors provided entrances and exits for
ghosts, devils, and other subterranean inhabitants.

The discussion of spectacle on the professional stage must be reserved to our consideration of the court shows, for the professionals naturally followed some distance behind the sumptuous and expensive productions of the court. But though the spectacle on the public stage was imitative of the court, it was far from meager. Processions, battles, embassies, were frequent and gave as much elaboration as possible. Those who think modern stage decoration incongruous with Shakespeare's plays forget to what extent he availed himself of the resources of his theater. Not to speak here of "Midsummer Night's Dream" and the "Tempest," plays frankly spectacular and adopting many of the devices of current court entertainments, there are in other plays ghosts, magicians, witches, and fairies; and in two plays besides the "Tempest" the machinery of the hut seems to have been employed: for the descending apparitions in "Macbeth," IV. i, and for Jupiter on the eagle in "Cymbeline," V. iv. The best idea of the resources of the stage in the way of fireworks, vanishings, ascents, and unusual costumes and properties, can be derived from Heywood's "Four Ages." In these, as generally in sixteenth-century plays, the "dumb shows" interspersed through the dialogue employ some of the most elaborate properties and machines. A few stage directions will indicate what the stage managers could do when they aimed at a spectacular performance.

Enter Saturne with wedges of gold and silver, models of ships, and buildings, bow and arrowes, &c. His Lords with him.

Enter Sibilla lying in child-bed, with her child lying by her, and her Nurse &c.

Hornes winded, a great noise of hunting. Enter Diana, all her Nimphes in the chase, Jupiter pulling Calisto back.

Sounde a dumbe shew. Enter the three fatall sisters, with a rocke, a threed, and a paire of sheeres; bringing in a Gloabe, in which they put three lots. Jupiter drawes heaven: at which Iris descends and presents him with his Eagle, Crowne and Scepter, and his thunder-bolt. Jupiter first ascends upon the Eagle, and after him Ganimed.

Sound. Neptune drawes the Sea, is mounted upon a sea-horse, a Roabe and Trident, with a crowne are given him by the Fates.

Sound, Thunder and Tempest. Enter at 4 several corners the 4 winds: Neptune riseth disturb'd: the Fates bring the 4 winds in a chaine, and present them to Æolus, as their King.

Sound. Pluto drawes hell: the Fates put upon him a burning Roabe, and present him with a Mace, and burning crowne.

Thunder and lightning. All the servants run out of the house affrighted, the two Captains and Blepharo, Amphitrio and Socia amazedly awake: Jupiter appeares in his glory under a Raine-bow, to whom they all kneele.

Hercules sinkes himselfe. Flashes of fire; the Divels appeare at every corner of the stage with severall fire-workes. The Judges of hell, and the three sisters run over the stage, Hercules after them: fire-workes all over the house. Enter Hercules.

Hercules kils the Sea-Monster, the Trojans on the walles, the Greekes below.

Two fiery Buls are discovered, the Fleece hanging over them, and the Dragon sleeping beneath them: Medea with strange fiery-workes, hangs above in the Aire in the strange habite of a Conjuresse.

Enter Mars and Venus.

Vulcan catcheth them fast in his net.

All the Gods appeare above, and laugh, Jupiter, Juno, Phœbus, Mercury, Neptune.

Hercules swings Lychas about his head, and kils him.

Enter Hercules from a rocke above, tearing downe trees.

All the Princes breake downe the trees, and make a fire, in which Hercules placeth himselfe.

Such performances reveal a medley of methods, properties being sometimes discovered and sometimes brought on, but add little or nothing to our knowledge of the methods of legitimate drama, though they may suggest how much the Elizabethan stage could offer its spectators beyond the spoken word and the impersonation of character. A word should perhaps be added in regard to the lighting, which was of importance in the regular as well as the spectacular drama and has aroused some discussion between symbolists and realists. For us accustomed to electricity, it is difficult to imagine the days when the gas-lit stage seemed of unsurpassable brilliancy, and still more difficult to imagine oil-lamps or candles as affording dazzling effects. There is record of the amazing rapidity with which the candle-snuffers wrought transformation from light to darkness on the eighteenth-century stages; and we may presume that the indoor theaters of the seventeenth century, the better of which were lit by wax candles, secured various lighting effects to the satisfaction of their audiences. Was the case different in the outdoor theaters when the performances were by daylight? There seems to have been no hesitation on the part of dramatists to use night and day, sunlight and moonlight, and pitch darkness. Indeed, there is a group of plays where the action represents persons mistaking one another on account of the dark night, and hence producing all kinds of entanglements. The "Merry Wives of Windsor," the "Two Angry Women of Abingdon," the "Merry Devil of Edmonton" (plays all acted at about the same time), have striking scenes of this sort.

I must confess I cannot see the difficulty here which some modern commentators have found.[1] Of course, darkness was symbolized rather than realized, just as it is to-day. The stage is never dark except for a moment. The action is intended to be seen. With our brilliant light, half-light can be used as a symbol of darkness more effectively than in past times, but we still have recourse to lamps, candles, moons, etc., to symbolize night-time. Elizabethans may have occasionally obtained effects of darkness by smoke or gauze, or by putting out lights, but in the main they only symbolized darkness. They brought candles or tapers on the inner stage to indicate that it was night-time in the chamber or study, and brought torches on the front to indicate that the night was dark. When darkness was required for the action, some of the dramatis personæ carefully stated that it was dark; candles or torches reiterated the illusion; if they went out it was certainly still darker; but the action was plainly visible to the audience. So it is to-day, and a long time must ensue before we give night scenes a realistic presentation. We act a "Midsummer's Night's Dream" on a brilliantly lit stage, or some-

---

[1] W. J. Lawrence, "Light and Darkness in the Elizabethan Theater," *Elizabethan Playhouse and Other Studies*, Second Series, 1913. John Corbin, "Shakespeare his own Stage Manager," *Century Magazine*, December, 1911.

times by amateurs outdoors in the afternoon sunlight, and no one is worried by the incongruity.

Although some special incidents of stage presentation have been touched on in this chapter, its main purpose has not been to deal with particular features, but to indicate the main principles which characterized the presentation of the drama on the professional stage. Some modifications of these principles in individual cases must be admitted, notably (1) in traces up to about 1600 of the multiple setting carried on from medieval times to the court entertainments, and (2) in influences on the professional stage from the very modern methods familiarized by the court masques after 1600. These modifications are to be discussed in the following chapters. But the development of Elizabethan stage presentation ran its peculiar and interesting course without substantial effect from either of these qualifying influences. The fixed and most important principle was the use of the projecting platform as a sort of neutral, vaguely localized territory, where almost anything might happen. The second principle was the use of the inner stage, with its curtains (and to some extent the upper stage), as a means to denote locality more exactly, to employ properties more readily, and to indicate changes of scene more effectively. In the development of the inner stage lie the main steps of a progress from the first simplification of the cumbrous medieval methods to the close approach to the Restoration presentation on a scenic back and a bare front stage. This particular process is, so far as I can discover, peculiar to the English theater, and had its effect on the creations of our greatest dramatist and his contemporaries.

CHAPTER VI

So far we have been considering the Shakespearian stage from the point of view of the professional companies and their theaters and public performances. We have not considered the performances of amateurs at court or university, the influence of the court on stage setting or acting, or the dramatic entertainments peculiar to the court. Yet, as we have seen, the Renaissance drama everywhere in Europe was at first an affair of the schools and court. If in England the professional actors finally took possession of the drama, there was a long period extending through three quarters of the sixteenth century in which school and court were the leaders and innovators. After that time, the universities and schools contributed little that was of importance in the history of the stage or the drama; but the court continued to exercise a varied and constant influence on the public theater. Even in a survey of the activities of the public theater, it is necessary to consider the influence of the court, not only on the matters of the stage presentation discussed in the preceding chapter, but also in connection with many matters of patronage and regulation which will come up as we proceed. We turn, therefore, to examine the stage and drama from the point of view of the courts of Elizabeth and James; and to understand the court drama of that period, we shall have to include the practices of the first half of the century, in the reigns of Henry VII and Henry VIII.

COURT SHOWS OF THE EARLY TUDORS

Performances at court may be conveniently divided into two classes, (1) shows of various sorts in which the dramatic interest was secondary to that of spectacle, music, and dance, and (2) regular drama. These shows were of many kinds, under many names; some without any speeches, others with a minimum of speech supplied by a prologue or other explanatory address, and others with considerable dialogue or even an elaborate libretto. Two forms of entertainment, however, are early distinguishable, then soon combine, and finally in combination experience a notable dramatic and literary development — the Disguising and the Pageant. The disguisings or mummings appear early at court and are among the favorite entertainments of the first Tudors. In their simple form, a band of gentlemen, disguised in fantastic fashion, enter a hall and give a dance, perhaps joining with some of the ladies present. The pageant was an elaborate movable device representing temple, palace, sun, moon, or what not. This was wheeled into the hall, and on it ladies and gentlemen in costume appeared in tableaux usually with some allegorical significance. Either a disguising or a pageant could get along with dumb show, but with either a certain amount of speech-making or dialogue might be involved. When the two were combined, a considerable court spectacle resulted, with an elaborate pageant, expensive costumes and properties, dancing, music, and possibly a play.[1]

[1] I know of no contemporary picture of one of these English spectacles, but their general character is shown in the print (1661) reproduced, facing

Such elaborate shows were common as early as the reign of Henry VII, though only one has been fully reported. It was given in Westminster Hall on the occasion of the wedding of Prince Arthur with Katharine of Spain on November 18, 1501. There were three pageants, a Castle, bearing singing children and eight disguised ladies, amongst whom was one "apparelled like unto the Princesse of Spaine," a Ship in which were Hope and Desire as Ambassadors, and a Mount of Love, from which issued eight knights who assaulted the castle. After this device, which was set forth by "countenance, speeches, and demeanor," the knights and ladies danced together.[1]

In 1513, there was introduced, according to the chronicler Hall, a dance disguise "after the maner of Italie, called a maske, a thyng not seen afore in Englande." Just what the innovation was is not clear, possibly the use of visors instead of hoods, or complete disguises.[2] At all events, the new "maske" or dance between ladies and gentlemen of the court henceforth became the central factor of most court revels. The other elements, the procession, the pageant, the pantomime, the music, the dialogue, continued as before. The records of the early years of the reign of Henry VIII, which have been preserved in the detailed accounts of Richard Gibson, sergeant of the King's revels and tents show an abundance of these court shows, given with great splendor.

In one, the pageant is a forest, 26 by 16 by 9 feet, with a castle on top, a maiden, foresters, armed

page 142, of an Italian entertainment in the gardens of the Pitti Palace, Florence. Hercules bearing the globe is the pageant.

[1] Chambers, I. 398. Collier, *H. E. D. P.*, new ed., i. 58.

[2] Chambers, I, 401-3.

A Pageant in the Gardens of the Pitti Palace, Florence

knights, all drawn by a great lion and 'olyvant.'
At another time, the pageant was "ye golldyn arber
in ye arche yerd of plesyer," a huge arbor with thirty
persons and 350 clusters of grapes of gold, so huge,
that it broke through the floor of the hall. In another,
the "Gardyn of Esperans" was exhibited, a garden
embowered with silk daffodils, columbine, iris, and
other flowers. With these pageants went songs,
dances, jousts, speeches, and perhaps plays. On
some occasions, as Christmas revels, or Mayday celebrations, there were elaborate series of revels, with
pageants, processions, dances, and plays intermingled.
In 1527, a House of Revel, called the Long House, was
built for such purposes.

These elaborate court shows are manifestly very
different from the regular dramas of their day. Interludes of various kinds, moral or farcical, were given
at the court of Henry VIII, as Medwall's interlude of
"Finding of Truth," Redford's "Wit and Science,"
and Heywood's plays. Of their stage presentation
nothing is known beyond what can be inferred from
their texts. The brevity of the interludes indicates
a simplification in staging, to which I have referred in
Chapter I; but presumably the court performances,
even when by professionals, would have retained properties and 'mansions' to an extent impossible with
the wandering actors. The distinction between on
and off the stage and a great reduction in the number
and importance of the 'mansions' must certainly
have marked even the court performances. But this
tendency toward simplification in the interludes and
humanistic plays was unquestionably opposed by the
prodigal elaboration that accompanied the disguisings,
pageants, and masques. Moreover, it is difficult

to tell whether a given performance was a show or a legitimate interlude; the terms 'ludus,' 'interlude,' and 'play' are by no means reliable guides. And, further, it is difficult to tell to what extent dialogue and dramatic action accompanied the masques and pageants. But it is certain that at the time of classical and humanistic innovations and professional simplification, the staging at court was also influenced by the elaborate settings, peculiar to the pageant but likely also to affect any kind of dramatic performance.

In the matter of performers, it is also impossible to separate regular actors, minstrels, and amateurs. The court shows were affairs of the ladies and gentlemen, but some minstrels were employed. During the reign of Henry VIII, the gentlemen (including the children) of the Royal Chapel take a leading part in the entertaining, and appear as performers apparently in regular plays as well as shows, and certainly in mixed entertainments, part pageant and part drama. The King's interlude players also appear, and in the reign of Edward VI are more frequently recorded, and these professionals act in masques as well as plays.[1] The growing importance of the professional actors can be traced, but the more distinctive feature of the court stage before Elizabeth is the importance of the child actors of the Royal Chapel. They were manifestly suited to the mixture of pageant, masque, and drama which seems most characteristic of the court as distinct from the professional theater.

COURT PERFORMANCES IN ELIZABETH'S REIGN

Before Elizabeth's accession all these court entertainments had been placed under the control of a

[1] See Wallace, *Evolution*, 72, 73.

permanent official, the Master of the Revels. The extension of his authority in connection with performances outside of the court has been discussed in another chapter and does not concern us here. The office of the Revels was separated from the Tents and Toyles on the death of Sir Thomas Cawarden in 1560, and considerable records of its activities during Elizabeth's reign have been preserved and published, first by Peter Cunningham, and more recently by Professor Feuillerat. In addition to the Master were various subordinate officials, the clerk, the clerk-comptroller, and the yeoman. Extensive quarters were provided at various places and finally in St. John's Hospital. The business of the office came mainly when plays and masques were given at court, especially at the Christmas season and at Shrovetide. For the rest of the year there was little to do but to see that the costumes were properly preserved. For weeks before court festivities, however, extensive preparations were made. Old costumes might be 'translated' or new ones provided; much miscellaneous material was purchased, and many workingmen employed. In a memorandum drawn up in 1572–73, "for the better management of the office," the "stuffe cheifely occupied in the Revelles" is enumerated as "wardrobe stuff (*i.e.* for garments), vizors, hair, lawn, fringe, lace, buckrames, thread, silve, wood, coals, lights, colors for painters besides many other things."[1] Carpenters, tailors, painters, haberdashers, basket-makers, and silk-weavers were among the persons regularly employed. There were also expenses for reading and revising plays, for designing costumes and devices, and for transporting the goods from the Revels office to the court. "The

[1] Feuillerat, p. 5, and note.

L

chiefe busynes of the office," according to the Memorandum already quoted, "resteth speciallye in three poyntes, in makinge of garmentes; in makinge of hedpeces, and in paynting." "The connynge (*i.e.* knowledge) of the office resteth in skill of devise, in understandinge of historyes, in iudgement of comedies, tragedyes, and shewes, in sight of perspective and architecture, some smacke of geometrye and other thynges."

To what extent were these court performances, masques and pageants, and to what extent regular dramas? To these questions the incomplete records furnish only partial answers. Masques and shows occur frequently, but as the years go on decrease relatively in comparison with the plays. After about 1572, the plays are the more numerous, and in the later years of the reign there are few records of masques. There is also a change from the practice of preceding reigns in the performers. The ladies and gentlemen of court continue to appear in masques and pageants; but the Children of the Chapel have now become a semiprofessional company, which along with the children actors of Paul's and of Windsor, appear frequently. Adult professional companies also appear with increasing frequency, until in the latter part of the reign, they crowd out the children. These changes in the actors indicate the changes in the development of the drama. The court shows, with amateur actors, continue, but become separated from and in a measure subordinated to the regular plays by the professionals. Meantime, during the course of this process, a peculiar species of drama comes into existence, a sort of union of comedy and court show especially suited to the children actors.[1] This combination of music, dance, spectacle, mythology, pastoral, allegory, and witty dialogue finds its chief development in the talent of John Lyly; and by him and his children actors is transferred to the public stage. Its importance there may be recalled by its further development in Shakespeare's "Love's Labor's Lost" and "Midsummer Night's Dream," and its influence might be traced much further in the course of Elizabethan romantic comedy. For the first twenty-five years of Elizabeth's reign the children were the chief purveyors of court drama, but after 1583 they appeared rarely at court and suffered various suppressions until their revival at the very end of the century. In 1583, when the best adult actors were gathered into a company under her Majesty's patronage, the professional actors may be presumed to have demonstrated their superiority. Their companies acted their plays first in public and then repeated them at court. The court, in the main, took what the public liked. By the time of Marlowe and Shakespeare, the court drama could no longer be separated from that of the Theater, Curtain, and Rose. The regular plays of the public theaters came more and more to supply entertainment for Elizabeth and her court.

The Revels accounts for Elizabeth's reign give us much information as to the court performances, but they do not discriminate between the three classes of our analysis. In the numerous details supplied, shows

---

[1] Professor C. W. Wallace has discussed at length the development of this class of plays. His views are very often at wide divergence from mine, but he has accumulated a wealth of material to illustrate the importance of the court in relation-to the drama. *Evolution of the English Drama up to Shakespeare*, Berlin, 1912.

and masques are often indistinguishable from plays, and there is rarely any basis for distinction between adult and children's performances. Further, it must be remembered that these accounts deal mainly with the period from 1558 to 1583 and are very scanty for the later period, when the influence of the public theater and professional company must have dominated at court. I shall first summarize the information available from the records, and then attempt to analyze its bearing on the nature of the divergent methods of court and public stage and on their mutual relations.

THE REVELS ACCOUNTS

The performances at court, at Greenwich, Hampton Court, or Whitehall, were indoors, usually at night, by artificial light. The stage seems to have been a platform, at one end of the hall, though masques and pageants were often given in the center of the room. No definite account of stage arrangements has survived, but in comparison with the public theaters, the stage was manifestly a variable quantity which could be altered, augmented, or rearranged to suit special requirements.

A large portion of the expenses of the Revels office went into the costumes. On these there was a lavish use of silk, velvet, damask, cloth of gold, tinsel, feathers, and spangles; headpieces, buskins, and gloves receiving careful attention. Among others, we have descriptions of costumes for mariners, Venetian senators, Turks, Venuses or amorous ladies, hunters, Moors, monks, friars, Diana and her nymphs, fish-wives, market-wives, amazons, knights, sages, and Albanese warriors. Diana appears to have worn "one upper garment and one nether garment, of purple cloth of silver tissue, the back side tinsel; the upper garment fringed with narrow fringe of Cologne (Cullen) gold, and the nether garment fringed with fringe of Venice (Vennys) gold with gilt bells." [1] Her six nymphs were costumed by couples in carnation, blue, and purple, respectively, all fringed with gold and garnished with gilt bells. All had purple kirtles, white ruffs and gloves, taffeta hose, and headpieces "of paste paper, gilded, silvered, and painted, garnished with green, gold sarcenet and woven silk, dyed and set with counterfeit stones." [2] It is not easy to find much fitness in the costumes designed for mythological personages, but a certain propriety is observable in the green suits for hunters, and the lamb skins for shepherds. One entry in 1574 [3] provides for a pastoral masque or play by Italian players, lambskins for shepherds, horsetails for wild men, arrows for nymphs, lights, shepherds' staves, hoops for garlands, scythe (syth) for Saturn, bay leaves, and flowers. The more elaborate costumes were generally designed for the amateur performers in masques, but frequent provision is also made for the children and adult players.

Minor properties and materials used may be sufficiently indicated by a list of the articles on which John Carow spent £14 11s. 1d. in 1571: "Spars, rafters, boards, puncheons, nails, vices, hooks, hinges, horse tails, hobby-horses, pitchers, paper, branches of silk and other garniture for pageants, feathers, flag brooches, tow, trenchers, gloves (black), scepters, wheat sheaves, bodies of men in timber, dishes for devils' eyes, devices for hell, & hell mouth, staves for banners, etc. Bows, bills, dagg[er]s, targets, swords, fanchions, firework, bosses for bitts, spears, paste, glue, packthread,

---

[1] Feuillerat, 43.   [2] Ibid., 43.   [3] Ibid., 227.

whipcord, holly, ivy and other green boughs, bays and strewing herbs & such like implements." [1] Sometimes a great effort was made for stage realism, as for the hobby-horses for the children of Westminster in the play "Paris and Vienna," [2] or in the play "Nascisses," where the hunters "made the crye after the fox (let loose in the Coorte) with theier howndes, hornes, and hallowing." [2] In connection with the same play, 22 shillings were paid to John Izarde "for his device in counterfeiting Thunder & Lightning." [3]

More important for our inquiry are the references to the larger properties which provided the stage setting. The records leave no doubt that elaborate structures were furnished. We hear frequently of houses, castles, cities, battlements, rocks, forests, trees, mountains, and clouds. Sometimes these properties seem rather crude, as in the note of "a payle for the castle topp," [4] and the machinery somewhat primitive, as "a cord and pulleys to draw up the cloud," [5] or "Double gyrtes to hange the soon (sun) in the clowde." [6] Sometimes, however, these structures were very elaborate, as in 1581, the Mount with a castle upon it,[7] "with falling sides, tree with shields, hermitage and hermit, savages, enchanter, chariot, and incidents to these," which called for an expenditure of over one hundred pounds. This edifice was evidently huge in size, of the sort often employed in the earlier pageants and later masques. The houses, cities, battlements and rocks employed in plays seem to have been of simpler construction and designed for use as a background, rather than to serve as a movable stage for the performers. They were constructed of canvas

[1] Feuillerat, 140. [2] Ibid., 141. [3] Ibid., 142. [4] Ibid., 203.
[5] Ibid., 307. [6] Ibid., 240. [7] Ibid., 345, 346.

fastened on a wooden framework and were painted to represent the objects intended. However crude these may have been, evidently much of the scenic effectiveness then as now depended on the painter.

Many plays are noted with the properties provided. Unfortunately, none of these titles can be positively, and only very few conjecturally, identified with extant dramas. Sometimes the setting is a forest, as in the unknown play charged "For provision and carriage of trees and other things to the court for a wilderness in a play"; [1] more often a castle and battlement, or a city and battlement, are the only large properties mentioned. [2] The history of "Sarpedon" by the Chamberlain's men, in 1579–80, required a great city, a wood, and a castle; the "Duke of Milan and the Marquis of Mantua," in the same season by the same company, required a country house and a city; the "Four Sons of Fabius" by the Earl of Warwick's men, a city and a mount; the "Five Plays in One," of 1584–85, by the Queen's men, a great cloth, a battlement of canvas, canvas for a well, and a mount; the pastoral of "Phillyda and Choryn," by the same company, one great curtain, one mountain, and one great cloth of canvas.

These edifices are charged as freshly prepared for each play. Other properties were provided from the Revels' stores, but occasionally the office was forced to borrow armor or a cloud. On one occasion, at least, the borrowing was from one of the public theaters, a well from the Bell inn in Gracious street for use in the play "Cutwell." [3] To what extent there was an exchange of favors between the court office and the public theaters, does not appear. It seems possible,

---

[1] *Ibid.*, 180.   [2] *Ibid.*, *passim*, see index.   [3] *Ibid.*, 277.

however, that for special occasions the professionals may have secured the loan of court properties and costumes.

Special interest attaches to two articles often mentioned in connection with plays, — painted cloths and curtains. Painted cloths were strips of canvas on which figures or scenes were painted, and they frequently served in houses in place of tapestries. Those in the court records usually occur in connection with the heavier properties, and seem to have been designed as separate backgrounds. It should be noted that they seem quite distinct from the canvas used on houses or cities. Thus, in 1580-1, there is a charge of £9 for painting by great of six small cities and three battlements, and immediately following this a charge of £7 for painting two great cloths.[1] Similarly, the cloths of canvas used for "A Game of Cards" are separated from the pavilions also provided, and the one cloth needed for "Beautie and Housewifery" is distinct from the battlement.[2] It may also be noted that the "frames," often mentioned in connection with the cost of carriage to court, may not always have been structures for houses and castles but possibly flats on which to stretch the painted cloths. The Earl of Leicester's men in 1576 seem to have required for heavy properties only "a paynted cloth and two frames."[3] We may recall that a knowledge of perspective was deemed necessary for the officers of the Revels, but it is doubtful whether the art had advanced very far in the Revels office of 1580. The painted cloths probably supplied appropriate backgrounds, after the fashion of tapestries, rather than realistic perspectives.

[1] Feuillerat, 338.   [2] *Ibid.*, 349.   [3] *Ibid.*, 266.

The frequent mention of curtain and curtain-rings in the Revels Accounts has sometimes been interpreted as indicating the use of front curtains similar to those on the modern stage. Curtains, however, were probably employed for the same purposes as occasionally in the drama from the twelfth century on, *i.e.* for concealment and discovery. Twice, indeed, such specific use is noted in the accounts: (1) "a hill for IX musses (muses) to sing uppon with a vayne of Sarsnett drawen upp and downe before them;"[1] (2) "for poles & shyvers for draft of the Curtins before the senat howse."[2] Curtains may at times have been drawn in front of the entire setting; but usually they seem to have concealed only a portion of the stage, containing special properties, as the back curtains were used in the professional theaters. The fact that there are so many notes in the Accounts for different preparations for curtains may be taken as evidence that they were fitted to specific purposes, and that there was no regular proscenium arch or front curtain on the court stage. Both of these were introduced much later in connection with the Masques of James I; and the uncertainty in the use of both arch and front curtain, 1603–10, is conclusive proof that the front curtain had not earlier become established in the court entertainments.[3]

PLAYS AT COURT BEFORE 1583

The general features of performance of a play at court before 1583 offer many differences from the kind of performances we have described as characteristic

---

[1] *Ibid.*, 117.   [2] *Ibid.*, 200.
[3] See T. S. Graves, *op. cit.*, 8–10, for many cases of curtains in court shows. None of these cases seem to be front curtains.

A Multiple Set on the French Stage, for Durval's "Agarite."

of the public theaters. A play appears to have been usually provided with a background made up of houses, presumably with doors for entrances and exits, or a castle or city with battlements, or a forest setting with divers trees, rocks, caves, etc. Possibly a painted cloth completed the background by furnishing a suggestion of street or landscape. Before any of the structures, curtains might be employed for concealment and discovery. Brilliant costumes and minor properties helped to complete a setting of pictorial vividness and considerable verisimilitude.

In this period, the court no doubt retained in part the medieval practice of special structures for different localities and of representing various places at once upon the main stage. As I have noted, such practices would inevitably be maintained at court longer than in the public performances. Even at court, however, there are signs of a simplification and an approach to the methods of the professional companies. The edifices that make up the background become fewer in number and show a great similarity, and the play seems clearly enough distinguished from the pageant. In such cases for comparison as are provided by extant plays, the elaborate setting of the court calls for little difference in presentation from that used in public. The one extant play in the Accounts for which properties are noted, the "Rare Triumph of Love and Fortune" (if, indeed, this is identical with "Love and Fortune" of 1582), is unfortunately not very helpful. The properties provided are one city and one battlement,[1] but these seem of no service except as a conventional background. Some other plays of the sixties that were performed at court, though not

---

[1] Feuillerat, 349.

specifically described, may better illustrate the practice. For example, in "Damon and Pithias," which was probably the "Edwardes Tragedy" acted at court in the Christmas season of 1564–5,[1] the Prologue seems to designate two distinct places.

So, here in Syracuse th' ancient toun, which once the
    Romans won,
Here, Dionysius palace, within whose court this thing
    most strange was done.

In the text also there are indications that some of the entrances and exits are intended to be through the gate of the city and "the court gate." On a public stage, these might be represented simply by doors. On the court stage they appeared as parts of edifices for city and palace; indeed there are payments recorded for "canvas to cover divers towns and houses." In either case, the neutral stage is the place of action and the medieval "houses" have become mere exits.

"Horestes," probably the "Orestes" acted at court, 1567–8, but prepared for professional performance with its twenty-five parts accommodated to six actors, contains the following stage directions.

"Go and make your lively battel and let it be longe, eare you can win the Citie, and when you have won it, let Horestes bringe out his mother by the armes, and let the droum sease playing and the trumpet also, when she is taken; let her knele doune and speake."

In public theaters, the gallery would take the place of the canvas city and palace that were provided at court.

What changes were brought about by the knowledge of the classical stage or of continental imitations must

[1] Feuillerat, 116.

be largely a matter of conjecture. Tragedies in Latin or English at university or court were doubtless given a sumptuous setting, with a palace background,[1] but the more spectacular features were confined to the dumb shows of the intermissions. The renaissance conception of the Satyr stage allowed a background of rocks, forests, fountains, and so on in pastorals; but as has been noted this really represented a single place though it might resemble a multiple set. The classical stage prescribed by Vitruvius for comedy, however, corresponded closely to the bare stage and rear doors of the public theaters. In any case, classical example and professional practice agreed in the distinction between on and off the stage, and the use of rear doors for entrances and exits.

The court stage, for the average play, appears, then, by 1580 or earlier, to have been a bare projecting platform with rear doors, and with only a few somewhat conventional edifices furnishing a background and some simple survival of a multiple set. When we add that curtains were freely used to conceal and discover these edifices, the likeness to the regular professional stage must seem very close.

The most striking difference between performances in court and in public was probably in the elaborateness of costumes and properties. This may be illustrated by Peele's pastoral, the "Arraignment of Paris," printed in 1584, after having been "presented before the Queen's Majesty by the Children of the Chapel." A large number of the Olympian deities were impersonated, and the boy actors were required to mimic the majesty of Juno and the beauty of Venus, "Lady

---

[1] See "Gismond of Salern" (1567), Brandl's *Quellen*, where the palace and Gismond's chamber are specified in the entrances and exits.

President of Love," as well as Vulcan, Neptune, Mars, Vulcan's Cyclops, and others. Three elaborate shows were presented by the rival goddesses.

IVNOES SHOWE

Heereuppon did rise a Tree of gold laden with Diadems & Crownes of golde.

PALLAS SHOW

Heereuppon did enter 9. knights in armour, treading a warlike Almaine, by drome and fife, & then having march't foorth againe, Venus speaketh.

VENVS SHOW

Here Helen entreth in her braverie, with 4. Cupides attending on her, each having his fan in his hande to fan fresh ayre in her face. Shee singeth as followeth.

In addition to these, the list of properties included: a lamb, a fawn, an oaken bough laden with acorns, fruit, an artificial charm of birds, a ball of gold, a wreath of poplar, a hearse for Colin, Venus's fan, a horn. The scene, too, was prepared with great care to represent Diana's grove on Mount Ida. Flora describes her preparation at the opening; and we may infer that thickets and trees formed the background, and that many colored flowers dotted the stage. Flora also presents three devices portraying the goddesses in flowers.

> This peice of worke compact with many a flowre
> And well layde in at entraunce of the bowre.

The bower of Diana appears to have been a commodious structure. Thither the goddesses repair during a storm of thunder and lightning, and here later Jove and the Olympian court take their seats. This bower, indeed, forms the only special locality indicated in the text. Whether or not it was concealed by a curtain, is not clear.

Though the costumes and properties are elaborate and expensive, the setting itself offers nothing different in principle from those common in pastoral plays on public stages. One setting does for the entire play, and on this setting one locality is given full properties. The public performance by the children would have been less showy than that before the Queen, unless they were permitted to retain the costumes and properties used at court. But any public stage could have managed the setting, and Diana's bower could have been readily arranged on the inner stage. It is rather stretching a point to consider this scene, with its groves of Ida, tree for Œnone, and bower for Diana, as a multiple set.[1] A pastoral setting of this sort is really one set for virtually a single locality, and not a multiple setting in the medieval sense. It was possible enough on the Elizabethan public stage, as it is familiar to-day in out-of-door performances of Shakespeare, or, indeed, in any performance of "A Midsummer Night's Dream."

By the time the first London theater was built, the multiple setting of the medieval stage seems to have undergone a simplification at court only a little less than in the hands of the professionals. From 1580 on, the adult theatrical companies appear at court with increasing frequency. Performances by amateurs become negligible in the history of the stage, and the main course of its evolution seems clearly determined by the professional companies. Whether because of

[1] Cf. W. J. Lawrence, *Elizabethan Playhouse*, 236.

the improvement of these companies or because of Elizabeth's parsimony, or for whatever reason, the number of court masques and pageants decreased, and the period of 1585–1603 was not one of elaborate court shows. At every Christmas, however, several plays were given at court by the professional companies, and we may be confident that before 1600 the methods of the public theater prevailed at court.[1]

THE INFLUENCE OF THE COURT ON THE PUBLIC STAGE. THE PLAYS OF JOHN LYLY

To what extent did this court stage determine or influence the practice of the professional theater in the eighties and nineties? Was the multiple set carried over and established in the Theater and the Curtain, the Globe and the Blackfriars? These questions, which have provoked a deal of controversy, may best be answered by a somewhat detailed examination of the plays of John Lyly. These plays, which carry on the development of the court entertainment up to Shakespeare's romantic comedies, were acted by children both at court and in their own private (*i.e.* indoor) theaters. They represent about all we know of the children's activities in the period 1580–1600, and they bear many marks of court influence. They have been analyzed by their editor, Mr. Bond,[2]

---

[1] So far as we have information concerning university performances, they seem to have undergone a similar change from medieval complexity to professional simplicity. Plays given in 1566 at both Oxford and Cambridge had multiple settings with a seat for the queen on the stage itself. In 1592, for Gager's *Ulysses Redux* at Christ Church, curtains seem to have been used to manage a change from an exterior to an interior. (Boas, *University Drama*, 215, 216.) Certainly, after 1590 the university drama is much influenced by the professional theaters.

[2] John Lyly, *Works*. Ed. R. W. Bond, Vol. II, 269 *et passim*.

for presentation on the professional stage, but Mr. W. J. Lawrence [1] has called attention to their adaptability to the multiple setting. Our survey of the stage thus far has perhaps prepared us to find their technic experimental and tentative, qualities characterizing both the court and public theaters of the eighties. Both would regard the outer stage as a neutral, vaguely localized place, and sometimes stretch a point to bring certain persons or incidents upon it. When a special locality was required, the court stage would have recourse to "mansions"; the public stage to the curtained recess; but neither would be employed very extensively.

"Campaspe," probably the earliest of his plays (c. 1581), illustrates the difficulty of determining between a simple multiple setting and the curtained recess. On the court stage there would presumably be three edifices, the city or market place, the palace, and Apelles' studio. This may have been carried over to the public stage with doors and a curtained recess taking the place of the three properties. But there is only one definitely localized place, Apelles' studio, and this is clearly shut off from the front stage by curtains. The imaginary transfers of place while the scene is in progress doubtless recall the multiple setting, but they offer no difficulty for the public stage. Alexander says, "We will go to see Diogenes. . . . And see where his tub is . . . Diogenes?" (II. ii. 119); and the modern editor says the scene has changed from Alexander's palace to the market place. With a multiple setting, Alexander might take a step or two from his palace toward the market place, or from one door toward the other. But with no multiple setting

[1] *The Elizabethan Playhouse,* 59 *et passim.*

M

the action would be the same; Diogenes would enter
the front stage from one of the doors. The incongruity
of the imaginary shifting of place depends largely on
the assumption that the main stage is some particular
spot. If your imagination is trained to regard it as
almost anywhere, there will be no difficulty in bringing Diogenes on to meet Alexander. In the other
plays, however, Lyly is more chary of these imaginary
shiftings.[1]

Three plays, "Sapho and Phao," "Endymion,"
and "Midas," all have some suggestion of the multiple
setting, but also lend themselves readily to the public
stage. In "Sapho and Phao," various localities may
be imagined, but the main stage is again neutral and
unpropertied, representing locality very vaguely. The
propertied localities are Sybilla's cave, Vulcan's forge,
and Sappho's chamber. That Sappho's chamber was
represented by the recess and revealed and concealed
by curtains is indicated by the stage directions in
III. iii. "Shee falleth asleepe. The Curtaines
drawne." Sybilla's cave was also doubtless represented by the recess; and probably Vulcan's forge.
In "Endymion," the main stage again represents
neutral indeterminate locality, here usually the vicinity
of Cynthia's palace. Specified localities, however, are a
grove with the bank on which Endymion sleeps, a foun-
tain, and the castle of Corsites. Each of these would
require a curtained space or a door. In IV. iii, Corsites
enters saying "I am come in sight of the lunary bank."
Presumably the curtain opened disclosing Endymion
asleep there. (He has been sleeping since II. iii, but
surely not without the protection of the curtain.)
Fairies enter, pinch him asleep, and then dance, sing

[1] See also I. iii. 110; III. iv. 45, 57.

and *exeunt*. Then Cynthia, Pythagoras, and others enter and converse for thirty lines. Mr. Bond considers this a transfer of scene to the palace gardens, but this is a modern way of viewing it. It is merely a transfer to the front stage — to neutral ground (while the curtains probably closed before the sleepers). At line 73, Cynthia says, "Behold Endymion"; the curtains open, and the action is henceforth before the bank, in a definite locality.

In "Midas," the first three acts are in a neutral place, which might be loosely described as the garden before the palace. The first scene of Act IV seems to require a forest background, and the remaining three scenes of Act IV and the first scene of Act V require a reedy place. If the forest and reeds were provided in the alcove, the curtains which had been open for five scenes would close for Act V, Scene ii, again indicating a neutral place near the palace, and would open for Act V, Scene iii, disclosing the temple of Apollo at Delphi.

In several other of the plays, as in "Endymion" and "Midas," a forest or garden setting may have been retained throughout, even though the recess was used to denote special localities. In the pastoral "Gallathea," there is no change of scene, but a forest setting with an oak tree continues through the five acts. In "Love's Metamorphosis," another pastoral, there also seems to have been a forest background throughout. Here, however, certain special localities are required, the temple of Cupid, Ceres' tree, and a large rock on which a Syren appears. These might be managed by means of the curtained inner stage, but the single pastoral setting seems probable, though this is the only play of Lyly's not acted at court. In the "Woman in the Moon" one of the planetary gods is always overlooking the action from above (in the balcony); so the scene remains fixed in the forest of Utopia.   In Act IV, Pandora makes appointments with three shepherds in three distinct places.   Later Stesias, disguised as Pandora, fulfills the three appointments, and Pandora herself appears with Gunophilus on the way to the seashore.   All these different places might conceivably fall under the survey of the planet Mercury, and apparently the front stage sufficed.

In "Mother Bombie" Lyly follows the Terentian model, and again keeps to one place, this time on a square, or open space, where all the action takes place, except that two windows (presumably of houses) are used.

Lyly appears to have used a multiple setting only in a simple form, and then rarely.   He may fairly be taken as illustrating a compromise between the simplified multiple setting still used at court in the eighties and the tentative technic of the public stage.   Such a compromise would most naturally have obtained at the children's indoor theaters, where the court influence would be most strongly felt.   Court properties may have been utilized occasionally at the early Blackfriars, and it would have been easy to manage the most elaborate of Lyly's pastoral settings, that of the "Love's Metamorphosis."   There is no indication that in the public performances the doors and curtained recess became fixed localities marked by signs, and thus did away with properties.   "Campaspe" might be so managed, but none of the other plays. The inner stage and the doors appear to have been used much as on the later professional stage; often indicating localities, but not fixed simultaneous localities.

ROXANA
TRAGÆDIA

A plagiarij
vnguibus
vindicatu,
aucta, et
agnita ab
authore
Gulielmo
Alabastro.

FRONTISPIECE OF "ROXANA," 1632

In "Love's Metamorphosis," while the siren is singing on her rock by the seashore and charming Petulius, Protea enters, scolds the lady, and commands her "Followe me at this doore and out at the other" (IV. ii. 96).   Evidently Lyly was thinking of the stage doors and not of any special localities by the sea shore.   His own practice seems to have been towards the elimination of shifts of place and toward the presentation of an entire play on what could be imagined as a single terrain, *i.e.* toward a unity of place, accommodated to the resources of an indoor theater.   The influence of the court appears in the mythological costumes and the nature and perhaps frequency of forest settings rather than in any distinct method of staging.   Lyly's methods do not seem essentially different from those of other playwrights in the eighties and early nineties. The main stage is used as neutral territory, with very vague localization; as, Utopia, Arcadia, a forest, near the palace, or anywhere beneath the planets.   Curtains are mentioned in two plays and are obviously used in others for discoveries, retirements, and for specialized places, as temples, caves, inner rooms. Traces of the multiple setting are to be found in the single pastoral set, or in a form so simplified that it would offer little departure from the inner-outer arrangement, by this time becoming familiar on the professional stage.

Lyly, in short, transferred a peculiar form of court comedy to the public stage.   The court, indeed, began to show a marked preference for the professional actors at just the time Lyly's earlier plays were produced. The children of the chapel do not appear at court after 1582, and the Paul's boys only rarely after 1581 until 1590, and then not again until 1600.   During most of the nineties, when the professional companies were attracting brilliant dramatists, the children were suppressed. The dramatic entertainment of court as well as of public was largely in the hands of the adult professionals.

PLAYS BY THE PAUL'S BOYS, 1600–03

About 1600, the chapel children began acting at Blackfriars and the Paul's boys at their theater. The influence of the court stage can be further traced in some of the plays produced by the Paul's boys. After a suppression of ten years, it might be expected that the children would exhibit somewhat archaic methods of staging, especially as a number of their plays were fantastic comedies, with music, singing, and dancing, after the fashion they had made popular a decade and more earlier. Since we happen to be able to identify a number of the plays which they acted in 1600–03, we have a chance to test the survival of court methods. They produced a Lylian pastoral, the "Maid's Metamorphosis," with a similar arrangement to that we have noted for his "Love's Metamorphosis." But the cases most often cited as evidences of a late multiple setting are two plays by William Percy, probably never acted, but written for the Paul's theater and preserved in manuscript.[1] The directions for staging follow.

THE FAERY PASTORAL, OR FOREST OF ELVES

THE PROPERTIES

Highest, aloft, and on the Top of the Musick Tree the Title THE FAERY PASTORALL, Beneath him pind on Post of the

[1] Printed by Haslewood for the Roxburghe Club, 1824.

Tree The Scene Eluida Forrest. Lowest off all ouer the
Canopie ΝΑΤΤΑΙΤΒΟΔΑΙΟΝ or Faery Chappell. A kiln of
Brick. A Fowen Cott. A Hollowe Oake with vice of wood
to shutt to. A Lowe well with Roape and Pullye. A
Fourme of Turues. A Greene Bank being Pillowe to the
Hed but, Lastly a Hole to creepe in and out. Now if so be
that the Properties of any These, that be outward, will not
serue the turne by reason of concurse of the People on the
Stage, Then you may omitt the sayd Properties which be
outward and supplye their Places with their Nuncupations
onely in Text Letters. Thus for some.

THE CUCKQUEANES AND CUCKOLDS ERRANTS

The Properties

Harwich, In Midde of the Stage Colchester with Image
of Tarlton, Signe and Ghirlond vnder him also. The
Raungers Lodge, Maldon, A Ladder of Roapes trussed
vp neare Harwich. Highest and aloft the Title The Cuckqueanes and Cuckolds Errants. A Long Fourme.

The "Faery Pastoral" is dated 1603 and was prepared for a court performance, as the prologue indicates. Its directions propose a simple form of the
multiple set, not different from that which we have
assigned to other pastorals, as the "Love's Metamorphosis" and the "Maid's Metamorphosis." The rear
curtain was apparently used in V. v. "Here they shutt
both into the Canopie Fane or Trophey together with
the banquet"; and also I think in II. i where a discovery seems implied.

The "Cuckqueanes and Cuckolds Errant" is more
puzzling, which may be due merely to Percy's eccen-
tricity. The Ms. is dated 1601, but the action of the
play is 1588; and its staging seems nearer to what we
might expect not long after that date. It is difficult

to tell whether Percy meant to have the doors marked 'Harwich' and 'Maldon' respectively, and the curtained entrance 'Colchester'; or whether he designed actual properties for these places. The former has been the usual interpretation, but a practicable property seems required for a fourth place, the Ranger's Lodge, and there is a fifth place, not indicated in his directions, which requires at least a door, "Dr. Pearle's house" (see II. 3, 5; III. 6, 7). The direction provides for a multiple set of five stations, but it seems probable that Percy designed to use the two doors for the two towns, and the central opening for the inn. He has applied to a non-pastoral a sort of multiple setting presenting points of similarity to that union of classical and medieval stage practices which we have discussed. Percy views the stage as a classical stage with doors, and strives to reduce his scenes to a unity of place, as Lyly did in such diverse schemes as "Mother Bombie" and the "Woman in the Moon."

Through a portion of the play he has marked the entrances, as from Harwich, from Maldon, etc.; but he has rarely marked the exits. One fears that he would have found it difficult to make these consistent. But to me the most puzzling stage direction is one for V. viii, which the various commentators on the play have neglected.

THE DIRECTION

FLORADIN, CLARIBEL, OLIUEL, LATRO, PEARLE, PIGOT made a maruellous Rutt at their commings furth, The Rest followed easily after them and stealingly, so as the whole Scene was insensibly and suddenly brought about in Castrophe of the Comœdy, And the whole face of the Scene suddenly alterd.

The persons named were supposed to be in the inn at Colchester (central entrance). As the direction indicates, they now rush or steal out on the front stage. As the action continues it belongs in front of the inn. The word "Scene" may be used as applying to the persons, but the words seem to indicate a change of scenic background. Possibly all that is meant is that the curtains were drawn, but it is difficult to see why any change of scene was desired.

The suggestion that signs take the place of properties in the "Faery Pastoral" and the implication that signs were placed over the doors in the other play, again may indicate the exigencies to which this form of multiple setting was sometimes reduced, but seems a very exceptional practice as late as 1600. Indeed, it is difficult to believe that signs could have actually taken the place of the kiln, the cott, the oak, or the well, all practicable constructions and necessary for the action. As for the "hole to creepe in and out," Percy wrote an alternative passage for Paul's omitting this property (V. 4).

The other plays acted by the Paul's boys about 1600 show no indication of signs, or, so far as I can see, of a multiple set. They do indeed display some curiosities of staging and often suggest their relation to the court-shows. In "Histriomastix," for instance, a curious spectacular play with some properties, the interval between acts is twice curiously managed. Between Acts II and III, the device is one used at court, a mist,

"Enter Pride, Vaine-glory, Hypocrisie, and Contempt: Pride casts a mist, wherein Mavortius and his company vanish off the Stage, and Pride and her attendants remaine."

Between Acts III and IV, the method is more unusual.

"They speake and fall asleepe on the Stage. Sound Musicke. Enter Envy alone to all the Actors sleeping on the Stage: the musicke sounding: she breaths amongst them."

Then after a soliloquizing of eighteen lines,

"They all awake, and begin the following Acte"

In Act I, Chrisoganus' study is apparently in the central alcove, and revealed by the curtain, but in Act V a special arrangement is introduced, apparently employing the two doors (the central space being left for the throne, revealed in Act VI).

"Enter Lyon-rash to Fourchier sitting in his study at one end of the stage: At the other end enter Vourcher to Velure in his shop."

In II. ii, there is a change of scene managed by a curtain.

"Enter Contrimen, to them, Clarke of the Market: hee wrings a bell, and drawes a curtain; where-under is a market set about a crosse."

· A throne is used in II. i, and at the close of the play; it seems to have been concealed by the curtains at the exit of Plenty in II. i, and to have been revealed in the final act only at the entrance of Plenty.

The other plays, "Antonio and Mellida," Parts I and II, "Jack Drum's Entertainment," the "Wisdom of Doctor Doddipoll," "Blurt Master Constable," the "Malcontent," and "What You Will," show no indications of a multiple set; and most of them could not possibly have been played with either a multiple

setting or with signs over the doors. The curtain is
mentioned in the "Wisdom of Doctor Doddipoll, I. i,
and "Blurt Master Constable," II. ii, text, and
seems to me likely to have been used frequently in
these and the other plays. At all events, there are
many manifest changes of scene, as from indoors to
outdoors, or between distant localities. "What You
Will," [1] indeed, I have already discussed at length in
Chapter V,[2] as affording a striking illustration of the
use of the curtained inner stage for the alternation of
indoor and outdoor scenes.

These Paul's plays, taken together, then, show
both some traces of the court stage and a general
similarity to the professional methods. Multiple settings are to be found particularly in the form usual
for pastorals and in the curious directions of Percy;
also some imitation of classical procedure in the observance of act divisions and attempts at unity of place.
Properties seem somewhat more frequent than in
contemporary plays by adults, but there is no indication of painted cloths; though it should be noted that
in "Cynthia's Revels," acted by the children of the
chapel about 1600, occurs one of the very few possible
allusions to a painted background.[3] The stage, however, is clearly indicated with three entrances, the
central entrance provided with a curtain which can

---

[1] *What You Will* is not assigned to any company by its title-page. It
was probably acted in the spring of 1601 by the Paul's boys; see R. A.
Small, *The Stage Quarrel between Ben Jonson and the so-called Poetasters*,
Breslau, 1899, pp. 101–114. Dr. Small also considers that the present
form of *Histriomastix* was acted by the Paul's Boys in 1599, pp. 67–90.

[2] P. 119.

[3] 3. *Child.* Slid the boy takes me for a piece of perspective, I hold my
life, or some silk curtain, come to hang the stage here. Sir Crack, I am none
of your fresh pictures, that use to beautify the decayed dead arras in a public
theatre. *Induction.*

disclose a considerable space, thus closely resembling the typical professional stage. The curtain is frequently employed for various purposes, and in one play at least in a notable scheme of alternation. If we had more knowledge of this private theater and of its rival playhouse of the Blackfriars children during the first years of their reëstablishment after 1600, I think it is safe to surmise that we should find (1) some of the last distinct survivals of medieval practices as these had been established at court, and (2) a rapid development in the use of the curtained inner stage. At least it is clear that in the indoor theaters, the inner stage soon came into frequent employment.

In the plays of Lyly and in those acted shortly after the reopening of Paul's in 1600, I have examined what must have been the main line of court influence on the professional stage. In the early eighties, when Lyly began to write, the court theater possessed a special class of actors drawn from the choir boys, a special group of dramatists, a special type of play, and special methods of stage procedure. But the further history of these plays, actors, and methods of staging, shows them losing their identity in the general development of the professional drama. After 1583, as we have seen, the court came to rely mainly on the adult companies; and both before and after their long suppressions, the children had become semi-professional companies appearing in the city theaters and accumulating a varied repertory. If Lyly more than any other dramatist, and the Paul's boys more than any other company, continued the tradition of court-entertainments, yet manifestly they minimized their differences from other companies and theaters. Their history adds further testimony to the establishment of a typical professional stage and principles of staging.

During the last twenty years of Elizabeth's reign, the influence of the court stage seems to have been rather intangible. It led to efforts for more decoration on the public stage, particularly in pastoral and fantastic comedy; and in all elaborate spectacles the professionals must have imitated as far as they could the practices of the court. That perspective backgrounds were occasionally used after the manner of the painted cloths seems to me possible, but without definite evidence. The indoor theaters of the children appear to have decreased the reliance on the bare front stage, and to have accelerated the freer employment of the curtained inner stage. It seems clear that, in whatever other ways the court influence was effective, it did not result in the establishment of the multiple setting.

If the Paul's boys in 1600 still exhibit some traces of the multiple set, this may safely be taken as the last of this peculiar influence of the court stage. For, with the accession of James I, in 1603, came a new development in court staging that departed even more radically from medieval principles than had the practice of the professional theaters. We must now turn to this late scenic development of the Court Masque and its effect on the theaters of Shakespeare and his successors.

CHAPTER VII

THE COURT THEATER IN THE REIGNS OF JAMES I AND CHARLES I

In the matter of stage decoration, the reign of James I exhibits an abrupt departure from that of Elizabeth. During the late years of her reign we have few records of elaborate theatrical entertainments; but from those which heralded the accession of James I, we may infer that there had been no noteworthy changes in the staging of pageants and masques for twenty years. On the contrary, in the reign of James, not only does the court masque take on a new importance as a dramatic spectacle, it achieves through the initiative of Inigo Jones, a new step in the evolution of stage presentation.

The progress from the Elizabethan to the modern stage has been often indicated in this volume. Instead of presenting a neutral place with occasional specified localities, the post-Restoration stage presents each scene as definitely localized. The neutral front stage becomes less and less important until it disappears. The curtained recess becomes the main stage. A play becomes a succession of definitely localized scenes. This step seems a natural consequence of the development in the public theater that we have studied; but there can be no doubt that the conception of movable scenes had its first realization in the elaborate spectacles of Italian courts, and that it was

PERFORMANCE OF THE LIBERATIONE DI TERRENO AT FLORENCE IN 1616.

After an etching by Callot. The arrangement is very similar to that of a Stuart Court
Masque in England.

made familiar in the court masques of James I and Charles I.

In a general way, this development seems to have been about as follows. The huge pageant carrying the masquers and brought into the hall on wheels, gave way to a fixed structure on an elevated stage at one end of the hall. This structure — palace, mountain, or what not, — was supplemented by a setting constructed in part by means of painted flats, according to the art of perspective, and finally by movable scenes. In the end the court masque was given a proscenium arch with a curtain and changing scenes, as, *e.g.*, in Shirley's "Triumph of Peace," 1634.

Some of the early conditions of court shows in the reigns of Henry VIII and Elizabeth have been touched upon. The detailed account of the development of spectacle, lighting, and scenes would require a very careful examination of methods used in the various courts of Europe, especially those of Italy. The initiative for the important development from changing sets to moving scenes seems to me to have come from the account in Vitruvius of the periaktoi of the Greek stage, but the further progress in scenery is not easy to trace with exactness. In England an authoritative survey of the development of the stage management of the masques has been provided in the works of Brotanek and Reyher. On many details it is impossible to speak with accuracy, though our information may be enlarged when all the views and designs by Inigo Jones are made accessible to students. It is clear, however, that in the hands of Inigo Jones the court masques went through a rapid development, and in elaborate staging equaled or perhaps surpassed similar spectacles in Italy and France. By the thirties the stage had complicated mechanism for moving scenes, a rising curtain, and a proscenium arch, and in these respects approached the picture-frame stage of the nineteenth century.

THE COURT MASQUES

The Court Masque of James I was an elaborate and expensive show given on festal occasions at court and often costing thousands of pounds. It had but a single, or at most, two performances, always at night, and might be preceded by an extensive procession or followed by a banquet. It was somewhat strictly distinguished from pageants, barriers, entertainments, and other similar spectacles, and came to have a distinct form. The kernel of the show was the masked dance, in which members of the court, even Queen and King, took part. This dance or masque proper came near the end of the show and was often elaborated into various dances. As accompaniments of this masque were (1) music, instrumental and vocal, (2) a dialogue, taking the form of a play of some length, usually with mythological or allegorical motive, (3) various grotesque dances by professionals, preceding the main masque, and often integrated with the play, and (4) a spectacular stage setting. All of these elements were given great care and expense, and are of interest in various ways. The masque is in many respects the forerunner of the opera. Our interest, however, is mainly with the element of the stage setting. I shall glance at its history and consider its effect on the public drama.

The masques were given in great halls in the various palaces or in the buildings erected at Whitehall for their special accommodation. In all cases the rooms

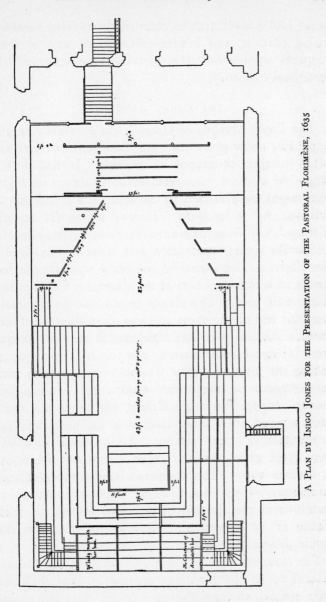

A PLAN BY INIGO JONES FOR THE PRESENTATION OF THE PASTORAL FLORIMÈNE, 1635

were rectangular, the Great Hall in the palace of
Whitehall, one of the smaller, measuring 89 by 39
feet, the new masking house of 1637, one of the largest, 112 feet in length, 57 feet wide, and 59 feet in
height.   The size of the stage in these two rooms
can be seen in the diagrams for the pastoral "Florimène" (p. 177) and the masque "Salmacida Spolia"
(p. 186).   The general arrangement of the hall appears
in the diagram on page 177.   At one end was the stage,
elevated 4 to 8 feet, on the other the seats for royalty;
on the sides, benches for the spectators; and in the
middle a place for the dancing.   Thither the masques
descended by machines or stairs from the stage.

The first extant masque [1] performed before James I
is the "Vision of the Twelve Goddesses" by Daniel,
presented January 8, 1604, at Hampton Court.   It is
interesting as an example of the old method of presentation, and thus serves as a point of departure for
succeeding innovations.   Just as formerly the pageants, after being wheeled into the hall, were placed
at various positions about the room; so here the several structures were placed on the floor, leaving the
center free for dancing.   At the lower end of the hall
was a mountain whence the masquers descended, and
opposite it, at the other end, were the Cave of Sleep
and the Temple of Peace.   The hall, wrote Sir Dudley
Carleton, was so restricted by the various machines
that they could admit only persons of quality.

This masque of Daniel's conforms to the preceding
methods of presenting pageants, or huge edifices
brought in on wheels and placed about the floor of

---

[1] First masque was performed on Jan. 1.   See Nichols, *Progresses of James
I*, IV, 1602; also, a letter by Carleton.   *S. P.*, James I, VI. a 21: Reyher,
356.   This masque had a curtain.

the hall. At the next Christmas season, Jonson's "Masque of Blackness" begins the series of innovations by which Inigo Jones transformed the staging of court spectacles. Jones had just returned from Italy and had already introduced changing scenes in the performance of a tragedy at Christ Church, Oxford, in August, 1605. These seem to have been ineffective and Jones did not repeat their mechanism at the court. But he did confine the elaborate decorations and scenery for the masque to one end of the hall.

A curtain, on which a landscape was painted, fell, and " an artificial sea was seen to shoot forth as if it flowed to the land." This was the main machine, a "greate stage fower foote highe from the grounde upon Trestles," [1] on which was "a great concave shell like mother of pearl," conveyed by sea monsters and containing the masquers. The back scene was a vast sea painted in perspective, so that it seemed to unite with the billows of the moving stage. In the upper portion was a night piece, where later "the moon was discovered in the upper part of the house, triumphant on a silver throne, made in the figure of a pyramid." For the dancing, another platform in the center of the hall seems to have been provided, as in Campion's masque of January 6, 1607. Indeed, it was not until some years later that the dancing was regularly performed on the floor of the hall.

For the next few years there are many variations, but the principles of staging become well established. The stage is elevated, and after a time it is set in a decorated frame or arch. A painted curtain may serve for the first scene before which an Induction is played. It is drawn, and discloses the main setting or machine.

---

[1] Reyher, 358, quoted from D. A. Audit Office, B 2419, R. 40.

Such disclosure, however, is usually not complete. In Campion's masque a curtain discloses one side of the setting, and the other side remains concealed for some time. Often the first curtain discloses only the lower portion of the scene, and clouds or dark curtains conceal the upper part, where later various deities are usually revealed. After several discoveries and transformations, the masquers descend from their mountain, island, heaven, globe, or whatever the main machine may be, and advance to the center of the hall, where they perform the dances. The introduction of antimasques, or grotesque dances preceding the main masque involved the necessity of further changes in decoration. After the curtain, a setting appropriate for the particular nature of the antimasque — witches, satyrs, animals, or what not — must be provided, and later this must be changed to give place to the grandiose decoration for the courtly masquers. Both Jonson's "Hue and Cry After Cupid" of February 9, 1608, and his "Masque of Queens," February 2, 1609, introduce antimasques and consequent changes of scene. Henceforth, both antimasques and changes of scene increase rapidly in number and popularity.

The features of the presentation which have been enumerated were all, however, in an experimental stage in comparison with their later development. Actors occasionally appeared off the stage in the hall, as in Jonson's "Masque of Beauty"; the height of the stage varied, as did the method of descent for the masquers from the main stage to the dancing place. Of special interest in connection with the later development of the stage are the proscenium arch, the curtain, and the changes of scene.

THE ARCH AND THE CURTAIN

There are no signs of any frames for the stage in the masques until 1606, in Jonson's "Hymen," when, on either side of the great globe two statues of Hercules and Atlas supported the firmament above. In 1608, in the "Hue and Cry After Cupid," "the scene was a high steep red cliff, advancing itself into the clouds." "Before which, on the two sides, were erected two pilasters, charged with spoils and trophies of Love and his mother . . . and overhead two personages, Triumph and Victory, in flying postures, and twice so big as the life, in place of the arch, and holding a garland of myrtle for the Key. All which, with the pillars, seemed to be of burnished gold, and embossed out of the metal." Whether or not "in place of the arch" implies an earlier use of a proscenium arch cannot be determined. There is no other indication of its presence until 1610, in Daniel's "Tethys Festival." Here the description is by Inigo Jones himself and leaves no doubt. The traverse or curtain was in front of the arch, and when drawn, "the scene was discovered with these adornments."

"First, on eyther side stood a great statue of twelve foot high, representing Neptune and Nereus. . . . These seagods stood on pedestals, and were al of gold. Behinde them were two pillasters on which hung compartments, with other devises: and these bore up a rich Freeze, whereon were figures of tenne foote long, of flouds, and Nymphs, with a number of naked children, dallying with a draperie, which they seemed to holde up, that the Scene might be seene, and the ends thereof fell downe in foldes by the pillasters. In the midst was a compartment with this inscription *Tethyos Epinicia*, TETHYS feasts of triumph. This was supported with two winged boyes, and all the worke was done with that force and boldnesse on the gold and silver, as the figures seemed round and not painted." [1]

Hereafter each new masque was provided with an appropriate frame or arch placed before the curtain, as in Jonson's "Lethe," February 22, 1617. Here the "front before the scene was an Arch Triumphal," surmounted with Humanity scattering flowers, with Cheerfulness and Readiness forming the sides. Later masques vied with each other in the ingenuity and splendor of such decorative frames.

That the front curtain as well as the arch was a novelty at court [2] is shown by the variety of usage in the early masques in the reign of James. In Daniel's first masque, as we have seen, there was no curtain. In Jonson's "Masque of Blackness" the curtain or scene falls; in Marston's Entertainment to the Countess of Derby, "a traverse slided away," and "the traverse that was drawn before the Masquers sank down." [3] Busino saw the curtain fall as late as 1618.[4] Often the "curtains are drawn" or "the scene opened"; and it is impossible to say just when the modern method of the rising curtain was adopted. The confused use of the words curtain, traverse, and scene leaves us in doubt as to the nature of the property. In the Ms. of his "Masque of Blackness," Jonson thus describes the scene: "In the end of the designed place, there is drawne uppon a downe right cloth, strayned for the scene, a devise of landscape, which openinge in manner of a curtaine, an artificiale sea is seene." [5] In the

---

[1] Daniel, *Works*, ed. Grosart, III. 310, 311.   [2] See p. 153.

[3] Marston, *Works*, ed. Bullen, III. 394, 398.

[4] Reyher, 363, Busino, *Anglipotrida*, preserved in the Records Office, Venetian Transcripts, CXLII. 70 ff.

[5] British Museum Ms. Royal 17 B xxxi. quoted by Brotanek, 228.

first edition (1608), however, this description is altered. "First for the scene was drawn a landtshcap (landscape) consisting of small woods — which falling, an artificial sea was seen, etc." In the next "Masque of Beauty" "a curtain was drawn in which Night was painted"; and in "Tethys Festival," the travers which concealed the entire decoration was "figured a darke cloude interior with certaine sparkling starres." Sometimes, as has been noted, there were two curtains, one usually concealing the lower and the other the upper half of the stage. All these varieties, however, gave way to a curtain within the outer decorated frame, which rolled up, disclosing the first scene. Jonson's "Chloridia," 1631, appears to be the earliest masque in which the arrangement is explicitly described.

CHANGES OF SCENE

The means used to present a change of scene also passed through an experimental period. In the tragedy at Christ Church, 1605, the three scenes presented were apparently arranged by means of turning triangular pillars, after the fashion of the Greek periaktoi. This method, as described by Sabbatini in his authoritative work of 1638, had been already used in France in 1596 for the "Arimène" of Nicolas de Montreux,[1] but was henceforth discarded by Inigo Jones. In the early masques, the changes of scene are limited; a front flat, which opens, the main machine, which may revolve or move or open in various ways, and the rear flats provide all needed permutations. A change of scene might be accomplished very simply, after the fashion used in the public theaters. For example,

---

[1] Leland, *Collectanea*, III. 631. Reyher, 365. V. Bapst, 208. Marsan, 213. For the passage in Vitruvius, see p. 16.

in the "Masque of Flowers," 1614, "a traverse painted
in perspective like the wall of a city . . . the traverse
being drawn, was seen a garden of a glorious and
strange beauty," [1] which furnished the setting for the
masque proper.   When one scene or setting was to be
changed for one equally elaborate, some device was
employed to distract the attention of the spectators.
In "Tethys Festival," such a device is described by
Inigo Jones himself.   "First at the opening of the
heavens appeared 3 circles of lights and glasses, one
with [in] another, and came downe in a straight motion
five foote, and then began to moove circularly : which
lights and motion so occupied the eyes of the spectators, that the manner of altering the scene was scarcely
discerned; for in a moment the whole face of it was
changed, the Poet vanished, and Tethys with her
Nymphes appeared in their severall Caverns gloriously
adorned." [2]   Again, a change of scenery was sometimes
concealed by mists made from perfumes,[3] or by drawing a cloud or some part of the scene.

Curiously, the front curtain does not seem ever to
have been lowered in order to hide the shifting.   Although a " back cloth " or a back scene opened or
closed for discoveries and concealments as on the professional stage, it apparently never occurred to any one
to employ the front curtain for these purposes.   In the
continental courts as well as in England, the problem
of concealing changes of scene stimulated much ingenuity.   The suggestion of Vitruvius that the periaktoi
might be revolved to the accompaniment of sudden

---

[1] Reyher, 368.   Nichols, 2, 735.   [2] Daniel, *Works*, ed. Grosart, III. 315.
[3] See Jonson's *Hymen:* "The air cleaving, in the top thereof was discovered Juno."   Ed. 1606.   "Mist made of delicate perfume."   Brotanek,
240.   Reyher, 379.

claps of thunder, may have encouraged the notion that some disturbance was necessary to distract the attention of the audience. At all events, it was many years before the front curtain was regularly used to mark a change of scene. The front curtain appears to have been used only at the beginning of the masque.

There was no decided change in the manipulation of scenery until late in the reign of James. Jonson's "Neptune's Triumph" (intended for January 8, 1624) presents a notable increase of scenes over any preceding performance. An abbreviated scenario follows.

1. "All that is discovered of a scene are two erected pillars." Induction: Poet, and Master Cook. A huge pot is brought in, or disclosed.

2. "Here the Anti-masque is danced by the persons described, coming out of the pot."

3. The scene opens. "The island of Delos is discovered, the Masquers sitting on their several ledges. The heavens opening, and Apollo, with Mercury, some of the Muses, and the goddess Harmony, make the music; while the island moves forward, Proteus sitting below, and Apollo sings."

The island joins itself to the shore and the Masquers land. The island goes back. The Masquers dance their entry.

4. "The first prospective of a Maritime Palace, or the house of Oceanus, is discovered with loud music. And the other above is no more seen."

"Then follows the Main Dance."

5. "After which, the second prospect of the Sea is shown, to the former music."

"The Revels follow."

6. "Which ended, the Fleet is discovered, while the three cornets play."

"The Antimasque of Sailors."

While the main machine, the "Island of Delos," is of a familiar sort, the succeeding "prospectives" seem to have been managed by moving flats. Henceforth most of the masques show many of these changes. There is, however, little indication of the way in which the changes of scene were arranged. In the French pastoral, "Florimène," produced at the English court in 1635, the wings were not changed, but only the back scene. This may have frequently been the case, or a method of changing the wings similar to that described in Sabbatini may have been used. Fortunately, careful drawings prepared by Inigo Jones for the "Salmacida Spolia," 1640, indicate very clearly his perfected method of moving and perspective scenes. This was the last masque given at the court of Charles; but the method of scenes sliding in grooves may have been in use for some years preceding. These designs explain themselves. Plan I shows the plane of the stage with side scenes and a back scene. Plan II shows a cross section of the stage. The side scenes (B) and the back shutters (D) each provide four different settings, the frames of the flat scenes moving in four sets of grooves. Corresponding to each scene on the floor is a parallel scene above (Plan II. R) for the clouds, the lower part of each cloud scene overlapping the scene on the floor below. These run in grooves in the ceiling. The ascent and descent of deities is provided for by a windlass (Plan II. W) under the stage. At the first change of scene, the first flat on each group slides back from the center and reveals the flat directly behind it, and so on. At the fourth change of scene, the back shutters disappeared, and the main machine (E) with seats for the masquers, King, and Queen, was discovered, with a background

furnished by the "back cloth" (H). The last flat of
each of the side groups still remained to complete the
setting.[1]

The various steps by which the moving scenes were
improved by Inigo Jones seem due to his invention.
As late as 1638 Sabbatini knows of no methods beyond those used by Jones either at Christ Church in
1605, or in his early masques. With the initiative
supplied by Vitruvius for changing scenes, however,
moving flats seem an inevitable outcome. The triangular pillars would prove ineffective, and some kind
of flat frames would naturally be substituted. For
the court spectacles some device like that of the sliding
grooves became desirable for the quick changes required. M. Reyher thinks that the Italian spectacles
had surpassed the technic set forth by Sabbatini;
and it is quite likely that in France, Spain, and Italy
court architects arrived at schemes for moving scenes
quite as effective as those of Jones. Still, it must
be remembered that the question is not of transformations and machines, but of a change of scene
by movable flat frames. In this particular I know
of no contemporary advance on the English court
masques.

By the thirties, then, there was instituted a method
of staging certainly very far removed from either the
multiple setting that still survived in the French theater or from the projecting stage and rear curtain of
the London playhouses. In comparison with the
modern stage, of course, the arrangement is in many
respects both cumbersome and restricted. The triangular perspective seems artificial and likely to be

[1] For full description and analysis, see Brotanek, 235 ff., and Reyher,
369 ff. The masque is printed in the *Works* of Davenant, II. 301.

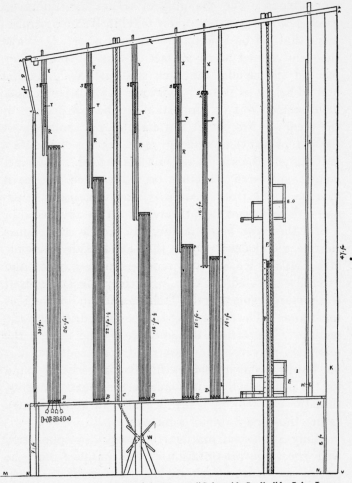

PLAN II. Design for the staging of the Masque "Salmacida Spolia," by Inigo Jones.

Profyle of ye sceane when ye sceane doth wholly change as well on ye sydes as at ye back shutters, and when ye syde peeces are made to change by running in groves.

The letters correspond to those in Plan I. Jones's additional directions abbreviated are: M, the ground line of the room; N, heighth of stage; Q, ye freese of ye front (proscenium arch); R, ye peeces of Clouds which came downe from ye roofe; S, grooves in which ye clouds went; T, clouds extending across the stage; V, upper back shutters; W, capstall of Engyne C by which ye Deityes were lett upp and downe; X, braces fastened to the roof of the sceane.

monotonous. The changing of scenes by sliding on grooves would not seem likely to fulfill Bacon's requirement that "it be quietly and without noise." [1] While the front scenes were 26 feet in length before they reached the clouds, the back shutters gave only the limited height of 14 feet. Masquers at this point must have seemed out of proportion to the perspective of the scenes.[2] Moreover, the machine (the survivor of the old pageant) is still the main feature of the decoration, and the scenes are subsidiary to it. Machine, scenes, and arch all must be made anew for each masque. The front curtain is more ornamental than useful. No permanent theater is yet established.

Still there can be no doubt that such a stage comes close to the modern stage. It establishes the principle of successive scenes, each representing a distinct and carefully pictured locality. Further, the stage itself is a picture-frame stage. The proscenium arch makes the frame. The front curtain goes up, disclosing the picture. The various scenes succeed, and though the masquers may come out of the frame to dance, it is not until the shifting scenes dissolve into a background for the main machine, introducing the courtly dancers, that the proscenium really becomes an arch of entry rather than the frame of a picture.

Many additional matters of interest in connection with the stage presentation of the masques must be passed over here. Such are the positions of the torchbearers and musicians, the manipulation of the cloud effects in the upper heavens, and the effects of disclosure and transformation obtained in the main machines. Only a word can be given to the very

---

[1] Cf. *Of Masques and Triumphs*. "It is true, the alternation of scenes, so it be quietly and without noise, are things of beauty." [2] Reyher, 380.

important features of lighting and costume. The hall itself was brilliantly lit, but there seem to have been no footlights on the stage.[1] In the decoration, however, much gold and silver and the brightest colors were employed, in order to reflect as much light as possible. The main machine was crowded with lights and often took a concave form, as M. Reyher has noted, the interior of shell, or globe, serving as a great reflector. Lighting from above also seems to have been used — "over all a serene sky, with transparent clouds, giving a great lustre to the whole work."[2] In this dazzling setting, the costumes of the masquers were the focus of all attention. Of gorgeous color, heavily laden with gold and jewels, they were the culmination of the extravagant spectacle. Mythological or allegorical personages were usually represented, and Ben Jonson exhausted his classical learning in his efforts to make the costumes and properties appropriate to the person or the allegory. Their appropriateness is not always as noticeable as their bizarre extravagance; and pedantic exactness often had to yield to decorative values or to the taste of the queen. But Inigo Jones knew the monuments of classical antiquity and the artistic achievements of Renaissance Italy as well as Jonson knew classical and humanistic literature. The living pictures were often no unworthy reproduction of the designs of Raphael and Michael Angelo, and were intended to rival the pictures with which Rubens had decorated the ceiling of the masquing hall. The costumes marked a new style in theatrical presentation by their appropriateness to both the decoration and the fable.

---

[1] The first footlights known in England appear in the picture in Kirkman's *Wits*, 1672.   [2] *Chloridia*, 1631.

INFLUENCE OF THE MASQUES ON THE PUBLIC STAGE

In what respects and to what extent did this elaborate stage and these new principles of presentation influence the public theaters? This question was raised over a century ago by Malone, who was inclined to think that the court performances must have rendered the bareness of the old public stage intolerable. While it is clear that the improvements in the playhouses were not as great as Malone supposed, his question still remains without a satisfactory answer. It is, indeed, a complex question which must be divided into many inquiries before answers can be found. The court masques, however peculiar in some respects, were a part of the general European change in staging arising in court spectacles, and eventually leading to the adoption of scenery and successive scenes in all theaters. This marked change was postponed in England until the Restoration. Before the Civil war, the possible period when the Masque might have influenced the public stage is confined to the reigns of James I and Charles I, and indeed the complete development of moving scenes is virtually limited to the reign of Charles, 1625-42.

Even in this period it is entirely clear that there was no general adoption of the stage and shifting scenes of Inigo Jones in the London theaters. Plays with such staging are to be found only in special performances. At the court and the universities and at other places before royalty, plays were sometimes presented with scenes. This was the case with the French pastoral "Florimène," of which a picture is given on page 194 and of several of the pastoral plays written for the court of Henrietta Maria. Inigo Jones devised scenes for a performance of Fletcher's "Faithful Shepherdess" at court in 1634, for Heywood's "Love's Mistress" in 1633, and Cartwright's "Royal Slave" in 1636–37. Strode's tragi-comedy, "The Floating Island," acted, like the "Royal Slave," at Oxford in August, 1636, was also provided with scenes. Henry Killigrew's "Conspiracy," 1638, acted at court for the nuptials of Lady Villiers and Lord Charles Herbert, also had scenery, though there is no indication of it in the printed text. Nor is there any sign in Habington's "Queen of Arragon" of the scenes with which it was provided at court. These were all exceptional cases, and there is no indication that performances of regular plays at court differed in staging from their performance in the London theaters.

Some of these plays just mentioned were also produced at the regular playhouses or by professional actors. Heywood's "Love's Mistress" was played by the Queen's men both at court and in public; and Cartwright's "Royal Slave," after its performance by the students of Christ Church, was repeated at Hampton Court by the King's men. In other cases, masques given at court were later performed in public, as the "Sun's Darling," by Ford and Dekker, and "The World Tossed at Tennis," by Middleton, and the "Microcosmus," by Nabbes. In none of these cases is there any indication in the text of shifting scenery. In fact, the use of such elaborate scenery as in "Salmacida Spolia" must have been rare even at court and Oxford. Of the four plays by William Cartwright, "the most florid and seraphical preacher in the university," three, the "Siege," the "Ordinary," and the "Lady Errant," have no scenes, though they employ a curtain for discoveries, and the "Lady Errant" seems to have had a background setting. Even in the "Royal Slave" the eight scenes or 'appearances' seem to have been, at least in part, practicable settings rather than perspective flats. The extravagant courtier, Sir John Suckling, wrote his "Goblins" and "Brennoralt" for a stage without scenery, though he spent much money for costumes and scenes for the performance of his "Aglaura" at Blackfriars in 1638.[1] This is the only case in which the use of scenery in a regular playhouse is recorded, and even here there is no indication in the text of its use.

Scenery in these plays, even more than in the masques, was far from possessing the verisimilitude of a later day. In Cartwright's "Royal Slave," for example, the six different appearances are: (1) "a temple of the sun," (2) "a city in the front and a prison on the side," (3) a stately palace, (4) a wood, (5) a castle, (6) "the sun eclipsed, and a shower of rain dashing the fire." The third of these, "a stately palace," served as a background for the second and third acts and parts of the fourth and fifth. As far as it affected the staging, it was simply a background with doors and windows, where the actors entered or looked on the front stage. The front stage, therefore, represented any room, or place in or about the palace, just as it might have in the Theater or Globe. In "Aglaura," the scenes were apparently quite similar to those just used for Cartwright at Oxford. There must have been a grove, a place with a cave, a tower room for Aglaura; but most of the scenes of the play took place before some 'appearance' of 'a stately palace,' as in the "Royal Slave." Indeed, if we take literally the

---

[1] Aubrey in his account of Suckling says that *Aglaura* "had some scenes in it, which in those days were used only at Masques."

o

directions in the alternative fifth act, which provided a happy ending for the court, the exigencies of the new scenery caused a reversion to primitive practices.[1] In the directions, "a state set out," "Table out," and "A bed put out, Thersames and Aglaura on it"; 'out' may merely mean 'ready' or 'outside' of the scenes; but if these properties were pushed out front when indicated, the state must have remained while the scenes changed from a grove to a room, and to the palace; and the bed must have been dragged on after the scenes had already indicated that the scene was the bedroom. There is not evidence enough to decide; but manifestly the first substitutions of scenery for the curtain must have introduced confusion in the management of properties. It would be some time before the stage could accustom itself to scenery.

Although it is clear that the masque staging was not transferred to the public theaters, it is also obvious that the public stage did adopt or imitate many elements of the masque performances. Masques — sometimes mere masked dances, but sometimes elaborate imitations of the court show — as in the "Tempest" and the "Maid's Tragedy," — are very frequent in plays. Special features, as clouds, transformations, personages flying through the air, rising mists, grotesque dances, were often imitated from the court. In court entertainments professional actors were usually employed in the antimasques. It was, therefore, natural that these comic dances and other elements should be repeated in the regular playhouses. In the "Two Noble Kinsmen" (1613), the May dance in iii. 5 was borrowed from the second antimasque in

---

[1] See Neuendorff, 204 ff. He takes the directions as an extreme but in some measure typical case of incongruity.

INIGO JONES'S DESIGN FOR THE PASTORAL OF "FLORIMENE," 1635

Beaumont's "Masque of the Inner Temple" and "Gray's Inn" given before the King on February 20, 1613.[1] I have elsewhere suggested that the antic dance of twelve satyrs in the "Winter's Tale" (iv. 4) was similarly borrowed from the antimasque of satyrs in Ben Jonson's "Oberon," given at court January 1, 1611.[2] In introducing the twelve dancers, the servant assures Polixenes "One three of them, by their own report, sir, hath danced before the King." Perhaps three of the King's men had recently taken part in "the antic dance full of motion and gesture" in the court entertainment on New Year's. Even the bear that devours Antigonus may have been one of the white bears that drew the chariot of Oberon.

The popularity and diversity of these antimasques at court led to emulation as well as imitation in the theater, as in Shakespeare's "Tempest," where the "strange shapes" and the "divers spirits in shape of dogs and hounds" may have been suggested by similar acting at the court masques.[3]

The borrowings from the court of costumes, properties, machinery, and decorations are more difficult to trace. Machines for clouds and aërial goddesses are found in early pageants and early plays, and their existence in seventeenth-century drama cannot be attributed solely to the masques. And the directions in printed plays do not give us specific or detailed information. We may suppose, however, that improvements in the court machines led to improvements in those used in the theaters, and that occasionally properties and costumes used at court may have

[1] *Two Noble Kinsmen*, ed. Harold Littledale, N.S.S. Series II. 1876–85. Introduction. *The Influence of Beaumont and Fletcher on Shakespeare.* A. H. Thorndike, 48 ff.   [2] *Ibid.*, 32 ff.   [3] *Ibid.*, 146, 147.

found their way to the Blackfriars and Cockpit. Certainly the spectacular plays of the seventeenth century suggest the influence of the Jacobean masques, just as plays like Heywood's "Ages" borrow from the court pageants of an earlier day.

One of the earliest plays to adopt a masque-like scheme is "The Four Plays in One" by Beaumont and Fletcher, which may date as early as 1608 or 1609.[1] The four plays are given the form of an entertainment before a king and his bride, and the Induction provides scaffolds crowded with spectators. The first three plays present many spectacular features, descending deities, and elaborate pantomimes, and processions with the accompaniment of music. In the first there is a change of setting, as indicated by the directions. "Solemn music, a mist ariseth, the rocks remove." The fourth play, the "Triumph of Time," assumes more definitely the structure and paraphernalia of the Masque. The theme is allegorical, and after an introductory dialogue, in response to the petition of Anthropos, "Jupiter and Mercury descend severally. Soft music"; and after their ascent to music, "Enter Plutus, with a troop of Indians singing and dancing wildly about him and bowing to him." The Indians are, of course, the antimasque, and they *exeunt* with a dance. Whether scenes were used is not stated, but the action calls for a somewhat complicated setting, and probably a changing background. After a song, Anthropos is set digging at a rock from which flames fly out. Then the main masque is introduced in this wise:

Enter Delight, Pleasure, Craft, Lucre, Vanity, etc., dancing (and masqued) toward the Rock, offering service

[1] *Influence of Beaumont and Fletcher on Shakespeare*, A. H. Thorndike, 84.

to Anthropos. Mercury from above. Music heard. One
half of a Cloud drawn. Singers are discovered; then the
other half drawn. Jupiter seen in glory.

After the dance and a song, the masquers *exeunt* in
the following procession.

Enter the Triumph. First, the Musicians. Then, Vain
Delight, Pleasure, Craft, Lucre, Vanity, and other of the
Vices: Then a Chariot with the Person of Time sitting in
it, drawn by four Persons, representing Hours, singing.

In other of Fletcher's plays, spectacular features
are clearly imitated from the masques, as in his "Proph-
etess" (1622). In II. iii. "Enter on a cloud, Delphia
and Drusilla, in a Throne, drawn by Dragons." In
III. ii. Delphia conjures up "a she-devil," and in IV.
i., in the dumb show, "Delphia raises a mist," and in
addition to other appearances and magic, there is in
Act v. a masque of shepherds and shepherdesses.
No other play of Fletcher's, however, goes as far as
the "Four Plays in One," in an effort to combine the
two species, romantic drama and the court masque.
For their successful union we must turn to Shakespeare's "Tempest." On the Elizabethan stage, as
in all subsequent eras, its performances must have been
spectacular. The masque structure appears in the
masque proper (IV. i.) danced by the reapers and
nymphs, and in the antimasques of "the strange
shapes" and "divers spirits in the shape of dogs and
hounds." The figures of Prospero, Ariel, and Caliban,
and the goddesses unite with the idyllic love story
and the plottings of the courtiers. Doubtless even in
Blackfriars the Enchanted Island was given a setting
to capture the eye as well as the fancy of the spectator.

Shakespeare's "Tempest" and "Winter's Tale" brought from Ben Jonson, in his "Bartholomew Fair" (1614), a characteristic protest against the mingling of species.

"If there be never a servant monster in the fair, who can help it, he says, nor a nest of antiques? he is loth to make nature afraid in his plays, like those that beget tales, tempests, and such like drolleries, to mix his head with other men's heels: let the concupiscence of jigs and dances reign as strong as it will amongst you; yet if the puppets will please anybody they shall be intreated to come in."

Jonson objected to dances, monsters, antics, and other masque elements in comedy. And his objection seems to have had some weight with his successors. At all events, there are few later plays which attempt to integrate comedy and masque. The influence of the court entertainment, which permeated romantic comedy from the days of Lyly, came to an end with Fletcher and Shakespeare. Henceforth there were pastorals and masques at court or in the theaters, but they were regarded as species distinct from regular comedy or tragi-comedy.

The effect of the court masques on the principles of staging in the playhouses must be regarded as incidental and occasional. Spectacular and special plays were affected; and there must have been some influence on lighting, costumes, properties, and other incidental matters, especially in the private theaters. That backgrounds were frequently used and that occasionally painted flats were substituted seems to me probable. Certainly in later plays there is an increasing tendency to localize scenes; but there is also a tendency toward continuity of place during an act or successive scenes. The public theaters were probably developing a principle of staging that presented action in definite places and successive scenes. But they were not yet ready for the revolutionary practice of the court masque. The plays of Shirley and Davenant and others in the last decade of the theater would hardly suggest to any one that their authors had written librettos for the elaborate scenic displays of Inigo Jones.

Throughout the Stuart, as in the Tudor, reigns the court entertainments in general kept a different stage from that of the theaters. In spite of the intimate relations between the court and the professional companies, the public houses were prohibited from the expensive experiments and elaborations of the royal shows. Comedy and tragedy remained the denizens of the platform stage. Pageant, pastoral, and masque resided mainly in the scenes and machines of Denmark House or Whitehall. But the splendor and audacity of the court performances helped to inspire more than one author to attempt in the public theater the visualization of dream or fantasy. To the child actors and fairylands of the court performances we owe something of the "Midsummer Night's Dream," and from the gorgeous enchantments of the court masques came some hint for the "Tempest."

CHAPTER VIII

GOVERNMENTAL REGULATION

The history of governmental regulation of the drama under the Tudors and Stuarts records a gradual change from heterogeneous local supervision to direct control by special officers of the court. By the time of Charles I, this control had become well defined by laws and patents and rendered effective through the office of the Master of the Revels. But for many years governmental regulation involved a conflict of authorities and uncertainty of administration. Few laws or proclamations seem to have been enforced strictly, and there was often the possibility of appeal from one jurisdiction to another. The authorities of the city of London, in particular, found their efforts to punish or prohibit plays frequently set aside by the court. This conflict between the city of London and the court forms, indeed, one of the most curious chapters in the history of the drama; but a similar conflict seems to have taken place in most of the towns. The mayor and his brethren found their efforts to regulate the intruding players subject to licenses, patents, letters, and proclamations from the court. London yielded to the court; but finally came the Revolution, the Puritans had their way, and the drama ceased. The regulation of the drama throws an interesting light on the increasing power of the crown, the growth of Puritanism and the demand of civil liberty; but our attention must be confined to the narrower concerns of the stage.

In connection with the theaters I have already glanced at various municipal regulations, and in connection with the court stage have encountered some of the court officials. Before going on to a consideration of the activities of the professional companies, it seems desirable to survey the entire field of the relations of the government to the drama. Regulation dealt with playhouses, actors, and plays. It determined when plays should be given, if at all, and what the plays should be. It might forbid plays on Sunday, or during Lent, or during the plague; or it might prohibit seditious or irreligious matters, or censure some particular play, or forbid play acting altogether. Some of the matters of regulation, both by court and city, as affecting the professional companies will be touched on again in later chapters. In this chapter, while surveying the whole field of government regulation, I shall also pay especial attention to the functions of the Master of the Revels, including that of censorship.

I. GENERAL REGULATION

When Elizabeth came to the throne, the chief problem in regard to the drama was the same as that which confronted her predecessors, to prevent sedition and heresy. On May 16, 1559, a proclamation prescribed a system of licensing plays, doubtless following the custom generally prevailing. All plays were forbidden [1] "eyther openly or privately, except the same be noticed before hande, and licenced within any citie or towne by the Maior or other chiefe officers of the same, and within

---

[1] Hazlitt, *English Drama*, 19–20. See Gildersleeve, 14, in regard to an April proclamation forbidding all plays, referred to in Holinshed, III. 1184.

any shyre by suche as shalbe Lieutenaunts for the
Queenes Maiestie in the same shyre, or by two of the
Justices of peax inhabyting within that part of the
shire where any shalbe played." Later on the proclamation specifies what should be censored, "that
they permyt none to be played, wherein either matters
of religion or of the governance of the estate of the
common weale shalbe handled, or treated; beyng no
meete matters to be wrytten or treated upon, but by
menne of aucthoritie, learning, and wisedome, nor to
be handled before any audience but of grave and dis-
creete persons." This system of censorship exercised
by the local authorities must have been conducted
with great laxity, although in 1574 we find the London
Common Council [1] making special provision for the
appointment of persons to read the plays, and putting
Puritan emphasis upon a kind of censorship not noticed in the royal proclamation, that of "inchaste,
uncomely, and unshamefaced speeches." A few
months earlier the court had taken steps to control
the censorship more effectively, by providing in the
patent of May 7, 1574, to Leicester's men [2] that their
plays be seen and allowed by the Master of the Revels,
an official of the King's household concerned only
with court plays and shows. In a patent of 1581 to
the Master, his powers of censorship were greatly
enlarged. "Whom we ordeyne, appointe, and au-
thorise by these presentes of all such Showes, Plaies
Plaiers, and Playmakers, together with their playinge
places, to order and reform, auctorise and put downe,
as shalbe thought meete or unmeete unto himself or

---

[1] Hazlitt, *English Drama*, 27–31.   Gildersleeve, 156 ff.
[2] Malone, *Variorum*, iii. 47.   Collier, *H. E. D. P.*, i. 208.   Hazlitt, *English Drama*, 25–6.   *Malone Soc. Coll.*, I. 262.

his said Deputie in that behalfe." [1] The Master of
the Revels, however, came only slowly to the full exercise of these powers. The London authorities still
censored plays, and the Bishop of London interfered
in the case of "Barnevelt" so late as 1619; but from
the accession of James I, the Master had control of
licensing plays and gradually assumed direction of the
affairs of companies and theaters. He was, however,
always subject to the higher powers of the court.
To quote from Dean Gildersleeve [2] : "Thus the
hierarchy of dramatic rulers ran, — King, Privy
Council, Lord Chamberlain, Master of the Revels;
and all the higher powers interfered at will, though for
the most part they left the exercise of authority to the
Master, the servant of the Crown."

In the meantime, while the censorship was gradually
becoming centralized, a series of statutes established
the status and the licensing of the players. In the
early Tudor period, actors had some definite connection with guild, town, nobleman, or court. Otherwise
they had no legal status. In the reigns of Henry
VIII, Edward VI, and Mary, enactments and proclamations concerning plays deal chiefly with the prevention of heresy and sedition. The licensing and
censorship of plays are provided for in the proclamations of 1551 and 1553, and occasionally plays of all
kinds are prohibited for a period, but the status of the
player is not specifically defined. There are frequent
indications, however, that the traveling players were
numerous and troublesome, and that they sometimes
wrongfully used great names for their protection. [3]
Elizabeth's proclamation of 1559, which we have just

[1] *Shaks. Soc. Papers*, III. i. Collier, *H. E. D. P.*, I. 247. Halliwell-
Phillipps, *Illustrations*.　　　[2] P. 19.　　　[3] Gildersleeve, 23–7.

found to provide in some detail for the licensing of plays by local authorities, also recognizes the responsibility of her "nobility and gentlemen" who have players as their servants. By this time the companies apparently often traveled about on the strength of a sort of license obtained from some nobleman or gentleman without having any very close relationship to this patron. The statute of 1872 — famous in the long series of poor laws — is often quoted because of the harsh penalties it imposes on unlicensed players; but its real significance lies rather in its establishment of a regular system of licensing for the companies either from "any baron of the realm or other honorable person of greater degree" or from "two justices of the peace at the least, whereof one to be of the Quorum, where and in what shire they shall happen to wander."[1] The professional companies wandering from their town or patron were thus provided with a definite legal status and enabled to escape from the class of rogues, vagabonds, sturdy beggars, and other undesirables who infested the highways. Mere gentlemen, who had previously authorized companies, could no longer do so under sanction of law; and a later statute of 1597(8)[2] took the privilege away from the justices of the peace. On the accession of James I, the power was restricted to the crown alone.[3] Nevertheless, many companies under license of noblemen continued to "wander abroad" throughout the reign of James I and even into that of his successor.

After 1603, however, the chief companies held their licenses directly from the court. These licenses varied

---

[1] *Statutes*, IV, pt. ii. 590. See also *Historia Histrionica*.
[2] 39 Elizabeth, cap. 4. *Statutes*, IV, pt. ii. 899.
[3] Cap. 7 (1604). *Ibid.*, 1024.

a great deal. The actors might be given a pass from the Lord Chamberlain to perform while attending the King on a progress;[1] a company might be authorized by the Privy Council to play in the provinces during a visitation of the plague in the city;[2] licenses, at least for the provinces, might be given by the Master of the Revels; or royal patents might be issued under the great seal. The earliest of these latter which we possess is that of 1574 to the Earl of Leicester's men. Attention should be paid to the extensive privileges granted — the company is authorized to act in London or anywhere else in England without interference from legal authorities or from previous statutes.

Later patents[3] follow this general model, but usually specify the regular places of performance in and about London. The 1619 patent for the King's men is the first extant which limits the playing in plague time by the number of deaths in the weekly bills. The company is authorized to act "when the infeccion of the Plague shall not weekely exceede the nomber of forty by the c't :ficate of the lord Maior of london for the time being as well within their two their now usuall houses called the Globe within our County of Surrey and their private house scituate in the precincts of the Black-friers within our City of london, As also within any Town halls or Moote halls or other convenient places within the liberties and freedome of any other City, University, Towne or Burrough whatsoever within our said Realmes and Domynions."

---

[1] Chalmers, *Apology*, 512 n.; and Malone, *Variorum*, 166, 167.

[2] Dasent, *Acts of the Privy Council*, XXIV. 209.

[3] All patents are printed in the *Malone Soc. Coll.*, I. 260–83. See also list in Gildersleeve, 231 ff.

It will be noted that these patents leave little authority in the hands of local authorities. Players traveling with such a license had the right to play in the moot hall or some fitting place. One performance at least was usually given in the moot hall before the mayor and aldermen, and properly rewarded. If the mayor and aldermen for any reason deemed it inadvisable for the company to act, they paid a liberal gratuity. Naturally, however, they came to be somewhat careful in inspecting the licenses presented. There was every temptation to actors to procure some kind of license by hook or by crook. But if authorized by the royal seal the traveling company was certain of a favorable reception in any town.

Except for the mention of the regular houses of the companies in their patents, there is no indication of national regulation of playing places. The conflict over the theaters in London will be discussed later, but it may be noted here that these royal authorizations mark the interference of the court in a matter where local authorities would most naturally desire entire control. Indeed the patent of 1619 seems to have been procured by the King's men because of an attempt by the Corporation to suppress the theater in Blackfriars.[1] Their patent of 1603 held good, but it did not mention Blackfriars house (occupied only in 1608) and they wished the security afforded by the royal seal.

On the whole, the national regulations and enactments gave support to the drama. It was recognized as desirable for the recreation of the King's loyal

---

[1] As Mr. E. K. Chambers suggests, *Malone Soc. Coll.*, I, 280. For documents on the attempts to suppress the Blackfriars, see *Malone Soc. Coll.*, I. 90.

subjects and for his own solace and pleasure. Actors were provided a legal status and finally brought under the direct patronage and control of the crown. Local authorities, especially those in London, were gradually deprived of their powers to interfere or suppress. The rogue and vagabond of the early days became the servant of a royal household authorized to act in certain playhouses and to present any plays of which the censor approved. I now turn to the varied functions which this officer performed.

II. THE MASTER OF THE REVELS

The Master of the Revels first appears in the reign of Henry VII as a court official in charge of revels, masques, and shows. Under the pleasure-loving Henry VIII the office increased in importance and was made permanent in 1545 by the appointment of Sir Thomas Cawarden, as "Magister Iocorum, Revelorum et Mascorum omnium et singularium nostrorum." We are to glance at the subsequent development of the Master's duties until he came to have a general power of licensing and regulating the drama. This development was due in part to the desire of the government for a centralized control, and in part to the desire of successive Masters to make the office as lucrative as possible. The patents conferring large but vague powers on the Master of Revels permitted him, according to the Elizabethan interpretation, to license what was in accord with the law and also to license what was otherwise forbidden. Somewhat as 'dispensing patents' gave certain persons the privilege and profits of giving licenses to exempt gambling and unlawful games, so the Master of the Revels was given the opportunity to increase his income by licensing violations or exemptions.   It must be remembered that virtually all governmental regulation was subject to this dispensing power.

Sir Thomas Cawarden died in 1559 and his place was given to Sir Thomas Benger, who continued from 1560 to 1577, though during the last five years of his term Thomas Blagrave served as Acting Master.   The office had fallen into some disorder and was reorganized in 1573.   The reports sent to Lord Burghley give an interesting account of the affairs of the office at that date and show that it was as yet solely concerned with court performances.   It was always a department under the Lord Chamberlain, of whom the Master was a subordinate.   The busy seasons were at Christmas and Shrovetide, with the occasional addition of some royal progress.   Tailors, carpenters, painters, haberdashers, joiners, wire drawers, etc., were employed in making costumes and properties under the supervision of a clerk, yeoman, and groom, as well as of the Master. The children who were employed in the entertainments caused considerable trouble in training and transportation.   Plays to be acted at court were " perused and reformed," and then rehearsed, usually at St. John's in the "grate chambere where the workes were doone and the playes rezited." [1]

This task of censoring the plays given at court was, as has been noted, greatly extended by a new patent of 1581, granted to Edmund Tilney, who became Master in 1577.   He is empowered to enforce service from the workmen required, to summon all players and playmakers that they may recite their plays before him, and to imprison any who are recalcitrant.

---

[1] See E. K. Chambers, *Tudor Revels*, for these reports and an account of the office at this time.

Still further, sweeping powers are confirmed to the Master, in the clause quoted.[1] Few records exist to determine in what ways Tilney exercised the general power conferred. He played no part in the agitation over the drama in the city of London during the years 1582–84, when the Privy Council acted directly; but players with his license appear in Leicester [2] and Gloucester [3] in 1583. In 1583 he was also called upon by the Lord Chamberlain to advise as to the selection of the players for the Queen's men. In 1589 he was actively interfering in the Marprelate controversy, advising the Privy Council to suppress all plays in London.[4] Later he was made one of a commission of three to license plays in London, of which he doubtless continued the active member. In 1592 the Aldermen complained to the Archbishop of Canterbury that Tilney had licensed the playhouses which before had been open to the statutes for the punishment of such disorders. The Archbishop treated with Tilney, and as a result the Master sought a "consideration" from the city. Possibly he received one, for the actors had a hard time in the years 1592–94. In these years Tilney was receiving considerable sums from Henslowe, owner of the Rose (without the city limits), for licenses both for plays and for the playhouse. The fee for the Rose, increased from 5s. to 6s. 8d. a week in 1592, had risen to 10s. in 1596, and after 1600 was £3 a week for the Fortune.[5] In 1598 the Privy Council acted through him in giving the Chamberlain's and Admiral's companies a monopoly about

---

[1] *Shak. Soc. Papers*, III. 1.   See p. 202.
[2] Kelly, *Drama in Leicester*, 211, 212.   [3] Murray, ii. 282.
[4] Letter, Lord Mayor to Burghley, Hazlitt, *English Drama*, 34, 35. *Malone Soc. Coll.*, I. 180.   [5] *H. D.*, II. 116–18.

P

London, apparently under bonds to the Master for their obedience to him. These companies enjoying special privileges from the Crown were directly under his control; and there are indications that by this time he was fully established as censor.[1] The London authorities and the justices of Middlesex and Surrey, however, still exercised authority over actors and theaters, and the Privy Council or Lord Chamberlain often went over the Master's head. By the end of Elizabeth's reign, the Master was receiving payments for licensing plays and playhouses about the city, and for licensing companies to travel. Apart from the regular emoluments, the office was now a lucrative one.

In the reign of James, some of the earlier anomalies appear, but the power of the Master steadily grew. Daniel the poet for a time had the right to license plays by the Children of the Revels,[2] which he neglected, at least in the case of "Eastward Hoe";[3] but the authority of the Master is reaffirmed in various patents.[4] Tilney was succeeded by Sir George Buc, who had the office in reversion in 1597, began to act as deputy by 1606, and took full control on Tilney's death, in 1610. Buc continued to license and censor plays for performance, and further licensed plays for publication, and on one occasion gave a license for building a playhouse, that in Whitefriars in 1613. He must have handed on the office in good condition to his successors, Sir John Ashley, who acted for only a few months in 1622–1623, and Sir Henry Herbert, who

[1] Gildersleeve, 60.   [2] See patent, Hazlitt, 40–41.   [3] Gildersleeve, 61.

[4] Prince's men, 1606; Queen's, 1609; Duke of York's, 1610; Palsgrave's, 1613; and, according to Herbert, in patents 1620–30. See Gildersleeve, 63, 64.

in July, 1623, purchased the office for £150 a year and continued to exercise all the authority he could muster until the outbreak of the Civil War.

His main sources of revenue outside of his regular services in connection with court entertainments were : (1) Licensing of companies in the country, but not in the city, these receiving authority directly from the Crown. (2) Special licenses of various sorts to the patented companies; for traveling, or for organizing special traveling companies, or warrants of protection assuring them against arrest. (3) Licenses of all sorts of traveling shows, ropewalking, trained animals, acrobats, and so on. Indeed, after the Restoration he seems to have claimed authority to license billiards, ninepins, and cock-fighting. (4) Licensing playhouses, or receiving gratuities from owners or occupying companies. From the King's men he had two benefit performances a year, afterwards compounded to £10 at Christmas and Midsummer. (5) Various fees, as Lenten fees, for permitting performances in this forbidden season, 44s. on one occasion from the King's men, or fees for special relaxations in plague time, etc. (6) Licenses of plays. He was now established as sole censor of plays about London, an authority strictly exercised at least over the patented companies; the fee for each play had been 5 to 7 shillings under Tilney, but was now £1, or double if special exertion was required. (7) Licenses for old plays, revived. (8) Licensing plays (and sometimes poems) for publication, up to 1638.

Herbert had to pay £150 a year to Ashley, but his business was so profitable that "by those means, as also by a good marriage, he attained to great fortunes for himself and his posterity to enjoy." After the

Restoration, when seeking to regain his ancient privileges, he implied that he had received £4000 a year
from the players. This is doubtless too large; but
his services in regulating the drama certainly brought
a handsome reward.

On November 20, 1622, the Lord Chamberlain issued
a warrant,[1] which seems to have defined and secured
the licensing power of the Master.   It recites that many
disorders have arisen from "diverse and sundry Com-
panyes of stage players Tumblers vaulters dauncers
on the Ropes And also by such as goe about with mo-
tions & shewes & other the like kind of psons by reason
of certaine grants Comissions & lycenses which they
have by secret meanes pcured both from the Kings
Ma[tie] & also from diverse noblemen"; and further
that these persons claim a "Kinde of licentious fre-
dome" without the approbation of the office of the
revels, and "greatly abuse their authority in lendinge
lettinge & sellynge their said Commissions."   The
local authorities are therefore commanded that unless
such players and entertainers have licenses under the
hand and seal of the Master of the Revels, they shall
forbid playing, seize all their licenses, and send them to
the Master.   The warrant further confirms the exclu-
sive authority of the office to license "playes, showes,
feats of activity and sights."   From this date, through
the energetic administration of Herbert, these provisions seem to have been enforced, and the provincial
records contain frequent references to licenses by the
Master of Revels.[2]   Such portions of Herbert's office

---

[1] A copy is preserved in the Mayor's Court Books at Norwich, printed by
Murray, ii. 351. Except through Herbert's later reference, this warrant
was unknown to Dean Gildersleeve, who summarizes its contents on p. 55.

[2] See records for Leicester and Norwich in Murray.

book[1] as survive give a vivid picture of his occupations and throw much light on the history of the drama from 1623–42.

III. THE CENSORSHIP

I turn now to the most important function of the Master, the censorship. In general, this duty was not so much moral as political. The statute of 1606 forbidding oaths gave the censor a good deal of pains, but in the main his efforts were devoted to the suppression of any contempt for authority. The government and the established religion, royalty, persons of high rank, these were to be guarded from attack or ridicule.

A few manuscripts of censored plays have been preserved, and are probably typical of the Master's general method, as far as he had any. The play, "Sir Thomas More," probably written before 1590, is preserved in a confusing manuscript, consisting of the copy corrected by the censor and three different sets of additions and alterations. Tilney's suppressions are numerous, but the wonder is that he should have permitted in any form a play celebrating an opponent of Henry VIII and intended to excite feeling against the foreigners dwelling in London.

The "Second Maiden's Tragedy" exists in manuscript with the erasures of both the Master, Sir George Buc, made October 31, 1611, and also those of the manager. Like many other Elizabethan dramas, the play represents a usurping and lustful tyrant, and Buc seems to have been somewhat particular in this case in deleting descriptions of royal lust. He is still

---

[1] This *MS. Herbert*, as it is sometimes called, was used by Malone (*Variorum 1821*) and Chalmers (*Supplementary Apology*). We must now rely on their extracts, as the original has been lost or destroyed.

more particular about oaths. A more significant instance of his censorship is to be found in the corrected manuscript of Fletcher and Massinger's "Sir John Van Olden Barnaveldt." The play was ready for production August 14, 1619, three months after Barnevelt's death, was at first suppressed by the Bishop of London, then permitted. For some reason it was not printed with the other plays by its authors. Buc's deletions are extensive but not very consistent. He complains that the Prince of Orange "is too much presented" and suppresses the vigorous closing speech declaring in unmistakable terms for political liberty against despotism; but he permits some similar protests to stand. The play was acted in spite of its obvious reflection on the recent execution of Raleigh, Spain's enemy, and the pro-Spanish policy of James I.

A more direct attack on Spain, Middleton's "Game of Chess," brought interference of the authorities, but was passed by Buc's successor Herbert. Massinger's "Believe as You List," however, was refused a license. We have many references by Herbert to his labors as censor, but no manuscript that shows his full corrections. Being an obstinate and fussy person, he seems to have spent much care in removing all oaths, including such expressions as 'Faith,' 'By Heaven,' 'By the Gods.' In the case of Davenant's "Wits," the author succeeded through Endymion Porter in bringing King Charles to his rescue. Herbert yields and notes, "The King is pleased to take faith, death, 'slight for asservations, and no oaths, to which I do humbly submit as my master's judgement, but under favour conceive them to be oaths, and enter them here to declare my opinion and submission." On one other occasion, the King's opinion was asked, in June, 1638, on Massinger's "King and Subject." Herbert's account of it seems likely to get the immortality he desired.

"At Greenwich the 4 of June, Mr. W. Murray gave mee power from the king to allowe of the play, and tould me that he would warrant it.

> 'Monys? Wee'le rayse supplies what ways we please,
> And force you to subscribe to blanks, in which
> We'le mulct you as wee shall thinke fitt. The Caesars
> In Rome were wise, acknowledginge no lawes
> But what their swords did ratifye, the wives
> And daughters of the senators bowinge to
> Their wills, as deities,' &c.

This is a peece taken out of Philip Messinger's play called The King and the Subject, and entered here for ever to bee remembered by my son and those that cast their eyes on it, in honour of Kinge Charles, my master, who, readinge over the play at Newmarket, set his marke upon the place with his owne hande, and in thes words:

> 'This is too insolent, and to bee changed.'

Note, that the poett makes it the speech of a king; Don Pedro king of Spayne, and spoken to his subjects."

Again, the wonder is that such insolence should not have brought punishment on the author's head.

These examples may illustrate the way in which plays were censored. The cases in which punishment was provoked by specific plays are more significant, but little is known of details. The Marprelate controversy in 1589 brought the stage to the side of the court and bishops, and we know from contemporary pamphlets that Martin was attacked and ridiculed in several non-extant controversial plays.[1] On November

---

[1] See *Works of Lyly*, ed. Bond, I. 52 ff.

26th the Privy Council ordered the suppression of all plays in and about London; but this probably did not long continue. The Paul's boys were "dissolved" in 1590 or 1591, but whether or not as a result of their share in the Marprelate affair, is a matter of conjecture. In 1597, another suppression of plays arose out of the "Isle of Dogs," in part by Nash,[1] apparently because of seditious matter. On February 7, 1601, the Essex conspirators arranged for the performance of Shakespeare's "Richard II" at the Globe, as an encouragement to rebellion. Queen Elizabeth showed herself very sensitive on the parallel with Richard II, and the abdication scene had been omitted in the quartos of 1587–8. However, notwithstanding the gravity of the rebellion with which Shakespeare's company was thus connected, the players seem to have come off lightly. Two weeks after the rebellion they acted at court before the Queen. The only other recorded cases of government objection to plays during Elizabeth's reign are the objection, traditionally from the then Lord Cobham, to the use of Oldcastle for the character renamed Falstaff, and an inquiry in the Privy Council on May 10, 1601, concerning persons of quality offensively represented at the Curtain.

In the early part of the reign of James there seem to have been numerous objectionable presentations of royalty on the stage. In 1604, Beaumont, the French ambassador, wrote of the condition of a prince "whom the comedians bring upon the stage, whose wife attends these representations to enjoy the laugh against her husband." A year later, on March 28, 1605, Calvert complained in a letter to Winwood that the players

---

[1] New light is thrown on this suppression in Wallace, "Swan Theater and Pembroke's Men," *Englische Studien*, 1911. See pp. 233, 281.

"did not forbear to present upon their stage the whole course of the present Time, not sparing either King, State, or Religion, in so great absurdity, and with such Liberty, that any would be afraid to hear them."

No extant plays bear out these statements, nor can we get any hint of such presentations in the several plays of this date that received censure. In December, 1604, the tragedy "Gowry," dealing with the rebellion of that nobleman, was acted by the King's men and was probably forbidden. Day's "Isle of Gulls," in 1605, according to Fleay, may have satirized royalty. "Eastward Hoe," in 1604, on account of mild satire of the Scots, got Jonson and Chapman into prison. Jonson had been in difficulties before over the "Poetaster" and "Sejanus," and it is not certain that the letters by the two authors in 1605 concerned the "Eastward Hoe" imprisonment. At all events, it is clear that two distinguished writers were imprisoned for some offense given by their plays, and that they escaped the more serious consequences with which they were threatened.

Chapman and the Children of the Revels, who acted "Eastward Hoe," soon committed another offense, concerning which we have some detailed information, the production of "Biron's Conspiracy and Tragedy," in 1608. Beaumont, the French Ambassador, writing on April 5, tells how the actors gave the play after they had been forbidden and "brought upon the stage the Queen of France and Mademoiselle de Verneuil. The former having first accosted the latter with very hard words, gave her a box on the ear. At my suit three of them were arrested; but the principal person, the author, escaped."[1] Two months later, however, the

[1] Von Raumer, *Sixteenth and Seventeenth Centuries*, II. 219.

two tragedies were entered for publication with the license of Sir George Buc, though not until after a spirited protest by Chapman and some severe mutilation by the censor. Dean Gildersleeve [1] suggests that it was the scandal attending upon these dramas which caused the edict "against the representing of any modern Christian kings in stage-plays." In Chapman's plays, one scene pictured the court of Queen Elizabeth, where the real Biron had actually been, and according to Beaumont's gossip, players had gone to scandalous lengths in representing James I. It would be interesting to know more of these plays ridiculing royalty, presenting the King as drunk, and cursing and swearing.[2] For a few years from about 1600 to 1607 the drama was given over to realism and satire; and it seems probable that attacks on persons and interests were more frequent and direct then than at any other period. Complaints of informers in the audience also become frequent in plays of this time. Except for the imprisonment of Jonson and Chapman, there is, however, no evidence of unusual activity of the censorship.

The punishment of scandalous or seditious performance is occasionally noted in the later years of James, but nothing definitely connected with an extant play until the famous case of Middleton's "Game of Chess" in August, 1624. Acted a few months after war had been declared with Spain, this sets forth a story of Spanish and Jesuit plotting, and gives a patriotic interpretation of the visit of Charles and Buckingham to the Spanish court. The black knight is a bitter caricature of the Spanish ambassador Gondomar. The play secured Herbert's license and was

---

[1] *Op. cit.*, 101.   [2] Von Raumer, *op. cit.*, II. 219, 220.

acted nine times in succession at the Globe, "followed with extraordinary curiosity and frequented by all sorts of people, old and young, rich and poor, masters and servants, papists, wise men, &c., churchmen and Scotsmen;"[1] and then suppressed by the Privy Council at the request of the King, upon the complaint of the Spanish ambassador. The players escaped with two weeks' closing of their theater. Indeed, the play was really an expression of popular approval for the crown's change to a protestant and anti-Spanish policy. Moreover, the players had received the permission of the Master of Revels, who obtained the backing of his superior, the Lord Chamberlain.

Nevertheless, further presentations of the "Game of Chess" were not permitted, and the play obtained publication surreptitiously. One fortunate instance of political criticism might escape punishment, but the example was a dangerous one. The next year, a plan to put "Amboyna" on the stage was stopped by the protest of the Dutch minister. There was reason for this fear of politics in the drama, for Massinger's plays were dealing under a thin disguise with England's foreign policy. It is in two of Massinger's plays, as I have noted, that we have in censored passages most striking protests against political despotism. The daring of the political matter thus presented by the King's own company must be taken not of course as a sign of disloyalty, but of the expression of political opinion unchecked by censorship.

Perhaps if all the Elizabethan plays were examined by an historian with the knowledge of Gardiner, many political allegories as close as those found in Massinger might be discovered. Certainly an interesting array

---

[1] Letter, Chamberlain to Carleton, Aug. 21, 1624.

of instances might be easily collected. Lyly's plays have yielded to modern observers elaborate presentation of important state affairs. Though any hint of civil discord was a forbidden theme, Marlowe, in "Edward II," wrote of rebellion and a feeble monarch; and in "Richard II" Shakespeare bettered his practice. In the play of "Woodstock" an anonymous writer made a popular hero out of Richard's brother, and dealt very frankly with the royal abuses of power. Though the Tudors and Stuarts strove to increase royal power, tyranny continued a favorite theme in tragedy; and the scandals concerning the favorites of James only increased the number and infamy of royal favorites on the stage. The new knights and the monopolies were frequent objects of comic satire, and the affairs of courtiers seem sometimes to have been brought into ridicule. Kings and queens filled the London stage, and while the divine right and the sanctity of royal persons were made much of as dramatic motives, the kings themselves are often portrayed as weak or vicious. Not only Shakespeare but even such court dramatists as Beaumont and Fletcher and such a court favorite as Suckling pursued their kings with rebellion and murder. The "Maid's Tragedy" had to be altered to avoid offense to Charles II; but the murder of a lawful king by his mistress and the overthrow of the government were presented without objection from James I or Charles I. Democracy of our twentieth-century type had few advocates in the sixteenth; and the serviceability of the People as a *dramatis persona* was limited to mobs and insurrections; yet in plays addressed to the working classes, as some of Dekker's and Heywood's, the observant reader may find many hints, which the Stuarts might well have heeded, of the growing political and social consciousness of the populace.

Evidently the drama was little hampered by the censorship, though the censor might occasionally prove annoying. It was certainly free enough so far as indecency of theme or language was concerned. As long as it paid due regard to church, state, and royalty, it was permitted a considerable range of political comment and philosophical speculation. Only when it became specifically impertinent and personal, did it clash with authority. As Dean Gildersleeve says, the Elizabethan drama was essentially non-controversial, and no dramatist was less controversial than Shakespeare. "When the manuscripts of his plays were submitted to the Revels office, the pen of Tilney or Buc, we may feel sure, marred with no considerable 'reformations' his unblotted lines; nor would his dramas have been materially different from what they are, had there been no necessity of guarding against the condemnation of the censor." [1]

IV. THE OPPOSITION OF THE CITY OF LONDON

We come now to the relations between the theater and the city of London. In general, as has often been noted, the city government, representative of the property-holding classes, was hostile to the theaters as sources of rioting, fire, the plague, and immorality; and the theaters relied on the support of individual noblemen and the court. In theatrical regulations, the Privy Council and the Lord Chamberlain were usually ranged against the city. Often, however, in special cases, the positions may be reversed, and the conflict of authorities offers many anomalies and

[1] *Op. cit.*, 136.

exceptions. It must be remembered, too, that the permanent theaters were erected outside of the jurisdiction of the city government. Those on the Surrey side were in the liberties of the Clink and Paris Garden; those to the north, in the liberties of Holywell and Finsbury. These came under the jurisdiction, respectively, of the Justices of the Peace of Surrey and Middlesex. More anomalous was the position of the theaters in Blackfriars and Whitefriars, districts surrounded by the city proper, yet liberties exempt from control by the city government, and from any local control. Not until 1608 did they come legally under the government of the city, and in the case of Whitefriars some vestiges of the old right of sanctuary were maintained until the very end of the seventeenth century. The regulation of the stage by the city, then, applied to several distinct conditions, (1) the playhouses and innyards within the city proper, (2) the playhouses in the suburbs outside of the jurisdiction of the city, and (3) those in the special liberties of Blackfriars and Whitefriars. A further distinction, which I shall have occasion to refer to again, grew up between 'public' and 'private' theaters, the latter at first occupied by the child actors, who as choir boys in service of the Queen were on a different footing from the 'common' players.

The efforts of the city during the reign of Elizabeth were directed toward a suppression of playhouses and an assertion of the city's authority in conflict with the Privy Council. The periods of greatest activity on the part of the city are 1572–79, 1580–85, and 1594–97. As a result of the earliest agitation, the players erected theaters outside of the city's jurisdiction. The result of the second campaign was the defeat of the city and the continuation of the theaters.

THE BANKSIDE
From Hollar's View, 1647.

The campaign in 1596 resulted, at the most, in the temporary restriction of the number of theaters. In the reigns of James and Charles the theaters and companies were directly under the crown, and the attacks of the city may be regarded as an irregular warfare rather than as sustained campaigns. The playhouses were legally without, virtually within the city; but efforts to increase their number were fought, and the regulations prescribed under Elizabeth's reign were continued. These regulations, in general, forbade playing on Sunday, in Lent, or during the prevalence of the plague. In particular, they might and did cover many matters, from regulation of the coaches before Blackfriars to interference in the rivalry between the theaters and the bear gardens. There is, however, one safe rule to keep in mind in regard to all these governmental regulations. They were never strictly enforced. However drastic the enactment, whether by Council or city, might appear, there was always a way out; through the interference of a powerful nobleman, through the special license of the Master of the Revels, or through a conflict of authorities, or through the unsystematic and inefficient character of the administration.

In the remainder of this chapter I shall glance a little more closely at the more important efforts made by the city to suppress or control the theaters, and at some of the specific measures of regulation, especially those concerning performances during the plague.

In 1572 "plays were banished for a time out of London." [1] In March, 1574, however, the demand for licenses to play in the innyards within the city had

[1] Harrison's *Chronologie* in Harrison's *Description of England, New Shaks. Soc.*, I. liv.

become so considerable, that the Lord Chamberlain proposed to grant a patent to one Holmes for such licenses. This would doubtless have been a profitable privilege, but the Mayor and Corporation, upon being consulted, interposed strong objections.[1] They pointed out the dangers of assemblies in the inns, the desirability that such licenses should be under city control, and the fact that "great offers" had already been made of sums to be paid to the poor in hospitals as payment for licenses to play. A few days later the Privy Council asked the Lord Mayor for a statement of "what causes he hath to restrain plays," but two months later, in May, the crown granted the patent to the Earl of Leicester's players, authorizing performances in London, except in "time of common prayers or in the time of great and common plague in our said city of London." Thus, at this early date, a patent from the crown was used to override the city government.

Perhaps the mayor was slow in yielding, for on July 22, we find the Privy Council requiring him "to admit comedy players to play within the City of London, and to be otherwise favorably used."[2] The plague was severe in the autumn and doubtless put a stop to the playing, and the City Council took the occasion to formulate careful regulations for dramatic performances when the plague should cease. The preamble of these regulations of December 6, 1574,[3] summarizes effectively the case of the city against the players in the innyards.

"Whereas heartofore sondrye greate disorders and inconvenyences have beene found to ensewe to this Cittie by the

[1] Gildersleeve, 153, 154.   [2] *Acts*, VIII. 273.

[3] Hazlitt, *English Drama*, 27–31. Collier, *H. E. D. P.*, I. 208–11. See Gildersleeve, 156, 157.

inordynate hauntynge of greate multitudes of people, speciallye youthe, to playes, enterludes and shewes; namelye occasyon of frayes and quarrelles, eavell practizes of incontinencye in greate Innes, havinge chambers and secrete places adjoyninge to their open stagies and gallyries, inveylynge and alleurynge of maides, speciallye orphanes, and good cityzens children under age, to previe and unmete contractes, the publishinge of unchaste, uncomelye, and unshamefaste speeches and doynges, withdrawinge of the Quenes Majesties subjectes from dyvyne service on Soundaies & hollydayes, at which tymes such playes weare chefelye used, unthriftye waste of the moneye of the poore & fond persons, sondrye robberies by pyckinge and cuttinge of purses, utteringe of popular, busye and sedycious matters, and manie other corruptions of youthe, and other enormyties; besydes that allso soundrye slaughters and mayhemminges of the Quenes Subjectes have happened by ruines of Skaffoldes, Frames and Stagies, and by engynes, weapons and powder used in plaies. And whear in tyme of Goddes visitacion by the plaigue suche assemblies of the people in thronge and presse have beene verye daungerous for spreadinge of Infection."

The act provides that plays in innyards or other places shall be read and allowed by persons appointed by the Lord Mayor and Aldermen, that the players shall be licensed by the Lord Mayor and Aldermen, that the places of playing shall be approved by them, and that the house owner shall give security for the preservation of order. Further, no plays shall be given during times forbidden by the city authorities, such as during the plague, or during Divine service on Sundays and holydays. Further, all licensed house-keepers shall contribute to the poor of the city. These regulations were apparently enforced with some severity; for at once the players erected the Theater and

Q

the Curtain outside of the city limits.[1] But the performances in the innyards within the city still continued, though pamphlets and sermons still thundered their denunciation against the drama.

Two orders of the Privy Council in 1578 and 1579 deserve notice here because of their bearing on the general regulation of the theaters. The second, in March, 1579, forbids performances during Lent.[2] Though this is notable as the first explicit law to this effect, the order apparently enforced an existing act and continued in operation until the closing of the theaters. It was, however, often not enforced. Of the three theatrical seasons fully recorded in Henslowe's Diary, two show the theater closed during Lent, the third shows performances daily during the Lenten season.[3] As early as 1617, the Master of the Revels was selling dispensations for performances in the forbidden period. The other order of the Council just referred to indicates another way in which any ordinance of the city or court might be overridden. In December, 1578, the Privy Council, apparently after a suppression owing to the plague, required the Lord Mayor to suffer six specified companies to play within the city, "and no company else." [4] These companies are to be allowed "because they are appointed to play this Christmas before her Majesty." This practice of special exemptions soon became well established. Six is rather a large number, but frequently the restrictions placed by the city on dramatic performances in general

---

[1] For the order prohibiting plays, formerly dated 1575, and held by Collier, Fleay, Ordish, Murray, and other writers using the wrong date, as the cause of the building of the Theater, see p. 228.   [2] *Acts*, XI. 73, 74.

[3] Closed Lent, '95 and '96, but open 12 days in '97 (Greg, *H. D.*, ii. 51) and in '98 (p. 85).   [4] *Acts*, IX. 435, 436.

were removed for the benefit of two or three companies
which had powerful friends at court or in council.

In 1580 the second campaign of the city against
the theaters opened with an appeal of the Lord Mayor
to the Middlesex Justices, which brought about the
indictment of John Braynes and James Burbage for
causing unlawful assemblages at the Theater and pro-
voking breeches of the Queen's peace.[1] On April
12, the Lord Mayor addressed the Privy Council on
the matter, and begged that plays might be forbidden
in the Liberties as well as in the city.[2] What happened
to Burbage and his theater we do not know; but in
May the plague was so severe that the Privy Council
forbade performances.[3] In June, the Mayor again
appealed to the Lords requesting their aid for the re-
dress of such things as were found dangerous "in
spreading the infection and otherwise drawing God's
wrath and plague upon us, as the erecting and frequent-
ing of houses very infamous for incontinent rule out of
our liberties and jurisdiction, also the drawing of the
people from the service of God and from honest exercises to unchaste plays."[4] Apparently the Curtain
and Theater were not closed.

In the following year the plague again caused the suppression of the theaters. On July 10, 1581, the Privy
Council ordered the Mayor and the Justices of the
Peace to suppress plays until September.[5] Presumably the Mayor and Aldermen closed the playhouses

[1] See indictments in the *Athenæum*, Feb. 12, 1887, quoted from Middlesex
County Records. It refers to assemblages on Feb. 21, 1580, and other days
before and after that date.

[2] *Remembrancia* (*i.e. Index*, as in all references), 350. *Malone Soc.
Coll.*, I. 46.   [3] *Acts*, XII. 15.

[4] *Remembrancia*, 330. *Malone Soc. Coll.*, I. 47.

[5] *Remembrancia*, 331. *Malone Soc. Coll.*, I. 49.

effectively; but in other measures against the plague they did not satisfy the Lords, and received sharp reproofs in September and October.[1] Yet on November 18, the Privy Council required the Mayor to "suffer the players to practice such plays, in such sort, and in the usual places, as they had been accustomed."[2] The city authorities seem to have delayed in carrying out this order, and on December 3 [3] the Lords again ordered the Mayor to permit certain unnamed petitioning companies to perform in and about the city, as they had been accustomed to do. The reasons given for the opening of the theaters are the usual ones, that the plague is abating, the players need the money, and they are to act before the Queen at Christmas. They are forbidden to play on Sundays. It should be noted that performances were resumed within the city as well as in the liberties. In this same month, December, 1581, the patent was issued that gave the Master of the Revels wide authority, apparently overriding the local control of the city government.

The city shortly proceeded to extreme measures, an act totally prohibiting plays within the city. This act was passed probably in 1582,[4] and is referred to in a municipal letter of 1584. Some action resulted, for Rawlidge's "Monster Lately Found Out," published 1628, states that soon after 1580 the citizens

[1] *Remembrancia*, 331.   *Acts*, XIII. 234.

[2] *Remembrancia*, 350.   *Malone Soc. Coll.*, I. 50.

[3] *Acts*, XIII. 269.   See Gildersleeve, 162, 163; and *Malone Soc. Coll.*, I. 50, note on IV.

[4] This order quoted by Collier, *H. E. D. P.*, I. 211-12, quoting from the undated pamphlet printed by Hugh Singleton, has been misdated because of the misdating of the Letters. See Gildersleeve, 163, 164, 172, 173. Chambers, *Academy*, Aug. 24, 1895.

expelled the players and "quite pulled down and suppressed" the playhouses in the city.[1] Yet in the spring of 1582, the Privy Council again requested the Lord Mayor to allow performances in the city, though they suggested appointing a censor and forbidding plays on holydays.[2] The Mayor had to submit, though he replied rehearsing the evils of plays.[3] In the following July, however, he refused to grant the request of the Earl of Warwick that his servant might give a fencing exhibition at the Bull in Bishopsgate street.[4]

On Sunday, January 13, 1583, the falling of a scaffold during a performance at Paris Garden injured many of the spectators. This judgment of God doubtless added vigor to the attacks of the city officials. But the Privy Council came to the aid of the players with the formation, on March 10, 1583, of a select company directly in the Queen's service. The plague interfered again with theatrical performances, and the Mayor again called upon the Privy Council to suppress the playhouses outside the city.[5] On November 26 and again on December 1, the Privy Council requested permission for Her Majesty's Players to act within the city.[6] In the following summer, however, the disturbances at the Theater and Curtain led the mayor to seek an order for the pulling down of those buildings. The lords consented, but Burbage, owner of the Theater, appealed to his patron, Lord Hunsdon, and was "bound over to the oyer and

[1] Quoted by E. K. Chambers, *Academy*, Aug. 24, 1895.

[2] *Remembrancia*, 351. *Acts*, XIII. 404. *Malone Soc. Coll.*, I. 52.

[3] *Remembrancia*, 351. *Malone Soc. Coll.*, I. 54.

[4] *Athenæum*, Jan. 23, 1869. *Remembrancia*, 351. *Malone Soc. Coll.*, I. 56–58. H. P., *Outlines*, I. 374.

[5] *Remembrancia*, 337. *Malone Soc. Coll.*, I. 63.

[6] *Remembrancia*, 352. *Malone Soc. Coll.*, I. 66, 67.

terminer."[1] The two theaters survived unharmed the order for their destruction.

The Queen's players now took up the battle for their profession and some time in the winter, probably of 1584,[2] they petitioned the Privy Council for leave to play within the city and also at the playhouses outside. Their petition was accompanied by "Articles" setting forth such regulations as they deemed advisable; these have been lost, but one of their proposals was that they should not act when deaths from the plague were above 50 a week. To this petition the city submitted an elaborate reply, reviewing the history of the municipal legislation, controverting one by one the contentions and proposals of the players, objecting to plays at all, and proposing in their turn a set of regulations entitled "The Remedies."

"That they hold them content with playeing in private houses at weddings, &c without publike assemblies.

If more be thought good to be tolerated, that then they be restrained to the orders in the act of common Counsel, *tempore* Hawes.

That they play not openly till the whole death in London haue ben by xx daies vnder 50 a weke, nor longer than it shal so continue.

That no playes be on the sabbat.

That no playeing be on holydaies, but after evening prayer, nor any received into the auditorie till after evening prayer.

[1] H. P., *Outlines*, I. 374, 375. *Malone Soc. Coll.*, I. 163. Gildersleeve, 169.

[2] Lansdowne Ms., reprinted *Malone Soc. Coll.*, I. ii; also reprinted in parts: Hazlitt, *English Drama;* Collier, *English Dramatic Poetry*. The petition and subsequent documents have been misdated 1574, as Mr. E. K. Chambers, *Academy*, Aug. 24, 1895, and Dean Gildersleeve, 171–72, have shown. The correct dating is of considerable importance in stage history, and the history of the Queen's Men. Collier, Fleay, Murray *et al.* have been led into serious errors by this misdating.

That no playeing be in the dark, nor continue any such time but as any of the auditorie may returne to their dwellings in London before sonne set, or at least before it be dark.

That the Quenes players only be tolerated, and of them their number, and certaine names, to be notified in your Ll^ps lettres to the L. Maior and to the Justices of Midd'x and Surrey. And those her players not to divide themselves into several companies.

That for breaking any of these orders their toleration cesse." [1]

Unfortunately we do not know the result of these communications. Dean Gildersleeve suggests that "it is probable that some compromise measure was adopted, including some of the municipal rules." [2] It is clear that plays were not kept out of London or confined "to private houses, weddings, etc." And it also seems clear that the regulation concerning the plague was not adopted, for in subsequent years we find that special orders for suppressing because of the plague are issued by the Privy Council, as heretofore.[3] The Master of Revels was gradually assuming control, but the city government continued ineffectual protests, and the Privy Council continued to interfere on occasions great and small. In 1589, because of the Marprelate controversy, they suppressed plays altogether, yet the Lord Strange's men disobeyed the Lord Mayor and "in very contemptuous manner departing from me, wente to the Crosse Keys, and played that afternoon." [4] On July 28, 1591, the Privy Council reproved the Lord Mayor for neglect of the order against playing on the Sabbath day, and

---

[1] *Malone Soc. Coll.*, I. 174. Collier, *H. E. D. P.*, I. 217.   [2] 174, 175.
[3] May, 1586, *Acts*, XIV. 99, 102. May 7, 1587, *Acts*, XV. 70.
[4] Hazlitt, *English Drama*, 34, 35.

added that the performances on Thursday were a "great hurthe and destruction of the game of beare baytings and lyke pastymes." [1] Therefore they direct that there be no plays permitted on those two days.

By 1592, as has been noted, the Master of the Revels had won a good deal of authority, but in the last dozen years of Elizabeth's reign, there are still many evidences of vigorous enactments by the Privy Council as well as by the city officials. The most important conflict of authorities is still on the question of playhouses. Each new building was stoutly opposed by the city, and an increase in the number of houses was usually forbidden by the Council, yet the Swan, Blackfriars, Globe, and Fortune were all built between 1592 and 1600. On November 3, 1594, the Mayor wrote to the Lord Treasurer protesting against the new theater on the Bankside (probably the Swan) urging especially the danger of disorder and rioting that had lately much prevailed in the city.[2] Apparently no action was taken by the Privy Council, but on September 13, 1595, the Mayor again urged the suppression of all plays about the city,[3] again without action by the Council, although they suppressed plays during the plague of 1596.[4] In the summer of that year a letter of Nash's complains, that "the players are piteously persecuted by the Lord Mayor and the Aldermen." [5] In November of the same year the inhabitants of Blackfriars petitioned the Privy Council against the "common playhouse" that Burbage was planning to build in that Liberty.[6] Nevertheless the playhouse was

---

[1] *Acts*, XXI. 324–5.   [2] *Remembrancia*, 353.   *Malone Soc. Coll.*, I. 74.
[3] *Remembrancia*, 354.   *Malone Soc. Coll.*, I. 76.   H. P., *Outlines*, 349–50.
[4] *Acts*, XXVI. 38.   [5] Collier, *H. E. D. P.*, I. 292.   Fleay, *Stage*, 157.
[6] *Remembrancia*, 353.   H. P., *Outlines*, I. 204.

completed, and flourished until the Civil War in spite of this and later efforts of the citizens of Black-friars to close it.   They called it a common theater; but as it was indoors and occupied by children actors, the players called it a "private house" and secured some protection from laws against "common playhouses."

In the next summer, the Lord Mayor made a more successful attack on the theaters, for his letters of July 28, 1597, to the Privy Council, asking for the "present staie and fynalle suppressinge of the saide stage playes as well as the Theatre, Curten and Banckside as in all other places in and about the Citie" [1] brought an order from the Lords on the same day prohibiting in the Queen's name all plays within three miles of the city until November 1 and that "all playhouses should be plucked doun."   Orders to the Justices of Middlesex and Surrey especially specify "the Curteyne and the Theatre nere Shore ditch" and "playhouses in the Banckside, in Southwark." [2]

The Lords in their orders declare "that there are verie greate disorders committed in the common playhouses both by lewd matters that are handled on the stage, and by resorte and confluence of bad people." It seems probable that among other cases they had in mind the performance of the "Isle of Dogs," declared in a letter of the Council on August 15 to be "a lewd plaie that was plaied in one of the plaiehouses on the Bancke Side, contayninge very seditious and sclanderous matter." [3]   On August 10, Henslowe in his Diary makes incidental reference to the restraint, which "is

[1] *Remembrancia*, 354.   *Malone Soc. Coll.*, I. 78.
[2] *Acts*, XXVII. 313-314.   H. P., *Outlines*, I. 356, 357.
[3] *Acts*, XXVII. 338.

by meanes of the playinge the Jeylle of dooges." [1] The imprisonment of some of the actors and the search of Nash's lodgings seem to indicate that the play's satire aroused serious charges of sedition. Two years later, indeed, Nash, who declares that he wrote only the induction and first act of the play, writes, "The straunge turning of the Ile of Dogs from a comedie to a tragedie two summers past, with the troublesome stir which hapned aboute it, is a generall rumour that hath filled all England." [2] The play has not been preserved; but neither the Lord Mayor's complaint nor the orders of the Council would indicate that any one play was the sole cause of the drastic orders. [3]

Drastic, explicit, and thoroughgoing as these orders were, they had the same fate as most orders affecting the theaters. There is no evidence that an attempt was made to enforce the order for the demolition of the playhouses. Performances were suppressed in all of the public theaters, [4] but the Rose reopened on October 11, [5] twenty days before the end of the restraint, Henslowe having obtained a license for the Lord Admiral's company. Another license was granted to the Lord Chamberlain's men at the Theater; and a third company which played for some time without a license was ordered suppressed on February 19, 1598, by the Privy Council. Presumably [6] the two

---

[1] *H. D.*, ed. Greg, I. 203.　　　　　　　　[2] *Lenten Stuff.*

[3] Because of Henslowe's reference, it has generally been assumed that the "Isle of Dogs" was acted at the Rose, but Professor Wallace has discovered documents that indicate that it was played at the Swan. "The Swan Theater and the Earl of Pembroke's Servants," *Englische Studien*, 1911.

[4] *Ibid.* See Documents in the lawsuit Robert Shaw *et al. v.* Langley.

[5] *H. D.*, I. 54.

[6] *Acts*, XXVIII. 327–8. The theaters of Blackfriars and St. Paul's were not occupied by the children until later.

favored companies had interfered to stop their intruding rivals who were probably playing at the Swan.

The erection of the Fortune theater in 1600 caused further difficulties. The Middlesex Justices opposed, but Edward Alleyn secured the support of his patron the Lord Admiral;[1] and also of the inhabitants of Finsbury.[2] On April 8, 1600, the Privy Council required the justices, by order of the Queen, to permit Alleyn to complete his theater.[3] The Lords stated that this house was to take the place of the Rose, which was to be pulled down. On June 22, they issued an elaborate order "for the restrainte of the imoderate use and Companye of Playehouses and Players." This laid down very precise rules; there are to be but two houses, one on the Bankside, the other in Middlesex. The Fortune is to be occupied by the Lord Admiral's men, and is to take the place of the Curtain (instead of the Rose), which is to be destroyed. On the Bankside the Globe is to be occupied by the Lord Chamberlain's men. There are to be no other theaters and no more performances in "any common inne for publique assembly in or neere aboute the Citie." These two companies are to act but twice a week, and never on the Sabbath or in Lent or in time of "extraordinary sickness" in or about the city.[4]

One might suppose that these orders would have amounted to something. But it is doubtful if any one tried to enforce them. Within a year the Privy Council had seemingly forgotten all about the order for the destruction of the Curtain, for in May, 1601, they received a complaint about a play in that theater and merely ordered the Middlesex Justices to investigate and

---

[1] *Henslowe Papers*, ed. Greg, 49–50.   [2] *Ibid.*, 50–51.   [3] *Ibid.*, 51–52.
[4] *Acts*, XXX., 395–8. H. P., *Outlines*, I. 307.   *Malone Soc. Coll.*, I. 80.

"take bond" of the players to answer before the Council.[1] In December, however, they remembered their orders of 1600, but simply to scold the mayor and aldermen and the justices for not enforcing them.[2] Three months later, March 31, the Lords have forgotten the prohibition of innyards and order the Mayor to permit several of the Earl of Worcester's and the Earl of Oxford's men to play at the Boar's Head in Eastcheap.[3] The Justices and the Mayor seem in this case not unfavorable to the companies, perhaps because of the payments which they by this time were accustomed to make for the poor in the parish where they were located.   Whether these orders of 1600 were intended to apply to the Children of the Chapel and the Paul's boys is difficult to say.   In an order delivered to the Mayor on March 11, 1601, in regard to closing for Lent, the Privy Council specify "especyally at Powles and in the Blackfriars," [4] and the municipal order of 1619 suppressing the Blackfriar house cites the orders of 1600 as limiting the theaters to two and "exempting thereby the Blackfriars.[5] But neither Blackfriars nor Paul's is specified in the order of 1600, and apparently both were open in that year.   No theater was demolished because of these orders, and performances appear to have continued regularly at the Blackfriars, Paul's, the Curtain, and Rose, and occasionally at the Swan and some of the innyards.

During the reigns of James I and Charles I, the local regulation of the drama was, as we have seen, largely under the control of officials of the court.   The leading companies, organized under the patronage of the

[1] *Acts*, XXXI. 346.

[2] *Remembrancia*, 354.   *Acts*, XXXII. 468–9.   *Malone Soc. Coll.*, I. 83. H. P., *Outlines*, I. 308.   [3] *Remembrancia*, 355.   *Malone Soc. Coll.*, I. 85.

[4] *Acts*, XXXI. 218.   [5] H. P., *Outlines*, i. 311.

royal family, received patents authorizing them to play at appointed theaters; and the licensing of their plays and administration of their affairs came more and more regularly under the supervision of the Master of the Revels. The opposition of the city was thwarted; nevertheless the municipal authorities did not abandon their efforts to limit or decrease the number of playhouses. Although on May 31, 1615, Philip Rosseter and others received a privy seal authorizing them to build a new theater in Blackfriars, the protests of the mayor and aldermen led to the reference of the patent to the Lord Chief Justice, and its revocation by the Lords of the Privy Council.[1] In 1619, on the petition of inhabitants of Blackfriars, the city authorities ordered the suppression of the Burbage-Shakespeare theater in Blackfriars. The King's men, who occupied the theater, succeeded, however, in obtaining a new royal patent expressly authorizing their use of this theater; and years later, in 1631–33 they were again successful in resisting an effort to close the theater. In this instance, the Privy Council, the King himself being present, was content with issuing detailed orders for the regulation of the traffic congested by the crowds of coaches waiting at the theater. Apart from these protests from Blackfriars, the city authorities were in the main quiescent, or at least ineffectual. The later playhouses, as the Cockpit and Red Bull, kept outside the mayor's jurisdiction, and the innyards seem to have been used but little. Though the city continued its Puritan dislike of the drama, the local administration through the Revels office left little cause for objection on the ground of rioting, fire, and plague.

[1] For this somewhat perplexing case, see Gildersleeve, 198–200.

V. SPECIAL REGULATIONS: THE PLAGUE

It remains to note some of the minor matters of regulation which helped to bring quiescence on the part of the city. First, the taxation of the companies for the benefit of the poor and sick undoubtedly went far toward winning the favor of local authorities. The practice had probably been instituted as early as 1574,[1] and was in full force by 1600 for the Bankside theaters,[2] and continued as late as 1621.[3] Regulations as to the hours of performance seem to have been reasonably satisfactory to local authorities. Sunday performances, much objected to during the reign of Elizabeth, were prohibited by the statutes of 1603. They continued to be a matter of complaint, however, as late as Prynne. There are also complaints against week-day performances during divine service. In general, it appears that the regular companies acted in the early afternoon and only on week days. The regulations in regard to acting during Lent have been noticed and afford the usual illustration of irregularity in the enforcement of statutes.

The regulations in regard to the plague require special attention because they have been used by historians of the stage as determining the dates of plays and the suppression of companies. Assuming that plays were prohibited when the deaths by plague were above a certain number, Mr. Fleay fixed certain periods when he assumed no plays were acted. In discussing this general theory and offering evidence

[1] See Letters of Mayor, March 2, 1573(4), and Hazlitt, *English Drama*, 30.
[2] Chalmers, *Apology*, 405.
[3] See documents quoted by C. W. Wallace, *Englische Studien*, 1911. These show payments to the overseers of the poor of the Liberty of Paris Garden in certain years, 1611–25.

against its specific application, I wrote in 1901.[1] "In the first place it is not clear just what the regulation was for closing the theaters. . . . In the second place there is no certainty that any regulation prohibiting theatrical performances during the plague was rigidly enforced." Miss Gildersleeve's essay on "Government Regulation" added weight to both these premises. To base the history of the companies on the assumption that the theaters were always promptly closed when the weekly deaths were above a certain number would seem to disregard all that we know of the history of government regulation. Nevertheless, Mr. Murray in his recent "English Dramatic Companies," having modified Fleay's interpretation of the regulations, has proceeded to use them in the same mechanical manner as his predecessor as a primary guide in his history of the companies.

The regulations in regard to the plague underwent various changes, which have been touched on in the preceding pages. In Elizabeth's reign, when the plague was severe, the Mayor and Aldermen frequently appealed to the Privy Council to suppress plays. When the plague began to decrease, the Privy Council in turn commanded the city authorities to permit the opening of certain theaters. Usually such prohibition was for the summer, and such resumption in the autumn. No definite regulation as to the number of weekly deaths is heard of until the controversy of 1584. Then the Queen's men proposed that plays should be allowed in London whenever the total number of deaths from the plague should be under fifty a week. In their reply the city authorities express dislike for what is apparently a novel method of regulating performances

---

[1] *Influence of Beaumont and Fletcher on Shakespeare,* 1901, pp. 14 ff.

in plague time; but if any such regulation is to be adopted, they wish to substitute the much more stringent limitation to when the ordinary deaths amount to "between forty and fifty and commonly under forty." In their "remedies" they propose "till the whole death in London have been by xx days under 50 a week, nor longer than it shall continue." What regulation, if any, was adopted by the Privy Council, we do not know. As we have seen, the Council continued as before to control the closing and opening of the theaters during plague time by special orders and apparently not in accord with any fixed rule.

/ In 1593, a great plague year, plays were prohibited by the Privy Council on January 28, in the city or within 7 miles,[1] and again on February 3, 1594,[2] within 5 miles of the city;/ yet, on October 8, 1594, the Lord Chamberlain requested the mayor to permit performances at the Cross Keys Inn.[3] Nothing is heard of regulating performances by the number of deaths in the weekly bills. On James' accession in the fearful plague year of 1603, the patent for the King's men provides merely that they may perform when the "deaths from the plague shall decrease." /The draft of the patent for the Queen's men, 1604, however, and the order of the Privy Council of April 9, 1604, mention 30 deaths per week as the limiting number. / The order of the Privy Council applies to the Globe, Fortune, and Curtain, says nothing whatever of the performances in Blackfriars and St. Pauls, and states the limitation as /"Except there shall happen to die weekly of the plague above the number of thirty within

---

[1] *Acts*, XXIV. 31–32.
[2] *Remembrancia*, XXI. *Malone Soc. Coll.*, I. 72.   [3] *Ibid.*, 73, 74.

the City of London and the Liberties thereof." [1] No provision concerning the plague appears in the royal patents from 1604 to 1619. In the patent of the King's men for 1619 and also in their patent of 1625 the number is fixed at forty. Some passages in Herbert's office book seem to indicate that later the number was fifty.

Contemporary references indicate that the order of the Privy Council of 1604, fixing the limit for three patented theaters, at 30 a week was in some measure enforced. But whether it applied to the private theaters, whether it was enforced rigidly, and for how many years it was enforced, are questions on which we have no sure information. So in regard to the less stringent rule of forty. In times when the plague was continuous, but not very severe, as 1605–10, we may be sure the players ventured on some infringement in the rules and were suffered by the Council.[2]

The one known instance which appears to have been in strict accord with the rule of forty occurred when the theaters opened on February 23, 1637, and closed

[1] Printed in *Henslowe Papers*, 61, 62.

[2] In the years when the question of closing of the theaters is of special interest to historians of the drama, we have some new and specific evidence. In August, 1608, Burbage took back the lease of the Blackfriars and presumably at once occupied it with the King's men. The deaths by the plague were then over 30 and continued over 30 a week and over 40 except for four isolated weeks of 39, 32, 33, and 36, until the week ending Dec. 7, 1609. Mr. Fleay and Mr. Murray, therefore, contend that the theaters were not opened in this period. In my *Influence of Beaumont and Fletcher on Shakespeare*, I advanced various evidence that the theaters were not closed for this entire period, and that Burbage's company did act at Blackfriars in 1608–09. The fact that the plague held about the same for 1605 to 1610, increasing in the summer and fall and decreasing in the winter, made such partial occupancy seem, *a priori*, possible. My more specific evidence was not sufficient to satisfy Mr. Murray, but new light on the subject is thrown by the documents in the lawsuit Keyser *v.* Burbage *et al.*, discovered by Professor

R

on March 2. The case came up in a meeting of the Privy Council described in a letter from Garrard to Wentworth.[1] This may serve to show that the plague regulations continued to be administered in 1637 about as they had been in 1580; and may stand as a final illustration of the manner in which the enforcement of most laws about the theaters was determined — or neglected.

"Upon a little abatement of the plague, even in the first week of Lent, the players set up their bills, and began to play in the Blackfryars and other houses. But my Lord of Canterbury quickly reduced them to a better order; for at the next meeting of the Council his Grace complained of it to the King, declared the solemnity of Lent, the unfitness of that liberty to be given, both in respect to the time and the sickness, which was not extinguished in the City, concluding that if his Majesty did not command him to the contrary he would lay them by the heels if they played again. My Lord Chamberlain [Pembroke and Montgomery] stood up and said that my Lord's Grace and he served one God and one King; that he hoped his Grace would not meddle in his

Wallace. Keyser brought suit to recover certain property which he had in the Children's company, dispossessed when Burbage took over the Blackfriars theater in August, 1608. The documents mention the sickness as preventing Keyser using his boys, but several passages indicate that Burbage was using the theater during the plague season of 1609.

The bill by Keyser was brought in February 8, 1610, and asserts that the Burbages, Heminge, Condell, et al. "have entred in and upon the said playe howse, and all the said goodes, apparell and premises and have soe Continewed in the possession for a longe tyme and made profitt theirof to themselves to the full valewe at the leaste of fifteene hundred poundes," elsewhere he says he has kept the boys for two years, i.e. since 1608. The defendants in their answer of Feb. 12, 1610, declare that since Evans surrendered the lease "about the tenth of August last past (1609 or 1608 ?), they the said defendantes have entred into occupied & enjoyed the said great hall or playhouse taken the benefytt and profytt thereof."

[1] Quoted by Gildersleeve, 214; and by Wheatley and Cunningham, *London Past and Present*, I. 200-1.

place no more than he did in his ; that the players were under his command. My Lord's Grace replied that what he had spoken in no way touched upon his place, etc., still concluding as he had done before, which he did with some solemnity reiterate once or twice. So the King put an end to the business by commanding my Lord Chamberlain that they should play no more."

CHAPTER IX

THE DRAMATIC COMPANIES

WITHIN the course of Shakespeare's life the quality or profession of actors gained a position of considerable importance in the social organization. Some of its members acquired wealth, a few fame, and many a good livelihood and the respect of the community. The prosperity that fell to the profession and the social status that it won were due in no small measure to its organization into companies. It was these professional companies that made the permanent playhouses necessary, that made dramatic writing profitable, and that maintained the theaters in spite of the protests of the city. Shakespeare himself was a member of one of these companies and wrote all of his plays for it. Other poets were similarly attached to other companies, and these organizations were the sole purveyors of the drama in its most brilliant period.

Although these companies were in a position of far greater prosperity and power at the time of Shakespeare's death than at the time of his birth, they were even then numerous and active and on the road to obtain a fixed place in society. Their ancestry goes far back to the wandering bands of entertainers, jugglers, acrobats, who added their quota to the amusement of the Middle Ages. Farther back still, perhaps to the mime and pantomime, themselves the degenerate offspring of the Roman theater. The descent from

Changling   Simpleton

French Dancing M[r]

S[r] I Falstafe   Hostes   Clause

FRONTISPIECE OF KIRKMAN'S "WITS," 1672

the professionals of Rome, scattered and outlawed by the triumph of Christianity, to the performers of the Middle Ages cannot be closely traced, but at any rate the latter continued, like the former, outlaws without the pale of the church. They were mere vagabonds, who carried on the scantiest of dramatic traditions and provided only the crudest and most unworthy dramatic entertainment. It has indeed been questioned whether the term dramatic can be properly applied to these buffoons and acrobats, for no certain records of their performances and no account of any plays have survived. But rudimentary drama in the form of clownage and mimicry, rising now and then to the level of farce can hardly have been absent from the wayside life of the Middle Ages and was probably not without effect on later farce and comedy when they emerge into the literature of the sixteenth century. It is evident that, though the vagabond actors had no ascertained connection with the religious drama of the Middle Ages or with literary drama of any kind, they maintained a sort of dramatic practice and were the direct progenitors of the wandering companies which begin to be heard of by the end of the fourteenth century.

Earlier than that, indeed, some of the more successful of the wandering performers obtained employment by king or noble, and were established as permanent members of royal households. Records of Henry VI for Christmas of 1427 show pageants to the 'entre ludes' of "Jake Travail et ses compaignons," and various noblemen supported companies in the fifteenth century.[1] As members of households they had of course a fixed place, at once removed from their

---

[1] Chambers, II. 186.

lawless brethren. If permitted to act on their own account from time to time, they received recognition from town or magistrate because of their master's license. A professional entertainer in the Middle Ages was without status unless he was somebody's man; only by attachment to the households of great nobles or kings could he achieve success or permanence in his vocation. By the beginning of the sixteenth century the number of professional actors increased very rapidly. They found more employment in shows and festivities at the courts of Henry VII and Henry VIII, and they won an increasing support from the public. Their status remained the same, they were vagabonds and outcasts unless they obtained protection under the livery of noble or king; but there was more employment, more pay, and a more definitely recognized profession. One person might still be minstrel, juggler, actor, servant of the king, and traveler about the towns; but as time went on, the profession of acting gained a place and recognition, not entirely independent of the court patronage, but mainly reliant on popular favor.

This rise of the class from traveling mountebanks to purveyors of the drama was not confined to England; but was paralleled in every nation of western Europe. The sixteenth century saw the actors attaining a place in the social organization, prospering under royal patronage, organizing themselves into companies, appealing to the public, determining certain methods of dramatic presentation, and encouraging certain forms of drama. The drama, which was passing from the control of guilds and societies which had long had charge of the religious plays, remained for a part of the century still largely in the hands of

universities, schools, and various organizations of
amateurs. It flourished at court or school for a time
and to different degrees in different countries, and
literature did not rapidly find its way to the public
stage. But the occasional performances of amateurs
were insufficient to supply the dramatic needs of
audiences or writers, or to meet the play-acting in-
stinct to which the Renaissance brought so many
incentives. Court and public both welcomed the
professionals, who gained patronage, monopoly, or
other support, and in one way or another succeeded
by the end of the century in taking charge of the
popular drama. In Italy the Commedia dell' Arte
resulted; in other nations literature found better
treatment from the professional companies who produced the dramas of Shakespeare, Lope de Vega, and
Molière.

THE ADULT COMPANIES 1500–1603

In England, in spite of the religious controversy and
troublesome times of Henry VIII, Edward VI, and
Mary, there was a rapid multiplication of professional
companies. The children's company, maintained at
court, occupied a leading position there, as Professor
C. W. Wallace has shown, but the records of traveling
adult companies are numerous. A company would
consist of four or five men and a boy or two,
who took the female parts. It might establish itself
in London for a season playing in some innyard; but
in summer months it wandered about the country
giving plays in some nobleman's hall, or in moot hall
or church, or on the village green. In the old play of
"Sir Thomas More," there is a scene which describes
a performance by such a company in connection

with an incident of More's youth. More is entertaining the Lord Mayor and Aldermen at supper and
arranges for a play by the Lord Cardinal's players
before the banquet (dessert). The company consists
of four men and a boy who takes the female parts.
The play announced as the "Marriage of Wit and
Wisdom" is really a medley of two interludes, "Lusty
Juventus" and the "Disobedient Child." Luggins,
one of the actors, is sent off for a beard which has been
forgotten, and when he fails to return, More himself
steps in and improvises the missing part. The play
dates about 1590 and the incident of More's improvisation, about 1500; but a performance similar to the
one described might probably have taken place at
any time between these dates. More's skill "ex-
temprically" amazes the actors; but improvisation
cannot have been unusual among the professionals.
We hear of the improvised wit of Tarleton and others
and of clowns who speak more than is set down for
them. Probably the clowns were the chief improvisers,
as at the first they were the chief actors and the main
support of their companies. With the short plays,
the few parts, the fixed types of character, and the
current jokes, there must have been a good deal of
improvising and a general tendency to disregard or to
supplement the text. The conditions in the profession
were not very different from those which gave rise to
the Commedia dell' Arte in Italy; but in England the
written drama fortunately adapted itself rapidly to
the histrionic conventions.

From the beginning of the sixteenth century some
connection existed between literary drama and the
itinerant companies. Plays were necessarily made to
fit the new conditions of acting, and as a result, the

prevailing type of drama was the Interlude, a short play, for a few actors, few properties, and actable anywhere. Longer plays, designed for a more elaborate performance were made over to suit the itinerants, so that by doubling parts, five-act plays like "Cambyses" and "Horestes" were made presentable by five or six actors on an improvised stage. Nevertheless, while some plays were doubtless written directly for these companies, and while they condensed and enlarged some of the school and court plays, we have no extant plays before 1585 which we know were written primarily for professional adults. Probably few of the non-extant plays had literary merit, but somehow these plays, acted by the thriving companies to the delectation of the public between 1557 and 1585, prepared the way for Marlowe, Greene, and Shakespeare.

It was in this period, too, that the adult companies were establishing themselves as largely independent of royal patronage and securing their main support from the public. Yet only sparing records exist of this process before the building of the Theater. Records of court performances are abundant and descriptions of performances of traveling actors before noble or king may be found in the "Taming of the Shrew" and "Hamlet" as well as in "Sir Thomas More." But the traditions and standards of acting accumulated by a generation of practice before an increasing public have gone unrecorded and must in the main be judged by the resulting activity in the London public playhouses in the eighties and the nineties. Some notion of the growing importance and independence of the professionals has already been derived from the history of their relations with law and the authorities.

We have seen that the famous statute of 1572 gave actors a legal status provided they were organized into companies under the license of a nobleman of the rank of baron, or of two or more justices of the peace. Although doubtless this regulation merely legalized the current practice, the immediate results must have been to diminish the number of companies and to strengthen the position of those remaining. Then, in 1574, two years after the statute, a royal patent was granted to Leicester's men, an organization which seems to have been the direct precursor of Shakespeare's company. After 1572 there was indeed a marked increase in the number of performances by professional companies at court. Instead of a single company, four or five usually appeared at the Christmas and Shrovetide festivals. For the next ten years, players of the Earl of Leicester, the Lord Chamberlain, the Earl of Warwick, Earl of Sussex, the Earl of Derby, and Lord Howard, were regularly employed. The profession of actor was already far advanced above the association of rogues and vagabonds.

The growing prosperity of the companies at this period is further indicated by the violent attacks upon them by the London authorities and by Puritan moralists. They could hardly have succeeded in their effort to establish themselves about the city without the active support of the Crown and the Privy Council. The first distinct victory for the players was marked by the building of the Theater in 1576 and of the Curtain in 1577. Even after these two playhouses were established in the outskirts of London, the city authorities by no means gave up the contest. Though the mayor and aldermen were compelled on various occasions to submit to the interference of the Privy

Council, they apparently succeeded, in the spring of 1583,[1] in suppressing all performances in the innyards within the city proper. The court, however, came to the relief of the actors and constituted a company, chosen from the best actors in the noblemen's companies, which was known as Her Majesty's Players, its members being taken into the Queen's service and "allowed wages and liveries as grooms of the chamber." Though the positive status of this company does not seem to have differed greatly from that of noblemen's companies which performed occasionally before the Queen, it had of course a decided prestige whether in London or traveling, and for ten years or so remained unquestionably the leading company. Shortly after its formation, moreover, the companies reëstablished themselves in their playhouses in the liberties and to some extent in the city innyards,[2] and were henceforth able to maintain themselves, despite the continued and occasionally violent opposition of the city authorities.

Whatever the causes may have been that led to the establishment of this Queen's company — and they are not wholly clear[3] — its formation illustrates an important tendency in governmental control. The statute of 1572, in attempting to regulate vagabondage, limited and controlled the licensing of actors. With the accession of James I the licensing power was limited to the crown alone. This is in accord with the general Tudor tendency away from local and towards central administration; but it was doubtless rendered desirable because, as time went on, the personal

---

[1] Gildersleeve, 166. Fleay, *Stage*, 54.   [2] Gildersleeve, 170–75.
[3] See Gildersleeve, 166–9, and Wallace, *Univ. of Nebraska Studies*, 1913, p. 242. Some difficulty of Burbage at the Theater may have contributed.

relations of the players to their patrons grew less personal and intimate. By 1583, the noblemen who licensed the players were not always sufficiently concerned with their retainers to save them from the interference of the city authorities or to warrant any responsible control over their actions. Although the establishment of a company under the Queen's direct patronage did not lead immediately to the abolishment of other patronage, and although the companies continued for twenty years more under licenses from individual noblemen, they were henceforth mainly under the direct control of the Privy Council or Lord Chamberlain. The assumption under James I of complete control by the court was only the legal adoption of a practice virtually established. It also resulted in the conferring of a monopoly on a few leading companies. It may be added that this monopoly, strengthened during the reign of Charles I, reëstablished by Charles II, has played a large part in English theatrical history and was not finally abolished until near the middle of the nineteenth century.

During the twenty years from 1583 to 1603, there was no monopoly, but a considerable variety of practice in the organization of the theatrical companies. Those that wandered about the provinces were often irresponsible, stealing, borrowing, or buying their licenses, and rarely attaining any permanence. In London the strife with the government, whether of city or Privy Council, still went on. Numerous regulations in respect to sedition, fire, or the observance of Sunday, affected the theaters; but the few companies that gained a permanent footing in London were established as servants of prominent noblemen and were strong enough to withstand any serious attacks upon them by the city. It is with these few companies and their successors who enjoyed monopoly under James and Charles that we are mainly concerned. In addition, however, certain companies of child actors became established in London and entered into competition and at times successful rivalry with the adult companies.

THE CHILDREN'S COMPANIES

The practice of play acting by children, so prominent in the dramatic activities of the reign of Elizabeth and James I, seems to have had a very ancient origin. School children, perhaps especially those of the singing schools, occasionally appear as actors in the miracle plays. These singing schools existed not only in connection with the cathedrals, but were numerous in villages and towns throughout England in connection with Chantries. Singing boys became frequent as performers at court or at noblemen's houses during the early Tudor reigns in disguises, tableaux, and pageants. By this time, however, the schools had a new incentive for the performance of plays. The schoolmasters were the leaders in introducing new classical influences both by composing and presenting dramas. In 1517, the boys of St. Paul's grammar school appeared at court, and by that date there were plays at Eton. In 1538 Ralph Radcliffe set up a theater in his school where plays were given by the children before outsiders. Later, Nicholas Udall encouraged play-acting at Westminster and Eton, and in connection with his head-mastership of one of those schools, wrote "Ralph Roister Doister." The authors of a number of the plays at the beginning of Elizabeth's reign were schoolmasters, and boys from the Westminster and Merchant Tailors' schools appeared at court.

The two most important companies of children, however, were under more direct royal patronage. It had long been the custom to select boys from the various cathedrals or elsewhere and bring them to London to sing in the choirs of St. Paul's and the Chapel Royal. This last choral organization was a very ancient one composed of both gentlemen and children, and even in the early Tudor period was sometimes called upon to furnish entertainments spectacular and dramatic as well as musical. Under Henry VIII the children of the chapel frequently took part in the elaborate shows at court and presumably in plays as well. By the time of Elizabeth, the children of the Chapel Royal, the children of Windsor, and the children of St. Paul's choir had been definitely organized for dramatic purposes and soon surpassed the child actors from Westminster and the Merchant Tailors. In the schools provided for these choir boys training seems to have been given in acting as well as in singing, and they were soon able to present a varied dramatic repertory, in which singing and dancing and spectacles, though important, were subordinate. The children of St. Paul's, under their master Westcott, appear to have been in special favor with Elizabeth, for they played when she entertained Mary at Hatfield House in 1557, and after her accession were the first company to appear before her at Nonesuch, August 7, 1559. From this date they acted at court regularly until 1581, and after that intermittently until 1590. The children of the Chapel, and those of Windsor were in almost equal demand, especially in the period from 1567 to 1584.

Apart from their appearance at court these three companies also appeared in public. Following long-established custom, the masters had the right to select children from the cathedral towns, and bring them to London for the choirs, and they seem to have acquired under Elizabeth the additional privilege of exhibiting the boys in public. The Paul's boys probably acted regularly in a room in their school and the Children of Windsor and Children of the Chapel, from 1576 to 1584, gave plays in a room in Blackfriars. These companies were in frequent difficulties, and near the end of Elizabeth's reign the manager of the Chapel children got into serious trouble because of kidnapping. By this time, if not earlier, the boys trained for acting were apparently separated from those trained for singing and were maintained solely for plays. At times their rivalry with the adult professionals was acute; the new companies of children were given royal patronage under James I; but in 1606 the warrant for taking up singing boys for the Royal Chapel expressly forbids their acting in plays.[1]

The positions of the adult and of the children's companies for a few years subsequent to 1576 have interesting points of similarity. From the numerous adult companies a few had secured legal protection, court support, and by the erection of playhouses an established position in London. Of the children of choirs and schools, two companies had likewise support

---

[1] This commission and one of 1604 are reprinted in the *Malone Soc. Coll.*, I. 4 and 5, pp. 357 ff., with an explanatory note by E. K. Chambers, correcting mistakes of Collier and Wallace. Earlier commissions for the chapel in 1562, 1567, and 1597 are reprinted by Wallace, *Children of the Chapel*, 61, 65. For the history of the children's companies 1600–1607, see pp. 322–328.

from the crown, permanent theaters, and professional attributes. The appeal to the public rather than to patron gave both classes of companies an opportunity for independence; and the building or leasing of theaters gave promise of permanency. With this opportunity for profit, capital became interested, and a new importance attached itself to the relations of the companies to the capitalist and manager.

In the case of the children's companies the master, instead of being merely singer, teacher, or dramatist, was likely to be also speculator or man of business. Of the St. Paul's boys we have few records; but the securing of a room in Blackfriars, 1576, by Farrant was a business venture entirely outside of his status as Master of the Children of Windsor. The subsequent history of the children of the revels is a series of efforts by various entrepreneurs to exploit the children for personal profit. This led to marked success especially in 1597–1604, but also to illegal practices in taking up the children, and finally to the killing of the goose that laid the golden egg. We shall return to the history of these children's companies in the next chapter; but it should be noted that the children themselves do not appear to have had any share in control or profits. The managers of these companies, with what capital or court support they could command, controlled the affairs of both theater and company.

BUSINESS ORGANIZATION OF THE PROFESSIONAL COMPANIES

In the adult companies, an organization was maintained independent of theater owner or promoter. Their internal organization seems to have remained the same from beginning to end. In the time of

Henry VIII, four actors and a boy sufficed, and this
number may have been sufficient for many of the later
provincial companies; but the Queen's Men in 1583
was composed of twelve actors; that was the number
of sharers in the King's Men at Shakespeare's death,
and seems to have been about the usual number for
the stronger companies. From the beginning, the
shareholders hired additional actors, boys, and helpers,
and they must have had managers or treasurers. Their
properties, costumes, and plays were held as company
property, and after the permanent theaters, this
became of considerable value, and the subject of
frequent lawsuits. As we shall see when we come to
examine the records of the individual companies, the
treasurer or business manager often seems to have
thrived at the expense of his colleagues. Many of the
transactions recorded in Henslowe's Diary show Henslowe acting on behalf of the company, advancing
money to authors, paying fees to the Master of the
Revels, purchasing costumes, etc. However, when
Henslowe personally appears, it is usually as creditor;
and though he grew rich, his management does not
seem to have established the company on a secure
financial basis. The companies did not always fare
any better when one of their own number served as
manager. One of Henslowe's companies, the Worcester's men, became involved in litigation with its
subsequent managers and was forced to disbandment,
either in order to avoid payment of its debts to one, or
because of the rascality of a second. On the other
hand, Shakespeare's company probably owed its continued prosperity in part to excellent business management, in which some of the leading members of the
company shared.

s

The builders of the theaters introduced a new factor
— the capitalist. The older Burbage was in continuous difficulties with Braynes, who had advanced
money to build the Theater, and records of lawsuits
have survived concerning the ownership of many of
the playhouses. The relations between the companies and the theater owners are various; but we
do not know of any instance of a company owning a
theater. The nearest approach to this is in the case
of the Globe and the Blackfriars, when the Burbage
brothers distributed shares in the ground leases and
buildings among a few of the leading members of the
company. To a considerable extent, by means of re-
arrangement upon the death of one of the owners, the
control of the theaters was kept in the hands of active
members. In the case of the theaters owned by
Henslowe and his son-in-law, the famous actor Alleyn,
the companies seem to have had no interest in the
land and buildings. In other cases, as the Swan,
the building was an enterprise undertaken by some
one unconnected with any company.

The usual arrangement between owners of the
theater and the sharers in the company seems to have
been for the sharers to receive all of the money taken
for general admission, and the owners to receive the
whole or part of the additional fees charged for admission to the galleries and boxes. In the lawsuits
brought in 1635 by some of the sharers in the King's
men against some of the housekeepers of the Globe
and Blackfriars, Cuthbert Burbage affirmed in defense. "The players that lived in those first times
[*i.e.* of the Theater] had only the profitt arising from
the dores, but now the players receave all the commings in at the dores and half the galleries from the

housekeepers." [1] Out of their proceeds the share-holders, of course, paid "all expenses for hirelings, apparel, poets, light, and all other expenses of the playhouses." Henslowe received regularly one half, or possibly at times the whole, proceeds of the galleries, as rent for the Rose,[2] and later one half the galleries from the Lady Elizabeth's men. On one occasion Alleyn received one eleventh of the entire weekly proceeds of the Fortune as rent,[3] but he later leased the house to the Palsgrave's men for £200 annual rental.[4] In any case, the capitalist or partners who risked money in the building were naturally the first to be taken care of, and the company had to pay a fixed amount, or a share of the receipts, or the intake from a certain portion of the house.

Henslowe figures both as owner of the building and as banker and business manager, and doubtless profited from the double function. Articles of agreement exist in imperfect form between him and his partner Meade and the Lady Elizabeth's Men.[5] Within three years the shareholders had brought suit against Henslowe, charging him among other misdeeds with taking £200 from them for play books, and yet retaining the plays. As banker and manager, Henslowe secured his rent, and was also in a position to get the better of all bargains with the shareholders. "The reason for his often breaking with us," they state he gave in these words, "Should these fellows come out of my debt, I should have no rule with them." [6] And they declare that "within three years he hath

---

[1] Halliwell-Phillipps, *Outlines*, I. 313.
[2] Greg, *H. D.*, II. 133, 134. *Henslowe Papers*, 87.
[3] *H. D.*, ed. Greg, I. 124. [4] *Henslowe Papers*, ed. Greg, 27, 28.
[5] *Henslowe Papers*, 23, 24. *Alleyn Memoirs*, 118. [6] *Henslowe Papers*, 89.

broken and dismembered five companies." In the Shakespeare-Burbage organization, the leading actors were both "housekeepers," or sharers in the playhouse, and "shareholders" in the profits of the company. We shall find those whose income was confined to the latter source taking legal means to secure partnership in the leases. Arrangements between owners and the companies must have varied greatly, and the division of the proceeds may often have been a complicated task. Shakespeare, for example, drew his income as part owner (or lessee) of two playhouses, as a shareholder in the company, as a playwright, as an actor, and perhaps also as stage manager or for some other services. Of the officials of the company, other than manager, treasurer, or doorkeeper, we know little. The important office of stage manager doubtless existed, but there are no details as to its duties or rewards. The theatrical business then, as now, was speculative and uncertain; but in spite of ups and downs, the profits of a sharer in one of the leading companies was enviable. The Palsgrave's men provided that any sharer retiring should receive £70 from the company, and if he died before retirement, his widow should have £50.[1] The widow of Thomas Greene claimed £80 as due from the company on the death of her husband. A share in a good company of course represented a considerable investment in costumes and plays. Lean years put the company in debt, but the fat years brought large dividends, and the actor who stuck to one company prospered. Shakespeare's company, the most prosperous of all, kept its organization intact from 1594 to 1642. Some actors

[1] *Henslowe Papers*, 64, Letter of Charles Massye to Edward Alleyn, 1613(?).

who had played with Shakespeare were still acting for the same company when the revolution stopped their profits and called them to the service of the King.

RELATIONS WITH PLAYWRIGHTS AND PATRONS

If a sharer took to playwriting, as many of them did in the earlier days, his value to the company might be largely increased. Certain playwrights, as Heywood, Shakespeare, Fletcher, and in a later period Dryden, were regularly attached to one company, presumably under some form of contract. Other dramatists, as Henslowe's hack-writers, were temporarily allied to one company and manager. But the companies seem to have been always ready to try a play wherever it might be found. The demand for new plays was always brisk. Ben Jonson seems never to have been attached to any company. Letters of Daborne that have been preserved show him bidding one company against another for plays not yet written. Even in the early days Greene was accused of selling the same play to two companies. In general, if the dramatist was not a sharer in a particular company, his relations were not very different from those of writers of to-day dealing with manager or publisher. The better dramatists were likely to become attached to particular companies, but such attachments were frequently broken. Stress needs to be placed on the variability, because Mr. Fleay's assumption that dramatists were always bound to this company or that have led to much muddling of the stage history. The rewards of the dramatists varied much and improved as time went on, as we shall see in a later chapter. There is some evidence of a practice which prevailed after the Restoration of giving the author certain share of the profits, or the proceeds of certain performances.

The plays usually became the property of the company and were carefully guarded from piratical booksellers or rival companies. So rapidly did the fashions change and so rapidly did the dramatic art develop that a play was often out of date within a year or two. Even Shakespeare's "Richard II," first acted in 1595, was considered an old play by 1601. An old play, however, could be revised and a really successful play could stand a revival with but little revision. Hence the repertory became of great importance to a company. In 1594, after Marlowe's death, the Admiral's men relied very largely for success on his plays which they possessed; and the preëminence of the King's men was doubtless greatly furthered by their possession of Shakespeare's plays. Popular plays were sometimes stolen, as in the cases of the First Part of the "Spanish Tragedy" and the "Malcontent." In 1627 we find the King's men paying the Master of the Revels £5 "to forbid the playing of Shakespeare's plays to the Red Bull company." Later the successors of the Queen's men secured a similar monopoly in their stock plays.

The companies' growing independence of their patrons has been alluded to; but we have little information as to the conditions of patronage in Elizabeth's reign. The patrons of the companies occasionally appear as their protectors in disputes with the mayor or magistrate, or even in the discussions of the Privy Council. The protection and prestige afforded by a great nobleman like the Earl of Leicester or by such an official as the Lord Chamberlain, were of course of the greatest value to the fortunate companies. In other cases the use of the nobleman's

license must have been about the beginning and end
of his relations with the actor, although it would not
be surprising in view of Elizabethan conditions if this
use of his name brought the nobleman an honorarium
from the company. The most striking case of personal relations between a patron and his company is
that of the Earl of Oxford, who leased the first Blackfriars theater for his company of boys, and then turned
the lease over to John Lyly the dramatist. When the
leading companies were brought under the patronage
of members of the royal family, they became members
of the royal household and shared in certain duties
and emoluments. Some lists of companies have been
preserved as recipients of rewards incident on the
death of one sovereign or the accession of the other.
In the time of Charles I the relations between the
King and the companies seem to have been closer and
more personal than in the earlier reigns. He supervised the censorship of plays, advised with the Master
of the Revels, and suggested themes and plots to
dramatists. There is little indication of such personal
concern with the affairs of the professionals by either
Elizabeth or James. A tradition says that the "Merry
Wives" was written in response to a request of the
Queen's, and Ben Jonson has borne admiring testimony
of

> those flights upon the banks of Thames
> That so did take Eliza and our James!

But no one has recorded how the sovereigns expressed
their appreciation.

The leading companies, however, constantly appeared
at court, and earned thereby large additions to their
incomes as well as the protection of the officials. The
court season extended from Christmas to Shrovetide

in February or March, and usually a number of plays were given. Elizabeth sometimes saw as many as nine, in the reign of James the number was larger, and the court of Charles I sometimes had as many as twenty plays by a single company. The regular pay for a play at court was £6 13s. 4d., increased by a reward of £3 6s. 8d. if the King was present. If the performance was given at Hampton Court or Richmond instead of one of the city palaces, the amount was doubled, amounting to £20. The King's men occasionally received over £200 for the court season. In addition there were other occasional performances in the houses of noblemen or before societies, as that of "Twelfth Night" in the Middle Temple in 1602.

TRAVELING IN THE PROVINCES

While our attention is confined mainly to the leading London companies, it must be remembered that these included numerically only a small part of the profession. The provinces had play-acting in abundance, and a large body of entertainers remained strolling actors without any secure attachment to a playhouse. The leading London companies themselves traveled from time to time when the plague was prevalent in the city or when for some other reason the season was unsatisfactory. If a city company failed or came into difficulties, its members who found no employment with the other companies were likely to take to the road. After the Queen's company, organized in 1583, ceased to act in London, numerous records of the Queen's companies appear in the provinces. Complaint had been made by the city authorities that players claimed the Queen's patronage without right "last year, when such toleration was of the

Queenes players only, all the places of playing were filled with men calling themselves the Queenes players "; and probably some of these provincial performances were by unauthorized players. At all events, there is much evidence of forging, buying, and stealing licenses by the traveling actors; and licenses by noblemen were used long after such licenses had been prohibited by James I. Sometimes a portion of a company seems to have traveled under the company's name and license, while the major part remained in London. Under James I two companies, indeed, appear to have secured licenses as Queen's men under Queen Anne, one acting regularly in the city and one in the country. Pembroke, the Lord Chamberlain, records that Swynerton and Slaughter, "being two of the Queens Ma^{ts} company of Playors hauinge sepa[ra]ted themselves from their said Company, have each of them taken forth, a severall exemplification or duplicate of his ma^{ts} Letters patents graunted to the whole Company and by vertue thereof they severally in two Companies wth vagabonds and such like idle psons, haue and doe vse and exercise the quallitie of playinge in diuse places of this Realme to the great abuse and wronge of his Ma^{ts} Sub^{ts} in generall and contrary to the true intente and meaninge of his Matie to the said Company."[1]

Other companies that appear from time to time in the provinces cannot be traced at all in London. The records of provincial performances, as collected by J. M. Murray, show a very large and continuous activity. Such towns as Bristol, Coventry, Leicester, Norwich, and Plymouth were visited yearly by several companies; and there were few places of any size

[1] Murray, II. 343.

which did not have an occasional opportunity to see the players. Norwich furnishes the fullest and most interesting records,[1] which may be glanced at for a moment as illustrations of general conditions.

The first payment recorded in the Chamberlain's Accounts is 6s. 8d. in 1534–35 "to the Kyngs players at Saynt Olaues gild." Frequent payments follow during the reign of Henry VIII to various professional companies, and for preparations — in 1541–42, 2d. "for sedge to strowe the Halle," 2d. for drink for the players, and 2d. to two "laborers that fechyd barrells and tymber and made a scaffold." In the next season 2d. was paid for perfume "for the chambyr whyche savord sore." The plays were usually given in the "common hall" or "assembly chapel"; though after the initial performance before the mayor, perhaps the companies acted elsewhere. Lord Sussex's players could not act in 1544–55 "bycause Mr. Mayer and his brethern was at no leyser to se them playe and also the comon halle at y^t tyme occupied w^t the Kyngs Greyne (grain)", and so received the very large gratuity of £2 5s. Once Mr. Mayor and his brethren saw a play "in Mr. Castyldens place," probably an inn. In 1546–47, two records occur of performances by other than professional actors: "to mr. byrde scolemaster of the gram scole for his scolers playeng an Interlude in the chappell of the comon halle the sonday aftr Twelfth Day," and again on a Sunday "to certen Spanyards and Ytalyans who dawnsyd antycks & played dyvrse other feets at the Comon Halle." Once in the reign of Mary, Mr. Burke, the schoolmaster received twenty shillings "for his paynes

[1] Murray, II. 335–72. On these records all statements in succeeding pages are based.

in makinge and playing an Interlude." In the early years of Elizabeth's reign children actors continued to compete with the adults. The children of the Duke of Norfolk received a gratuity when Mr. Mayor and his brethren dined at his grace's. The school-masters and their scholars played at night, in 1564–65, causing an expense of 3*s*. "for Torches to show lighte in the chappell," and in 1580–81, the Earl of Oxford's boys paid Norwich a visit.

After 1575 the Chamberlain's Accounts are supple-mented by the Mayor's Court Books. The earliest entry records the suit of the Company of the Waits of the city who were permitted to act generally except in the time of divine service and sermons. In 1583 the Earl of Worcester's men, having received 26*s*. 8*d*. *not* to act because of fear of the plague, "yet did play in an inn"; whereupon it was ordered that they should never receive any reward again and that their Lord should be notified. "But afterward upon their submyssion & earnyst intreaty, it is agreed that their L. shall not bee certyfyed thereof." Two years later the players of the Earl of Essex were in a similar difficulty; and in 1588, the Earl of Leicester's players received 40*s*. on condition that they should play only twice. In 1590, one of Lord Beauchamp's players was imprisoned because after receiving 20*s*. on con-dition they should not play, they set up their bills and played in the church. Leave to play a few times was usually granted, but in many cases gratuities were given to prevent the performances. Probably all the companies that acted in Norwich are not re-corded, but the books are sufficient to indicate the same sort of conflict against players and playhouses that we have seen in London. The regular playing place seems to have been the White Horse Inn; forbidden "either now or hereafter" in 1601; evidently in use but again forbidden in 1617, "not at Powles (Powl being the host of the White Horse) but in the Chappell nere the Newhall"; open the next year;[1] and in operation surreptitiously in April, 1624.

There are many illustrations of the way licenses were used and misused. In 1612, Ralph Reve came with the King's patent for Rossiter and others, and at first affirmed that he was Philip Rossiter. His boys were not permitted to act, but he seems to have received 40s. as a reward.[2] The next year Nicholas Long appeared with Rossiter's patent and a deputation from Rossiter, but the commission was only to teach and to instruct, not to travel; therefore he was not allowed to play, but was given 20s. The following year, 1614, Long appeared with other players of the Lady Elizabeth's company; "and beinge demauned wherefor their cominge was, sayd they came not to ask leaue to play But to aske the gratuetie of the Cytty." Probably they received this, though there is no record. The company was back again the next year and were allowed to play two days, the mayor and his brethren apparently being tired of the gratuity plan. But when the following year (1616) the company again returned to this fruitful field, forty shillings were promptly dispatched to them at the White Horse, "an extraordynary gratificacion by reason they are absolutely forbidden to play." The company, however, appeared regularly for a number of years longer, sometimes being allowed to play, and sometimes forbidden, and in 1620–21 apparently both playing and receiving gratuities.

---

[1] Murray, II. 343.   [2] *Ibid.*, 339 n.

Swynnerton with his company acting under the license of the Queen's men appeared in 1614, 1615, and 1616, but in the latter year confessed that only he and Robert Lee of the actors mentioned in the patent were present. "He was desired to desist from playing & offered a benevolence in money wch he refused to accept"; so he was allowed to play. Two months later he was back again though with no patent. He was finally persuaded not to play by the usual means of a gratuity. The next year (May 31, 1617) Robert Lee appeared with the license of the Queen's men, and got permission to play; but a letter was received from the Lord Chamberlain Pembroke, denouncing Swynnerton and his companions as using the license to which they had no right; so the city authorities revoked their permission. The letter also denounced companies illegally using the licenses of the King's Revels, the Prince's men, and the Prince Palatine's company. It is interesting to note that the next year when four actors appeared with a royal patent, two, Lee and Long, had already been proved untrustworthy in their dealings with the city, and a third, William Perry, had been particularly denounced by Pembroke. Presumably they had found means to appease the Master of the Revels.

The subserviency of the city authorities to the actors with royal patents was natural enough, but as time went on their opposition to plays increased, though they still bought off the traveling companies, however dubious the licenses. In 1623 they appealed to the Privy Council, protesting that the players were especially prejudicial to the town because of its manufactures from which multitudes of people were drawn away to see the plays, and secured an order, dated

May 27, forbidding "Companies of players, tumblers, or the like sort of persons to act any plays or to shew or exercise any other feats and devices within that city or the liberty of the same until you shall receive further order from this Board."   In spite of this order, Francis Wambus of the favored Lady Elizabeth's company appeared with the company's patent and peremptorily affirmed that "he would play in this City and would lay in prison here this Twelvemonth but he would try whether the Kings command or the Counsells be the greater."   He attempted to play at the White Horse, was arrested, imprisoned for one month, then freed on the request of the Master of the Revels, but refused damages.   Traveling companies were given gratuities not to play in 1624 and 1625; but in 1630, if not earlier, plays were again permitted.   In 1634, William Perry, an old offender in purloining licenses, appeared as one of the King's players, was permitted to act fifteen days, and then insisted on acting eight days longer; whereupon the city authorities decided to protest again to the Privy Council or else directly to the King.   Plays continued, but in 1640, the city received an order from the Master of the Revels requiring the Mayor and officers to forbid all plays and giving them power to imprison offenders and take away their licenses.

In these records of a provincial town we can discover that growth in the power and prosperity of the professional companies which has been the subject of this chapter.   At first the rivals of local companies and children, they soon were able to lord it over the local authorities, and their royal patents secured them from interference.   It would not appear that many of the genuine London companies visited Norwich, but even those masquerading under their colors received tolerance and gratuities. But the success and arrogance of the professionals doubtless helped to hasten the triumph of those who regarded them as "the vagrant and licentious rabble by whose means and devices the purses of poor servants and apprentices and of the meaner sort of people are drained and emptied."

TRAVELING ON THE CONTINENT

A word should be added in regard to the foreign travels of the English actors. They are heard of in France and Italy, but the principal field of their operations was in the Scandinavian and Germanic countries. In 1585, a portion of the Earl of Leicester's company, including Kemp, Bryan, and Pope afterwards colleagues of Shakespeare, acted at the court of Denmark, and thence journeyed to the court of Christian I of Saxony. In 1590 Robert Brown a member of the Earl of Worcester's men was in Leyden, and two years later, with other members of the company he made an extensive tour, acting at Wolfenbüttel, Cologne, Frankfurt, and Nuremberg. From this expedition there developed various companies which had long careers in Germany. Brown and his associate Jones returned to England in 1593, but part of the company remained under the service of Count Moritz von Hersen. Brown was back at Cassel in 1596, and his company can be traced until 1620. Sackville, another of the original members, established a company of his own, and later became a rich goldsmith at Frankfurt. From Brown's organization came other companies headed by Green, Webster, and Reynolds; and a company of unknown origin appeared in 1604 headed by Spencer. These companies were at times attached to courts, but they traveled much, going as far afield as Stockholm, Riga, Warsaw, Vienna, and Gratz. Those that became established learned the language, and they carried through Germany an extensive repertory of Elizabethan plays. Their history can be traced until about 1660.[1]

[1] For matter in this paragraph see E. Herz, *Englische Schauspieler und englisches Schauspiel zur Zeit Shakespeares in Deutschland.* Leipzig, 1903.

RICHARD BURBAGE
After a picture at Dulwich College.

CHAPTER X

OF the great number of companies, some records of which have been preserved, only a few attained lasting reputations or exercised an important influence on the drama. The bulk of our knowledge of theatrical matters during Shakespeare's lifetime is connected with the leading London companies. During the later part of Elizabeth's reign these were: (1) the Queen's Men, from 1583 to about 1594; and after that date (2) several companies more or less under Henslowe's management; (3) Shakespeare's company; (4) two Children's companies of the Chapel Royal and St. Paul's. Under James I, most of these companies survived under different names. Shakespeare's company became the King's men; one of Henslowe-Alleyn's companies became Queen Anne's men; another the Prince's men. From the two companies of choir boys came various children's companies. In this chapter some matters additional to the general discussion of Chapter IX will be presented in regard to the companies during the reign of Elizabeth.

I. *The Queen's Men*

The companies preceding the Queen's men in 1583 require only a brief notice here. When Elizabeth came to the throne, she continued as members of the royal household four interlude players, who are frequently heard of in the provinces as the Queen's players, and make their final appearance, as a company of eight, in a record of payment in the household book of 1585. Before this date, however, other professional companies had apparently won greater favor at court, for we have records of performances there by servants of the Earl of Leicester, Earl of Warwick, Lord Clinton, Lord Charles Howard, and Lord Derby. Of these companies the most important was that of the Earl of Leicester, which acted at court regularly, 1572–83, and then furnished some of the players for the new Queen's men.

Robert Dudley, Earl of Leicester, had players under his patronage as early as 1559; but names of the actors first appear in a list of 1572.[1]

James Burbadge	William Johnson
John Perkinne	Roberte Wilson
John Laneham	Thomas Clarke

The company received a royal patent under date of May 10, 1574.[2] The Signet Bill in connection with this patent names the first five of the actors in the list of 1572.[3] In 1575 the company probably took part in the famous entertainment to the Queen at Kenilworth, and in 1576 James Burbage, with money supplied by his father-in-law, John Braynes, built the Theater. Here the company probably acted until about 1583, when Laneham, Wilson, and Johnson joined the new Queen's men. Burbage was in constant difficulty with Braynes,[4] and also, about 1582,

---

[1] Printed by E. K. Chambers in the *Malone Society Collections*, I. 348. Murray prints this list (I. 28–29), but dates it incorrectly in 1574.

[2] See above, pp. 204, 205.   [3] See Collier, I. 203–04.

[4] See full records of lawsuit in documents published by C. W. Wallace, First London Theater, *University of Nebraska Studies*, 1913.

with one Peckham, who claimed ownership of the Theater property, and tried to oust the tenants by force. According to testimony in lawsuits, this caused some of the players to leave the company; but Burbage apparently did not join the new Queen's men. He seems to have shortly organized a company under Lord Hunsdon's patronage, which continued at the Theater or, in conjunction with the Lord Admiral's (Howard's), at the Theater and the Curtain until about 1592.[1] The Lord Hunsdon's men appeared at court in 1582 and 1586, and occasionally in the provinces, 1582-90. Shortly after 1590, they probably disbanded or combined with other companies. In 1594, Lord Strange's men secured the patronage of Lord Hunsdon, who was then the Lord Chamberlain.[2] After the formation of the Queen's men, Leicester's men must have been reorganized; for they are heard of in England and, accompanied by a recommendation by the Earl, traveled in Denmark, 1585–86, and later in Saxony, 1587.[3] The English company played at Stratford, 1586–87; and, on Leicester's death in 1588, probably joined Lord Strange's men. It is possible that Shakespeare joined Leicester's men at the time of their visit to Stratford.

The new Queen's company was formed early in 1583 of actors from several companies selected by the Master of the Revels.[4] "Out of which companies,"

---

[1] *Ibid.*, 240–42.

It has been conjectured by Fleay, Murray, and others, that Burbage joined the Queen's Men, since they appear at his theater in 1584; but the owner of the Theater then announced himself as Lord Hunsdon's man. The owner must have been Burbage. Further, as Mr. Wallace notes, there is no reference to Burbage as one of the Queen's Men.

[2] See below, p. 294.   [3] Murray, I. 34.

[4] Cunningham's *Revels Accounts*, 186.

according to Howes' account, "There were twelve of the best chosen, and at the request of Sir Francis Walsingham, they were sworn the queenes servants and were allowed wages and liveries as groomes of the chamber. . . . Among these twelve players were two rare men, viz., Thomas [Robert] Wilson, for a quicke, delicate, refined extemporall witt, and Richard Tarleton, for a wondrous plentifull pleasant extemporall wit, he was the wonder of his tyme." [1] In "Malone Society Collections," I. 345–6, Mr. E. K. Chambers published a certificate of 1599 giving as the Queen's Players :

Richard Tarleton	John Adams
John Laneham	John Garlande
William Johnson	John Dutton
John Towne	John Singer, and

Lionel Cooke

John Perkins, Trompeter, is also mentioned as dead. This may possibly be the John Perkins of Leicester's Men, 1572.[2] Of the new company, Laneham, Wilson, and Johnson were from Leicester's Men, Dutton from

---

[1] Stow, *Chronicle*, ed. Howes, 1615.

[2] In "The First London Theater," *Univ. Nebraska Studies*, 1913, p. 11, Mr. C. W. Wallace writes : "I shall later publish in extenso a license granted by the City to the Queen's Men, dated 28 November, 1583, wherein we learn for the first time that the twelve chosen actors were 'Robert Wilson, John Dutton, Rychard Tarleton, John Laneham, John Bentley, Thobye Mylles, John Towne, John Synger, Leonell Cooke, John Garland, John Adams and Wyllym Johnson,' and their playing places were to be 'at the Sygnes of the Bull in Busshoppesgate street, and the sygne of the Bull in Gratious streete and nowhere els w[th]in this Cyttye' for the time being." It will be noticed that nine of these names are the same as in Mr. Chambers' list. Of the others, Wilson, who died about 1588, is known through the account of the company in Stow's *Annals*, and Bentley through his appearance at Norwich, 1583. Thobye Mylles, I believe, is not known except in the promised document.

Warwick's; the others have not been traced. The year 1582 had been marked by suppression of acting in the city and by vigorous measures against the actors on the part of the city authorities. The formation of a company of leading actors directly in the Queen's service must be regarded as an intervention by the court on behalf of the profession. Apparently the company played at once in London, although the plague was increasing, but they were soon driven to the country.[1] At Norwich, in June, one Wynsdon tried to gain admission without paying, and in the brawl which followed was killed, though not by a member of the company. They were back in London in the fall, and on the intervention of the Privy Council were permitted to act in the city,[2] and gave two plays at court that Christmas.[3]

The history of the company in the next few years is derived mostly from documents concerning the conflict between the court and the city over the London playhouses, and has been discussed in Chapter VIII. The actors proposed certain articles of regulation, which have been lost; but the vigorous replies of the city have been preserved. These oppose plays altogether and note the power of restriction of players to the Queen's company is "less evil than to grant more." They declare "Last year when stage toleration was to Queen's players only, all the places of playing were filled with men calling themselves the Queen's players. The terms offered by the city are discussed in another chapter.[4]

[1] Gildersleeve, 167. Letter of the Mayor to Walsingham, May 3. *Remembrancia.* See Murray, I. 8, for a slightly different statement, ignoring the letter of May 3.   [2] *Remembrancia*, 352.   *Malone Soc. Coll.*, I. 66, 67.
    [3] E. K. Chambers, "Court Performances before Queen Elizabeth," *Mod. Lang. Review*, October, 1906.   [4] See p. 230. Gildersleeve, 174.

The dispute was probably settled by a compromise
not unfavorable to the companies. At all events, the
Queen's men seem to have continued acting in the
city, and appeared at court every year from 1583, to
1591. The reference to the pseudo Queen's men indicates how loosely the licenses of the companies were
supervised, and in the provinces probably the Queen's
authority was evoked even more freely than in the
city. From 1588 to 1591 there seem to have been at
least two companies acting under the Queen's license,
one in London, and the other touring the provinces.
At Ipswich, in May, 1591, two different companies
of Queen's men received payment within four days.[1]

After 1591 the company apparently lost its pre-
eminence. Lord Strange's men took its place at
court in 1592. Some of the Queen's men still held
together, for Dutton is mentioned as the chief player
in Cambridge in September, and Mr. Dutton's players
were at Coventry in November. On January 6, 1594,
the company appeared at court, and for a time,
in April, joined Lord Sussex's men at the Rose, performing the old "King Leir" among other plays.
On May 3, 1593(4), Philip Henslowe records a loan,
"Lent vnto frances Henslow the 3 of Maye, 1593 to
laye downe, for his share to the Quenes players when
they broke and went into the countrey to playe." [2]
The company is not recorded again in the city, though
their title is used for provincial performances until
the death of Elizabeth.

Of the plays acted during the ten years' existence
of the company we, unfortunately, know very little.
The five court plays that are known are non-extant.
Greene is the only dramatist that can surely be

----

[1] Murray, I. 11–12.   [2] *H. D.*, ed. Greg, 4.

identified with the company; but it is probable that some plays of Wilson, Kyd, Peele, and Marlowe were acted by the Queen's men before 1592.

II. *Henslowe's Companies*

Henslowe's Diary, recording miscellaneous financial transactions with various companies and their members, is the most important document for the Elizabethan theater.[1] Of these companies, that of the Lord Admiral was the chief; and, in consequence, it is the only Elizabethan company of which we have full records for a number of years. Its patron was Charles Howard, Baron Howard of Nottingham, later Earl of Nottingham, appointed Lord Chamberlain 1583, and Lord High Admiral in 1585. The company acted at court as early as 1574, and henceforth was heard of frequently in the provinces. It returned to court in 1585, after an absence of eight years, and in 1587 was ranked by a spy of Walsingham's as among the leading London companies. After 1583 and before 1590, the famous actor, Edward Alleyn, his brother John, and James Tunstall (Dunstan) had joined the company from Worcester's men.[2] From records of lawsuits published by Mr. Wallace[3] we know that John Alleyn, brother of the famous Edward, and probably Tunstall (Dunstan) were servants of the Lord Admiral's about 1590, and that this company was then acting jointly with another company, probably Lord Hunsdon's, at the Theater and the Curtain. A joint arrangement had been made by Burbage of the Theater and Henry Laneman of the Curtain in 1585

---

[1] The edition of this document by Mr. W. W. Greg is a model of editing and is the main source for this section.   [2] Murray, I. 44–48.

[3] *University of Nebraska Studies*, 1913, pp. 97, 98.

and apparently continuing to 1592.[1] In 1589 the Admiral's was involved in the Marprelate controversy, but apparently its position as the leading London company was secure. Presumably, the acting of Alleyn and the plays of Marlowe had given it supremacy over the Queen's men.

As yet, so far as we know, the Admiral's men had no connection with Henslowe. Alleyn married his stepdaughter on October 22, 1592, and the Admiral's men began acting at the Rose, Henslowe's Bankside theater, May 14, 1594. In the interval the history of the company is obscure. The Admiral's men disappear from court along with the Queen's men in 1591, and their places are taken by several new companies, Sussex's, Hertford's, Pembroke's, and Strange's. Pembroke's men may have secured some plays of the Queen's men. At any event, when in difficulties in 1593 they sold to the booksellers, or to rival companies, chiefly to Strange's, the "Taming of a Shrew," "Titus Andronicus," the "True Tragedy of Richard Duke of York," and possibly the old "Hamlet." The Admiral's men apparently were temporarily dispersed, some going abroad and others to the provinces. Some kind of union was probably made with Strange's men. At all events, Alleyn heads the list of Strange's men, May 6, 1593, though he is still described as "Servant to the Right Honorable Lord High Admiral."

Such changes and combinations are found in all the companies in this period of tribulation. In these years, 1592–94, the plague was severe, and the companies in great difficulty. As a result of these difficulties, companies ceased or were reorganized, and a

[1] *University of Nebraska Studies*, 1913, pp. 126, 149.

large number of plays were published. This year (1594) thus becomes an epoch-making date in dramatic history. Henceforth, until 1603, the Strange-Chamberlain's and the Admiral's men were undoubtedly the leading companies and the chief rivals, and during this period the Admiral's men continued at the Rose and then at the Fortune under the Henslowe-Alleyn management.

In 1597 some of the players quit Henslowe and helped to form a new company, Pembroke's, acting at the Swan; but in the summer when all the theaters were inhibited, on account of the "Isle of Dogs," they were glad to return. The Pembroke's men, who for a while acted with the Admiral's, in the fall of 1597, seem to have been composed of these prodigals.[1] The Admiral's men continued at the Rose until November, 1600, when they moved to their new house, the Fortune, their place at the Rose being taken by the Earl of Worcester's company, probably newly reorganized. At the accession of James I, the Admiral's men were licensed as the Prince Henry's men, and Worcester's as Queen Anne's men.

In Henslowe's Diary, the records of the Admiral's company are kept regularly from January 15, 1594, to July 13, 1600, with the exception of certain rather large intervals. For long periods they are fairly complete, giving date, name of the play, and receipts for each performance. After 1597 they are less complete, though they supply weekly receipts, names of new plays, and the purchases of play books, costumes, and

---

[1] See C. W. Wallace, "The Swan Theater and the Earl of Pembroke's Servants," *Englische Studien*, 1911. The information given in these documents supplants the accounts in Fleay, Murray, and Greg of the Admiral's and Pembroke's men in 1597-98. See p. 233 *ante*.

properties. As there are no corresponding records of
any other company, our knowledge of the repertory
of a theatrical company or its offering for a season
rests almost wholly on Henslowe's accounts.

The first full season of the Admiral's men at the
Rose extends from June 15, 1594, to June 28, 1595,
over a year of continuous acting, with the exception
of a month's intermission, March 14 to April 21.
They seem to have played every week day, rain or shine.
They had as attractions a practically new theater, the
greatest actor of the day, Edward Alleyn, and nearly
all of Marlowe's plays, and they seem to have been
successful from the start. For the first season they
naturally relied largely on Marlowe's plays, in which
Alleyn had already won a name in the chief parts.
The "Jew of Malta," which they had already acted
in May at the Rose and again in company with the
Chamberlain's men in Newington Butts, was acted
nine times. The "Massacre of Paris," revived June
19, was given ten times. Part I of "Tamburlaine"
was revived, perhaps with new alterations or new
spectacle, August 25, and performed fourteen times;
Part II, revived on December 19, was given six times.
"Dr. Faustus," revived September 30, ran for twelve
performances. These runs, it must be remembered,
did not consist of consecutive performances. A play,
after the first performance, would not be acted again
for several days, and not for a third time until after
another interval. The ten performances of the "Massacre" extended from June 19 to September 25;
"Tamburlaine" and "Faustus" were performed off
and on throughout the entire year. The five plays by
Marlowe had a total of 51 performances, about one
fifth of the entire number.

Outside of Marlowe's plays, the repertory of the company was not a rich one, but it included the following plays, all non-extant, which had considerable popularity: the "Rangers Comedy" (9 times), "Cutlack" (10), "French Doctor" (9), "Grecian Comedy" (12), "Warlam Chester" (7), and the "Siege of London" (7). In all there were 38 plays, of which 17 were old. A new play was supplied at fairly regular intervals of about a fortnight. The following list gives the date of the first performance of the new plays of 1594–95 and the number of times each was acted. It may be taken as fairly representative of the Admiral's offering in a season. Of these 21 new plays, it will be noted that two were acted only once each and that eleven others were not given in either of the subsequent seasons. Only eight were repeated later. The most successful of all ran into a total of 32 performances in three seasons.

New Plays 1594–5

Bellendon, 8 (10) June, 17; 1 in 1595–6; 7 in 1596–7.

Galiaso, 26 (28) June, 9.

Philipo and Hippolito, 9 July, 12.

Godfrey of Bulloigne, 19 July, 11; 1 in 1595–6.

Merchant of Emden, 30 July, 1.

Tasso's Melancholy, 11 (13) Aug., 12; revised 1601–2.

Venetian Comedy, 25 (27) Aug., 12.

Palamon and Arcyte, 17 (18) Sept., 4.

Love of an English Lady, 24 (26) Sept., 2.

Knack to Know an Honest Man, 22 (23) Oct., 16; 4 in 1595–6; 1 in 1596–7.

I Cæsar and Pompey, 8 Nov., 8.

Dioclesian, 16 Nov., 2.

Wise Man of West Chester, 2 (3) Dec., 16; 13 in 1595–6; 3 in 1596–7; bought of Alleyn 19 Sept., 1601.

Set at Maw, 14 (15) Dec., 4.

French Comedy, 11 Feb., 6.

Mack, 21 Feb., 1.

Selio and Olimpo, 5 March, 6; 4 in 1595–6; possibly Heywood's Golden Age, 1611.

I Hercules, 7 May, 4; 7 in 1595–6; probably Heywood's Silver Age, 1613; appears in later entries, 16 May, 1598, 16 July, 1598; 14 and 18 Dec., 1601.

II Hercules, 23 May, 3; 5 in 1595–6; probably Heywood's Brazen Age, 1613; appears in later entries with I Hercules.

Seven Days of the Week, 3 June, 5; 12 in 1595–6; 5 in 1596–7.

II Cæsar and Pompey, 18 June, 2.[1]

Of all these plays only two can with certainty be identified with extant plays. The first and second parts of "Hercules" seem to be the same as the "Silver Age" and the "Brazen Age," by Heywood, which were not published until long after, in 1613. These very spectacular plays are mentioned in an inventory of the company made in 1598, and were apparently for a long time profitable stock plays. So also must have been "Long Meg of Westminster," possibly new when produced on February 11, which is referred to in Field's "Amends for Ladies," 1618, acted about 1611, and the "Wise Man of Westchester," for which the company paid Alleyn two pounds as late as 1601. The net result of the season seems to have been some eight or nine plays added to the repertory.

As we do not know under just what conditions Henslowe shared in the receipts, his figures cannot be interpreted exactly. They vary widely from a few

---

[1] See List, Greg., *H. D.*, II. 339, 340. Various apparent differences between his summary and that given here will be explained from a study of the entries in the Diary. It is not always clear what plays were new, or the exact number of times each was acted.

shillings to several pounds. The amount received from a new play is almost always large and may indicate a large attendance or extra prices, or that Henslowe had a special share in the first day's receipts. Even the two unsuccessful plays, the "Merchant of Emden" and "Mack," brought the manager three pounds eight shillings, and three pounds, respectively. The great houses of the season, however, seem to have been drawn by the two parts of "Hercules" and the "Seven Days of the Week." Although put on late in the spring, these plays average three pounds for an afternoon. The Hercules plays were highly spectacular, and we may imagine "Seven Days of the Week" was also. Then, as now, the theatrical management had recourse to something besides the regular drama.

The records of the other two seasons show similar conditions. During the year running from August 25, 1595, to July 18, 1596, 37 plays were produced, of which 18 are old and 19 new. Marlowe's plays were acted less often than in the preceding year; but some popular plays of the preceding year had good successes. Of the new plays, three had but a single performance each, and 14 were not acted in the following season, although such popular plays as "Crack Me a Nut" and "Harry the Fifth" were probably revived again later. Dekker's "Fortunatus" was apparently an old play revived in this year. "Tamar Cam," perhaps a rival of "Tamburlaine," "Chinon of England," "A Toy to Please Chaste Ladies," and the "Blind Beggar of Alexandria" ran over into the next season. By the third season, which extended with a few intermissions, from October 27, 1596, to July 19, 1597, the company had acquired a considerable repertory; in fact, until December 4 no new play was offered.

Henceforth new plays came rapidly and at the end of this season of 184 performances, 34 plays had been offered, of which 14 were new. Among the old plays was "Jeronymo," the "Spanish Tragedy," acted for the first time by this company, which had 13 performances. Including this among the new plays, the fifteen occupied 131 out of the 186 performances recorded. Even the possession of a large repertory did not lessen the demand for novelty. The table gives the names of the new plays acted each season with the number of performances.

NEW PLAYS AUGUST, 1595–JULY, 1596

Longshanks, 29 Aug., 14; bought of Alleyn in 1602; perhaps a revision of Peele's "Edward I."

Crack me this Nut, 5 Sept., 16; properties purchased for it in 1601; bought from Alleyn in 1602.

New World's Tragedy, 17 Sept., 11.

Disguises, 2 Oct., 6.

Wonder of a Woman, 15 (16) Oct., 9.

Bernado and Fiammetta, 28 (30) Oct., 7.

Toy to Please Chaste Ladies, 14 Nov., 7; 2 in 1596–7.

Henry V, 28 Nov., 13; probably a revision of the "Famous Victories."

Chinon of England, 3 Jan., 14.

Pythagoras, 16 Jan., 12; bought from Slaughter in 1598.

II Seven Days of the Week, 22 (23) Jan., 2.

Blind Beggar of Alexander, 12 Feb., 13; 9 in 1596–7; properties bought in 1601.

Julian the Apostata, 29 April.

I Tamar Cam, 6 (7) May, 9; 1 in 1596–7.

Phocas, 19 (20) May, 7; bought from Slaughter in 1598.

II Tamar Cam, 11 June, 4.

Troy, 22 (25) June, 4.

Paradox, 1 July, 1.

Tinker of Totness, 18 (23) July, 1.

New Plays, October, 1596–July, 1597

Valteger, 4 Dec., 12; probably identical with Hengist of 22 June, 1597; bought from Alleyn in 1601.

Stukeley, 11(10) Dec., 10.

Nabuchodonozor, 19 (18) Dec, 8.

Alexander and Lodowick, 14 Jan., 15; marked 'ne' again on Feb. 11.

Woman Hard to Please, 27 Jan., 11.

Guido, 19 (21) March, 5.

Five Plays in One, 7 April, 10.

French Comedy, 18 April, 11.

Uther Pendragon, 29 April, 7.

Comedy of Humours, 11 May, 13.

Henry I, 26 May, 6.

Frederick and Basilea, 3 June, 4.

Martin Swarte, 30 June, 3.

Witch of Islington, 14 July, 2.

In the following year there is no daily record of performances, but a somewhat full record of expenses. The chief items are payments for plays and costumes. There were also fees for the Master of the Revels, small sums spent at the tavern when the company met to hear a play read, advances to free a delinquent author from prison, and occasional special expenditures. In the season from Oct. 14, 1589, to July 10, 1600, Mr. Greg makes the amount recorded as £222 5s. 6d. Of this sum a little over half was paid to playwrights for some twenty plays. The expenditures for costumes was about £80, an unusually small sum; of this £38 were spent for a single play, the "Seven Wise Masters," £20 of this for silk and taffeta. The Master of the Revels received 7s. each for licensing plays; Haughton was bailed from the Clink; and a drum and trumpet were purchased "to go into the country." It was worth while to pay £2 "to stay the printing of Dekker's Patient Grissel." During the year Henslowe also paid the Master of the Revels £3 a month and gave William Paschall £10 at the appointment of the Lord Chamberlain.

From October 21, 1597, to March 12, 1603, the record is fairly consecutive. In this time 178 plays are mentioned, many of which are old. In the six years recorded there is an average of 20 new plays a year. In producing so many new plays, often some of these at short notice, the services of a considerable number of dramatists were necessary. Henslowe had, during these years, Chettle, Dekker, and some others writing constantly, and other dramatists writing occasionally. The number of dramatists 1598 to 1603 is 26. Of these Chettle was busiest, having to his credit 52 plays in little less than five years, 18 in the year of 1598; but no one of these plays was written without collaborators. During the same period Dekker had a hand in 45 plays. The great majority of Henslowe's plays were made by collaborators — Chettle, Dekker, Day, Drayton, Hathaway, Haughton, Wilson, Smith, and Munday.

It would be dangerous to assume that Henslowe's management was a typical one; but it is the only one of which we have any records, and it concerns one of the two chief companies of the period 1594–1603. One notes the large number of new plays each year, the number of dramatists writing, the large proportion of plays that apparently were never printed and the comparatively few plays reproduced year after year. We shall see reasons for surmising that Shakespeare's authorship provided his company with permanent successes and saved it from such a reliance on hack writers as Henslowe's accounts indicate. On the other hand, these accounts deal with seven years of very rapid change and development in the drama; and, though Henslowe's management does not seem the best suited to encourage literary genius, it is probable that a good deal of similar experimentation was carried on by all the companies.

The Lord Admiral's Company gave three plays at court in the Christmas season of 1594–5, four plays in 1595–6, two in 1597–8, three in 1598–9, two in 1599–1600, three in 1600–1, one in December 27, 1601, and three in 1601–3.[1] None of these plays is named in the records, but references in the Diary and on title pages make it certain that Dekker's "Fortunatus," "Shoemaker's Holiday," and "Phaeton" were given. The two "Earl of Huntingdon" plays were probably given in 1598–9, and "Merry as May Be" and Greene's "Friar Bacon and Friar Bungay" in 1602–3.

The members of the company are known from Henslowe's Diary and from the plot of Frederick and Basilea, 1597. In December, 1594, this list was entered by Henslowe.[2]

Edward Alleyn	Martin Slaughter
John Singer	Edward Juby
Richard Jones	Thomas Dutton
Thomas Towne	James Dunstan

There were various changes in membership. Alleyn gave up acting for a time after 1597. Slaughter, Jones, Dutton, and a later member, Spenser, deserted Henslowe in 1597 to join the Pembroke's company

---

[1] The lists in Fleay and Murray must be supplemented by the additional references given in Chambers' article in the *Mod. Lang. Review*, October, 1906.   [2] *H. D.*, ed. Greg, 5.

at the Swan,[1] but were back with the Admiral's men in the fall, except Slaughter, and with the addition of Borne (Bird) and Shaw. Spenser was killed by Ben Jonson in September, 1598. Alleyn now seems sometimes to have acted with the company, as shown by the plot of "Tamar Cam," c. 1602. Shaw and Jones appear to have left the company for good early in 1602. Of the share holders who signed their names in February 7, 1602, four had been members since 1594.

Thos Singer	Thomas Towne
Thomas Dounton	Humphrey Jeffs
William Byrd	Anthony Jeffs
[John Singer]	Samuel Rowley
Edward Juby	Charles Massy

In this same year, 1602, Henslowe records the organization of another company of the Earl of Worcester's men, and the company appeared at court in January and February. The names of the following actors occur incidentally in the accounts. The first four seem to have joined this company from the Chamberlain's men; Heywood had been employed by the Admiral's men; the others were probably members of the earlier Worcester's company.

John Duke	John Thayer
William Kemp	John Lowin
Christopher Beeston	Richard Perkins
Robert Pallant	Thomas Heywood
Thomas Blackwood	Underell
Cattanes	

The career of this company belongs to the reign of James I.

[1] C. W. Wallace, *Englische Studien*, 1911.

III. *Shakespeare's Company — The Strange-Chamberlain's Men*

The origin of Lord Strange's company and its history during the theatrical confusion 1589–94 has received much attention; but the data furnished by the records is insufficient for more than a conjectural outline.[1]

Ferdinando Stanley, Lord Strange, was patron of a company acting in the provinces from 1576 on. This, or another company under his patronage, appeared at court January 15, 1580,[2] as Lord Strange's Tumblers, and the same acrobats again in 1581, 1583, 1585, and 1586. Once they are called "Boyes." On December 29, 1588, and February 11, 1589, the Lord Admiral's men were paid "for showing other feats of activity and tumbling," and again in the season of 1589–90. In 1590 and 1591, other feats of activity[3] are assigned in the pipe rolls to Ld. Strange's men and, by the Acts of the Privy Council, to the Admiral's. It has been suggested that some sort of a union had been formed between Strange's tumblers and the Admiral's men.

By this time, however, a combination had been made between Strange's and Leicester's men. The Earl of Leicester died in 1588, and when we first have a list of Strange's men, 1593, it contains the names of Kemp, Bryan, and Pope, formerly of Leicester's company. As we have already seen, James Burbage, the owner

[1] See Fleay, Greg, Murray, and others. My account is somewhat different from any of these. The fact is that no one of them is complete. Chambers and Greg have corrected many points in Fleay. Murray has new evidence, but is neglectful of Greg at this point. Some further suggestions come from Mr. Wallace's documents, *Univ. Nebraska Studies*, 1913.

[2] E. K. Chambers, "Court Performances before Queen Elizabeth," *Mod. Lang. Review*, October, 1906.

[3] E. K. Chambers, *op. cit.* W. W. Greg, *H. D.*, 71.

of the Theater, had probably reorganized part of the
company under the patronage of Lord Hunsdon by
1583.[1] This company is not heard of after 1589–90,
although in 1594 Lord Strange's men secured the
patronage of this same Lord Hunsdon. Later, Burbage and his sons were actively concerned with this
new company. It seems probable, therefore, that
the earlier Lord Hunsdon's company furnished some
actors to Strange's men. I suggest that out of the
close relations existing between the proprietors of the
Theater and the Curtain there resulted some reorganization about 1590, Leicester's men and Lord
Hunsdon's men contributing to form a new company,
the Lord Strange's men, which for a number of years
was evidently closely related with the Lord Admiral's
men.

In November, 1589, Strange's men, however constituted, were summoned before the Mayor on account of
the Martin Marprelate controversy and ordered to
stop playing until further notice; but they treated
the Mayor's orders with scorn and "went to the Cross
Keys and played that afternoon." [2] Whereupon they
were again summoned, forbidden to play, and two of
their number sent to the country. Presumably, the
Cross Keys Inn was their regular playing place within
the city, though they may have had others.

In 1591–92 the company gave six plays before the
Queen; and on February 15, 1592, opened at Henslowe's newly reconstructed Rose, where they acted
until inhibited by the Privy Council on June 22 (23),
due to a riot on a Sunday.[3] They received permission
to play three days a week at Newington Butts, but

---

[1] Cf. p. 275, above.   [2] Hazlitt, *English Drama*, 34–35.
[3] W. W. Greg, *H. D.*, ii. 51–54.

refused and finally gained a warrant for a reopening of the Rose in August; but they did not open there until December 29th, when they continued until February 1, 1593. They acted at Hampton Court through the winter and received a warrant to travel on May 6. This warrant contains only six names, headed by that of Edward Alleyn, who, however, is described as "a servant of the Lord Admiral," but had possibly been acting with the Lord Strange's men for some time. The others, doubtless shareholders, are: William Kemp, Thomas Pope, John Heminges, Augustine Phillipps, George Bryan.

Another list of actors in the company is furnished by the plot of the second part of the "Seven Deadly Sins," found by Malone among the papers of Edward Alleyn at Dulwich College.[1] To Fleay we are indebted for the identification of this performance, with the "Four Plays in One" acted by Strange's men March 6, 1592, and probably in part with the "Five Plays in One" and "Three Plays in One" acted by the Queen's men, 1584–85. The list apparently gives the actors and supernumeraries of Lord Strange's men in 1592.[2] Three of the names on the warrant of 1593 reappear with the prefix 'Mr.': Bryan, Phillipps, and Pope. T. Belt, Sander [Cooke], Nick [Tooley], R. Go[ugh], Ned, and Will [Tawler], are designated as 'boys.' The others are: Rich. Cowley, John Duke, Rob. Pallant, John Sinkler, Rich. Burbadge, Tho. Goodale, Will Sly, Harry [Condell], Kit [Beeston ?], John Holland, and Vincent. No actors are named for the

---

[1] Facsimiles by Halliwell-Phillipps, and reprinted in *Henslowe Papers*, ed. Greg.

[2] Tabulated by Fleay, *Stage*, 84. Greg, *Henslowe Papers*, 152. Murray, *Dram. Companies*, I. 79.

parts of Henry VI and Lydgate in the Induction, and Fleay conjectured that these were taken by Shakespeare and Hemings.

The progress of the company in the country can be traced through the provincial records and through Alleyn's correspondence with Henslowe. While still traveling, on September 25, 1593, their patron became the Earl of Derby, a title which the company used until his death, April, 1594.[1] They then soon procured the patronage of Henry Carey, Lord Hunsdon, who was Lord Chamberlain, an all-important official for the drama. On June 3, Henslowe's Diary records their appearance as Chamberlain's men at Newington Butts, where they acted jointly with the Admiral's men, — their last connection with Henslowe. Here were produced various plays, formerly belonging to Pembroke's men (perhaps earlier to the Queen's), of special interest in connection with Shakespeare.[2] On October 8, their new patron wrote to the Lord Mayor asking for permission for them to play within the city at the Cross Keys, which from this letter seems to have been their regular winter house. On March 15, 1595, Kemp, Shakespeare, and Burbage, servants to the Lord Chamberlain, received payments for plays acted December 26, and 28 (27), 1594. This is the first reference to Shakespeare as a member of the company. Lodge's "Wit's Misery"[3] alludes to "Hamlet" (Kyd's play) at the Theater, where the company was now established. There was probably some connection between the Theater and the Cross Keys Inn as early as 1579, for Burbage was arrested

[1] See title page of *Titus Andronicus*, quarto eds., and the Records of Coventry and Leicester.
[2] See above p. 280. [3] Entered S. R., May 5, 1596.

on his way to play at the Cross Keys in this year.[1] Possibly the company used the Theater in the summer and the Cross Keys in the winter.

On July 23, 1596, the Lord Chamberlain died, and his son George Carey became Lord Hunsdon and gave his patronage to the company, which was known as Lord Hunsdon's men until March 17, 1597, when George Carey became Lord Chamberlain and the company resumed their old title. The company remained in the Theater until the expiration of Burbage's lease in 1597, and apparently for some time after that, perhaps even until its demolition in 1598. They may have occupied the Curtain as a makeshift while the new Globe was being erected out of the timbers of the Theater.[2]

James Burbage, before his death, February, 1597, had made a deed of gift of the lease of the Theater to his son Cuthbert. When the Globe was built, Cuthbert Burbage and Richard the actor took half the shares in the new enterprise; the other half was divided among five of the principal actors, William Shakespeare, August Phillipps, John Hemmings, Thomas Pope, and William Kemp. Various lawsuits, of which records have been preserved, give the interesting but incomplete history of the ownership of this theater and Blackfriars, up to the civil war. I note here that

[1] See *Univ. Nebraska Studies*, 1913, 89-90.

[2] Cuthbert Burbage declared that he retained possession after the lease expired and paid rent "for divers years." It seems possible, however, that the company occupied the Curtain; but the conjectures to this effect by Halliwell-Phillipps, *Outlines*, I. 358, Fleay, *Stage*, 134, 148, and Murray, I. 96-7, rest on slight evidence. The "Curtaine plaudeties" in Marston's *Scourge of Villainy* (S. R., Sept., 1598) is a general reference to theatrical applause and does not say or imply that Romeo was acted at the Curtain. All theaters were closed, by an act of the Council, July 28, 1597; the Rose opened October 11.

the including of some of the actor members of the company as housekeepers in the theater was a principle henceforth maintained throughout the history of the company. The distribution of the shares will be discussed in Chapter XI in connection with the lawsuit of 1635.

Of the plays acted by the company from 1594 to 1603 we have little information, except for those by Shakespeare. In 1594 they seem to have had a repertory of old plays gathered during the company reorganizations of 1592-4, including a number that furnished opportunity for Shakespeare's revision. "A Warning for Fair Women," published in 1599, "Thomas Lord Cromwell," 1602, the "Alarum for London," 1602, Dekker's "Satiro-mastix," 1602, and Jonson's "Every Man in His Humour" and "Every Man out of His Humour," acted in 1598 and 1599, are the only extant non-Shakespearian plays written between 1594 and 1603 that can certainly be assigned to the company. Doubtless the very names of many plays have gone to oblivion, though we may doubt whether the company equaled the Admiral's men in the number and variety of new plays. Beyond question, the Chamberlain's men came to rely more and more on the plays of their fellow, Shakespeare. He averaged two plays yearly, and his plays soon formed the most valued portion of the company's stock. The success of the company is shown by their appearance at court every year from 1594 to the end of the reign. They were paid for two plays in the Christmas season of 1594-5, five in 1595-6, six in 1596-7, four in 1597-8, three in 1598-9, three in 1599-1600, three in 1600-01, four in 1601-2, and two in 1602-3. No doubt many of these were Shakespeare's.

Two lists of actors are furnished in the Folio edition of Jonson's "Every Man in His Humor," and "Every Man out of His Humor," the first acted in 1598, the second in 1599. The second list has only six names, all of which are included in the first.

Will. Shakespeare	Tho. Pope
Ric. Burbage	Will. Slye
Aug. Philips	Chr. Beeston
Joh. Hemings	Will Kempe
Hen. Condel	Joh. Duke

It will be noticed that all these names are found on preceding lists. Cowley, Cooke, Tooley, Gough, and Sinkler, who appear in the plot of the "Seven Deadly Sins," also appear in later lists and were probably connected with the company in 1598, 1599. There seems to have been little change in the membership until 1602, when Kemp, Duke, C. Beeston, and Robert Pallant of "Seven Deadly Sins" appear as members of the reorganized Worcester's Men.

IV. *Children's Companies in Elizabeth's Reign*

The Paul's Boys

From the first recorded performance before Queen Elizabeth at Nonesuch, August 7, 1559, the Children of St. Paul's appeared at court nearly every year through the Christmas season of 1581. In that year their master Sebastian Westcott died, and there is nothing certainly known of the company until April 26, 1585, when their new master, Thomas Gyles, received a writ authorizing him "to take up XX apte and meete children.[1]   In the interval the Paul's boys

---

[1] Collier, i. 258, 259. Hazlitt, 33, 34.

may have combined with the Children of the Chapel
to perform Lyly's "Campaspe" and "Sapho and Phao"
at court. They were at court again in the Christmas seasons from 1586–7, to 1589–90, when they
must have presented other of Lyly's plays. They
seem to have been mixed up in the Marprelate controversy,[1] which brought the companies into difficulties
in 1590. Sometime after September 29, of that year,
the company made a solitary provincial appearance
at Gloucester, and in the printers' address to the
1591 edition of "Endymion" we learn that "the
plays in Paul's were dissolved." We next hear of
a Paul's company in 1600, when it acted "Jack
Drum's Entertainment,"[2] and appeared at court on
New Year's, 1601. It probably continued without
interruption and was acting at the singing school
when James I came to the throne. Its history will be
considered in the next chapter.

The Children of the Chapel

Bower, master of the Chapel children at Elizabeth's
accession, was succeeded, in 1561, by Richard Edwards, who was given a commission to take up children. Edwards was a poet, the author of "Damon
and Pythias" and the non-extant "Palamon and
Arcite."[3] On his death, in 1566, he was succeeded by
William Hunnis. Two years earlier, Richard Farrant
had been appointed master of the children of Windsor

---

[1] See Lyly's "Pappe with a Hatchet" (1589, c. Sept.), "If it be shewed at
Paules it will cost you foure pence."

[2] See Fleay, II. 175, and R. A. Small.

[3] C. W. Wallace, *Evolution*, 109, assigns *Appius and Virginia* to Edwards, conjecturing that the R. B. of the printed page is a slip for R. E. On
Misogonus, see Fleay, Brandl, Murray, and Wallace.

Chapel; and henceforth Hunnis and Farrant and their two companies were closely associated.[1]

The Children of the Chapel appeared at court in the Christmas seasons of 1559, 1564, 1568, and henceforth frequently.[2] The Children of Windsor acted every season from 1566-7 to 1576-7. On December 20, 1576, Farrant leased rooms in the Blackfriars monastery for a theater, "sixe upper chambers, loftes, lodgynges or Romes lyinge together." The theater proper seems to have been a small room 46 by 25 feet.[3] After Farrant's death, in 1580, his widow sold the lease, December 20, 1581, to Hunnis and John Newman. Hunnis, however, was soon in difficulties over the lease, which he turned over to Henry Evans, who sold it to the Earl of Oxford, who made a present of it to John Lyly about June, 1583. Lyly and the children were turned out of the theater in 1584. We may conclude that the children of the Chapel and the children of Windsor occupied the theater under some joint arrangement before Farrant's death and also after Hunnis' succession, *i.e.* from 1576 to 1581. After that date it is impossible to trace the arrangement of companies under Evans, the Earl of Oxford, and Lyly. The Paul's boys, Oxford's boys, the Chapel children and the children of Windsor all seem to have been in existence, but probably under shifting combinations.[4]

[1] See Wallace, *Evolution*, 199-225. Hunnis, though master of the Queen's chapel, does not appear in the court payments after 1575 until 1582-3, Farrant apparently receiving pay for both companies of children, 1576-80.

[2] In the imperfect records they do not appear in 1568-9, 1572-3, 1573-4.

[3] See p. 62.

[4] Our data are viz.: *Sapho and Phao* and *Campaspe* were published in 1584, with title pages stating that they were played before the Queen by her Majestie's Children and the Children of Paules. Campaspe on new yeares day by night (Some copies give the date as Twelfth Night, a statement

After performances ceased at Blackfriars, the Children of the Chapel are heard of at Norwich, 1586–7, and at Leicester, 1590–1, and were probably the children's company appearing at Croydon in 1591 and 1592. Oxford's children, now under the management of Henry Evans, appear at court December 27, 1584, and are heard of in the country until 1590. Whatever organization may have been maintained, the Children of the Chapel seem to have disappeared as a London company shortly after the closing of Blackfriars. Nathaniel Gyles (brother of Thomas, master of Paul's) succeeded Hunnis as master of the Chapel.

On July 15, 1597, this Nathaniel Gyles obtained a patent to take up children for the Queen's chapel and united with Robinson and Evans to establish again a theater in Blackfriars. Evans leased from the Burbages a new and large theater there for twenty-one years from September 29, 1600. Soon after Evans and the others were in trouble from kidnapping boys

repeated in the edition of 1591.) Sapho and Phao on Shrovetuesday. Each has a "Prologue at the Blackfriars." In 1581–2, plays are recorded at court by the children of the Chapel on New Year's Eve and Shrove Tuesday, which may be Lyly's plays, as Bond supposes. One by the Paul's boys on December 26, 1581, has no name for the master. In 1582–3, the Children of the Chapel acted on December 26, and were paid through Hunnis; and the Merchant Taylors' boys appeared on Shrove Tuesday. In 1583–4, the Children of the Chapel were paid through their master (not named) for plays on January 6 and February 2; and the Earl of Oxford's servants were paid through John Lyly for plays on New Year's day at night and on Shrove Tuesday, which may have been *Sapho and Phao* and *Campaspe*, as Mr. Chambers conjectures and Mr. Wallace accepts. It seems improbable, however, that the Children of the Chapel (who gave plays that season by themselves) should when combined with the Paul's boys thereby become designated as Oxford's servants. Oxford's boys acted on December 27, 1584, with payment to Evans. Peele's *Arraignment of Paris*, pub. 1584, was acted at court by the Children of the Chapel.

for their company, and Evans made over the lease to his
son-in-law Hawkins. This new company is known from
the actors' lists in Jonson's "Cynthia's Revels," 1600,
and the "Poetaster," 1601. It included some of the
most famous of the boy actors, and was indeed one of
the leading companies at the accession of James.
Nathaniel Field, John Underwood, Salathiel Pavy, and
Thomas Day are mentioned in both plays; Robert
Baxter and John Frost in the earlier; William Ostler
and Thomas Martin in the later.

It seems clear that for some years after 1590 there
was a cessation of public performances by children in
London. About 1600, there was an important revival, the Paul's boys acting probably in their singing
school, the Chapel children at the new Blackfriars.
The boys at Blackfriars at once established a formi-
dable competition with the adult companies. It is to
this rivalry of the reëstablished children that Shakespeare refers in "Hamlet." The account that Rosen-
crantz gives of the players manifestly applies to the
London children. The adult actors have been forced
to travel because of the "late innovation," the "aery
of children" who are now in fashion. Or as the first
quarto (1603) puts it more baldly:

> For the principall publike audience that
> Came to them are turned to private plays,
> And the humour of children.

The children, we further learn, indulge in satire, an allu-
sion to the so-called "war of the theaters," but are
winning out even against "Hercules and his load," *i.e.*
the sign of the Globe playhouse. Discussion of the
plays and dramatists who coöperated with the children
for 1600–10 may be conveniently postponed to the

reign of James I.   Here it will be sufficient to glance
at the plays acted by the children in the earlier period,
1560–90.

Of the nature of the plays presented by the children
we are forced mainly upon conjecture, since most of
them are non-extant.   Of the many recorded performances at court, only some thirty have names of
the plays, and only two of these can be identified
with extant plays, "Edwardes tragedy" of December, 1564, as "Damon and Pythias," and "Orestes" of 1567–8 as "Horestes."   The titles of these
thirty plays by children suggest no especial differences from those by adult actors, nor do the
records in the Revels Accounts indicate distinctions
in character.   But some of the characteristics that we
should expect in the repertory of children acting
primarily for the court appear in the few extant plays
probably designed for children, as "Misogonus"
(1560?), "Queen Hester" (1561), and "Appius and
Virginia."   The children's plays were probably usually
distinguished by singing, dancing, spectacle, and a
large number of female parts.   Later plays, as the
"Arraignment of Paris" (Children of the Chapel, before 1584) and "Triumphs of Love and Fortune" (pr.
1589) indicate the development of a particular kind of
refined comedy, of which Lyly is the chief exponent.
The opportunity for the development of this kind of
comedy doubtless came mainly from the court patronage of the child actors, and it was Lyly's comedy
that was the forerunner of Shakespeare's.   So far
as Lyly is concerned, the credit must go to the
Paul's boys, who produced all of his eight comedies,
with the possible exception of the "Woman in the
Moon," probably between 1580 and 1590.   No author

of importance can be assigned to the other children's companies.[1]

In addition to the companies discussed in this chapter, we have records of a few others in London after 1583. The following appeared at court: Earl of Sussex's, 1583, 1592; Earl of Hertford's, 1592, 1603; Lord Hunsdon's, Lord Chamberlain (Henry Carey), 1586; Earl of Derby's (William Stanley), 1601. The Earl of Sussex's men have been mentioned in connection with their appearance at the Rose. Of the other companies nothing is known of their London careers beyond these appearances at court. They are all heard of at various places in the provinces.

[1] See Wallace, *Evolution, passim,* for a different view of the importance of the children and court.

CHAPTER XI

THE LEADING COMPANIES IN THE REIGNS OF JAMES I AND CHARLES I

I. *The King's Men*

JAMES I arrived in London May 7, 1603, and on the same day issued a proclamation against monopolies and also against various exercises, pastimes, including common plays on the Sabbath day. Two days later he had authorized the companies to act,[1] and on May 19, a patent licensed the Lord Chamberlain's men as the King's Servants, mentioning the following shareholders:[2]

Laurence Fletcher	John Henings
William Shakespeare	Henrie Condell
Richard Burbage	William Sly
Augustyne Phillippes	Robert Armyn
Richard Cowly	

This list is headed by Laurence Fletcher, an actor who had won the favor of James in Scotland.[3] Armin had joined the company by 1600, soon taking Kemp's place as leading comic actor. Pope and Bryan had retired. The others had been connected with the company since 1592, or earlier.[4]

From this date, the organization of the King's men was uninterrupted until the closing of the theaters. The changes in membership can be traced with exactness,

---

[1] W. W. Greg, *H. D.*, 190.
[2] Halliwell-Phillipps, *Outlines*, II. 82. *Malone Soc. Coll.*, I. 264.
[3] Murray, I. 104 n. [4] *Ibid.*, 146; II. 30 and 31.

owing to the lists of actors given in many plays and other documents, and these changes have been effectively tabulated by Fleay[1] and Murray. New actors were admitted from time to time: Lowin and Cooke by 1603; Ostler, Underwood, and Eccleston, taken over from the Revels Children in 1608; Nat. Field, the famous boy actor, a little later; Taylor on Burbage's death, 1619; but the original shareholders long held their places. Shakespeare does not seem to have acted after 1603; but Burbage continued until the year of his death, and Hemings and Condell attended the funeral of James I, and appear in a new patent granted by Charles I.

The new patent, of 1603 under the direct patronage of the King, may be taken as a special mark of His Majesty's favor in recognition of the leadership of Shakespeare and Burbage's organization among the London companies. For forty years this primacy was unbroken. The company gave a number of performances at court annually until 1615–16, without any interruption because of the plague; in one year presenting twelve plays, another fifteen, another twenty. After 1616 records are less frequent, though we often hear of more than twenty plays at court in a season, and no other company appeared with anything like this frequency.

In 1608 Burbage took back the lease of Blackfriars, from Evans, and immediately occupied the theater with the King's men.[2] Henceforth the company occupied two playhouses, using the Blackfriars mainly as a winter theater and winning the custom that had formerly gone to the children. The difficulties of the Queen's Revels had virtually ended that company

[1] *Stage*, 268, 269, 323, 324. Murray, I. 172 ff.   [2] See p. 241 n. *ante*.

x

before Evans, their manager, surrendered his lease. The Whitefriars children united with Burbage to pay 20 pounds a year, to prevent the St. Paul's boys from acting;[1] thus adopting monopolistic methods that we usually consider peculiarly modern. The King's men at Blackfriars consequently had but a single children's company as a rival, and these Whitefriars Revels boys in the end succumbed. ⟨The Globe, after its rebuilding in 1613, retained its prominence among the public outdoor theaters; but the Blackfriars soon surpassed it in the favor of the fashionable, and in the end was recognized as first of the private theaters. ⟩ The company traveled occasionally in the provinces, visiting Oxford with notable frequency, especially in the years 1603–9. After 1609 it seems to have kept pretty closely to London.

The company, though under the direct patronage of the King was often in hot water with the authorities. It was in difficulties over the "Tragedy of Gowry" in 1604; again for playing in Lent, 1616; again because of an attempt of the inhabitants of Blackfriars to close the theater in 1619; and in the same year because of Fletcher and Massinger's "Sir John Van Olden Barnaveldt," in 1624 for Middleton's "Game of Chess," and later for Massinger's "Spanish Viceroy." In 1631 the company successfully resisted another effort to close the Blackfriars.

Of the plays acted by the company in the first years of the reign of James we have few records. The tendency to give domestic plays, already shown by the "Warning for Fair Women," continued in the "Miseries of Enforced Marriage," the "Yorkshire Tragedy," and the "London Prodigal." The old play of "Mucedorus"

---

[1] W. C. Wallace, *Univ. of Nebraska Studies*, 1910.

was revived. These plays are sufficient to show that the company catered to the taste of the crowd as well as did Henslowe. But even while Shakespeare was writing, the company was producing plays by other leading authors of the time: "Sejanus," "Volpone," the "Alchemist," "Catiline," by Jonson, the "Duchess of Malfi" by Webster, and "Philaster," the "Maid's Tragedy" and "A King and No King," the great successes of Beaumont and Fletcher. Shakespeare's place as chief dramatist was taken by Fletcher, who seems to have collaborated with Shakespeare after Beaumont's retirement in 1612; and during the years 1612–25 the company relied on his pen in much the way it had on Shakespeare's from 1594 to 1612. During Fletcher's later years, Massinger and others frequently collaborated with him, and after his death Massinger took his place. On Massinger's death, Shirley appears to have transferred his services from the Queen's men. In the years after 1625, however, where we have considerable information as to the plays acted, nearly all the principal authors appear on the list: Jonson, Ford, Davenant, Brome, Carlell, and others. From 1603 on, the repertory of the company was manifestly of great value, and it was eager to secure its monopoly in this famous list of plays. Beaumont and Fletcher's plays were carefully kept from publication, and not issued by the company until 1647. Shakespeare's plays, although published in folio, 1623, by his fellow actors, were still withheld from other companies. In 1627 the King's men paid the Master of the Revels five pounds to forbid the playing of Shakespeare's plays by the Red Bull company.[1] In 1637 we find the company

[1] Malone, *Variorum*, III. 229.

securing a similar restraint to prevent the printing of any of their plays without their consent.[1]

Though we have no record of a season's performance, as for the Lord Admiral's men, we may form some estimate of its nature from the list of twenty plays given at court 1612–13: Philaster, the Knot of Fools, Much Ado about Nothing, the Maid's Tragedy, the Merry Devil of Edmonton, the Tempest, A King and No King, the Twins' Tragedy, the Winter's Tale, Sir John Falstaff [Merry Wives of Windsor], Moor of Venice [Othello], Nobleman [Tourneur], Cæsar's Tragedy [Shakespeare's Julius Cæsar], Love Lies a Bleeding [Beaumont and Fletcher's Philaster], A Bad Beginning Makes a Good Ending, the Captain, the Alchemist, Cardenna, Hotspur [I Henry IV], and Benedicte and Bettris [Much Ado]. Seven plays are by Shakespeare, including two recent and five old. Four are recent plays by Beaumont and Fletcher. "Cardenna," the lost play, is reported to have been by Shakespeare and Fletcher. Three plays are anonymous and non-extant. They may have been new plays. Except possibly these and "Cardenna," none of the twenty plays were acted for the first time in 1612, but some half dozen of the number had been acted within a year or two. The lists of plays given at court between 1618 and 1625 give the names of plays for twenty-five performances. Only five of these were by Shakespeare; the majority were by Fletcher.

In 1641 a warrant from the Lord Chamberlain[2] (Essex) confirms the company's ownership in sixty plays and forbids any one to print these without their consent. This list represents the stock plays of the King's men which were not already in print. It

---

[1] Collier, H. E. D. P., II. 83–84 n.   [2] Malone Soc. Coll., I. 364.

includes twenty-seven or twenty-eight later printed
as by Beaumont and Fletcher and more recent plays
by Massinger, Middleton, Davenant, and others.
To this repertory must be added many plays already
printed but still frequently acted by the company,
and including all of Shakespeare's, many of Jonson's,
and some of the most popular of Beaumont and
Fletcher's.

This long-continued prosperity of the company must
be credited in some measure to the sagacity of
the business management. In distinction from the
rival companies, its members seem to have worked
together in harmony, and the leading actor-sharers
in the company were also housekeepers: *i.e.* sharers
in the leases of the playhouses. In 1599 the two
Burbages transferred one half interest in the Globe
to Shakespeare, Hemings, Phillipps, Pope, and Kemp;
each of these actors holding a one-tenth interest in
the playhouse.[1] Apparently some agreement was
made by which a sharer on death or withdrawal from
the company was to transfer his share back to the
other housekeepers. On Kemp's withdrawal his share
was so transferred; but on the deaths of other of the
sharers there were difficulties. It is not known what
happened on the death of Pope, 1603,[2] but after the
death of Phillipps in 1606, his widow's second husband,
Witter, brought suit against Hemings and Condell.
From their reply it appears that Condell and Slye
had been given one-sixth shares in the moiety; and
later Ostler had one seventh, and still later Field one
eighth. This division into sixteen shares seems to have
held from about 1616 to 1635. Some of the other

---

[1] Witter *v.* Hemings and Condell, pr. by Prof. Wallace, *Univ. of Nebraska Studies*, 1910.   [2] For his will see Collier, *Memoirs of Actors.*

leading actors, Taylor, Lowin, and Shank had then secured shares, but those of Richard Burbage and Condell had gone to their widows. In 1635 three actors, Benfield, Swanston, and Pollard, brought suit[1] against the largest shareholders, Cuthbert Burbage, his sister, and Shank an actor who had "surreptitiously" bought Hemings' holding, asking for a compulsory sale of one share to each of them. The Lord Chamberlain granted their petition on the basis of the former custom of the company. The housekeepers henceforth were:

C. Burbage 2½	Taylor 2
Mrs. Robinson 2½	Lowin 2
Mrs. Condell 2	Swanston 1
Shank 2	Pollard 1
Benfield 1	

A similar petition was offered by Swanston, Pollard, and Benfield for the division among the three of one of Shank's shares in the Blackfriars. This was granted, but the case is not quite clear. The shares in this theater had been divided in 1608 among Cuthbert and Richard Burbage, Shakespeare, Hemings, Condell, and perhaps others. According to the petitioners of 1635, the property was held in eight shares of which Shank had two, C. Burbage and Mrs. Robinson, Mrs. Condell, Taylor, Lowin, and Underwood, each had one.

/ The statements in these lawsuits in regard to the values of shares, leases, and profits are often contradictory. In Witter's suit the profits of a share ($\frac{1}{14}$) in the Globe before the fire are estimated at £30 to £40 yearly. In 1634 an actor shareholder in the King's

---

[1] Halliwell-Phillipps, *Outlines*, I. 312. Sidney Lee, *Life of Shakespeare*, new ed., 305 ff. Shares in the Curtain were held by Pope and Underwood.

men is said to have received £180, and a housekeeper holding one-eighth interest in the Blackfriars £112. The Globe shares seem to have been worth about double those of the Blackfriars. If Shakespeare had been living in 1635, his income would have been a handsome one. ⸢ These figures may be compared with valuations made in 1631 by a committee appointed to appraise the Blackfriars property with a view to removing the playhouse. The committee reported that the players demanded £16,000 and presented an itemized account of £21,990. The committee valued the property as follows: fourteen years' lease in the theater at £50 yearly, £700; adjoining tenements and yard at £81 annual rental, £1134; the interests and damage of housekeepers and actor-sharers, £66 13s. 4d. each, (though the players demand £150) or £1066 13s. 4d. in all. Theatrical values were largely speculative, but it is evident that the King's men had a profitable enterprise.

The position of this company had, indeed, been steadily maintained and improved from the day of Shakespeare's first connection with it. Its rivals came and went, but it remained easily the chief company. With its well-established theaters and its splendid repertory, its general reputation and financial standing had never seemed better than in 1635.

II. *Successors to Henslowe's Companies*

A. The Prince's Men

The following Admiral's men appeared as Prince Henry's Servants on the entry of King James into London, March 15, 1604.[1]

---

[1] *New Shakes. Soc. Publ.*, 1877–79. Appendix II. 17. Murray, I. 207.

Edward Alleyn	Samuel Rowley
William Bird	Edward Juby
Thomas Towne	Humphrey Jeffes
Thomas Dutton	Charles Massey
Antony Jeffes	

All of these had been members of the company for some time; but there is no clear evidence that Alleyn acted after this date. Among the additions to the company before 1613 were Shank, afterwards an important member of the King's men, and Cartwright, who had been connected with Henslowe as early as 1598, and who was remembered in the "Historia Histrionica," 1699. The company continued to act at the Fortune, and frequently at court, until the death of their patron in 1612. By this time Towne had died, and A. Jeffes had sold his share in the company for £70.[1] On January 11, 1613, they received a new patent as the Servants of the Palsgrave, who had recently arrived in England for the purpose of marrying the Princess Elizabeth. The following shareholders appear in this list.[2]

Thomas Downton (Dutton)	William Cartwright
William Bird	Edward Colbrand
Edward Juby	William Parr
Samuel Rowley	William Stratford
Charles Massey	Richard Gunnell
Humphrey Jeffs	John Shancke
Franck Grace	Richard Price

In 1618 the company leased the Fortune of Alleyn for 41 years, at a yearly rental of £200 and 2 rundlets of wine. In 1621, they entertained the Spanish

---

[1] Warner, *Cat. Dulwich Mss.*, 36, 138.
[2] *Malone Soc. Publ.*, I. 3, 275; Collier, *H. E. D. P.*, i. 366; and Hazlitt, 44.

ambassador, Gondomar, at a banquet in the garden adjoining the theater. A few months later the play-house was burned, but shortly rebuilt by Alleyn, who leased the shares for long periods, usually for 51 years. Among the shareholders were Gunnell, Charles Massey, Juby, and Price. The prices paid indicated that the Fortune was a profitable enterprise.[1]

On May 29, 1630, Prince Charles was born, and the Palsgrave's, or the Fortune company, came under his patronage, probably on December 7, as the Prince's men. Apparently, the Prince's men and the King's Revels companies at once changed theaters, for Shirley's "Changes" was licensed for the King's Revels at Salisbury Court on January 10, 1632, and on January 26, "Holland's Leaguer" was entered as "lately and often acted" by the Prince's men at this same theater; and its prologue seems to allude to the transference of the King's Revels to the Fortune. Possibly there was some joint arrangement for an occupancy of the two theaters, one public and one private.[2]

The further course of the Prince's men is not easy to trace. They were prominent at court, 1634–39, and are mentioned in the "Historia Histrionica" as occupying Salisbury Court, yet we find them at the Red Bull in 1639 and at the Fortune, 1640, and the Queen's men seem to have occupied Salisbury Court after 1637.[3]

---

[1] Warner, *Cat. Dul. Mss.*, 243–7.

[2] Cartwright is mentioned in the *Historia Histrionica* as the leading member of the Prince's men at Salisbury Court, though he was at the head of the King's Revels. The new Prince's men contains only two actors connected with the company since 1622. See Murray, I. 217–19, and Fleay, *Stage*, 330, 331.

[3] See Murray, I. 219–24; and Fleay, *Stage*, 330, 331, 353–359, for explanations.

The company was still regarded as a prominent one, but it is not possible to trace any strict continuity of organization.[1] Its plays are reported to have been destroyed in the fire of 1621, but we know of very few before or after that date which can certainly be ascribed to this organization.

B. Queen Anne's Men

The Earl of Worcester's men were received under the patronage of Queen Anne in 1603, a rough undated draft of a patent being conjecturally dated in that year.[2] This names the Boar's Head Inn and the Curtain as the regular theaters. The members of the company were:

Thomas Greene	John Duke
Christopher Beeston	Thoman Swynerton
Thomas Hawood	James Hoult
Richard Pyrkins	Robert Beeston
Robert Pallant	Robert Lee

In 1605, the company leased the Red Bull theater, which was apparently a new building, from Holland.[3] Traveling companies were formed to act in the provinces: one under a license of 1605, headed by Lee, Slater (Slaughter), and Barfield; another later in 1612, headed by Lee and Swynerton. This practice of maintaining extra companies, in which the Queen's men seem to have taken the lead, brought about in 1616 an order for the suppression of such companies.[4]

---

[1] It seems to me that in these later years, joint arrangements between companies were doubtless made. Further, it is probable that organizations were maintained by theaters fully as much as by companies.

[2] *Malone Soc. Coll.*, I. 265; also Collier, *H. E. D. P.*, i. 336; Halliwell-Phillipps, *Illustrations*, 106.

[3] Wallace, *Univ. Nebraska Studies*, 1909.   [4] See p. 265 *ante*.

The London company obtained a new patent in 1609, mentioning "as their now usual houses the Red Bull and the Curtain." The Boar's Head was doubtless discarded when the Red Bull was leased in 1605. The members of this company in this patent are the same as in that of 1603–4.

The will of Thomas Greene in 1612 mentions Beeston, Perkins, and Heywood, but in the litigation growing out of this will many new members of the company appear. In 1617 the company appears to have occupied the new Cockpit, a private theater in Drury lane, though they probably continued to use the Red Bull as a public theater. The company was already in trouble with Christopher Beeston, their manager, who had failed to account for sums of money.[1] In 1619, Queen Anne died, and the actors attending her funeral included representatives of the provincial companies as well as the London shareholders. The first seven were shareholders in 1603 ; Slaughter headed a provincial company in 1605; the others appear also on a list of 1617, except Edmonds, of Slaughter's provincial company, Sanderson, and Garrett. Up to this time the organization had been well maintained.

Robert Lee	Ellis Worth
Richard Perkins	John Cumber
Christopher Beeston	Thomas Basse
Robert Pallant	John Blaney
Thomas Heywood	William Robins[on]
James Holt	John Edmonds
Thomas Swinnerton	Thomas Drew
Martin Slaughter	Gregory Sanderson

John Garrett[2]

[1] *Univ. Nebraska Studies*, 1909, Smith *v.* Beeston *et al.*
[2] Collier, I. 397.   Murray, I. 196, 197.

There had, however, already been signs of a decline in the company's prosperity, and there now set in a rapid disintegration. A number of the leading actors were licensed as the King's Revels, with the power "to bring up children in the quality." [1] But this company soon disappears; the actors reappear in various places, but there is some reason to think that an amalgamation was made with the Princess Elizabeth's men, who succeeded at the Cockpit. To understand the peculiar circumstances, we must return to the will of Greene, who stood at the head of the company, 1603–12. His will led to long litigation, the papers in which throw some interesting light on the affairs of the company.[2] Greene left claims against the company valued at £117, of which £80 were the value of his share; but his widow failed to obtain anything except promises. Baskerville, whom she married in 1613, arranged with the company for an annuity for himself and wife, which was renewed, till finally fixed at 3s. 8d. per diem in 1617, and guaranteed by the signatures of twelve shareholders in the company. In 1623, three of these, Worth, Cumber, and Blaney, applied in Chancery for relief, on the ground that the payment was to continue only so long as any four of this Queen Anne's company should act together in a London playhouse. The court refused this petition. It is impossible to determine with certainty what was the truth in the case; but by 1623 the organization seems to have lost that integrity which it had kept from 1603 to 1619. Mr. Fleay's suspicion that a virtual amalgamation with Lady Elizabeth's men had taken place cannot be

[1] Malone, *Variorum*, iii. 62. Murray, II. 192 ff. *Malone Soc. Publ.*, I. 3, Appendix. [2] Fleay, *Stage*, 192 ff., 270 ff. Murray, I. 193 ff.

proved;[1] but Beeston, formerly manager of the Queen's men, was at the head of the Lady Elizabeth's men in 1622.

In 1625, a new company, Queen Henrietta's, succeeded Lady Elizabeth's at the Cockpit, and four of the old Queen's men enrolled as members — Beeston, Blaney, Perkins, and Robinson, enough, apparently, to be responsible for Mrs. Baskerville's pension. We may, however, doubt if she ever received the money, and conclude that the breaking up of the Queen Anne's men shortly after their patron's death was somewhat facilitated by the company's willingness to escape their legal obligations. Beeston now appears as manager of the Cockpit, and on friendly terms with the men who had sued and denounced him.

Heywood seems to have been the chief author for this company, in which his relation was perhaps similar to that of Shakespeare and the King's men. Many of the plays were probably passed along to Queen Henrietta's company. Of the relations of Henslowe and Alleyn to the Queen Anne's company after 1603, we have few records. The company acted at court frequently from 1604 to 1614.

C. The Lady Elizabeth's Men

One other company, under Henslowe's control, played a prominent part in the time of James I. Under the patronage of the Princess Elizabeth, who later married the Elector Palatine and became the Queen of Bohemia, this company received a patent April 27, 1611;[2] and on August 29, the following members signed a bond to Henslowe.

---

[1] See Murray's criticism of Fleay, I. 199 n.
[2] *Malone Soc. Coll.*, I. 274. Murray, II. 340.

John Townsend	John Rice
Will Barksted [Baxter]	Robt. Hamlen
Joseph Taylor	Will Carpenter
William Eccleston	Thomas Besse
Giles Gary [Carey]	Joseph Moore
Thomas Hunt	Allexander Foster

[Francis Wam(b)us] [1]

In March, 1613, they united with Rossiter's second
Queen's Revels, Field, Taylor, Benfield, Eccleston,
Read, and Basse being among the actors; and this
company, or its successors, under Henslowe's management, acted "Bartholomew Fair" in the new Hope
theater, 1614.[2] An attempt to build a new theater
in Blackfriars for this company failed; but Field's
"Amends for Ladies" was acted in the incompleted
theater.   By 1622, probably after some further changes
in organization and possibly after a union with the
Queen's men, the company was installed in the Cockpit, with Beeston at its head.[3]   After 1625, they gave
place to the new Queen Henrietta's men; but acquired
a new license in 1628 and continued for some years
mainly in the provinces.   I have elsewhere glanced
at some of the experiences of this company, at Norwich.[4]   Evidently more than one organization was
using the company's license.

From 1614–16 the Prince Charles' (i.e. Charles I)
men were closely associated with Lady Elizabeth's

---

[1] There are two bonds of this date, one reprinted by Collier in his *Alleyn
Papers*, 98.   Warner notes both bonds in his *Cat. Mss. Dulwich College*, 239,
340, but makes up the lists of actors from the reverse of each bond.   Murray,
I. 243 n., follows Warner.   Greg, *Henslowe Papers*, 18, 19, 111, prints both
bonds with signatures and lists on the reverse.   The first bond omits the name
of Eccleston on the reverse.   The second omits Barksted and Gary but adds
Fr. Wamus among the signatures, but includes Gary's name on the reverse.

[2] See Agreement between Henslowe and Field, for the company, Greg,
Henslowe Papers, 23 f.   [3] Malone, *Variorum*, iii. 59–60.   [4] p. 268–270.

men, also under the control of Henslowe and Alleyn, and after Henslowe's death, in 1616, they seem to have occupied the Curtain [1] until they succeeded the Queen's men at the Red Bull.

During its heydey, with Field, Taylor, Benfield, and other famous actors, Lady Elizabeth's company was one of the best in London. Taylor, the water poet, declared —

> Such a company, I boldly say,
> That better nor the like e'er played a play.

They attracted many of the best writers, and they and their connected companies produced plays by Beaumont and Fletcher, Field, Middleton, Rowley, and Ford. Apparently their repertory continued in the possession of Beeston, and was used by Queen Henrietta's men. Next to the King's men they seem to have had the best list of plays, and frequently acted at court during the reign of James I.

Henslowe died in 1616, and Alleyn before this ceased to exercise any active management of the companies. Neither had a successor, and neither the lease of the Fortune nor the legal obligations incurred by the Red Bull company secured a firm organization such as that of the King's men at the Globe and Blackfriars. Alleyn's death in 1626, coincident with the accession of Charles I, saw the end of the long control exercised by the great actor and wealthy bear-master.

The new Queen Henrietta's company, which acted usually at the Cockpit, continued in some measure the plays and actors of some of the earlier Henslowe organizations, and the Prince's men at the Fortune

[1] Fleay, *Stage*, 301. Chalmers, 213. Chambers, *Mod. Lang. Review*, 1909, 165, 166.

and the new Salisbury Court were the successors of the
company once made famous by Alleyn's acting.   Christopher Beeston, manager of the Cockpit, seems to have
been the most influential person in the managing of these
companies, but their changes are somewhat obscure.

When in 1637 Beeston, with his kinsman William,
formed a new company at the Cockpit, he retained
many of the plays of the Queen's men in his possession.   In 1639 an order from the Lord Chamberlain
confirmed this company of Beeston's boys in the ownership of the following plays, and forbade all other companies to act them: "Wit without Money, the
Nightwalkers, the Knight of the Burning Pestle,
Father's Own Son [Monsieur Thomas], Cupid's Re-
venge, the Bondman, the Renegado, A New Way to
Pay Old Debts, the Great Duke of Florence, the
Maid of Honor, the Traitor, the Example, the
Young Admiral, the Opportunity, A Witty Fair One,
Love's Cruelty, the Wedding, the Maid's Revenge,
the Lady of Pleasure, the School of Compliment
[Love Tricks], the Grateful Servant, the Coronation,
Hyde Park, Philip Chabot, Admiral of France, A Mad
Couple Well Met, All's Lost by Lust, the Changeling,
A Fair Quarrel, the Spanish Gypsy, the World [Tossed
at Tennis], the Sun's Darling, Love's Sacrifice, 'Tis
Pity She's a Whore, George-a-Greene, Love's Mis-
tress, the Cunning Lovers, the Rape of Lucrece, A
Trick to Cheat the Devil, A Fool and her Maidenhead
Soon Parted, King John and Matilda, A City Night
Cap, the Bloody Banquet, Cupid's Vagaries, the
Conceited Duke, Appius and Virginia."

This represents the best repertory that could be
gathered in 1639 to oppose the stock plays of the King's
men, though two or three other companies probably

still possessed old plays. The first five on the list are all in part by Fletcher and written as early as 1614. The second five are by Massinger, written in the twenties. Thirteen or fourteen are by Shirley, nearly all written for the Queen's men after 1625. Others are by Middleton, Ford, Davenport, Webster, and Brome. As Mr. Fleay noted,[1] many of these plays had come down to Queen Henrietta's men in two streams, "either from Queen Anne's through the Revels men, or else they came directly from the Queen's Revels boys which joined the Lady Elizabeth's in 1613." The stage history of several of these plays is interesting as illustrating the vicissitudes of the companies. 'George-a-Greene," was written probably as early as 1590 and was performed by Sussex's men as an old play on December 29, 1593, at the Rose, and four subsequent performances during the ensuing month are noted in Henslowe's Diary. The company apparently broke in 1594, and "George-a-Greene" was entered for publication in 1595 but not printed so far as we know until 1599. The Richard Perkins mentioned in the text may have been the actor, and the play may have followed him in his career through the Worcester's men, Queen Anne's men, and the Revels at the Red Bull, to Queen Henrietta's company. Probably few plays written in 1590 were still kept in repertory in 1639. Beaumont and Fletcher's "Knight of the Burning Pestle" was probably written for the Blackfriars children in 1606–7.[2] From these children on their disruption in 1608, it must have passed to the children at Whitefriars, from them to the Princess Elizabeth's company, on to Queen Henrietta's, by whom it was acted at court in 1636.

---

[1] *Stage*, 356.   [2] Chambers, *Mod. Lang. Review*, January, 1909.

Y

In the reigns of James I and Charles I, it is clear that no other company equaled the King's men in reputation and profits, although at any given time there were always two or three prominent rivals. The somewhat obscure history of the various successors of Henslowe's companies points to one reason for their failure to secure permanent positions. They never seem to have attained a sound business organization and were usually at the mercy of capitalist or manager.

III. *The Children's Companies*

On the accession of James I, the two children's companies were evidently at the height of their success. The Paul's boys retained their old organization; but the Blackfriars children received a license, January 30, 1604, as the Children of the Queen's Revels. Their position was somewhat different from earlier days. The boy actors were apparently separated from the choir boys and used constantly for professional performances and the profit of their managers. These managers soon got into difficulties, through kidnapping and other violations of law, and in consequence the history of the different organizations becomes very complicated and impossible to trace with the data which we possess.[1]

The Paul's boys, apparently still acting at their school, produced many plays from 1600 to 1606. In 1606, Kirkham, formerly of the Children of the Revels, was paid at court as their manager. By 1607 they disbanded and a number of their plays were printed,

---

[1] Chamber's account in *Mod. Lang. Review*, 1909, is the best but must be supplemented by the evidence of Keysar's law suit printed by Wallace, *Univ. Nebraska Studies*, 1910.

but a new company, the King's Revels,[1] appeared, which acted somewhere in Whitefriars. Plays acted by this company were published 1607–11. This White-friars company agreed to pay Peirce, the master of Paul's Boys, £20 a year, on condition that the Paul's Boys should not act. It seems to be the same company of Revels alluded to in the lawsuit of Androwes *v.* Slater[2] managed by a partnership in which Drayton the poet and Martin Slaughter, a well-known actor, were prominent members.

Meanwhile the Queen's Revels, under the management of Kirkham and others, were acting at Black-friars, controlled by Evans or his father-in-law. Their plays, however, were to be approved by Samuel Daniel the poet. Already in 1603–04 Evans was negotiating with Burbage about transferring the lease to him, though without result. In spite of Daniel's oversight, the company was twice in trouble in 1604–5, first, over Daniel's "Philotas" and, second, over "Eastward Hoe," by Jonson, Chapman, and Marston. The authors and some of the actors were imprisoned for the second offense, and the company inhibited. They were soon playing again at Blackfriars, although they seem to have lost both court favor and their title as Queen's Revels. In 1606 there was further trouble over the "Isle of Gulls," and probably a re-organization with Keyser as manager. In 1607–8, the company was again in serious trouble over Chapman's "Byron." Evans, in August, 1608, surrendered the lease to Burbage, and the King's men took over some of the boys and entered in possession of the Blackfriars.

---

[1] Sharpham's *Cupid's Whirligig*, acted by this company, was published in 1607, so it may have existed earlier.

[2] N. S. S., *Transactions*, 1887–92, 269.

Burbage also agreed to share with the Whitefriars company the £20 which they paid yearly to keep the Paul's Boys from activity. The only persons who were not satisfied were those who held some shares in the old Revels company. Keysar brought suit against Burbage and according to his statements, he was in possession of some boy actors, but neither properties nor theater.

It seems probable that this remnant of the old Queen's Revels may have come to some agreement with the King's Revels of Whitefriars. Keysar received payment for two performances of the "Children of the Blackfriars" at court in the Christmas season of 1608–9, and for five plays by the "Children of the Whitefriars" in 1609–10. Nothing is heard of either after Christmas, 1609, but a new company of the Queen's Revels received their patent, January 9, 1610, to act "within the Whitefryers in the suburbes of our Cittie of London, or in any other convenient place," with "Phillip Rossetter and certain others" as managers. Field and Baxter of the 1601 list of Chapel Children are both in the lists of Jonson's "Epicœne," acted 1609, and of Beaumont and Fletcher's "Coxcomb," acted about 1610. Carey, Attawel, Richard Allen, also appear on these two lists.

This second Queen's Revels company was now the only children's company left in London, and some of the 'children' must have been ready for the adult companies. A traveling section of the company appeared at Norwich in 1611 and again in 1612, but was not permitted to act. In 1612–13, they combined with the Princess Elizabeth's men under Henslowe.

Henceforth, children actors are of slight importance. A third Queen's Revels appeared in the provinces in 1615, and was one of the three companies that secured

a privy seal in that year permitting Rossiter and others
to build a new theater in the Blackfriars. This theater
was demolished before it was completed, but on October 31, 1617, a new Revels company was organized,
which, however, is not heard of in London, but maintained itself in the provinces until 1627. A more
important children's company was that established in
1637 by Christopher Beeston and known as "Beeston's
Boys" or "The King and Queen's Company" acting
at the Cockpit. Through Beeston, this company
inherited a notable repertory of plays. Christopher
Beeston was succeeded by William Beeston, who was
superseded, in 1640, by William Davenant, who held
the position in 1642 and resumed his function of dramatic manager with the Restoration.

The success of the children actors in the early years
of the seventeenth century is of interest in more ways
than one to the history of the drama. In opposition
to the forces of both Henslowe and Burbage, the children won favor from audiences probably less popular
than those of the public playhouses, and established
theaters in the heart of the city. They stimulated
the production of plays and perhaps helped to raise
the rewards for the dramatists. Daniel and Marston
were sharers in some of the Blackfriars companies, and
Drayton in the Whitefriars enterprise of 1608–10. In
the end, however, the children succumbed to the adults,
and were absorbed in the Burbage and Henslowe
combinations. Thirty years later, the organization
of Beeston's boys seems to have been a repetition of
the earlier effort to break the supremacy of the adult
companies by means of children.

During the success of the Paul's and Blackfriars
boys from 1600 to 1607, they attracted the services

of the leading dramatists. At first the children seem to have revived some old plays, including the "Spanish Tragedy" or a substitute for the First Part, and some of Lyly's plays. New plays, such as the "Maid's Metamorphosis" and Jonson's "Cynthia's Revels" also follow the fashion familiar in Lyly's earlier plays for the Paul's boys. But the plays soon ceased to depend upon any of their old peculiarities of dance, music, and spectacle; and were undistinguishable in character from those acted at the public theaters. Indeed the children companies initiated, or at least encouraged, the current taste for realistic and satiric comedy. In addition to the personally satirical plays concerned with the 'War of the Theaters,' they produced some of the most revolting satires and grewsome tragedies to be found in the drama. The following list of extant plays may be interesting as showing what keen competition they were offering to the King's men in the years when both Burbage and Shakespeare were at their best.

Plays Acted by Children's Companies, 1600–1610

The dates are those of publication. A few of the plays may have been first acted by Rossiter's revels after 1610, and in a few other cases the ascription to a particular company is uncertain.

Paul's:

Anon. Jack Drum's Entertainment, 1601. Maid's Metamorphosis, 1600. Wisdom of Dr. Doddipoll, 1600. Abuses, n. e. The Puritan, 1607. Histriomastix, 1610.

Beaumont. Woman Hater, 1607.

Chapman. Bussy d'Ambois, 1607.

Dekker. Satiromastix, 1602.

Dekker and Webster. Westward Ho, 1607. Northward Ho, 1607.

Marston. 1 and 2 Antonio and Mellida, 1602. What You Will, 1607. Fawn (Parasitaater), 1606 (also at Blackfriars).

Middleton. Blurt Master Constable, 1602. Phœnix, 1607. Michaelmas Term, 1607. A Mad World My Masters, 1608. Trick to Catch an Old One, 1608 (also at Blackfriars).

Percy. Necromantes. MS.

Blackfriars' Children:

Anon. Sir Gyles Goosecap, 1606.

Beaumont and Fletcher. Knight of the Burning Pestle, 1913. Cupid's Revenge, 1615. Coxcomb. Scornful Lady, 1616.

Chapman. The Gentleman Usher, 1606. May Day, 1611. Monsieur D'Olive, 1606. All Fools, 1605. Byron's Conspiracy and Tragedy, 1608. Widow's Tears, 1612. Revenge of Bussy d'Ambois, 1613.

Chapman, Jonson, and Marston. Eastward Hoe, 1605.

Daniel. Philotas, 1605.

Day. Isle of Gulls, 1606. Law Tricks, 1608.

Jonson. The Case is Altered, 1609. Cynthia's Revels, 1601. Poetaster, 1602. Epicœne, S. R., 1610; acted 1609.

Lyly. Love's Metamorphosis, 1601 (first acted by Paul's).

Marston. Dutch Courtesan, 1605. Fawn, 1606. Malcontent, 1604. Sophonisba, 1606. Insatiate Countess, 1613.

Middleton. Trick to Catch the Old One, 1608 (also at Paul's). Five Witty Gallants, (S. R., 1608).

Middleton and Rowley. Match at Midnight.

Sharpham. Fleire, 1607.

Whitefriars (King's Revels):

Armin. Two Maids of Moreclack, 1609.

Barry. Ram Alley, 1611.

Day. Humour out of Breath, 1608.

Markham. Dumb Knight, 1608.

Mason. The Turk, 1610.

Middleton. The Family of Love, 1608.

Sharpham. Cupid's Whirligig, 1607.

A word may be added in regard to the closing of the theaters. On January 6, 1642, the King's men performed Beaumont and Fletcher's "Scornful Lady" before the prince at Whitehall. The King and Queen were not present, and this was the last play acted at court. On September 2 the order of Parliament was issued, prohibiting stage plays. In 1647 a folio edition of Beaumont and Fletcher's plays was issued by eight actors who had belonged to the King's men, and two who had been members of either the Queen's men or Beeston's boys. In 1647 and again in 1648 actors attempted to give plays in the Cockpit and the Red Bull, but were promptly suppressed. There were, according to Wright, some surreptitious performances later but there is no definite record until Davenant's beginning in 1656. In the closing years of Charles I, however, the managers had already appeared who were to continue the theater after the Restoration, and actors were being trained at Blackfriars and the Cockpit who were to revive the Elizabethan plays in the time of Charles II.

CHAPTER XII

THE DRAMATISTS

THE Elizabethan theater was a school of poets. The playhouses and the professional companies furnished a livelihood for men of letters, supplied incentives and rewards to the profession of dramatists, and gave encouragement and welcome to the work of genius. For the first time in the history of modern Europe a great literature found its support in the people rather than in the patronage of the great. Poetry had for its patrons London and the English nation. If the permanent greatness of this popular drama warrants comparison with the glories of Athens, it was achieved in a more heterogeneous democracy, with a less fully developed culture, and with no corresponding national triumph in the other fine arts. Even in its supreme achievement, the plays of Shakespeare, the English drama betrays its experimentation, its lack of determined standards, and its confusion of artistic ideals with the demands of the populace. The democratization of literature was already producing its mixed effects, and these effects were disturbed by the mediums of stage and actors through which the imagination of the poets responded to the appeals of the public. Yet the richness of this drama as well as its crudities owes much to the conditions in which it was produced. Its theater interests us to-day not only as the home of Shakespeare but also as the first means found by a modern nation for creating a popular regard for literary art.

It is the purpose of this chapter to emphasize this service of the public stage to poetry by a discussion of the relations of the dramatists to the companies. But one must admit that the support offered by the people was not always either whole-hearted or sufficient. We have seen that the theaters were opposed by a large section of the more respectable citizens, and owed a considerable amount of their backing to the court. Individual dramatists often sought and sometimes obtained patronage of the nobility. Others earned a living only by combining hack work for the theatrical managers with hack work for the booksellers. The profession of playwriting was a varied and shifting one. Its financial returns, literary prestige, and social status vary with individual writers and from decade to decade. Indeed, the rapidly changing life of the English people in this era, which we have seen reflected in the varying conditions of drama and theater, is also reflected in the relations of dramatists to actors and audiences. We shall glance at changes which cover a period of only eighty years, but carry the profession of dramatist from isolation in court or school, through an increasing recognition and applause from the national public, back to subserviency to a party and a class.

For twenty years after Elizabeth's accession very little is known of individual dramatists. The few names that have escaped from oblivion are connected with university or court. The scholars at the universities, like Dr. Gager, who wrote Latin dramas, hardly come within our survey; but now and then a university man produced an English play, as Wager, author of "Mary Magdalene" or Thomas Preston, who while a fellow at Cambridge so delighted the Queen by his acting of Dido and his skill in disputation that she gave him a yearly pension of twenty pounds and the title of "her scholar." A year or two later, possibly as a token of his gratitude, he wrote the tragedy of "Cambyses," which was destined to enduring fame through a phrase of Shakespeare's ridicule. Preston has been conjecturally credited with other plays, but eventually he forsook the drama and became master of Trinity Hall, Cambridge.

On the court side there were Thomas Norton and Thomas Sackville, later Lord Buckhurst, the authors of "Gorboduc," performed by the gentlemen of the Inner Temple as a part of their elaborate Christmas entertainment for the Queen in 1561-2. And there was George Gascoigne, famous in his day as poet, soldier, and spendthrift, who lived the varied sort of life characteristic of the time, and yet found opportunity for several dramas and entertainments. In the "Princely Pleasures of Kenilworth" he gave notable examples of his skill as author and actor and courtier. Dressed as a Sylvanus, god of the woods, he met the Queen as she was riding to the hunt and delivered a long address as he ran alongside of her horse. The Queen graciously offered to stop so that he might be at less expense of breath, but he promptly replied that he could run and speak all day in her Majesty's praise. Happily a few rods further made an end of this trial of devotion, for he led her Majesty to a bush where Leicester was concealed, costumed as "Deep Desire," and ready with another address.

The most distinctive group of dramatists, however, that emerges from the court records of the time is composed of the men in charge of the children of the Chapel and other companies of choir boys that

performed before the Queen. These men were all musicians of considerable note and teachers of their boys,
and also dramatic managers and authors. Under
their direction, as we have seen, a peculiar species of
drama developed, suited to the children actors, mingling song, dance, and spectacle, and preparing the way
for the comedies of Lyly and Shakespeare. Earliest
of these musicians was Richard Edwards, author of
"Damon and Pithias" and the non-extant "Palamon
and Arcite," which was produced with great success
in Christ Church Hall at Oxford; so that the "Queen
laughed heartily thereat and gave the author great
thanks for his pains." [1] In his five years of service
(1561–66) as master of the children of the Chapel he
doubtless produced other plays or "pithie and learned
inventions." He won much contemporary praise for
his "tender tunes and rhymes" and for his comedies,
which took the palm from Plautus and Terence. He
was declared to be

> The flower of our realm
> And Phœnix of our age. [2]

Sebastian Westcott, master of the Paul's boys,
presented plays at court from 1552 to his death in 1582,
and doubtless took an important part in the composition and devising of these entertainments, but the
records present few details of his management. They
give us more information about William Hunnis,
Edwards' successor as master of the children of the
Royal Chapel, and Richard Farrant, master of the

---

[1] A. Wood, *Athenæ Oxonienses*, I. 354.   Nichols, *Progresses of Elizabeth*,
I. 212.

[2] See Barnaby Googe, Turbeville's *Epitaphs* (containing one by Twine
from which the lines above are quoted), Puttenham, and Meres.

children of Windsor. Under these three masters, the choir boys became organized into companies that gave public performances in regular theaters. Farrant, best known as a composer of anthems, appears frequently in the court records as presenting plays, though we have no direct evidence that he wrote any; and in 1576 established a theater in rooms formerly occupied by the Revels Office in Blackfriars. Hunnis was keeper of the Queen's gardens at Greenwich, and in 1572 was paid for supplying "46 bushels of roses, 33 bushels of more roses," and many other flowers for a banqueting house;[1] and in 1774-5 presented a play requiring horns, collars, leashes, dog hooks, bawdricks, timber work, holly, ivy, firpoles, and moss for a rock.[2] He won praise from a contemporary for "Thy enterludes, thy gallant layes, thy roundlets, and thy songs." He seems to have coöperated with Farrant in the Blackfriars, and succeeded him for a time in its management. It should be noted that both of these men, gentlemen of the Royal Chapel, held court offices, and devised their plays under court patronage for court favor. Before the end of their careers other dramatists were writing for the children. Their successors in the management of the children's companies, Nathaniel Giles, Thomas Giles, Henry Evans, and Edward Kirkham, carried on the exploitation of the choir boys as public actors, but do not appear as dramatists.

One of their successors as manager, John Lyly, was an important dramatist. After leaving the university and gaining notable literary success through his novels, he obtained some position under the Earl of Oxford, himself a poet and dramatist, from whom he received

---

[1] Feuillerat, *Revels Accounts*, 165.   [2] *Ibid.*, 244.

considerable gifts. He came under the notice of
Elizabeth, held a seat in parliament, but after long
years of waiting failed to secure the mastership of the
Revels or any other position of importance at court.
In 1583 he was given the lease of Farrant's theater by
the Earl of Oxford, and early in 1584 appeared at court
as manager of the Earl of Oxford's company of children.[1] His career as master and manager, however,
extended only over a few months. His two earliest
plays, "Campaspe," and "Sapho and Phao," both published in 1584, were acted at court by the children of
the Chapel and the children of Paul's.[2] The remaining six plays were all acted by the Paul's boys and four
were given at court. Recent researches into the
biography of Lyly have thrown much light on his relations with his patron, the Earl of Oxford, and his
years of unrewarded writing for royal favor; but they
have not made clear just what were his relations as
dramatist for the children. The epithet "Vicemaster
of Pauls," one of the many derogatory titles applied
to him by Gabriel Harvey, may not have been his
actual title;[3] but it seems probable that after his
brief experience with Oxford's boys at Blackfriars, he
may have been employed as teacher and dramatic
trainer of the Paul's boys, under some arrangement
with Thomas Gyles, who succeeded Westcott as their
master and in 1585 received a royal warrant for taking
up children.[4] Lyly's plays smack of the schoolmaster
as well as of the courtier. As a dramatist, however,

---

[1] Wallace, *Development*, 170–2. Chambers, *Mod. Lang. Review*, Oct.,
1906, p. 7.   [2] See p. 299 n.

[3] See Feuillerat, *John Lyly*, 196 n., for objections to assigning Lyly to this
position, advanced by Baker and Bond. See also Wallace, *Development*,
173.   [4] Wallace, *Children of the Chapel*, 67.

he appears to have succeeded by appeal to popular audiences as well as by the applause of the court. In the support which he received from the Earl of Oxford we have one of the most notable cases of the reward that literary success might win from patronage; but in Lyly's letters and complaints to Burghley we have an interesting record of the failure of court patronage to supply permanent support for literature. In writing for the children's performances in public, Lyly was doubtless eking out a livelihood.

If Lyly is connected with the singing masters who wrote court plays for children, he belongs in other ways with the group of so-called "university wits," who went from Oxford and Cambridge to the service of the public theaters. One of this group, Peele, had a hand in dramas at the university, and wrote at least one play, a pastoral, the "Arraignment of Paris" (pr. 1584), for performance at court by the children of the chapel. The others, Marlowe, Greene, Lodge, and Nash, wrote for the professional companies. There are many points of similarity in the lives of all of these men as well as, more specifically, in their dramatic careers. They were all of humble or middle-class rank in life, all graduates from the universities, and all turned to letters as a career. They tried novels, poems, and pamphlets, and sought with only partial success for patronage. From aspiration for fame and position, they found themselves driven to a Bohemian and squalid life in London, dependent on the booksellers and the theater for means of support. Greene, Peele, and Lodge were nearly of the same age, Marlowe and Nash some years younger; all made their introduction to the drama between the years 1587 and 1593. Greene's career is the most fully illustrative of the struggle for a livelihood through letters and Marlowe's best indicates the opportunities that the theaters gave for literature.

Greene took his A.B. in 1578 and his A.M. in 1583; already (1580) the first part of his novel "Mamillia"

ROBERT GREENE
From " Greene in Conceipt," 1598.

was entered for publication. Henceforth he kept the booksellers busy with novels of one sort and another, moral tales, love stories — prodigal son, euphuistic, arcadian, and pastoral stories. Opportunity was usually left for a continuation, and Part II followed hard on the success of Part I. A promise to abandon love stories for more edifying material would apparently quicken the demand for one more tale of sentiment. Pamphlets exposing the tricksters and sharpers of London made a hit and led to a series in which he successfully exploited the interest in immorality. An occasional repentant pamphlet with personal confessions helped to excite the public interest in the author. In the midst of this busy trafficking with booksellers with a commercial adroitness worthy of our day of popular magazines, Greene saw the possibility of extending the market for his wares. In the stories of two of his prodigals he has romanticized on his experience. In "Never too Late," Francesco is brought to ruin by a faithless courtesan:

"In this humour he fell in among a company of players, who persuaded him to try his wit in writing of comedies, tragedies, or pastorals, and if he could perform anything worth the stage, then they would largely reward him for his pains. Francesco, glad of this motion, seeing a means to mitigate the extremity of his want, thought it no dishonour to make gain of his wit or to get profit by his pen : and therefore, getting him home to his chamber, writ a comedy ; which so generally pleased all the audience that happy were those actors in short time that could get any of his works, he grew so exquisite in that faculty."

In "A Groatsworth of Wit" the incident is amplified. Roberto ("whose life in most part agreeing with mine, found one self punishment as I have done ") has been betrayed by a courtesan and his lamentations are overheard by a stranger who offers assistance to a scholar in distress. Roberto asks how he may be employed.

"'Why, easily,' quoth he, ' and greatly to your benefit; for men of my profession get by scholars their whole living.' 'What is your profession ?' said Roberto. 'Truly, sir,' said he 'I am a player.' 'A player !' quoth Roberto ; 'I took you

z

rather for a gentleman of great living; for if by outward habit men should be censured, I tell you, you would be taken for a substantial man.' 'So am I where I dwell' quoth the player 'reputed able at my proper cost to build a windmill.' Roberto again asked how he was to be employed. 'Why, sir, in making plays,' said the other, 'for which you shall be well paid, if you will take the pains.' Roberto, perceiving no remedy, thought it best to respect his present necessity, [and] to try his wit, went with him willingly.''

We are familiar with Greene's wickedness and subsequent remorse through his abundant confessions, and we have a vivid picture of the squalor and wretchedness of his last illness from the pen of his enemy, Gabriel Harvey. Greene is known as the poet "who saw and practiced such villainy as is abominable to declare," the associate of cutthroats and sharpers, who hid his poverty under gorgeous cloak and doublet, who alternated between excess and penitence, and at thirty-five died miserably under the charitable care of a poor shoemaker and his wife. In the long list of pathetic deaths in literary Bohemia, there is hardly one more moving than his. Unvisited by his literary companions, except the malevolent Harvey, deserted except by the charitable Isams and his miserable mistress and their son, Fortunatus, he made his end in filth and poverty, praying, repenting, writing to his deserted wife, borrowing money for a pot of malmsey, and begging his hostess to crown him when dead with a garland of bays. The really remarkable thing about Greene's life, however, is not its dissipation or dreadful end, but its industry. When we consider the difficulties of rent, heat, light, paper, and ink with which he must often have struggled, the amount that he wrote in the course of ten years would seem to have left little time for wickedness. This industry was carried on constantly under pressure and in response to the immediate demands of the public. There were a few unsuccessful bids for patronage, but virtually all the labors of those ten years of putting ink on paper were in the effort to win pounds, shillings, and pence from the growing public that patronized the book stalls and playhouses. He gave them what they would buy, — but this included poetry and idealized heroines.

Marlowe, too, is supposed to have led a dissolute life, and he had a miserable death. His reputation for atheism was probably in large part due to the character of his plays ; but his association with a group of men who were doing some independent thinking and talking on matters of religion led to serious charges of blasphemy.[1] The consideration of these charges by the Privy Council was interrupted by Marlowe's death at the age of twenty-nine in a tavern brawl at Deptford by the hand of a "bawdy servingman." His few plays, however, had revolutionized the drama and made poetical tragedy a popular success. They took the theaters by storm, aroused every dramatist of the day to imitation, and left for others the inspiration of "brave, translunary things."

The records of theatrical companies are too incomplete to enable us to trace with any exactness the relations of the university wits to the particular companies. Fleay's efforts in this direction have been more productive of error than of knowledge. The general conditions, however, are clear. When Greene, Peele, and Lodge graduated from the universities, the two indoor theaters for children and the two outdoor

---

[1] See the accusation by Richard Baines, reprinted in Boas' ed. of Kyd, cxiii. See also Introduction, lxxi, lxxii.

playhouses for the professionals were all in operation, in addition to various innyards. In 1583, by the time they had won some foothold in London as writers, and Marlowe was graduating at Cambridge, the Queen's men were established under special favor, and some of the other professional companies were nevertheless holding their own. There was a larger and more certain demand for plays than ever before, and the theaters offered a quicker and more profitable appeal to the public than the booksellers. Marlowe does not seem to have left the university for good until 1587, when he received his A.M. degree, and in that year he won an instantaneous success with his "Tamburlaine." Henceforth poets, or at least men who could "hodge up a blank verse," were in demand; and the young university men, hanging about London without definite means of support, were drawn into the service of the companies.

The poets and wits soon became professional dramatists. The playwright came to write for particular companies, and his progress in dramatic technic was rendered rapid by the intimate association with actors and audience that the public theaters afforded. But if a few found regular employment in writing for the companies, there must have been many others who were incited by the success of Marlowe, Greene, and Peele, and composed plays in their manners without obtaining any permanent relations with the actors. Efforts to assign all the plays of the years 1587–93 to four or five well-known dramatists must be viewed with skepticism. The large number of anonymous plays published about 1594 usually show the influence of Marlowe, or Kyd, or Peele; but the majority were probably written by unknown imitators. The names of many playwrights as well as of many plays have doubtless perished; but there seems no question that a half dozen young university men were chiefly responsible for endowing the popular drama with poetic quality and literary ambition. In the main, they were probably free lances selling their plays where they could; but the more successful would naturally become attached to the leading companies and chief actors.

For a time the Queen's men seem to have attracted the best writers, including Peele and Greene. Marlowe's heroes were impersonated by the great tragic actor, Edward Alleyn, and his plays were probably written originally for Alleyn's company. At all events, they were carefully guarded by that company, and on the establishment of the Admiral's men at the Rose in 1594, formed the most valuable part of their repertory. Greene's plays seem to have been scattered upon his death and the breaking up of the Queen's men. Another group of plays, including the two parts of the "Contention of York and Lancaster" (2 and 3 Henry VI), the "Troublesome Reign of King John," the early "Hamlet," the "Taming of a Shrew" passed by somewhat uncertain paths into the hands of Shakespeare's company and furnished material for his revision. The university wits had supplied the companies with repertories.

The deaths of Greene and Marlowe mark the closing of the epoch of the university wits. After the reorganization of companies in 1592–94, the dramatists seem more definitely attached to fixed companies and writing more distinctly at the dictates of manager and actors. Such a change may naturally have followed. At all events, Henslowe's Diary has provided us with full records of the relations of the

dramatists to one manager, from 1597–1600. During
these years, as we have noted, the Admiral's men produced about twenty new plays annually, and these
were written mainly by half a dozen dramatists, working often in collaboration and in haste. We know that
other conditions governed Shakespeare's company,
and also the children's companies. Probably no other
company employed collaborators as extensively as
the Lord Admiral's; but it would be unsafe to consider Henslowe's practice as wholly peculiar. Somewhat similar conditions must have obtained at all
times in the professional companies.[1] A certain number of new plays were needed annually, and men who
knew the actors, had the trick of suiting the public,
could write rapidly, and were certain to have the
fifth act completed on a given day, would be the
dramatists preferred. Similar requirements are made
to-day by editors of newspapers and magazines of their
contributors. Two or three years without any plague
or governmental interference probably raised the
prices and attracted men of talent and writers of reputation; and the possession of one writer of lasting popularity would doubtless be preferred to the service of
half a dozen clever hacks, who could guarantee immediate but not lasting sales. Probably Henslowe
valued highly Marlowe's plays and would have been
glad to possess Shakespeare in his company. In lack
of such sure money earners, he experimented freely
with many.

Henslowe has often been pictured as a merciless
slave-driver and speculator; but, as Mr. Greg has
shown,[2] he acted for the company in dealing with
authors. An author usually received a payment "in

[1] See p. 289. Fleay, *Stage*, 117. Greg, *H. D.*, II. 111 ff.   [2] *Ibid.*, II. 110 ff.

earnest" or "in part," the sum being advanced as a part of the total price, and the company being secured by the deposit of a portion of the manuscript. In case the author failed to complete the play, his unfinished manuscript could be turned over to some one else. Some twenty dramatists, apart from authors of single pieces, wrote for the Lord Admiral's men during the years 1597–1603, when the Diary records payments to authors. Among these were poets and scholars of distinction, as Chapman, Drayton, and Jonson; but others who wrote many plays, as Haughton, R. Wilson, and Hathaway, are known to us only because this cash book of the manager happened to be preserved. The usual price for a play was £6; but this sometimes dropped to £5, and in the later years often rose to £7 or £8, — once in the case of "Patient Grissel" rising to £10 10s. The majority of the plays were the work of collaboration, four men often working on a single piece. In the year 1598, for instance, Chettle, Dekker, Drayton, and Wilson wrote only in collaboration; Chettle having a hand in eighteen plays, Dekker in sixteen, Drayton in fifteen, and Wilson in eleven. Some of them were old plays, which required only slight alterations; but the labor of these dramatists cannot be considered light.

A summary of the payments made to Dekker during this year will indicate the circumstances of employment more fully. On January 8, Dekker received 20s. for an unnamed book; but this order was canceled. On January 15, he received £4 toward "Phaeton." On February 4, he received £2 to discharge him from the Counter, where he was imprisoned, presumably for debt. On March 1, he was paid £5 for the "Triplicity of Cuckolds"; on March 13, £6 5s. in shares with Chettle and Drayton for the "Wars of Henry I, containing the part of a Welshman." The reading of the play in the Sun tavern with suitable refreshment cost 5s., which Henslowe advanced to the company. On March 25 and 30, £6 were paid for "1 Earl Godwin" by the same authors; and between March 30 and April 7, £2 for "Pierce of Exton." In May and June, Dekker divided with Chettle, Drayton, and Wilson, £7 for "1 Black Bateman" and £4 for "2 Earl Godwin." On June 31 (30) he shared with Drayton and Wilson £3 "in earnest of a book called the "Madman's Morris," later raised to £6; and on July 17–28, £6 10s., with the same authors for "1 Hannibal and Hermes"; on July 28–August 10, £5 10s. for "Pierce of Winchester." On August 19 he may have shared in the payment of £6 for "Chance Medley"; and he divided with Drayton, August 30 and September 4, £5 for "2 Hannibal and Hermes"; on September 29, £6 for "1 Civil Wars in France"; October 16, 20, £6 for "Connan Prince of Cornwall"; November 3, £6 for "2 Civil Wars in France"; November 18, December 30, £6 for "3 Civil Wars in France." It would not appear that even as busy a year as this, making allowance for omissions in Henslowe's records, brought Dekker over £30, equivalent to between $1000 and $1500 to-day.

The price of plays was advancing in the later years of the Diary, and it must have continued to rise rapidly. A correspondence between Henslowe and Daborne, dating 1613, has been preserved, which reveals a very different market from that of fifteen years before.[1] This third-rate dramatist is in destitute circumstances and appealing to Henslowe, now manager of the Lady

[1] *Henslowe Papers*, ed. Greg, 67–86. See also *H. D.*, II. 144.

Elizabeth's men, for loans and advances; yet he gets
£20 for a play and threatens to sell one to the King's
men for £25.   For another play, he and Tourneur are
to have £12 and "the overplus of the second day."
This expression raises the question whether dramatists received the proceeds of a benefit performance.
There is no reference to anything of the sort in the
Diary.   Dekker in the prologue of "If It be not Good,
the Devil is in It," acted 1611, speaks of the concern
of the dramatists for "a cramm'd third day," as if
the practice were a novelty.[1] A few of the plays
allude to an author's benefit for the second or third
day.   Later, the benefit performances for the Master
of the Revels indicate that the practice may have been
in more general use.   Further, the fact that benefits
for dramatists were an established custom in the
Restoration suggests that they were in vogue before
the closing of the theaters.   Just what Daborne's
"overplus" was, we can only guess, perhaps all above
a fixed sum.   There can be little doubt that the companies often used some such scheme for enabling the
author to share in the profits.   But the size and nature
of the benefit doubtless depended on various conditions.   The low price paid by the Admiral's men hints
that some additional recompense may have been provided for their regular authors; but such reward, if it
existed, was not sufficient to keep most of them from
poverty and debt.

A survey of Henslowe's Diary gives a vivid idea of
the demand for new plays, and the industry practiced
by both playwrights and actors.   But such conditions
as prevailed in the Admiral's company must have

---

[1] Collier, *H. E. D. P.*, III. 424–6.   W. J. Lawrence, *Elizabethan Playhouse*, 2d series, 97 n., 101.

failed to maintain or incite the best talent. A few notable plays, as Dekker's "Shoemaker's Holiday," resulted; but the great bulk of plays were never printed and probably deserved their fate. Written in haste to meet the needs of the day, they represent the efforts of writers who had no share in the profits of the company and no hope of personal distinction through such piecemeal collaboration. We turn from such hack work to more favorable conditions.

In the first mention of Shakespeare that has come down to us, Greene accused his younger rival of plagiarism, and taunted him with being an actor. Greene felt it presumptuous for an actor to attempt to rival the university wits and to make over their plays. Contemptuous references to Shakespeare the actor winning popular favor as poet and dramatist are also to be found in the university plays, "1 and 2 Return from Parnassus." But the stage had become a democratic institution, and men of all classes, callings, and degrees of education were trying their hands at plays. If R. W., the author of two interesting comedies of the eighties, "Three Ladies of London" and "Three Lords and Three Ladies of London," was Robert Wilson, the famous actor of the Queen's men, he antedated Marlowe and Greene and offers the first notable case of an actor who turned playwright. There were many later, but very few maintained the double employment, or continued to profit from their share in the company and their pay for the plays. There are only two of importance, Heywood and Shakespeare.

Heywood probably began to write plays as early as 1594, and appears frequently in the Diary as collaborator. He was also an actor, and on March 25, 1598, bound himself as Henslowe's covenant servant for two years. His first appearance, however, as a share-holder in a company was with the Worcester's men, in 1602. After James' accession, Heywood continued as a shareholder in the company, now under the patron-age of Queen Anne, until her death in 1619. His further connection with companies cannot be traced, although he seems to have written regularly for the Queen Henrietta's men, and he continued to write plays, pageants for the Lord Mayor's shows, and many non-dramatic works until his death, about 1640.

Heywood may have been a university man; at all events, he was an omnivorous reader and wrote about everything. For twenty-five years, at least, he was both an actor and playwright, and he continued to write plays after he had given up acting. Less than forty plays extant and non-extant can be assigned to him; but in the preface to his "English Traveller," 1633, he writes of "this tragi-comedy, being one reserved amongst two hundred and twenty in which I have had either an entire hand, or at the least a main finger." This statement has been questioned by Fleay and others, but there seems no reason for doubting it. If we recall that Dekker had a main finger in as many as sixteen plays in a single year, Heywood's forty years of writing might easily account for over two hundred. There are modern writers of popular plays who have equaled or surpassed his output. Like Dekker, Hey-wood often wrote hastily, with an eye to the vulgar and uncritical audiences; but like Dekker again, he was a poet of "sweetness and gentleness." He was guilty of some extraordinary vulgarizations of classical story and of plays like the "Bold Beauchamps" that delighted the apprentices but stirred the laughter of Beaumont and Fletcher. But he was also the author of "A Woman Killed with Kindness." Few men have worked more industriously; or, if we may judge from his writings, lived more genially.

Of Shakespeare's first experiences as an actor we know nothing; but by 1592, the date of Greene's attack, he was presumably well known in London both as an actor and a playwright. The next two years saw the appearance in print of his two narrative poems, and a growth of a friendship with a noble patron, the Earl of Southampton. The first reference to him as a member of a company comes in the record of March 15, 1595, when along with Kemp and Burbage, he received payment for the performance of two comedies before the Queen at Greenwich in the Christmas season of 1594. He was thus already recognized as a leading member of the company to which he remained attached until his retirement from the theater. Whether through a patron, as a doubtful tradition has it, or, as is more likely, through profit as an actor and playwright, he acquired position and property so rapidly that in 1596 his father, probably at his instigation, applied to the College of Heralds for a grant of arms, and on May 4, 1597, he purchased New Place in Stratford for sixty pounds.

This rapid rise in financial prosperity has more parallels among actors than among dramatists. Alleyn acquired a great fortune, and Burbage and most of the members of Shakespeare's company left comfortable estates. But it is a factitious distinction that credits his fortune to his acting and makes nothing of the profits of his pen. Shakespeare's income came largely as a member of a theatrical company, but there can be no doubt that his value to that company was as a maker rather than as an actor of plays.

His financial success may be in part credited to his business acumen, but some credit must be given to the management of the company in which he was so long a leading member. The history of the Lord Chamberlain-King's men shows, as we have seen, some striking contrasts with that of their chief rivals, the Lord Admiral-Prince's men. Instead of mulcting the shareholders for the benefit of the theater owner and entrepreneur, the leading members were given shares in the theaters; and instead of employing a host of hack writers, they seem to have relied largely on the genius of one leading dramatist. When Shakespeare's name appears in the court records along with those of Burbage and Kemp, it must be taken as a recognition of his services as an author, for certainly his reputation as an actor did not compare with that of his two colleagues. When with a few other members of the company, he was given shares in the Globe, and later in the Blackfriars, we must again consider these profitable transactions as recognitions of his great value to the company. At all events, the company was so conducted that it received Shakespeare's undivided services as a dramatist, and it gave him such a share in its profits that he was able to retire from the theater as a landed gentleman before he was fifty.

On what terms he wrote for the company we do not know; but it would be absurd to estimate his returns at the rates paid by Henslowe. We have seen that members in a company might receive, in addition to the profits from their shares, salaries as managers or actors, or for other specific services. There may have been some sort of continuation contract, by which Shakespeare was bound to write only for the company, and in return received an extra share in the proceeds, or a fixed sum for a play. Certainly as soon as any authors had benefit days, he received the same privilege. Further, as his services continued, his receipts for a play doubtless increased. After 1603, when his name appears as an actor in "Sejanus," we hear no more of him as an actor; but no doubt his income continued as a shareholder in the company and as a housekeeper in both the Globe and the Blackfriars. He seems to have written with great regularity, usually bringing out two plays a year, thirty-seven plays in twenty years, and nearly all without collaborators. While his company appreciated the money-making value of his dramas, he was not forced to any such rate of productivity as Dekker or Heywood. His income in the later years has been estimated by Sir Sidney Lee at £700.[1] The evidence is too conflicting for any accurate estimate of the receipts, which of course varied greatly from year to year; but the total sum seems a little excessive.

The conditions under which Shakespeare wrote his plays may well seem humble in comparison with the splendor of their enduring reputation. But no other Elizabethan dramatist was so well paid or wrote under circumstances more favorable to successful drama. As Professor Brander Matthews has suggested,[2] the conditions are strikingly similar to those under which Molière wrote a few years later. Each dramatist was an actor, a leader in his company, living on terms of intimacy with his fellow actors; each was attentive to the requirements of actors and audiences, and each was a master of stage craft. Both profited from the patronage of the court as well as from the favor of the public, and neither seems to have been concerned

---

[1] *Life of Shakespeare*, new ed., 315.   [2] *Molière*, chap. xxi.

about printing his plays or conscious that they would bring him lasting fame. Each shared the rich life of his observation and imagination with his theater and company, careless whether it passed on through the printed page to posterity. And although both were aware of the inadequacy of their theaters to represent the worlds of their imaginations, they were intent on making the very most of such means as the stage afforded. If Molière's theater was the more highly developed, Shakespeare at least had the best advantages that the Elizabethan stage offered.

Some years after Shakespeare and Heywood had established themselves as playwrights, the inducements offered to that profession seem to have undergone a marked improvement. The revival of the children's companies and the establishment of the Chapel children in Burbage's Blackfriars theater about 1600 furnished a new market for plays. The children no longer confined themselves to a particular class of plays, but rivaled the adult companies in all kinds, and attracted the services of a brilliant group of dramatists — Chapman, Jonson, Middleton, and Marston. The accession of James I also brought virtual monoply to the leading companies, and more peformances at court. There is a marked improvement in the profits and standing of dramatists. The increase in price is shown by Daborne's receiving £20 for a play from Henslowe. The improvement in general standing is shown by the efforts for literary fame made by such dramatists as Chapman and Jonson, and by the accession of men of birth and social position, as Beaumont and Fletcher. The profession of dramatist had won a higher status, whether judged by financial, social, or literary standards.

Jonson's career as a man of letters illustrates some of these differences. Of humble birth, without university education, for a time an actor and a writer for Henslowe, he succeeded in winning high estimation at court as well as in the theaters, and among distinguished scholars as well as among his fellow dramatists. He was happy at times to "leave the loathed stage" for the more secure support of court or patrons, and for many years wrote nothing for the public theaters. He devoted much time and his best energies to the composition of librettos for the elaborate entertainments into which he and Inigo Jones had developed the court masques. Yet his main work was done for the public theaters. As a dramatist he was an avowed reformer, seeking to bring classicist principles and precepts to bear on the contemporary stage, and he prided himself on writing as a scholar and a poet, and without too much regard for popular favor. He represents a conscious effort to give the drama literary aims and values, and he was the first of the Elizabethan dramatists to take pains as to the publication of his plays.

Though he had probably been writing plays for several years, he is first heard of as a dramatist in Henslowe's records for December 3, 1597, and he appears there as receiving payments from time to time until June 22, 1602. His services, however, were not monopolized by Henslowe; for in 1598 his "Every Man in His Humour" was produced by the Chamberlain's men, and followed the next year by a companion piece, "Every Man Out of His Humour." By 1600 he had also formed somewhat close relations with the Children of the Chapel at Blackfriars; for in that year they produced "Cynthia's Revels"; and in 1601 the "Poetaster," plays dealing in personal satire and

involving Jonson in the quarrel among the companies
as well as the poets. Nevertheless, in 1601–2, Jonson
was again writing for Henslowe, and in 1603 the King's
men produced his "Sejanus" with Shakespeare as
one of the actors. In the last half dozen years of
Elizabeth's reign, Jonson was selling plays to three
leading companies; and though during part of this
time he may have been an actor, and though he seemingly engaged in the rivalries of the companies, yet he
clearly maintained himself free from dependence upon
any one of them.

The first decade of the reign of James was Jonson's
best period. It was not free from trouble, as he was
twice in prison over difficulties about his plays, and
once in danger of more serious punishment. But it
was the time of his best comedies and of many
masques and other court entertainments. His plays
were no longer sold to the Prince's (Admiral's) men;
but to either the King's men or the Blackfriars' children, though in 1614 he wrote for Henslowe, now
manager of the Lady Elizabeth's company. Jonson
prided himself on his care in dramatic writing, boast-
ing of two years spent on one play; and the list of
plays and masques of this decade suggests that the
recompense was sufficiently large to permit some leisure in composition.

1603. Sejanus.   King's men at the Globe.
        Entertainment for the King at Althorpe.
        Entertainment for the Coronation (in collaboration).
1604. Eastward Hoe (collab.). Children at Blackfriars.
        Entertainment at Highgate.
1605. Volpone. King's men at Globe, and at both uni-
            versities.
        Masque of Blackness.

2 A

1606.   Speech to the King at Merchant Taylors' school.
         Masque of Hymenæi.
         Barriers.
1607.   Two Entertainments at Theobalds.
         Masque of Beauty.
1608.   Hue and Cry after Cupid.   Court Masque.
1609.   Epicœne.   Children at Blackfriars.
         Masque of Queens.
1610.   Prince Henry's Barriers.
         Alchemist.   King's men.
1611.   Catiline.   King's men.
         Masque of Oberon.
         Love Freed from Ignorance and Folly.   Masque.
1612.   Love Restored.   Masque.
         A Challenge at Tilt.
1613.   The Irish Masque.
1614.   Bartholomew Fair.   Lady Elizabeth's at the Hope.

As the usual payment for a masque was £50, his income from plays and masques must have averaged
£60 or more a year, and he doubtless received additional gifts.   For much of the period he was living
with Lord d'Aubigny, and in 1613 he was in France as
tutor of Sir Walter Raleigh's son.   Manifestly, his
plays were written for the stage under very different
circumstances from the sixteen in which Dekker
collaborated during a single year, or from the two which
Shakespeare produced annually for his fellow shareholders of the King's men.

Jonson soon after 1614 gave up the stage for a time,
was the recipient of pensions, and seems to have enjoyed more of the favors of patronage than any other
Elizabethan dramatist.   In the end, his quarrel with
Inigo Jones lost him the lucrative employment of
writing masques; there was a cessation of royal favor,

and he was forced back to the theater for means of livelihood. But he proved as arrogant as ever toward the public to which he returned for support.

Other men of letters, as Chapman, Daniel, and Drayton, wrote for the stage, but found their main employment outside of the theater. The career of Fletcher, on the other hand, illustrates the circumstances under which the leading regular dramatists wrote in the reigns of James I and Charles I.

Fletcher, the son of one of Elizabeth's favorite bishops, began writing as a sort of disciple of Jonson. His plays were almost from the beginning popular successes, and soon obtained for him a reputation as a poet equaling if not surpassing that of any contemporary. His popularity on the stage, however, was won from somewhat different audiences from those which kept Heywood busy. He wrote for the more fashionable circles, the courtiers and their imitators, those who crowded the streets about Blackfriars with their coaches. Indeed, he probably greatly contributed to the changes which made Jacobean drama less representative of the national temper as a whole and more responsive to the court and its followers than the Elizabethan. He began writing plays soon after the accession of James and contributed to various children's companies as well as to the King's men. The great plays of the Beaumont-Fletcher collaboration, however, were written for the King's men at the very time that this company was also producing the mature triumphs of Jonson and Shakespeare. Beaumont ceased writing for the stage by 1612, and Fletcher continued to write for other companies as well as the King's men until about 1613. In that year the King's men acted "Henry VIII" and the "Two Noble Kinsmen," both probably written by direct collaboration between Fletcher and Shakespeare. And the complete retirement of Shakespeare from the stage seems to have resulted in Fletcher's taking his place as chief dramatist for the company. To the great repertory which they already possessed, Fletcher added some four plays each year until his death in 1625. From 1619 on, our records are sufficiently full to establish the dates of twenty-two of these plays; from 1613–18, the dates rest on insecure evidence but indicate a similar rate of production, since there are seventeen plays to be assigned to these six years. A large part of his work was in collaboration; of the sixty plays in which he had a share about one third were by him alone; so his rate of production was not much greater than Shakespeare's.

Of the business relations between Fletcher and the company we have no direct information. He was neither an actor, nor a shareholder, nor a lessee of the theater. It seems probable, however, that he had some kind of continuation contract with the company and had some share in the profits which he helped to create. We may be sure that he received more for a play than any other dramatist of the time. He did no other writing, not even masques; and, so far as we know, had no patron and held no position from court or city. He lived in intimate relations with some of his fellow dramatists, and he certainly knew his theater and his audience. There are no indications in his case of the extreme poverty of the earlier playwrights, and we may presume that his four plays a year brought him adequate means of support.

Fletcher began collaboration with his intimate friend Beaumont, continued with Shakespeare and others, and then for a large number of plays with

Massinger. In most cases it seems likely that a scenario was first prepared, then the scenes divided between the two authors, and that each author wrote without much coöperation from the other. Owing to the distinct and mannered style of Fletcher, modern criticism has been able to separate his share with some certainty; and in most cases it is confined to definite scenes or portions of scenes. This method of collaboration appears to have been common throughout our period, and was indeed sometimes enforced upon the dramatists by Henslowe's system. Fletcher was not subject to that kind of compulsion, and in some of his plays with Beaumont the collaboration seems to have been more intimate and the writing not easily to be disentangled. In many cases, of course, and in some of the Beaumont-Fletcher-Massinger group, collaboration was not direct but consisted in the revision by one author of an old play by another.

The relations of the dramatists to the companies after the death of Fletcher offer few innovations. Though the social and literary status of the profession of dramatists was far higher than forty years earlier, it still included a very heterogeneous body of writers — courtiers, scholars, poets, lawyers, and preachers of various degrees of ability and reputation. Shirley might receive personal advice from King Charles in regard to the plot of his "Gamester"; or Ben Jonson's servant Brome might as a dramatic disciple surpass his master in popularity. In the main, the companies seem to have relied on a few poets, as Massinger and Shirley, who wrote regularly and who were well trained both in the traditions of the drama and the habits of the stage. The standing of the theater both in literature and at court served, however, to excite a large number of amateurs and dilettantes to try playwrighting. Young preachers at Oxford and young courtiers at London tried their hands at tragedies, tragi-comedies, and comedies designed to win both a place on Parnassus and the favor of the King. These plays were usually given at the university or at court; but some of them got a hearing at the public theaters. Sir Nicholas in Shirley's "Witty Fair One," 1633, queries, "What makes so many scholars, then, come from Oxford and Cambridge with dossers full of lamentable tragedies and ridiculous comedies, which they might here vent to the players, but they will take no money for them?" It is not clear whether Shirley means that the authors cannot hire the actors to perform these plays, or merely that the companies will not buy them, but it is certain that had Oxford preachers, as Goffe and Cartwright, and favorite courtiers, as Killigrew, Carlell, and Suckling never succeeded in having their plays performed, the English drama would be little the loser. The leading companies were now, like the patented companies of the eighteenth century, in possession of large repertories, and a main part of each season's offering must have consisted in stock plays. The favorites of Ford, Massinger, Heywood, Beaumont and Fletcher, Jonson, and Shakespeare might be given many times each year and were frequently called for at court. The demand for new plays was therefore considerably restricted; and imitation of the masters became inevitable on the part of both the amateurs and the best writers of the day. The theaters were the administrators of a great inheritance but they no longer attracted the more daring imaginations. Men wrote plays under the inspiration of Jonson or Fletcher or Shakespeare, to please the portion of the public dominated by the court.

Something remains to be said in regard to the ownership, licensing, and publishing of plays. The dramatist
usually surrendered ownership of a play to the company.
The actors submitted a copy to the Master of the
Revels and, if approved by that official, paid a fee for
a license to act. In addition to the manuscript presented to the censor, at least one other copy was
required to be cut up into parts for the actors, and one
copy remained in the archives of the company. In
some cases other copies were made and distributed
among friends or patrons of the author.[1] If the play
was successful on the stage, it was carefully guarded
from the booksellers.

Plays came into the booksellers' hands in various
ways. If a company broke up, its plays were sold to
other companies or the booksellers, hence the large
number of quartos printed in 1594, after the great
plague year 1593, and the breaking of several companies; and again in 1607–8, after the cessation of
the Paul's boys and Blackfriars children. Sometimes
plays were obtained surreptitiously either by buying
manuscripts, or by sending stenographers to the theaters. Several statements by Heywood refer to this
practice of stealing popular plays by stenography, and
also to other conditions governing the printing. One
occurs in the preface to his "Rape of Lucrece," 1630:

To the Reader. — It hath beene no custome in mee of all
other men (courteous Reader) to commit my plaies to the
presse: the reason though some may attribute to my owne
insufficiencie, I had rather subscribe in that to their seuare
censure then by seeking to auoide the imputation of weaknes
to incurre greater suspition of honestie: for though some haue

---

[1] For example, see prefaces to Beaumont and Fletcher's *Knight of the
Burning Pestle*, *A King and No King*, *Philaster*, quarto of 1622.

vsed a double sale of their labours, first to the Stage, and after to the presse, For my owne part I heere proclaime my selfe euer faithfull in the first, and neuer guiltie of the last: yet since some of my plaies haue (vnknowne to me, and without any of my direction) accidentally come into the Printers hands, and therefore so corrupt and mangled, (copied only by the eare) that I have bin as vnable to know them, as ashamed to chalenge them, This therefore, I was the willinger to furnish out in his natiue habit: first being by consent, next because the rest haue beene so wronged in being publisht in such sauadge and ragged ornaments: accept it courteous Gentlemen, and prooue as fauorable Readers as we haue found you gratious Auditors.   Yours T. H.

The second is in Heywood's "Pleasant Dialogues and Dramas," 1637, the prologue to "If you know not me, you know no bodie"; Or, "The troubles of Queen Elizabeth."   It is as follows:

A Prologue to the Play of Queene Elizabeth as it was last revived at the Cock-pit, in which the Author taxeth the most corrupted copy now imprinted, which was published without his consent.

PROLOGUE

Playes have a fate in their conception lent,
Some so short liv'd, no sooner shew'd than spent;
But borne to-day, to morrow buried, and
Though taught to speake, neither to goe nor stand.
This: (by what fate I know not) sure no merit,
That it disclaimes, may for the age inherit.
Writing 'bove one and twenty: but ill nurst,
And yet receiv'd as well perform'd at first,
Grac't and frequented, for the cradle age,
Did throng the Seates, the Boxes and the Stage
So much: that some by Stenography drew
The plot: put it in print: (scarce one word trew:)

And in that lamnesse it hath limp't so long,
The Author now to vindicate that wrong
Hath tooke the paines, upright upon its feete
To teache it walke, so please you sit, and see'st.

The third passage occurs in the address to the reader prefixed to "The English Traveller," 1633 :

True it is that my plays are not exposed to the world in volumes, to bear the titles of Works (as others). One reason is that many of them by shifting and changing of companies have been negligently lost; others of them are still retained in the hands of some actors who think it against their peculiar profit to have them come in print; and a third that it was never any great ambition in me in this kind to be voluminously read.

Heywood implies that dishonesty was practiced in selling the same play to the stage and to the press, and declares that he had obtained the special consent of the theatrical company to the publication of a correct edition. Most of the dramatists, especially before 1600, shared Heywood's indifference to publication, and few quartos appear with the direct authorization of the authors; and then only when a pirated edition forced the publication of a more correct copy. The practice of Ben Jonson seems to have aided in making authors more regardful of publication. In the years 1600–12 nine of his plays appeared in quarto shortly after they were acted, and in most cases under his direction. In 1616 appeared a folio edition of his "Works" carefully revised by him. The numerous cavils by his contemporaries on plays printed as 'Works' perhaps indicate the unusual character of the proceeding. Seven years later, some of the leading members of Shakespeare's company published the

collected edition of his plays, drawn in most instances
from copies in possession of the company. The
issuing of quartos with dedications to some patron had
already become frequent, and continued to be a source of
some profit to the dramatist. A play that failed on
the stage was often given a trial with the press. Yet
the leading dramatists took very little interest in publication, and the companies continued to guard their
manuscripts from the booksellers. No play with
Beaumont's name on the title page appeared before
the year of his death. The two published, anony-
mously, the "Woman Hater" and "Knight of the
Burning Pestle," had been released by the breaking
of the children's companies. Indeed, only nine of the
fifty-six plays of the Beaumont-Fletcher folio had appeared before Fletcher's death; and the "Maid's Tragedy" and "Philaster" were issued ten or twelve years
after they were first acted, and then in pirated and
corrupt editions. The first collection (incomplete) in
folio did not appear until after the civil war, and
twenty-two years after Fletcher's death.

It seems probable that the chief reason why the authors did not publish was because the company wished
to preserve the plays from the public. The booksellers
found the issuing of plays profitable, and not only obtained manuscript surreptitiously, but did not hesitate
to put attractive names, as Shakespeare, on the title
page of anonymous plays. A quarto was a small
pamphlet which sold for sixpence. The profits have
usually been assumed to have gone to the booksellers.
It seems evident, however, that when the booksellers
were so eager to print they would have paid good sums
for manuscript either to the company or the author.
Heywood's charge of dishonesty indicates that some

authors sold their plays to booksellers as well as to the theaters, and we may be certain that there were honorable ways by which the author might share in the profits of his quartos. If those profits seem small, we must remember the price paid for a play by the actors was sometimes as low as £5; a 10 per cent royalty on a basis of 1000 quartos would bring £2. Still, it is manifest that no dramatist made considerable proceeds from the publishing of his plays.

Our survey of the careers of a few dramatists has illustrated some of the changing conditions, but must also have suggested some common characteristics which distinguish the lives of dramatic poets during the entire period. Modern writers have often commented on the violent and Bohemian qualities of this existence; and we have noted many instances of quarrels and poverty. Greene lived in dissipation and died in misery; Dekker spent much time in prison; Marlowe was charged with blasphemy and killed in a brawl; Jonson killed a fellow actor in a duel, and was like to lose his ears because of libel; Nash, Chapman, and Middleton were in serious danger from the authorities of the law. Litigation was frequent in the life of Shakespeare, and lively quarrels in the career of Jonson. Tales of drinking and adultery are among the traditions that Dame Gossip has attached to the names of nearly all the playwrights. It was a violent age in comparison with our own. Vices and virtues jostled one another in the street as well as in literature. Variety of experience and intensity of emotions were the very characteristics of the age that craved for literary expression. Other times, other vices; and perhaps on the mere issue of personal morality, our Elizabethans could make out a case for themselves in comparison

with the romanticists who, from the fall of the Bastille
to the Reform Bill, were the glory of our literature.
But no one will attempt to make out a clean bill of
morals for these men of an age, cruder than our own
but perhaps better suited to encourage vigorous per-
sonality and imagination.   It is, however, worth while
to observe that their Bohemia was not a place mainly
for quarrels and brawls, but for friendly association
and appreciation.

In the small city with its few theaters these makers
of plays necessarily lived on terms of intimacy   And
the record of friendships surpasses that of enmities.
Among writers, jealousy is supposed to be the prevailing vice; but there are many words of admiration
from the Elizabethans for their fellows.   Ben Jonson
quarreled with nearly every one and he left some
sharp words of criticism for many of his friends; but
he made up most of his quarrels and wrote the most
eloquent eulogy of the time on his great rival, Shakespeare.   He was indeed the acknowledged king of those
festivals of wit and comradeship in the Mermaid tavern, that Beaumont lovingly described:

> What things have we seen
> Done at the Mermaid ! heard words that have been
> So nimble, and so full of subtle flame,
> As if that every one from whence they came
> Had meant to put his whole wit in a jest,
> And had resolved to live a fool the rest
> Of his dull life.

To the many praises of this convivial felicity from
Jonson's disciples, we may append the sketch that
Dekker drew in "A Knight's Conjuring" of the poets
in the Elysian fields, a Bohemian Elysium.

In another company sat learned Watson, industrious Kyd, ingenious Atchlow, and, though he had been a player moulded out of their pens, yet because he had been their lover and a register to the Muses, inimitable Bentley; these were likewise carousing to one another at the holy well, some of them singing pæans to Apollo, some of them hymns to the rest of the gods, whilst Marlowe, Greene, and Peele had got under the shades of a large vine, laughing to see Nash, that was but newly come to their college, still haunted with the sharp and satirical spirit that followed him here upon earth; for Nash inveighed bitterly, as he had wont to do, against dry-fisted patrons, accusing them of his untimely death, because if they had given his muse that cherishment which she most worthily deserved, he had been fed to his dying day on fat capons, burnt sack and sugar and not so desperately have ventured his life and shortened his days by keeping company with pickle herrings. . . . He had no sooner spoken this, but in comes Chettle sweating and blowing by reason of his fatness; to welcome whom, because he was of old acquaintance, all rose up and fell presently on their knees, to drink a health to all the lovers of Helicon: in doing which they made such a mad noise that all this conjuring, which is past, being but a dream, I suddenly started up, and am now awake.

Nor were the dramatists without friendships outside the limits of Bohemia. Even in the early days, the free-thinking club that Marlowe frequented may have brought him into association with Sir Walter Raleigh. Jonson's patrons and friends numbered many of the great lords and ladies, and his friendships included all that was best in English scholarship and letters. The plays of Fletcher and Shakespeare are enough in themselves to testify to their authors' wide acquaintance with many varieties of ladies and gentlemen.

It is the relations of the dramatists with the actors, however, that is of most concern to a history of the stage. In discussing their connections with the companies, we have found varying conditions, but in all cases indications of intimacy. It is a mistake to suppose, as did Fleay, that every playwright was at any given period attached to a single company; nevertheless few dramatists wrote without having a given group of actors in view. The greater dramatists were nearly all associated for long periods with particular companies and their plays were unquestionably conditioned by their actors' abilities and wishes. The universal practice was that familiar in stock companies down to recent times. A dozen actors with boys and supernumeraries presented an extensive repertory, and undoubtedly to each actor was assigned similar parts in the many plays. We can surmise with some certainty who took the leading tragic and comic parts in some of the plays of Shakespeare[1] and Fletcher; but we cannot trace the many ways in which their knowledge of the actor's capabilities and peculiarities influenced their creation of situation and character. Certain it is that in no period of our theater were actors and poets more closely associated.

The part played by patronage is not easy to estimate, and varied, of course, with individual writers. It might come through large gifts such as Lyly, Jonson, and perhaps Shakespeare received. It might involve the poet in political entanglements and partisanship, as in the cases of Jonson and Massinger. It might result in pensions and appointments, as for Jonson, Middleton, and Davenant. It is clear, however, that there was no Macænas, and no great rewards.

[1] Brander Matthews, *Shakespeare as a Playwright*, chap. ix.

Patronage extraneous from the theaters, given to men as individuals or poets, had, so far as we know, little influence one way or another on their dramatic writing. Another kind of favor came from the successful performance of plays at court, and was shared by both dramatists and actors. Jonson has spoken of Shakespeare's flights that captivated Elizabeth and James; and doubtless some of the most triumphant moments of his experience were when he saw his words win from the great Queen the same tributes of laughter and tears that they had aroused in the crowded Globe. The plays of Fletcher, and after him of Shirley, seem to have been no less popular at court than in the city. But these dramatists won their rewards from the court through the companies and after they had succeeded in the regular theaters.

The first decision came from the public. The stage was the direct avenue from poet to people. Through it came money, prestige, and fame. If the poets were on intimate terms with the actors, they had a hardly less close acquaintanceship with their audiences. And though they wrote to please actors, audience, or patron, or King, they never forgot their calling as poets. Even the sorriest of them had some visions of the beauty of words and the melody of verse. It was often this delight in poetry that brightened the long hours of poverty and gave dignity to drudgery, or asked for its crown of bays at the moment of squalid death. It was Dekker who in old age wrote, "I have been a priest in Apollo's temple many years; my voice is decaying with my age."[1] The bright god was with them in prison, court, or tavern, and they made the playhouses his temples.

[1] Dedication, *Match Me in London*, 1631.

CHAPTER XIII

ACTORS AND ACTING

In other chapters we have considered the organization of the actors in companies and their relations with the government, the theaters, and the dramatists. Here I shall examine what little data there is that bears on the character of the acting and glance at what is known of the careers of some representative actors.

At the beginning of the sixteenth century, though the profession of the actor was not well established, the practice of play acting had a long tradition. The Miracle plays had given abundant experience to a considerable portion of the population both as actors and as audience; and many of the most effective situations in both tragic and comic drama had received presentation on the medieval stage. Abraham's sacrifice of Isaac, the Maries at the cross, Noah's wife and her gossips, and the effrontery and exposure of Mak may serve to remind us of the opportunities for the dramatic art enjoyed by generations. There can be no doubt that the medieval actors acquired great competence in the mimicry of emotion and in the clear enunciation of verse.

The established practice of acting, however, grew and changed rapidly in England from about 1500 on, both as an amateur and a professional exercise. In the main, the amateur's acting need not detain us

368

EDWARD ALLEYN

From the picture at Dulwich College.

except to note its prevalence and its effect on the professional. The performances at schools, universities, and courts were the chief, but by no means the only exhibition of amateur skill. Every schoolmaster was a Holofernes and many a band of English mechanics had a histrionic leader in some Bottom. The situation might be compared with athletics in England during the last generation or two. At first reserved mainly for the upper classes and schools and a few professionals employed by them, dramatics soon became the employment and interest of the general public, which, as in the case of football, soon preferred the part of an audience but supported professionals of increasing prowess. Indeed the professional actors in sixteenth-century England relied on an appreciative public interest not unlike that which professional athletes receive to-day in Great Britain and in the United States.

What strikes the modern student in the records of these amateurs is their extraordinary audacity. They hesitated at nothing and remained unconscious of what seem to us absurd improprieties. Holofernes' effort to present the nine worthies and Bottom's essay at Pyramus and Thisbe, lion, wall, and moonlight, are doubtless burlesques that came close to truth. Hardly less absurd are the actual records of some of the performances.

Amateur acting is rarely free from absurdity and misdirected ambition; but that of the sixteenth century lacked the restraints and proprieties that custom establishes. The new worlds of the Classics and the Americas that had dawned on men's imaginations stimulated histrionic ambition without imposing any restraining guides. After a time, certain things became recognized as difficult if not impossible on the stage, and there came to be certain ways of representing the Olympian deities, fairies, and Indians, as well as kings, villains, and clowns. For a time, however, acting, as well as literature, must have been romantic in the sense that it let aspiration and fancy run beyond knowledge. Jupiter and Venus descended upon many an amateur stage; nymphs and Turks cavorted in the court masques; and a mermaid or satyr might pop out from any bush to offer an address to traveling royalty. The traditions of the medieval stage gave license to the presentation of almost anything, and the new matter brought from school and court only added fuel to the fire. The professionals soon developed a technic and repertory of their own, but amateur practice had made it inevitable that the repertory should be extensive and the technic daring.

One class of actors, the children, both as amateurs and professionals, are peculiar to the Elizabethan theater. In the courts of the Tudors we have seen that choir boys gained prominence as actors and after a time gave public performances in rivalry with the adult professionals. In the hands of these children a particular kind of play arose, with songs and dances, mythological persons and plots, many female parts, and with a lively and witty dialogue, in which pages were the leaders. As the drama was developing, one of the first divisions of labor was to give over to the children some of the mythological, fanciful, and romantic presentations that fitted ill with the habits of the traveling actors. Such plays as Edwards's "Damon and Pithias," "Appius and Virginia," Peele's "Old Wives Tale" and "Arraignment of Paris," and all Lyly's pieces are typical children's plays. In this comedy of Lyly, verbal wit and fanciful language are suited to children, and neither the passions nor characters are presented with a depth or subtlety requiring mature experience. This is true even of such a successor to Lyly's plays as Shakespeare's "Midsummer Night's Dream," which must have been intended, in the fairy parts, for children, and which must also have been devised for a court entertainment.

One other division of labor had, at a still earlier date, assigned to boys all female parts. Each adult company had two or three to take the parts of women or pages. In the children's plays, these female parts are often numerous, but in plays by adults there are rarely more than two of any length. The length is indeed much restricted, Shakespeare's heroines being much less talkative than his heroes. The fact that there were no woman actors and that all the elements of interest which actresses bring to the stage were left in the hands of boys had, of course, great influence on the drama. The Elizabethan drama is, in comparison with that of later periods, a very masculine affair. Yet Shakespeare's women could hardly have been conceived, if the boys had not been skillful and charming in their parts.

In one particular indeed, the influence of the boy actors is noticeable, the tendency of the heroines to masquerade as pages. Julia, Portia, Nerissa, Jessica, Viola, Rosalind, and Imogen appear on the stage as handsome youths, and in this respect found admirable portrayal. Quince's assurance to Flute that he may wear a mask has been taken to indicate that masks were often worn, especially in female parts; but they were rare, we may be sure, except in such companies as Quince and Bottom presented at the court of

Theseus. Even after the Restoration Kynaston played the heroine with great acceptance. In Fletcher's "Loyal Subject," Pepys records that "he made the loveliest lady that ever I saw in my life." And of his power to excite sympathy and pity, Downes in "Roscius Anglicanus" declares "it has since been disputable among the judicious whether any woman that succeeded him so sensibly touched the audience as he."

The skill of the boys as actors led to a revival of the children's companies toward the end of Elizabeth's reign. These companies now had little more than nominal connection with the choirs, and were made up of boys especially chosen and trained for acting, and in the private theaters of St. Paul's, Blackfriars, and Whitefriars they essayed all kinds of plays. Music was still a feature of their performances, but mainly as a supplementary concert or piece between the acts. The plays themselves were no longer confined to spectacular and refined drama, but included the most gruesome tragedies and most immoral comedies. We have very little information that bears on their way of acting or on the reasons that won the popular favor. In "Hamlet," Shakespeare speaks of their popularity and their part in satirical plays, and Ben Jonson has left a well-known tribute to Salathiel Pavy, one of these little eyases.

> Weep with me, all you that read
>   This little story
> And know, for whom a tear you shed
>   Death's self is sorry.
> 'Twas a child that so did thrive
>   In grace and feature
> As heaven and nature seem'd to strive
>   Which own'd the creature.

Years he number'd scarce thirteen
  When fates turn'd cruel,
Yet three fill'd zodiacs had he been
  The stage's jewel;
And did act, what now we moan,
  Old men so duly,
As, sooth, the Parcæ thought him one
  He play'd so truly.
So, by error to his fate
  They all consented
But viewing him since, alas, too late!
  They have repented:
And have sought, to give new birth,
  In baths to steep him;
But being so much too good for earth,
  Heaven vows to keep him.

The passage just referred to from "Hamlet" suggests that the children are likely to "grow themselves to common players," and the prince notes that the young lady of the traveling company that came to Elsinore "is nearer heaven than when I saw you last by the altitude of a chopine." Part of the interest in the child actors must have arisen, as in the case of little Salathiel, from the oddity of children in parts of elders; but another part of the interest came from the increasing power and skill of the growing boys. When in 1608 Burbage took over the Blackfriars theater, he took several of the best of the boy actors into the King's company. These boys, now twenty or more years of age, were already famous actors and long continued on the stage. I shall recur again to the general value of this training. For female rôles, it had a special utility, for certain boys were kept playing women from the age of twelve until they had passed to middle age. Like the Japanese men actors, from childhood they were trained in voice, gesture, and manners to women's parts.

The professional actors at first had very varied duties. They were acrobats, minstrels, entertainers in many ways. Even in the early years of Elizabeth's reign, tumbling and other acrobatic performances seem expected from the traveling companies; while singing and dancing, though special features of the children's plays, were also usual accomplishments of the adult actors. Any study of the plays written during the first three quarters of the sixteenth century will disclose the prominence given to one particular kind of acting, that by the clowns. Almost every play has a clown's part; and the horseplay, fisticuffs, and gross jokes have a manifest similarity in all. Often the clown, whether Vice in the moralities, or tricky servant in the Plautian imitations, is more than mere buffoon and may be essential to the plot. He may supply the mainspring of the action, and usually his antics keep him well to the front of the stage.

TARLETON AS CLOWN

Two of these clowns were among the first actors to gain a national and even an international reputation, Richard Tarleton and his successor, William Kemp. What little information has been preserved of their exploits comprises about all that we know of the methods of the clowns, and throws some light on two interesting features of the stage, the improvising by actors and the performance of jigs, dances accompanied by music and comic song.

Tarleton, according to Fuller, was tending his father's swine when discovered by one of the Earl of Leicester's servants who was so delighted with the swineherd's "happy unhappy answers that he brought him to court, where he became the most famous jester to Queen Elizabeth." [1]

According to several references in plays, he was a tavern keeper; at any rate by 1570 he had won enough fame to have his name attached to a ballad. By 1583 his position as the chief comic actor of the day was well established and he became a member of the new Queen's company. He took the part of Derrick in the old "Henry V," and in 1585 contrived for the company the play of the "Seven Deadly Sins," of which a plot has been preserved as it was later revived. It should be noted that this plot does not indicate an impromptu play, as Collier surmised, but is, like other plots preserved, an outline of entrances and exits for the use of the prompter. [2] Nothing further is known of his connection with the regular drama, but his popularity, which was enormous, seems to have been due largely to his improvisations.

Themes or verses were suggested by the audience, and Tarleton extemporized doggerel on the themes or capped the verses. To such exhibitions, which continued long after his death, Gabriel Harvey gave the name of their chief performer, accusing Greene of "piperly extemporizing and Tarletonizing." Howes, the annalist, declared that "for a wondrous plentifull

---

[1] Fuller, *Worthies of England*, II. 311.　　[2] *Henslowe Papers*, ed. Greg.

extemporall wit, he was the wonder of his time."
"The people began exceedingly to laugh," wrote
Nash, "when Tarleton first peept out his head."
After his death, a collection, "Tarleton's Jests" (c.
1592) attributed to him many well-worn jokes and
stories. His laurels were still green, when Meres
wrote in "Palladis Tamia" (1598), "As Antipater
Sidonius was famous for extemporal verse in Greek,
and Ovid for his *Quicquid conabar dicere versus erat,* so
was our Tarleton, of whom Dr. Case, that learned
physician, thus speaketh in the seventh book and
seventeenth chapter of his *Politics:* — *Aristotles suum
Theodoretum laudavit quendam peritum tragædiarum
actorem; Cicero suum Roscium; nos Angli Tarletonum,
in cujus voce et vultu omnes jocosi affectus, in cujus
cerebroso capite lepidæ facetiæ habitant."*

He seems also to have given great popularity to jigs.
Only one has been published, "The jigge of the horse
loade of fooles," and that unfortunately has for its
authority a manuscript of Collier's; but the music of
several has been preserved at Cambridge University.
Two years after his death there appeared "Tarleton's
Newes out of Purgatorie. Onely such a jest as this
Jigge, fit for Gentlemen to laugh at an houre." [1] Various ballads also celebrated his repentance, his fare-
well, and the visitation of his ghost. Additions to
his fame have been attempted down to the present.
Not without plausibility, he has been identified with
Spenser's "pleasant Willy."

> And he, the man whom Nature selfe had made
> To mock her selfe and Truth to imitate

and with Hamlet's Yorick of infinite jest.

---

[1] Reprinted, *New Shakespeare Society,* ed. Halliwell.

William Kemp, Tarleton's successor, seems to have followed closely in the practice of his master. Heywood wrote in his "Apology for Actors," 1612, "Here I must needs remember Tarlton, in his time gracious with the Queen his sovereign and in the people's general applause; whom succeeded Will. Kemp, as well in the favor of her majesty as in the opinion and good thoughts of the general audience." He apparently began acting as a member of the Earl of Leicester's company, and was the leader of that portion of the group which in 1585 went to the continent. "Will, the Lord of Leicester's player" is mentioned by Sir Philip Sidney writing from Utrecht as a bearer of a letter to Walsingham; and Kemp was with the others at Elsinore.[1] In the summer of 1586, however, when the others went to the court of Saxony, Kemp returned to England, and in the next year he may have been with that portion of Leicester's company which visited Stratford and may have carried Shakespeare with them to London. On Leicester's death, he probably joined the Lord Strange's men, in the traveling license of which company in 1593 he is mentioned. He and Burbage and Shakespeare were the members of the same company (under its new patron the Lord Chamberlain), who received payments at court on March 15, 1595. With Shakespeare's company he probably remained until about 1602,[2] when he appears in Henslowe's Diary as a member of Worcester's men, with whom he continued, as far as we know, until his death, sometime before 1609.

Kemp's most famous performance was dancing the

[1] Murray, I. 34–5. Herz, *Englische Schauspieler und englischen Schauspiele zur Zeit Shakespeares in Deutschland*, 1903, pp. 3, 4.

[2] Murray, II. 125, 126.

morris from London to Norwich. According to a common custom, he paid out sums of money on odds of 1 to 3 that he would accomplish this feat, and later complained that the greater part of the bettors "I cannot see, nor will they willingly be found." He left London on the first Monday in Lent, and, accompanied by a taborer, a servant, and an overseer, danced his way to Norwich. Because of fatigue and bad weather, the journey occupied twenty-three days, although he danced for only nine. He received a reward and a pension from the Mayor of Norwich and on his return to London published an account of his exploit, "Kempe's Nine Daies Wonder Performed in a Daunce from London to Norwich," 1600.[1] The dedication is to Anne Fitton, maid of honor to the Queen, and by some supposed to be the only dark lady of Shakespeare's sonnets.

The author of "An Almond for a Parrot," 1589, had dedicated this attack on the Martinists, "To that most comicall and Conceited Cavaliero, Monsieur du Kempe, Jestmonger and Vice-regent-generall to the Ghost of Dick Tarlton," and had pretended that Kemp's fame had already penetrated Italy. In the year after the morris to Norwich, Kemp seems actually to have traveled by way of France and Germany to Rome. The chief evidence of this is a quotation made by Halliwell from a manuscript not now discoverable,[2] which mentions Kemp's return from Rome where he had been with the famous Antony Shirley. There are, however, other references to his continental adventures, and Day's play, the "Travels of Three English Brothers," 1607, presents Kemp with Shirley at

---

[1] Reprinted by the Camden Society and in Arber's *English Garner*.
[2] N. S. S., *Ludus Coventriæ*, ed. Halliwell, p. 410.

Venice and assisting in an "extemporal merriment."
It is presumably on his return from this prolonged
excursion that he was with Burbage and other of the
Lord Chamberlain's men at that imaginary interview
with Cambridge students described in the university
play, "Return from Parnassus." One of the students
inquires, "What, Mr. Kempe! how doth the Emperor of Germany?" and another cries, "God save

KEMP DANCING THE MORRIS

you, Mr. Kempe: welcome, Mr. Kempe, from dancing a Morrice over the Alpes." To whom he perti-
nently replies, "Is it not better to make a fool of the
world, as I have done, than to be fooled of the world,
as you scholars are?"

There are frequent allusions to Kemp's jigs, and
four, not now extant, were entered for publication in
the Stationer's Register, one, the jig of the broom man,
another of the kitchen stuff woman, and a third of a
soldier, a miser, and Sym the clown. The play, "A
Knack to Know a Knave," acted for the first time by
Lord Strange's men, on June 10, 1592, was printed

in 1594 "with Kemp's applauded Merriments of the
Men of Goteham in receiving the King into Goteham."
These merriments are very slight, but perhaps Kemp
added to them in the performance. The practice of
interpolations by actors is defended by a character in
Brome's "Antipodes."

> That is a way, my lord, has been allowed
> On elder stages, to move mirth and laughter.

but is answered,

> Yea, in the days of Tarlton and Kemp
> Before the stage was purg'd from barbarism.

Every one will recall Hamlet's advice to the players on
this particular, and it is interesting to note that this
was probably written just before Kemp left the company for Worcester's men. Possibly Shakespeare had
some offenses of Kemp in mind when he wrote,

And let those that play your clowns speak no more than
is set down for them; for there be of them that will themselves laugh to set-on some quantity of barren spectators to
laugh too, though in the mean time some necessary question
of the play be then to be considered. That's villanous, and
shows a most pitiful ambition in the Fool that uses it.
II. ii. 42.

Though Kemp seems to have had a very active time
"making a fool of the world" across the channel and
with "mad jigs and merry jests" at home, it must be
remembered that most of his days were probably occupied as a regular actor in Shakespeare's company.
In the 1599 and 1609 quartos of "Romeo and Juliet,"
in IV. v, we have, "Enter Wil. Kemp" instead of
"Enter Peter"; and in the 1600 quarto and 1623
folio of "Much Ado," IV. ii, a similar slip prefixes

the speeches of Dogberry and Verges with Kemp and Cowley. Hence we know that Kemp played the parts of Peter and Dogberry, probably from their first appearance. In the "Return from Parnassus" already quoted, he undertakes to teach one of the students to act "a foolish justice of peace," which led Malone to infer that he was the original Justice Shallow.[1] As the leading low comedian of the company during the first years of Shakespeare's writing, it seems likely that he also played one of the Dromios, Launcelot Gobbo, and Launce.[2] From 1598–1602, if still a member of the company, he was pretty much occupied with traveling, and by the earlier year, Armin had joined the company and succeeded to some of his parts. Kemp apparently did not play Falstaff. Of his career as a member of the Earl of Worcester-Queen Anne's men we have no information; but he evidently kept up his reputation as a dancer of jigs and low comedian, until finally, as an epitaph maker proclaimed:

> Thou'st danc'd thee out of breath,
> And now must make thy parting dance with Death.

Kemp was by no means the only successor to Tarleton. Robert Wilson, one of Tarleton's fellows in the Queen's men, was famous as a comic actor and praised by Howes and Meres for his "extemporall wit."[3] John Singer and Thomas Pope, one of the leaders of Shakespeare's company, were other famous clowns.[4]

[1] *Variorum*, XVII. 114.
[2] Brander Matthews, *Shakespere as a Playwright*, 195.
[3] Stow, *Chronicle*, Howes' Continuation, 1583. Meres, *Palladis Tamia*, 285.
[4] Samuel Rowlands, *Letting of Humours Blood in the Head Vein*, 1600. Quoted by Collier, *Actors*, p. 121. See Ross on burning of Globe, 1613. H. P., *Outlines*, I. 310; II. 290–2.

Robert Armin, to whom reference has been made as succeeding Kemp, was in a peculiar way the follower of Tarleton. In Tarleton's "Jests," one story relates how the boy Armin serving as apprentice to a goldsmith had made some verses about his master, which were capped by the actor, who prophesied that the boy should succeed him.

> My adopted son therefore be,
> To enjoy my clown's suit after me.

"And so it fell out," the story goes. "The boy, reading this, so loved Tarleton after, that regarding him with more respect, he used to his plays, and fell in a league with his humour : and private practice brought him to present playing, and at this hour performs the same, where, at the Globe on the Bankside, men may see him."

Tests of improvised wit still continued on the stage, and jigs were frequently given as afterpieces. At the Fortune and the Red Bull they proved great drawing cards until the closing of the theaters. A comic afterpiece for tragedies or serious plays became, indeed, a fixture that lasted until within the memory of many. But these diversions came to be considered outside the field of legitimate drama, and the dramatists seem to share the sharp contempt with which Massinger speaks of "jigs and bawdry."[1] Tarleton and Kemp represent theatrical conditions that were rapidly changing. The drama continued to require some clownage, but it learned to keep its buffoonery subordinated to more serious interests or relegated to the jigs and drolls. Henceforth there were greater distinctions for actors than such fame as Tarleton and Kemp had won.

[1] *Roman Actor,* Preface.

The change was proclaimed in Marlowe's stirring prologue to "Tamburlaine" acted about the time of Tarleton's death.

> From jigging veins of rhyming mother wits
> And such conceits as clownage keeps in pay
> We'll lead you to the stately tent of war
> Where you shall hear the Scythian Tamburlaine
> Threatening the world with high astounding terms.

There was to be an opportunity for tragic and stately action instead of jigs and clownage, and for blank verse and high astounding terms instead of jigging rhymes and conceited prose. Henceforth, for a time, the stage was given over to histories and tragedies, declamation, and spectacle. Moreover, "Tamburlaine" was a play of one actor, centering its interest on the protagonist. Up to this time, it is difficult to find a modern play dependent for its success on a great emotional actor of a single part. Henceforth there are many such plays, including all of Marlowe's and many of Shakespeare's tragedies. "Richard II," "Hamlet," "Othello," "Macbeth," "Coriolanus," Jonson's "Catiline" and "Sejanus," Chapman's "Bussy D'Ambois" and "Biron" are, as manifestly as "Tamburlaine" and "Faustus," designed for great tragedians. Actors had been found who could declaim poetry and represent passion.

Edward Alleyn, the creator of Tamburlaine, is said to have been "bred for the stage," which would imply that he had acted as a boy. He was a member of a regular company by 1586, and was soon established in renown as the greatest actor of the time. Tarleton was ugly, with a squint, a face suited to his clownish parts, but Alleyn was of splendid physique, nearly seven feet in height, and best in majestic parts. He probably created all of Marlowe's protagonists and may have acted in some of Shakespeare's earliest plays. His biography is an extraordinary example of the variety and incongruity that characterized life in Elizabeth's reign and of the rapidity with which men carved out their own careers. An owner of theaters, a partner of his father-in-law Henslowe, a manager of companies, he rose quickly in fortune and soon added greatly to his income by his joint management with Henslowe of the bear baiting. In a few years, he was able to undertake the purchase of the manor of Dulwich by the expenditure of some £10,000, and later to carry out his great benefaction, the foundation of the College of God's Gift at Dulwich. His correspondence affords interesting glimpses of a prosperous activity, buying dogs and bulls, attending sermons, befriending the poet Dekker, dining old players and new acquaintances among the nobility, purchasing Shakespeare's Sonnets for 5*d*., and ever planning the details of his pious foundation. Amiable, religious, a model husband and friend, and a man of dignity and integrity, it is curious to recall that his fortune was made in part from baiting bulls and bears, and that even after he had retired from the stage, Alleyn occasionally officiated in those brutal entertainments. It is easier to imagine the stately figure of the portrait at Dulwich stepping from its frame to thunder Marlowe's mighty line or depict the "pangs of abdicating royalty," or in his last recorded appearance in public when as Genius "with excellent action and a well-tuned, audible voice," he delivered an address to James I on that monarch's entry into London.[1] Or, perhaps his final appearance

[1] Dekker's *Magnificent Entertainment*, 1604.

should be considered on September 18, 1619, when a distinguished company, including Lord Chancellor Bacon and Inigo Jones, assembled before dinner in the chapel of the college to listen first to a sermon and then to Alleyn's reading of the deed of foundation.

Of Alleyn's excellence as an actor, we have testimonies from Nash, Heywood, and Ben Jonson, but no detailed description of his method or list of his parts. It is clear, however, that his impersonations gave a new meaning to the art of tragic acting and that his successful life reflected somewhat of its merit on the profession in which he had his training.

While still at the height of his success on the stage, Alleyn found a worthy rival in Richard Burbage. The son of an actor and theater owner, he was bred in both the art and the business of acting. Of about the same age as Shakespeare, both young men doubtless found incentives to their future careers in the first successes of Marlowe's plays, with Alleyn in the leading parts. In 1594, they were at court, according to a record of payment, and presumably several years earlier they had already established their partnership as author and actor. We have references to Burbage as Romeo, Richard III, Hamlet, Othello, and Lear, and it seems probable that he played the leading heroic and tragic parts in all of Shakespeare's plays from "Love's Labour's Lost" to "Henry VIII." He must indeed have taken leading rôles in all plays acted by his company from about 1592 to his death in 1619. We hear of him as Jeronimo in Kyd's "Spanish Tragedy," Malevole in Marston's "Malcontent," and Ferdinand in the "Duchess of Malfi." In one transcript of the funeral elegy that gives us much information about his acting, he is alluded to in various other

2 c

parts, some of which are in plays never acted by his company. As this transcript rests only on Collier's authority, it must be regarded as spurious or garbled. From various references and lists of actors, we know that he appeared in Jonson's "Every Man in His Humour," "Every Man out of His Humour," "Sejanus," "Volpone," "Catiline," the "Alchemist," and in Fletcher's "Captain," "Valentinian," "Bonduca," "Queen of Corinth," "Loyal Subject," "Knight of Malta," and "Mad Lover."

While some of these plays are comedies, there are no allusions to Burbage as a comic actor. He won admiration mainly in tragic parts. An epitaph calls him "The best tragedian ever played," and the long elegy commands the poets to write no more:

> Or if you doe't, let't bee
> In comic scenes, for tragic parts you see
> Die all with him.

A further quotation from an authentic version of the elegy gives us our most specific account of his acting.

> He's gone, and with him what a world is dead,
> (Which he revived to be renewed so
> No more.)   Young Hamlet, old Hieronymo,
> Kind Lear, the grieved Moor, and more beside
> That lived in him, have now forever died.
> Oft have I seen him leap into a grave
> Suiting the person (which he seemed to have)
> Of a sad lover, with so true an eye,
> That then I could have sworn he meant to die.
> Oft have I seen him play his part in jest
> So lively that spectators and the rest
> Of his sad crew, while he but seemed to bleed
> Amazed thought that he had died indeed.[1]

[1] Mrs. C. C. Stopes, *Burbage and Shakespeare's Stage*, 118.

From this and other eulogies we may conclude that Burbage's art excelled in the variety and interest of his mimicry of emotion. If Alleyn was the Kemble, he was the Kean of their theater. For the statement that he was short and stout, there is no basis, so far as I can find, except Collier's verses and conjectures.

Of Burbage's activities as a theatrical manager and proprietor, sufficient note has been taken elsewhere in this volume. He was a painter as well as an actor, and was a citizen of repute and property, leaving on his death £300 yearly in land. He acted until a few weeks before his death, March 13, 1619, which caused an outburst of elegies and epitaphs. One writer took the Londoners sharply to task for mourning so much more for him than for Queen Anne, who had died a few days earlier. The Earl of Pembroke, writing to the Ambassador to Germany, records, on May 20th, "My Lord of Lennox made a great supper to the French Embassador this night here, and even now all the company are at the play, which I being tender-hearted, could not endure to see so soone after the loss of my old acquaintance Burbage."

Our attention has often been called to the close connection at every step of this development between the literary drama and the theater. The great popularity of comedians like Tarleton and Kemp is testimony to the spreading success of the professional actors rather than to any intellectual or artistic merit in their impersonations. But Lyly's refined and fanciful comedies appearing at the culmination of twenty years of successful performances by children's companies are a convincing evidence of the skill and ingenuity of the boy players. And the simultaneous advent of Marlowe and Alleyn and of Shakespeare and Burbage are proof that the art of acting developed rapidly along with the art of play writing. If the great tragedies inspired the actors, it must also be true that the great acting directed and assured the efforts of the poets. The fame won by Alleyn and Burbage in the department of their profession requiring the most unusual and varied gifts, is, of course, an indication of the rapid growth in subtlety and range of the histrionic art. But even leaving these two tragedians out of consideration, the multiform development of the drama during the first ten years of Shakespeare's career would in itself be sufficient proof of a corresponding progress in the art of acting. If we look over the repertories of two leading companies, headed by Burbage and Alleyn, upon the accession of James I, and if we consider the plays written in the next few years for the London theaters, we shall be convinced that actors have never had a more varied opportunity. The range of emotion, the classes of characters, the changes of diction, dialogue, and verse, the abundance of situation, the intensity of the contrasts that distinguished these plays imperatively challenge the most multifarious resources of the actor's art.

Attention should be called especially to the growth in variety and length of the female parts. Marlowe wrote no long parts for women, and even Lyly, when writing for the children, put little emotional stress into the lines for his ladies, nymphs, and goddesses; but by the time of "Romeo and Juliet," we may be sure that Shakespeare had found a remarkably competent boy actor. Shortly after, the revival of the children's companies gave a new opportunity for their training; and the increased number of women in the audiences of the private theaters probably gave a new encouragement to the rendering of feminine emotions. The plays of the boys did not differ much from those of the adults except that they employed female characters more freely. These children, who, if we may judge from the age of Nathaniel Field, their leading actor, ranged from thirteen to twenty, in the years 1600–1608, certainly acquired a very large range of difficult women's parts, including prostitutes, faithless wives, and tragic queens. In 1608, Shakespeare's company took over the leaders of the company, Ostler, Underwood, and Eggleston. The conjecture may not be wholly fanciful which connects the part of Cleopatra with the accession of some one of these well-trained boys to Shakespeare's company.

Incidentally, notice may be taken of a very different kind of histrionic proficiency. Disguise is a large factor in Elizabethan comedy, and a group of plays with multiple disguises indicates that the "rapid-change artist" had his success in that day. These plays were all acted within a few years for the Lord Admiral's company, and were apparently written to fit the ability of some actor to assume manifold rôles in rapid succession. In one of these, "Look About You," the character called "Skink impersonates, first, a real hermit whom he has slain; second, a stammering porter's son; third, the Earl of Gloucester; fourth, Prince John; fifth, an alehouse drawer; sixth, the hermit again; seventh, a falconer; eighth, the hermit; and last he is discovered as Skink." [1]

There was a chance for every kind of talent; but a severe and prolonged training was the road which led to opportunity. Alleyn, Burbage, and nearly all of the later actors were bred in the profession. The

[1] Freeburg, *Disguise Plots in Elizabethan Drama*, 1915.

children's companies, revived late in the sixteenth century, became the schools of the great tragedians and comedians of the next generation. The boys employed in subordinate or female parts by the adult companies became first the hired actors and then the shareholders and leaders. The companies traveling about the provinces picked up aspiring youths, and only the fittest survived to win the plaudits of the city. The profession had its apprenticeship, its stages, and degrees. Moreover, all actors went through the peculiarly valuable discipline of a stock company. As we have seen, Henslowe's companies gave as many as forty plays in a season, half of which were new. Each play had many parts, so that few of the twelve stockholders or their hired men and boys could get through a season without having played as many as thirty parts, and the next season possibly twenty new ones.

In Shakespeare's company, this discipline gained a unique value because of the character of its repertory. Every member of the company from 1590 to 1642 had to play in some of Shakespeare's dramas. The boy actor went to Shakespeare to learn his trade. Apart from the discipline afforded by the merit and the number of the plays in which he must act, the young actor was associated with veterans, and mayhap with the leaders of the profession, with Alleyn or with Burbage, and he might have as comrades of the tiring room dramatists like Heywood and Shakespeare. And the dramatists doubtless played their part in training the actors. We may be sure that Ben Jonson supervised his productions carefully, and he seems to have regarded himself as the teacher and sponsor of some of the children actors, Pavy and Field.

Shakespeare's skill in rehearsing the company is manifest from Hamlet's advice to the players.

The lives of the actors have left records of that violence and excess which characterize most Elizabethan biography. Many of them were handy with the rapier and the sword, and many of them were guilty of the faults to which their profession has always peculiar temptation. One of the very few stories about Shakespeare that goes back certainly to his own day recounts how he anticipated Burbage in an assignation with a citizen's wife and defended his priority on the ground that William the Conqueror preceded Richard the Third. This is the kind of story sure to be told and likely to be true of actors. Some of the Elizabethan players, like members of their profession in other days, lived loosely, ostentatiously, and unthriftily. But the scant records they have left are also surprisingly full of indications of industry, integrity, and thrift. The life of John Lowin, one of the chief actors of the reigns of James and Charles, may be taken as an illustration of the considerable consequence the better actors attained, and of the vicissitudes which befell the profession because of the Civil War. It also may serve to emphasize the training which an actor received in this later period and the way in which Elizabethan traditions were passed on to the modern stage.

Lowin was born in 1576 in the parish of St. Giles, Cripplegate, where the Fortune theater was later built. If Collier's evidence is correct, he was the author of a strange pamphlet for an actor, which finds "the ordinarie dances, used every where in these days . . . to be partly vain and partly prophane," and "so much artificiall that the human minds can not be intended or attentive to the art of dancing and to the praise of God together." He seems to have written nothing else and to have devoted himself very attentively to his profession. He is first heard of in Henslowe's Diary, where he appears as a member of Worcester's men from November 12, 1602, to March 12, 1603. He joined the King's men in time to act in Jonson's "Sejanus" in 1603, along with Shakespeare. He was not yet a shareholder in the company, since his name does not appear in the patent of May 19, or in the list of March 15, 1604. Perhaps, indeed, he may have joined the company to fill the place of Shakespeare, who is not thereafter recorded as acting. At all events, the lists in the quartos show that he acted in the "Malcontent," 1604, "Volpone," 1605, "Alchemist," 1610, and "Catiline," 1611. Undoubtedly he also took part in the performance of Shakespeare's plays. In this period he lived in Southwark near the Globe theater.

In the patent of 1619, he appears fourth on the list of twelve shareholders, and in the same year he took the part of Barnevelt in the censured tragedy, and in that year or earlier played Bosola in the "Duchess of Malfi." Lowin was now one of the leading members of the company and a man of some standing. He is mentioned eleventh in the list of actors appended to Shakespeare's plays in the folio, and his name appears in all but one of the lists of actors appended to twenty-one plays in the Beaumont and Fletcher folio. After the death of Burbage, in 1619, his name always appears in one of the first three places. Taylor was perhaps the leading actor in the younger parts. Among the parts which Lowin took we note Domitian in the "Roman Actor," 1626, Eubulus in "The Picture,"

1629, Jacomo in Carlell's "Deserving Favorite," Flaminius in "Believe as You List," and Belleur in Fletcher's "Wild Goose Chase." In 1629 he was one of the twelve shareholders in the company, held one share out of eight in Blackfriars, and one share out of sixteen in the Globe theater.[1]

Some note of the last years of Lowin and his companions in the King's men has been preserved in the dialogue "Historia Histrionica," 1699. In discoursing on Collier's recent attack upon the stage, Trueman, "an old Cavalier," recalls the great days of Blackfriars, when they, of all the companies, "were men of grave and sober behavior," and when the actors, Lowin, Taylor, Pollard, and some others, "were almost as far beyond Hart and his company as they are beyond those now in being." Then "Lowin used to act, with loud applause, Falstaff, Morose, Volpone, Mammon in the Alchemist, Melantius in the Maid's Tragedy."

With the outbreak of the Civil War most of the actors "either lost or exposed their lives for their king," except Lowin, Taylor, and Pollard, who were superannuated. Lowin took part in the surreptitious performance of "Rollo" at the Cockpit in 1649, playing Audbrey to Taylor's Rollo, when the soldiers carried the actors off to prison. In 1652, Fletcher's "Wild Goose Chase" was printed for the benefit of Taylor and Lowin. In his latter days, he kept an inn, the Three Pigeons, at Bretford, where he died very old, and his poverty was as great as his age. This actor, who had played with Shakespeare and under his eye taken leading parts, lived almost to the Restoration. He was probably the original Henry VIII, for Downes

[1] Halliwell-Phillipps, *Outlines*, I. 313.

in the "Roscius Anglicanus" states that Betterton was instructed in the part by Davenant, "who had it from old Mr. Lowin that had his instructions from Mr. Shakespeare himself." Unquestionably he learned many Shakespearian parts under the direction of Shakespeare, or of the actors who had first interpreted them. For forty years he acted regularly in Shakespeare's company, helping to create and to preserve its traditions, and these traditions he passed on with his own lips to three following generations.

In what respects did the acting differ from that of the present? We have definite information only concerning one particular, and that the incidental one of costume. No stage ever cared more for fine clothes than the Elizabethan or lavished on dress a larger portion of its expenses. Henslowe's Diary records many purchases of silk, velvet, copper lace, and tinsel, and frequent payments to the silk man, the little tailor, and the mercer. For every new play there was an outlay for new clothes; "Cardinal Wolsey," for example, requiring £38.12.2, for coats, velvets, satins, copper lace, etc., in August, 1601, and additional payments later. Many of the costumes were brilliant affairs, as a "flame-colored satin doublet," for which 45s. were paid on January 5, 1598, "a doublet and a pair of hose laid thick with gold lace," "a pair of Venetians of cloth of silver wrought in red silk," another "pair of crimson satin Venetians with a stripe of gold lace." The costumes for women were no less elaborate; the "skirts of a woman's gown of silver camlet," costing 55s., and "skirts of white satin laid with white lace," 33s. 4d. The two angry women of Abingdon had taffeta gowns costing £9, taffeta and tinsel for the bodice of Alice Pierce's gown cost £1, and a gown of black velvet for Mrs. Frankford in the "Woman Killed with Kindness" cost £6 13s. Some of the other records are more curious, as "a robe for Time," "coats for giants," "black buckram to make a suit for a fire drake," "for William Kemp to buy buckram to make a pair of giant hose," "lent Thomas Heywood to buy him a pair of silk garters," "a canvas suit and skins for the black dog of Newgate," "suits for devils, spirits, and a witch's gown for the play of 'Two Brothers.'" One entry indicates that a shift was made to repair old clothes, 7s. 6d. being paid "for mending of Hugh Davis's tawny coat, which was eaten with the rats." Another indicates a peculiar need for new indispensables, 14s. for "a pair of hose for Nick to tumble in before the queen."

Our fullest information in regard to stage costumes comes from the inventories made by Henslowe in 1598. These include the costumes and properties of the Admiral's men, among other items, a doublet and velvet gown for Henry V, wings for Mercury, Tamburlaine's coat with copper lace, his breeches of crimson velvet, Dido's robe, and "a robe for to go invisible." One section of the inventory is reprinted here to indicate the variety of the wardrobe.[1]

1 senator's gown, 1 hood, 5 senators capes.

1 suit for Neptune, firedrakes suits for 'Dobe.'

4 Janisaries gowns, 4 torch-bearer's suits.

3 pair red strossers [tight hose], 3 fairies' gowns of buckram.

4 Herowdes [? Heralds'] coats, 3 soldiers coats, 1 green gown for [Maid] Marian.

6 green coats for Robin Hood, 4 Knaves' suits.

2 pair of green hose and Anderson's suit, 1 white 'shepen' cloak.

1 *Henslowe Papers*, ed. W. W. Greg, App. I.

2 russet coats, 1 black freize coat, 3 priests' coats.

2 white shepherds' coats, 2 Danes' suits, 1 pair of Danes hose.

the Moor's limbs, Hercules' limbs, Will Summer's suit.

2 'Orlates' suits, hats, and gorgets, 7 anticks coats.

'Cathemer' suit, 1 pair of cloth white stockings, 4 Turks' heads.

4 friars gowns, 3 hoods to them, 1 fool's coat, cap, and bauble, Branholt's bodice, Merlin's gown and cap.

2 black say gowns, 2 cotton gowns, 1 red say gown.

1 'mawe' gown of calico for the queen, 1 cardinal's hat.

1 red suit of cloth for [John] Pyge, laid with white lace.

5 pair of hose for the clown, 5 gerkins for them.

3 pair of canvas hose for 'asane', 2 pair of black strossers.

1 yellow leather doublet for a clown, 1 'whittcomes' doublet 'pope' [wide-sleeved ?].

Eve's bodice, 1 pedant trusser, 3 dons' hats.

1 pair of yellow cotton sleeves, 1 ghost's suit, 1 ghost's bodice.

18 copes and hats, Verone's son's hose [Chapman's *Humourous Day's Mirth*].

3 trumpets, a drum, a treble viol, a bass viol, a bandore, a cittern, an ancient [flag], 1 white hat.

1 hat for Robin Hood, 1 hobby horse [for the Morris dance].

5 shirts, 1 'serpelowes,' 4 farthingales.

6 head tires, 1 fan, 4 rebatos, 2 'gyrketruses.'

1 long sword.

The inventory points to some degree of propriety in costume. The foresters wear green, the shepherds white; and doubtless senators, heralds, soldiers, friars, clowns, serving men, kings, and queens wore clothes with a certain appropriateness. The costumes for janisaries, fairies, Neptune, and Dido are more dubious, but seem to have had some distinctiveness, and conjecture is excited by Eve's bodice and a gown for to go invisible. For historical appropriateness no effort was made. Cleopatra calls on Charmian to cut her stays and was doubtless as formidably bodiced as Queen Elizabeth. Though Roman senators might wear robes, it seems likely that Julius Cæsar, Coriolanus, Cymbeline, Macbeth, and Romeo all wore doublet and hose of the extravagant fashion affected by the Earl of Southampton. What was wanted was display. Splendid coats retrieved from the court shows, new garments buckramed and spangled in the latest fashion, added to the spectacle, and helped to satisfy both actors and spectators. The stage, then as now, tried to be the glass of fashion, and one of the arts of the actor was the art of wearing clothes. The group of men and boys performing on the projecting platform had little to separate them from the surrounding audience. Their gay clothes helped to make of them the picture on which all eyes focused.

Though it is possible to form some picture of the actors in costume, it is very difficult to draw distinctions between their methods of acting and those of our day. Trueman in the "Historia Histrionica" declares that they were far better than those of the late seventeenth century. " It is an argument of the worth of the plays and actors of the last age, and easily inferred, that they were much beyond ours in this, to consider that they could support themselves merely from their own merit, the weight of the matter, and goodness of the action, without scenes and machines."

The absence of scenery and the scantiness of properties have sometimes been held to give little chance for stage business. But while the stage directions give little indication of business, it is easy to recall many notable provisions for it. Cleopatra helps Antony to

don his armor (IV. iv). The mirror in "Richard II,"
which the king dashes to the floor, affords business
almost exactly paralleled in Rostand's "L'Aiglon."
The knocking at the door in "Macbeth" has become
a sort of test and model for actors. The comic scenes
which interpose their contrasts in tragedy are often
very largely business, as the drunken porter in "Macbeth" and the gravediggers in "Hamlet." Many of
the familiar incidents in Shakespeare's tragedy are
indeed less original than these, and are his adaptations
of bits of business long conventionalized on the stage.
Such are the swearing on the sword, the midnight
striking of the clock, the entry reading a book, the
handling of a skull in "Hamlet." Certain classes of
scenes familiar in both Shakespeare and his contemporaries manifestly developed a considerable amount of
pantomime : as banquet scenes, receptions of ambassadors, carousals, funerals, games of chess or cards,
and so on. The amount of business provided for
tragic soliloquizers is especially interesting because it
indicates the feeling of a need of some action and
movement to break the long meditative speeches.
The soliloquizer often enters reading a book, or with
some other object in his hand — a dagger if he medi-
tates on suicide, or he wanders in the graveyard or
charnel house. In the midst of his soliloquy he may
fall down, like an emotional actress to-day, and pro-
claim his passion from the floor.

The prevalence of business led to the same sort of
conventionality that is such a detriment in the acting
of every age. A certain gesture or a bit of by-play
comes into constant use, like the chambermaid in the
opening scene, or the cigarette of the adventuress.
A curious Elizabethan example of this has been noted

in the case of the entrance with a book. The "Span-ish Tragedy" furnishes the first instance of this, but nearly fifty other examples have been collected.[1] After such a convention is well established, it soon be-comes the object of burlesque; and in a late play by Shirley it is not the tragic protagonist, but a clown who enters with a book which he uses in his fooling.

The long popularity of dumb shows in the Elizabe-than plays may be taken as evidence of the liking of the audience for business as well as for spectacle and pantomime. Certainly, although there may have been less stage business then than now, there was a good deal, and much of it had become fixed into conventions.

It would seem, however, that the absence of dis-tracting scenery and of long waits between the acts would fix the attention of the audience more exclu-sively upon the actors than is the case to-day. And the discomforts of the theaters, especially the fact that a large part of the audience was standing, would necessitate a more rapid action and more varied ef-fects than we in our comfortable seats require. There was certainly much that was horribly crude or gross in the plays to meet the needs of impatient ground-lings; and in an age when emotions were freely expressed and quickly resolved into action some of this inten-sity and abandon might well have been transferred to the stage. Lovers, scapegraces, roarers, villains, sentimentalists, men of fashion, jealous husbands, modest maidens, prostitutes, false wives, saucy girls, mighty queens, and whoever else, doubtless played their parts with vigor and emphasis rather than with restraint. In the poorly lighted theater, the lifting of an

[1] R. S. Forsythe, *Relations of Shirley's Plays to the Elizabethan Drama,* 1914, pp. 84, 85.

eyebrow would scarcely have conveyed much emotion, and the reticence that modern taste prefers in emotional scenes could not have carried the applause of the standing pit. Yet it is again Shakespeare who urges the actors to disregard these same groundlings and to avoid tearing a passion to tatters. "For in the very torrent, tempest, and whirlwind of passion, you must acquire and beget a temperance that may give it smoothness."

Another difference between Elizabethan and modern acting has been found in the greater importance then given to the spoken word. Dramatists and actors had to gratify an audience, unable or unused to read but accustomed to gathering jokes, stories, and information by the ear rather than the eye. The plays abound in verbal displays of all kinds, quibbles, puns, repartee, stichomythia, descriptions, soliloquies, orations. An exit was made to the tune of a rhymed couplet. One may conclude that the stylistic exuberance of the plays was due not only to the authors' poetic adventuresomeness, but not less to the desire of the actors for telling passages. The earlier plays in particular are diffuse, ornate, fantastic, or declamatory in manner, and evidently designed to give to the comedian such chance as the monologist has today in vaudeville, and to the tragedian the commanding opportunity of set declamations. The attitude of the author, and hence of the actors, is often frankly that of telling the audience something. Servants, messengers, and others deal in pure narrative. Expository and connecting scenes occur merely in order that the audience may be told of what has happened somewhere behind the scenes. An emotional crisis is elaborated not by business but by argument and rebuttal. A lady defending her chastity often indulges in an oration. The evolution of the last act is accomplished by a court of justice with extended pleas for plaintiff and defendant. As time went on, there was less exuberance in style and many indications of an effort toward naturalism in diction and dialogue. But even the most condensed and rapid of Elizabethan plays have nothing of the paucity and bareness of words that characterize one of Ibsen's; though perhaps the more discursive hardly surpass Shaw and Brieux in their fullness of utterance.

The effect of this fullness of utterance on the acting was further conditioned by the fact that all the tragedies and some of the comedies were written in blank verse. The actor spoke his lines standing close to his audience with no tragic buskins or mask to give him elevation and importance, and with no footlights or scenery to separate his world from theirs. On the modern picture-frame stage the scenery of a romantic or tragic play at once carries the spectator from the pit to the imaginary realm of the picture. On Shakespeare's stage not even the platform separated the actor from the audience on its three sides, for sometimes spectators sat about the stage itself. We have indeed noticed the utility of the rear stage for action absolutely requiring some aloofness from too searching observation, but the greater part of every play was spoken far down front. Desdemona might be murdered in the rear alcove, but Iago's deviltry and Othello's jealousy were enacted in the very arms of the audience. Voice was the only medium through which the spectators passed from the crowded pit to the palace of the Doges. The impression of actuality was heightened by the very intimacy between actors and audience. The passions of the Moor and his crafty ensign were the passions of men elbowing them. No Athenian Œdipus or modern Hamlet could secure quite the same sort of verisimilitude. But the illusion of aloofness which on the modern stage, as on the Greek, accompanied the illusion of actuality, — the impressions of dignity and grandeur, of human significance, — must in the Globe have come largely through the verse.

In this sense, the effect of the drama was that of literature in a degree that it rarely is to-day. Or rather, the effect of acting on the emotions and imagination was to a peculiar extent due to rhythmic and melodic recitation. It is easy to believe that actors read blank verse much better than they do to-day. They were all trained to it, and the audience was accustomed to it. The opening lines of one of Shakespeare's plays strike not only the key of the action, but of the very pitch and melody of the measured syllables that are to free the fancy and purify the passions. The full value of Othello's magnificent tirades was perhaps never better appreciated than in the theater for which they were designed, where the meaning and greatness of the action rested so largely on Burbage's rendering of the overtones of their noble music. Perhaps even "Lear," under those conditions, might have been acted with an imaginative grandeur which Lamb found so lacking even in the mimicry of Kean. For the play was not intended to rely on our paraphernalia of scenery, lights, and decoration, but to force its entry into our imaginations through the beauty of its spoken lines. To the Elizabethans the King was a broken old man like one of themselves, but he was also the very music of passionate suffering, the voice of poetry.

It is tempting to speculate on the characteristics of the acting through which, and not by means of print,

Shakespeare saw his plays presented to other men's imagination. But such speculation cannot be very profitable in exact information. The qualities of Elizabethan acting can hardly be re-created in detail or even in confident summary. We know that the plays, longer than ours to-day, were acted usually within two or three hours before an audience, part of which was standing. These plays are not only longer than ours but more crowded with incidents and persons, more varied and incongruous in their action. The actors played almost in the middle of the audience, without scenery, and with comparatively few properties. Manifestly, there must have been a certain condensation and rapidity of action in comparison with ours; and a greater value and importance must have rested on the spoken words, especially on the reading of verse. In recent years many interesting attempts have been made to revive these Elizabethan conditions, but they have usually rested content with abolishing scenery and long waits, and with retaining most of the text. A real revival is probably impossible. It would require that actors should receive long training in speaking blank verse; that they should be brought very close to the audience; that they should speak their parts rapidly without much interruption for business, but with careful attention to such business as the lines indicated; that every means of facial expression and gesture should be employed in the depiction of emotion, making the action somewhat more intense than in the modern manner. In addition, it would require an audience trained to this kind of acting. It is possibly in this close and long-continued intimacy between actors and audience that the Elizabethan acting gained its most characteristic quality.

CHAPTER XIV

THE AUDIENCE

WHEN Shakespeare peeped through the curtain at the audience gathered to hear his first play, he looked upon a very motley crowd. The pit was filled with men and boys. The galleries contained a fair proportion of women, some not too respectable. In the boxes were a few gentlemen from the Inns of Court, and in the lords' box, or perhaps sitting on the stage, was the young Earl of Southampton with a group of extravagantly dressed gentlemen of fashion. Vendors of nuts and fruit moved about through the crowd. The gallants were smoking, the apprentices in the pit were exchanging rude witticisms with the painted ladies in the lower gallery. If the play was "Titus Andronicus," the spying author may well have smiled at the impropriety of the opening lines which were to seek attention from the noisy throng.

> Noble patricians, patrons of my right,
> Defend the justice of my cause with arms.

Or, if the play were "Love's Labour's Lost," the opening speech would hardly have seemed less incongruous.

> Let fame that all hunt after in their lives
> Live regist'red upon our brazen tombs.

Shakespeare has left little criticism or compliment of his audience, and when he addressed it directly he

did so in the terms of gentle courtesy or pleasant
raillery. In "Hamlet," however, he does let fall the
opinion that the groundlings "for the most part are
capable of nothing but inexplicable dumb-shows and
noise." One may wonder whether recollections of the
pit of the Globe did not add vigor to his ridicule of the
Roman mob in "Julius Cæsar" and "Coriolanus."
Whom else had he in mind when he penned the tart
denunciation of Caius Marius?

> I had rather have one scratch my head i' the sum
> When the alarum were struck, than idly sit
> To hear my mouthings monster'd.

Many of his fellow dramatists expressed their contempt of the audience in no uncertain terms.

> Non ego ventosae plebis suffragia venor,

boasts Jonson at the end of the epilogue of "Every
Man in His Humour." Massinger protests against
"such as are only affected with jigs and ribaldry," [1] and
Webster declares that "most of the people that came to
that playhouse resemble those ignorant asses who, visiting stationers' shops, their use is not to inquire for good
books, but new books.[2] Yet the criticism of the
authors is directed as often against the affectations of
the gallants and would-be critics as against the crowd.
It is against these "genteel auditors" that most of
the satire is turned in Jonson's Inductions; and they
are the objects of ridicule in Dekker's "Gull's Horn
Book." General condemnation of the audience usually
occurs only when an author is excusing the failure of
his play, or writing condoling verses on the failure of
a brother dramatist. On the other hand, the prefaces

---

[1] Preface to the *Roman Actor*.   [2] Address to the *White Devil*.

and inductions of Jonson and others often premise a large amount of intelligence and reading on the parts of their audiences. Marlowe in his prologue to "Tamburlaine" proclaims an innovation. Marston for his tragedies and Jonson for his comedies bespeak from the audience a most serious appreciation of the authors' aims and art. In short, the Elizabethan dramatists, like those of any period, had their moods both of irritation and of confidence with their audience; but on the whole there was a growing unwillingness to trust their wares unreservedly to the public verdict.

The theater was a popular institution, and the audience representative of all classes of London life. Admission to standing room in the pit of the public theaters was a penny, and an additional penny or two secured a seat on a bench in the galleries. For seats in the 'rooms' or boxes set off from the galleries, or for stools on the stage, still more was charged. Later, and especially in the private theaters, considerably higher prices prevailed, ranging from sixpence to half a crown. These are the prices mentioned in the Induction to "Bartholomew Fair," acted in 1614 at the Hope, a public theater; but it was a new play, for which an extra charge was customary. It is difficult to translate these prices into money values to-day, for while the purchasing power was much greater then than now, the ratio varied widely. Labor, and especially unskilled or agricultural labor, was very much cheaper; but the cost of clothing was not much less then than now. The purchaser of a $2 seat in the orchestra of a theater to-day pays the cost of one day's unskilled labor or the cost of a shirt. The gallant who paid a shilling for a seat on the stage at

Blackfriars paid the cost of several days of unskilled labor, but only a fraction of the cost of his shirt. The penny meant to the apprentices and mechanics and mercantile employees somewhat less than what 25 cents does to-day; the shilling to the members of the middle class corresponded to $2 at present. The relative cost of theatrical entertainment was about the same then as now and varied as greatly among the different theaters.

The attendance at the theaters was astonishingly large. There were often five or six giving daily performances, which would mean that out of a city of one hundred thousand inhabitants, there were thirty thousand or more spectators at the play within a week. When we remember that a large class of the population disapproved of the theater, and that women of respectability were not frequent patrons of the public playhouses, this attendance is hard to account for. There has been no such patronage of the drama since until the present success of the moving pictures. In its ability to interest all classes and to afford at a low price an unfailing amusement, the Elizabethan stage may very well be compared with the movies. Like them it had novelty in its favor, and for twenty years or more after the first professional playhouses, many Londoners were theater mad.

The arrangements for the comfort of the spectators were meager, and they were often disorderly. Playbills seem to have been posted about town and in the theater, and the title of the piece was posted or announced on the stage. These bills, however, contained no lists of actors, and there were no programs, ushers, or tickets. There was usually but one door for the audience, where the admission fee was deposited in a box carefully watched by the money taker, and additional sums were required at the entrance to the galleries or boxes. Three o'clock was the usual hour for beginning a performance, which was announced by trumpets sounded thrice. At the third sounding, the prologue speaker appeared. The assembled audience had been amusing itself by eating, drinking, smoking, and playing cards, and sometimes continued these occupations during the performance. Pickpockets were frequent and if caught were tied to a post on the stage, according to Kemp's comment in his "Nine Days Wonder." The duration of a play is usually spoken of as two hours, though there is mention of three hours; but there was an additional concert at the private houses, and often a concluding jig at the public theaters. At these respectability was distinguished by its absence or its quietness. The moving, jostling groundlings were the dominant element, just as the gallery gods were in later days of the stage. After an hour or so of standing, their appetites must have been blunted for anything except low comedy, or rapid and sensational action. Disturbances were not infrequent, which sometimes ended in general rioting. In our quiet times, it is difficult to find a parallel to the pit of the public theaters, but perhaps the audience at a professional ball game comes as near as anything we have to the crowd that assembled in the Curtain and the Theater.

The Elizabethan audience was fond of unusual spectacle and brutal physical suffering. They liked battles and murders, processions and fireworks, ghosts and insanity. They delighted in seeing the conquered monarchs draw Tamburlaine about in his chariot. They liked Richard III surrounded with ghosts, or fighting many Richmonds in the battle field. They enjoyed the horrid stories of rape and revenge like "Titus Andronicus." They would endure seeing Gloucester's eyes torn out, or Hieronymo's tongue torn from his mouth, or a child's brains dashed over the stage. A dance of madmen, a chamber of horrors, a burning town, were interesting. They wanted to be thrilled, they liked physical activity, emotional excess. They expected comedy to abound in beatings and tragedy in deaths. They liked villany expressed not merely by plots and poisons, but in terms of rape, incest, and mutilation. There was doubtless more cruelty and brutality in those days of the St. Bartholomew massacre and the public burning of heretics than we like to acknowledge exists in our civilization. Men were at least more openly cruel, more bestial in the expression of passion. But if the theater reflects all this, it was following rather than leading its age. | The audience at the Globe expected some sensation and physical horror, but they did not come there primarily for these. They could get real blood and torture daily at the bear baiting near by, and public executions were by no means uncommon spectacles. The theaters attracted others than seekers after brutal sensation.

In the early days the audience was distinctly masculine, and there were few women and no young girls. Shakespeare never played before any audience largely composed of women unless at court. But the citizens' wives soon took to attending the play, and after the establishment of the private theaters there was a large increase in the number of women. Their presence may remind us that the audience was not without refinement. There were very few public entertainments offering as little brutality as the theaters.

There were no museums, libraries, or concerts. The rivals of the theaters were cockfights, exhibitions of acrobats, trained animals, monsters, puppet shows, and the bull and bear baiting. Those who craved less literary or more brutal entertainment could have it for their penny; but those looking for food for the imagination had nowhere to go but to the playhouse. There were no newspapers, no magazines, almost no novels, only a few cheap books, ballads, and romances, and the theater supplied the desire for story and discussion which is now met by thousands of printed pages. If it began with an audience no better than the average of the London population, and if it catered in some degree to their brutality, grossness, and ignorance, yet it also represented for them romance and imagination, idealism, and art.

Much was made in contemporary comment of the difference between the groundlings and the more judicious spectators. And it must be remembered that, while the upper middle class long opposed the theater, young nobles and Templars were among its most enthusiastic patrons. Lyly found a patron in the Earl of Oxford, and Shakespeare in the Earl of Southampton, and both young gentlemen were held by common gossip to be wasting time and means at the theaters. The leading companies not only played at court but attracted many of the upper classes to the stage and boxes of the playhouses. And if the law students and lordlings came to the theater, it may fairly be supposed that it was the poetry and invention which attracted them from the bear gardens and cockfights. Yet too sharp a distinction should not be drawn between the taste of the nobles and of the groundlings. Doubtless some incentive to literary ambition arose from the approval and criticism of men of taste and reading who came to frequent the theaters. But the young lords of Elizabeth's court were not greatly distinguished by taste and learning, and probably not much superior to the apprentices in their liking for obscene jokes and bad puns. The striking thing about the Elizabethan Londoner was his mixture of many interests. If a great noble like Raleigh was poet, courtier, buccaneer, freethinker, historian, so the sorriest apprentice might have in him a response for Titania as well as for Andronicus.

In comparison with almost any audience to-day, that of the Globe was illiterate. A large number probably could not read, and certainly only a very few read much. The average college graduate of to-day, ill read though he be, knows more of books than did the entire pit. One newspaper contains more information of some social or human consequence than was accessible to London in a month. With our democratization of literature moving on apace, we hear frequent complaints of making literature to meet the intelligence and interests of the million instead of elevating it to the author's own standards, but the million of to-day is superior to the thousands for whom Shakespeare wrote in knowledge of history, science, and letters.

The Elizabethan audience had the scantiest background of culture. A humanist like Sir Philip Sidney looked with disdain at the professional stage, ignorant of all the traditions of the classical drama. There was at first no thought in the mind of any scholar that a popular form of entertainment could produce great literature, itself to furnish the cultural training of the future generations. It is the constant complaint of

the dramatists themselves that they must submit
their wares to those without sufficient knowledge for
judgment. When Fletcher's "Faithful Shepherdess"
failed on the popular stage, both the author and his
friends joined in a chorus of explanations and ejacu-
lations at the ignorance of the public who did not know
Guarini's "Pastor Fido," or indeed what a true pastoral
or a true tragi-comedy might be. A direct knowledge
of the classics and of the Italians, and the many incentives which this knowledge offered to literary initiative,
were confined to a very few persons. But it is extraordinary the way in which this new knowledge became
a leaven working through popular thought and imagination. The theater became a means of education.

The most remarkable case is probably that of English history. The growth of national patriotism cul-
minating in the victory over the Armada had been
accompanied by the publication of many chronicles.
The interest might have remained antiquarian or literary, but the popular patriotism gave the dramatist
a chance to use this historical material, and for the fifteen years from the Armada to the death of Elizabeth,
the stage was crowded with plays based on the events
of English chronicles. If many of these exhibited only
a superficial desire to please the current national pride,
others undertook a more searching interpretation of
historical persons and events. Within a few years the
public was supplied with so much information on the
course of English history that Shakespeare could complete a whole tetralogy of the Wars of the Roses, and
could begin his "Richard II" in the middle of that
monarch's reign without bothering over much initial
exposition. A familiarity with English history had
become a cultural asset of the London crowd; and of

course Shakespeare's great series of historical plays has continued to supply a large part of whatever knowledge popular patriotism has required. This vogue of English chronicles on the stage stopped abruptly with the death of Elizabeth, but it had prepared the way for other historical information, for Chapman's plays on French affairs, Jonson's Roman tragedies, and especially for Shakespeare's plays from Plutarch. Only with an audience trained to an interest in history could the world contests of Cæsar and Brutus, Augustus and Antony have had a thrilling reality. It is due primarily to the dramatic genius of Shakespeare, and secondarily to the genius of Plutarch, but at least in a tertiary degree to the interest in the past which the drama had already developed in the London public, that, of all subjects of antiquity, Roman history was the one most effectively vitalized in our literature. Other matters of antiquity were less successfully presented, but the Homeric story and the Greek myths, however vulgarized, carried some information and mental enlargement.

One contrast with the audience of to-day must, however, be insisted upon. The vast amount of miscellaneous information which any audience of newspaper readers possesses — about railways, geography, mechanics, legislation, recent inventions, preventive medicine, popular science, etc. — was all unknown to the Elizabethans. It is this sort of information which has made possible the thesis play of the modern stage dealing with some question open to the intelligence and knowledge of the newspaper reader; and it is this sort of information which has banned anything remote from the present or unknown to its daily fare. An Elizabethan dramatist was not much limited by the general information of his audience. He probably would not go quite so far as to affirm that water would run up hill, but he could do about what he pleased with the solar system, or the geography of Bohemia, or the habits of the crocodile. On the other hand, he could expect the attention of his audience for Bonduca or Alexander the Great.

One exception must be made to this indifference of the audience to the matter of common information. In the field of law, the Elizabethan public seems to have been pretty well informed. A good deal has been made of the legal knowledge shown in Shakespeare's plays and of his personal fondness for litigation. It must be granted, however, that many dramatists, certainly Middleton and Massinger, show as much acquaintance with legal technicalities, and that there were a great many Elizabethan citizens equally involved in litigation. Something must be allowed to the influence that the great development of civil law in the sixteenth century exercised upon the daily life of the London citizen. He had to know some law in his business, and the lawyer was as indispensable an adjunct to his household as the physician. The law court became as effective on the stage as the battle field, and legal diction as readily understood as the metaphors of arms. Theology, another great influence on popular knowledge and culture, was too dangerous for lay discussion and played little part on the stage. The preference of the drama for law must also be attributed in some degree to the law students who were great patrons of the theaters and often turned playwrights.

On the whole, then, though the cultural background of the audience was very scanty, the dramatists did not hesitate to cultivate it whenever opportunity offered. The ignorance of the multitude did not prevent it from taking an interest in new information, not entirely of the kind that a modern person desires; or from offering a receptive hearing to a popularization of the accumulated lore of lawyer, historian, humanist, and antiquary. The amount of cultural training involved may easily be underestimated; for even in this age of universal education, we should hardly select for popular dramatization the Wars of the Roses, the orations of Cicero against Catiline, the myth of Endymion, the character of Coriolanus, or the trial and death of Sir Thomas More.

The audience, groundlings and lordlings alike, was used to the spoken word, and it soon became trained to blank verse. It was not well read but it was familiar with sermons. It found listening easier than reading; it was quick to respond to oratory or repartee. It liked sonorous declamation and it liked slangy billingsgate. It enjoyed hearing Friar Lawrence spin out a long speech about his herbs, it delighted in Mercutio's description of Queen Mab. It would have been pleased with our vaudevilles, monologists, our college debates, our acrobatic revivalists, our stump speakers, and our Chautauquan orators. Its delight in style was oral but none the less keen. It liked to hear new words, new phrases, classical allusions that it did not understand. It delighted in the clown's malapropisms, in Tamburlaine's ranting audacities, in his mellifluous enumeration of strange proper names, from Persepolis to Mexico; it enjoyed the Stygian vocabulary of the revenge tragedies or the stylistic redundances and burlesques of "Love's Labour's Lost." Its fancy was trained in listening to a speech. It felt at home with

ancient puns and familiar metaphors, but it was quick
to detect a new conceit or an adventurous figure. In
a time when language was changing rapidly, it was
careless of written propriety but keen for spoken
novelty. It responded to verse, it heard the fall of
the accent, the march of the measure; its heart beat
with the throb of the decasyllables. It delighted in
the musical monotony with which Peele told the tale
of David and Bethsaba; it loved the music as well as
the sentiment of the balcony scene in "Romeo and
Juliet." The public had long been accustomed to
acting, and to acting in which the spoken words were
listened to with attention. The new poetry and the
great actors who recited it found an audience sensitive
to whatever effects they could produce. There were
many moments during a play when spectacle, brutality, action, and story were all forgotten, and the
audience fed only on the words.

But, after all, the audience went to the theater less
for information, or sensational spectacle, or recitation,
than for story. The stage supplied stories of all sorts,
all strange and new. It essayed the whole range
of secular fiction and history. It made real and vivid,
for an age that had only begun to read, all the tales
of Greece and Rome, of Italian novelists, of English
history, and of contemporary London. It took the
place now filled by the novel, the short-story, the drama,
the newspaper, and the moving picture show. It
gradually accumulated a repertory that included all
the famous stories, and it added new ones at a prodi-
gious rate.

Under Henslowe's management the Rose was producing a new play every fortnight, and if the other
theaters did nearly as well, there were two new stories

every week for Londoners. They liked variety. If they saw Oberon and his fairies one day, they would the more willingly see a dramatization of a contemporary murder on another. They liked incident and action, and they preferred to have the emotions mixed. If they wept over distress, they desired an immediate relief in laughter. They enjoyed horrors but they preferred them mixed with fun. The more gruesome the tragedy, the more need for the jigs. They liked stories of strange lands, past times, and heroic deeds ; and they liked stories of the shoemakers, clothiers, and grocers of London. But beyond these somewhat natural and universal joys, they set few rules. They expected a story to have some order, some scheme ; the very pleasure of a story is partly that it has a beginning and an end. They expected to have the persons introduced, and after two hours of vicissitude to be finally disposed of — married or buried. They could enjoy a serial, two or three or even four plays on the same theme, but it must end, and everything be explained, settled, finished. But beyond this simple requirement there was little demand for formulas. They liked stories which purported to be true and those which purported to be false. The "Miseries of Enforced Marriage," drawn from a contemporary murder, and "Old Fortunatus" with his magic wishing cap, were all one. They were neither romanticists nor realists and had no fixed criteria. They did not even insist much on a happy ending or the triumph of virtue. After a time, moralists, and classicists, and naturalists and others began to introduce order and system and propriety of various kinds into these dramatic fictions. But in the early days of the theaters the audience seems to have been simply hungry for stories.

2 E,

By story, however, we must understand persons as well as plot. The drama, after all, is primarily impersonation. And the perennial interest in story is primarily an interest in our fellow human beings. The Elizabethan audience never lacked the keenest delight in human nature and consequently in its dramatic representation. This interest in human nature seems to remain about the same through the centuries and to find imaginative response of unsurpassable greatness under very different conditions and in periods far remote — in Aristophanes and Euripides, in Molière and Racine, in Balzac and Scott; and it is difficult to say just how the interest of one public differs from that of another, except in terms of the literature created to meet their demands. But the Elizabethan period was preëminently a period of individuals, a time when the individual man was working out his own progress and salvation as never before in England. He was escaping from the class of society into which he was born, or from the trade to which he was apprenticed, or the faith in which he was reared, he was carrying out new careers for himself in many new ways. He was less a cog in the machine, an item in society, a member of a class, a party, a sect, than ever before, and perhaps than he has ever been since. He came to the theater to hear and see the exploits, successes, trials, and defeats of other individuals like himself. He brought that curiosity about human nature which the adolescent youth feels, — dreaming of his own future. It was, indeed, the young men who crowded the theaters to hear stories and to see visions of what they themselves might do and become. The interest in motive and character was not much directed by formula or based on knowledge and culture, or narrowed by a strict morality; but, in that day, when the individual seemed looking on ever-widening horizons beneath which everything grew near and possible, that interest had an insistence and freshness hardly to be found in later epochs of readers.

In many ways this Elizabethan audience seems youthful to our more sophisticated tastes. Its ardent interest in experience, its curiosity about the ways of men, its liking for incongruous emotions, are the tastes of youth. There seems something improper to our taste in mixed metaphors, something indecent in the close juxtaposition of farce and pathos, grossness and innocence. We like our entertainment ordered and arranged and classified, and we are not much overjoyed at the extravagant or the impossible. It is the children who enjoy "Peter Pan"; but if Sir James Barrie could have been a little less self-conscious about his dog, fairies, and pirates, he might have carried many a theater full of Elizabethan adults along with him. Peele's "Old Wives' Tale" would hardly delight any court to-day, but it might be made into a charming extravaganza for our children. The nonsequitur interferes with our pleasure at the theater in the way that it does not to children and did not to the Elizabethans. We ask that the exposition be convincing and that the play develop from its premises. The Elizabethan asked that he be given a story which excited his imagination. As we grow more solemn and scientifically minded, perhaps we shall reject Shakespeare's romantic comedies, as did the early eighteenth century. It must be granted that they are fantastic and contain a good deal of nonsense and not much definitely labeled morality. But the Elizabethan audience, if it lacked that background of culture which encourages intellectual definitions and psychological precision in the drama, and that miscellaneous information which tends to sophistication, yet possessed that attitude which we find oftenest in children listening to stories — a mixture of impatience and responsiveness, a willingness to let one's imagination go and an eagerness to have it spurred. Something of this continues in every person who loves the play. But there can never be another age when the public goes to the theater, without much previous schooling or reading, and discovers there for the first time the whole world of stories.

What has been written so far in this chapter applies to the audiences that greeted Shakespeare's earliest plays rather than to those of the closing years of his career. Many changes have become manifest by the opening of the reign of James I. Some of them are directly connected with the private theaters. Others seem the result of growing prosperity, others of the growth of Puritanism. In every chapter of this volume, in matters of stage presentation, court performances, government regulation, management of the companies, important changes have been indicated, and the theater of 1640 has been found very different from that of 1610, and that still different from the theater of 1587. In a similar way, the audiences were undergoing rapid changes.

The private theaters, which became finally established during the first decade of the seventeenth century, were small in comparison with the public theaters and charged high prices. Seats were placed in the pit, or, as the "Historia Histrionica" has it, "Here they had pits for the gentry and acted by candlelight." This change means not merely that the auditors were more comfortable, but that the entire character of the audience was changed. The acting was no longer to the standing populace but to the gentry seated in the front benches. The prices, which seem to have increased further as time went on, effectually barred out the larger public, which still continued to throng the open-air theaters. The Fortune and the Red Bull, "were mostly frequented by citizens and the meaner sort of people." [1] The Globe maintained its reputation but was now used only as a summer house; in winter the King's men acted at the Blackfriars. This theater had become the resort of fashion, and regulations had to be made to control the great crowd of coaches waiting in the yard and streets outside. Moreover, women seem to have formed an increasingly large portion of the audience. It was now the private theaters which determined the plays to be acted at court, and which in general controlled the course of the drama.

The presence of fashion at the theater was not without difficulties. Dekker's "Gull's Horn Book" gives a satirical advice for the conduct of a gallant, which though prescribed for both the public and private playhouses, seems likely to have found more tolerance at the latter. Quotations may be permitted from the well-known passage, which constitutes the fullest contemporary account of a London audience.

Whether therefore the gatherers of the publique or private Play-house stand to receive the afternoones rent, let our Gallant (having paid it) presently advance himselfe up to the Throne of the Stage. I meane not into the Lords roome (which is now but the Stages Suburbs): No, those boxes, by the inquity of custome, conspiracy of waiting-women and Gentlemen-Ushers, that there sweat together, and the

---

[1] *Historia Histrionica*, Dodsley, xv. 407.

covetousnes of Sharers, are contemptibly thrust into the reare, and much new Satten is there dambd, by being smothred to death in darknesse. But on the very Rushes where the Comedy is to daunce, yea, and under the state of *Cambises* himselfe must our fethered *Estridge*, like a piece of Ordnance, be planted valiantly (because impudently) beating downe the mewes and hisses of the opposed rascality. . . .

Present not your selfe on the Stage (especially at a new play) untill the quaking prologue hath (by rubbing) got culor into his cheekes, and is ready to give the trumpets their Cue, that hees upon point to enter: for then it is time, as though you were one of the *properties*, or that you dropt out of ye *Hangings*, to creepe from behind the Arras, with your *Tripos* or three-footed stoole in one hand, and a teston mounted betweene a fore-finger and a thumbe in the other: for if you should bestow your person upon the vulgar, when the belly of the house is but halfe full, your apparell is quite eaten up, the fashion lost, and the proportion of your body in more danger to be devoured than if it were served up in the Counter amongst the Powltry: avoid that as you would the Bastome. It shall crowne you with rich Commendation, to laugh alowd in the middest of the most serious and saddest scene of the terriblest Tragedy: and to let that clapper (your tongue) be tost so high, that all the house may ring of it: your Lords use it; your Knights are Apes to the Lords, and do so too: your Inne-a-court-man is Zany to the Knights, and (mary very scurvily) comes likewise limping after it: bee thou a beagle to them all, and never lin snuffing, till you have scented them: for by talking and laughing (like a Plough-man in a Morris) you heap *Pelion* upon *Ossa*, glory upon glory: As first, all the eyes in the galleries will leave walking after the Players, and onely follow you: the simplest dolt in the house snatches up your name, and when he meetes you in the streetes, or that you fall into his hands in the middle of a Watch, his word shall be taken for you: heele cry *Hees such a gallant*, and you passe. Secondly, you publish your temperance to the world, in that you seeme not

to resort thither to taste vaine pleasures with a hungrie
appetite : but onely as a Gentleman to spend a foolish houre
or two, because you can doe nothing else : Thirdly, you
mightily disrelish the Audience, and disgrace the Author :
marry, you take up (though it be at the worst hand) a strong
opinion of your owne judgement, and inforce the Poet to
take pity of your Freakenesse, and, by some dedicated son-
net, to bring you into a better paradice, onely to stop your
mouth.

The success of the private theaters indicates that
there was a large class now willing to pay larger prices
and desirous to exercise their judgment and taste.
As early as 1607, Beaumont and Fletcher's "Knight
of the Burning Pestle" ridicules the citizen plays and
citizen audiences. The increase of wealth in Elizabethan London seems to have been very rapid, and
the court of James I rather lent encouragement to the
increase of luxury which follows an era of prosperity.
There had also been a rapid growth in general education. The audience of 1610 had much more of that
miscellaneous information which we expect in any city
audience than had that of 1590. London was taking
on the airs of a modern city. It was becoming sophisticated, worldly, and intensely interested in itself.
Moreover, it was rapidly dividing into two parties, that
of the court and that of the Puritans. Already in the
reign of James I, the plays are full of satire on the
Puritans, and it is the court party on which the drama
manifestly relies for its support. By the reign of
Charles I, the theaters are still more intimately attached to the court and completely divorced from the
growing majority of sober-minded citizens.

The increased patronage of the educated classes is
shown by more frequent appeals to them in prefaces

and dedications, and by the pretensions which the drama now makes to literary excellence and by its challenge of comparison with Plautus and Seneca, Aristophanes and Sophocles. Rant and bombast are discountenanced, style becomes less ornate and less exuberant, language loses its novelties and approximates a standard, the standard of upper-class London and the court. Beaumont and Fletcher, Dryden declares, understood and imitated the conversation of gentlemen much better than Shakespeare. Comedies of manners set forth the social life of the upper classes; and the stage no longer discloses the pitched field but the presence chamber or the drawing room. Politics receive increased attention, but democracy is less outspoken.

Some changes of this kind were inevitable with the passing of time. The audience was growing old. It had long been used to the theater. There was less novelty now, and there were no more new stories. The new generation was more critical, for the old masterpieces had established standards, and it was more knowing, for it had seen many plays. The audience, like the dramatists and the actors, had now established traditions of its own. It expected certain themes and methods. It no longer welcomed absolute novelty and experiment. It looked for imitation, refinement, adaptation, and slight departure. It was susceptible to fashion and criticism, as directed by the upper classes.

A marked indication of the change in the interests of the audience may be found in the large number of plays of social satire that appeared in the very decade in which the private theaters were establishing themselves. The day of fairies and ghosts was almost past on the stage; the growing sophistication of the public demanded realism; literary men found their incentive in a corrupt society waiting to be exposed. Merchants, lawyers, courtiers, citizens' wives, Puritans, all came in for attack, and the satire sometimes takes an extraordinary bitterness. Only a society far more self-conscious and critical than in the days of "Tamburlaine" could have welcomed such plays as Marston's "Malcontent" and Jonson's "Volpone." The chief topic of both satire and realism had become matters of sex. A large number of plays set forth scenes in houses of ill-fame, and adultery is the ever-recurring theme of tragedy and comedy. Even Shakespeare is affected by the change. "All's Well," "Measure for Measure," "Troilus and Cressida," have, if not a satiric, a bitter tone, and they all deal with adultery. It is impossible to find any of the plays that he wrote in the nineties which present such a view of sex as these three plays.

The change must mean, not necessarily that adultery was more prevalent than before, but that the Londoners now had more leisure to employ their minds on questions of sex. Some of the plays indeed are neither satiric nor salacious, but very much like modern problem plays, gaining their interest less from story than from the question which the play discusses. Heywood's "A Woman Killed with Kindness," perhaps the most notable example of this class, makes the erring wife the subject of sympathy as well as of debate; and Dekker's "Honest Whore," and, in some degree, Shakespeare's "Measure for Measure," may be included in the plays which make sexual relations the subject for discussion as well as for story. The fashion for these satiric and realistic plays soon wore itself out, and the theaters turned to the light-hearted, if not innocent, romances of Beaumont and Fletcher; but sex continued a dominant theme of the drama. And its dominance tended to narrow the wider range of stories demanded by the ardor of the earlier days. Tragedy, history, romance, and nonsense no longer mingled in one fantastic medley. Each kept to its own field and became merely an approach to the dominant interest. The audience had lost some of its childishness; it went to the theater, as how many audiences have gone since, expecting stories that would deal with that eternal subject of our curiosity, the entanglements of sex.

The intrigues of citizens' wives or the coquetry of ladies of fashion became the themes of realism, and the code of honor and the sanctity of the King's person the themes of romance, all involved in the dramatic presentation of adultery. There was little in the politics or morals of such a drama to mitigate the opposition of the Puritan. The stage had completely removed itself from the interests of that half of the nation which was soon to behead its king and close its theaters. Most students of the stage are fain to admit that the Puritans had a good deal of reason on their side. One cannot deny the truth of the words of the ordinance of the Long Parliament that closed the theaters for nearly twenty years. "Public sports do not well agree with public calamities, nor public stage plays with the seasons of humiliation, this being an exercise of sad and pious solemnity, and the other being spectacles of pleasure, too commonly expressing lascivious mirth and levity." The audiences that went to many of these later plays found neither morality nor decency. After the Restoration, the two theaters then established continued largely representative of the court and its followers; and it was not until the beginning of the eighteenth century that the drama began slowly to win back the support of the great body of sober-minded, middle-class Englishmen.

Yet, sixty years later at the time of Collier's castigation of the immorality of the stage, an aged apologist could look back on the years just preceding the Civil War as the halcyon days. "Then the prices were small (there being no scenes), and better order kept among the company that came; which made very good people think a play an innocent diversion for an idle hour or two, the plays themselves being then, for the most part, more instructive and moral."[1] To us, looking down from the earlier days, this later theater seems very close to that of the Restoration, but looking back from the playhouses "extremely pestered with vizard-masks and their trade," the audiences of the time of Charles I seemed seekers after innocent diversion, instruction, and morality.

In the specific matter of indecency, the drama in our period certainly grew steadily worse. There is sufficient grossness in the earlier plays, but it is the frank grossness of the streets. In the later days it has become the studied indecency of the profligate. The appeal of the plays is often to the entertainment of a corrupt society. It would be a mistake, however, to convict the entire audience on this evidence. The theaters were thronged to see Shakespeare's plays and the more moral of Massinger and Shirley as well as those reeking with adultery and seduction. But as the dominating portion of the audience became more and more representative of intelligence, fashion, and

[1] *Historia Histrionica.*

the court, while it banished the absurd wonders, vulgar histories, and extravagant romances of its early taste, it provided no new interests and enthusiasms. Politics and religion were bones of contention too bitter for free discussion in a theater regulated by the government. Business, trade, advance in wealth, were themes now relegated to the less fashionable theaters. Sex was the only theme left which had an interest for every one and an especial appeal to the ladies and gentlemen of the court and their imitators.

In considering the audience as it passed from the London of Drake to the London of Buckingham, we are naturally struck by the changes, but there was no break in the continuity of its existence. The persons who came one day to a theater came the next day or the next week, and they found there the same actors and the same plays. The apprentice who attended all the new plays in the nineties followed the success of his favorites Shakespeare and Burbage until their deaths, and in after years tried to persuade his children that Taylor and Lowin were far inferior in the great parts that Burbage had made his own. In the small city the intimate relations that existed among authors and actors applied in a measure to the audience as well. It would probably be impossible under the most favorable conditions of the present day to establish stock companies and community theaters as directly responsive to this public as these of London. A host of dramatists eager to write new plays, five or six established stock companies ready to produce new and old without great cost for scenes or advertising or stars, and a public that attended the theaters regularly and was uncontrolled by court or criticism — these are conditions under which the drama must respond to the public demand. Effective as is this public demand at the present time, it has no such chance for direct and immediate influence as it did under Elizabethan conditions. The drama attained its greatness through this opportunity for free experimentation, responding to fleeting moods and fashions as well as to profound social movements. In consequence we have very rapid changes in the character of the plays. For a few years everything is chronicle history, then realistic social plays, then romantic, and so on. The success of any kind of new departure is sure to be followed by several plays of the same sort. Any dramatist is sure to begin with some of the types of drama prevailing, though within a year or two he may have made successful innovations of his own. As the epoch developed, experimentation became less varied, and both audience and dramatist came to feel the effects of custom and tradition; but the period as a whole was certainly characterized by the sensitiveness of the drama to its public.

The Elizabethan audience has sometimes been extravagantly praised for its quick-wittedness and appreciation of poetry and sometimes extravagantly blamed for forcing its vulgarity on the plays of Shakespeare. Evidently it deserves a greater share of credit than audiences generally do for both the merits and the defects of the drama which it patronized. Taine was perhaps the first to point out with discriminating eloquence the full effect of the influence of the audience on the drama. So far as it affected Shakespeare, this influence has been ably analyzed in the recent criticism of M. Jusserand, Robert Bridges, and Professors Wendell, Bradley, Lounsbury, and Brander Matthews. Its general effect on Shakespeare for bad or for good is indeed unmistakable. No great dramatist reveals so plainly the lack of any standards of criticism or culture in his audience, the lack of a fixed body of social conventions or public opinion. If the audience must share in the censure for some lapses and excesses that result, it must also receive some share of the credit for the breadth and multiplicity of life which his plays present and which his Elizabethan audiences welcomed. And of the Elizabethan drama in general, it may be said that its greatest merit is similarly in its abundant and diversified presentation of human character; not in the main by social types, though these are found in some of Jonson's plays and elsewhere, nor in accord with literary formula, or religious creed, or moral and social conventions, but as individuals recognized and welcomed by the plaudits of a heterogeneous public. As has been hinted in an earlier chapter in this volume, the great tribute to the Elizabethan audience is the host of persons created for its recognition.

Shakespeare and his contemporaries may be deemed fortunate in having an audience essentially popular. Unusually attentive to the music of the spoken word, and eager for the newly unlocked storehouse of secular story, it possessed also the independent individuality and virility of Elizabethan Englishmen. Intimate and constant in its intercourse with theaters and actors, it impressed its demands and tastes upon the dramatists, but at the same time showed a quick and generous receptivity for whatever experiment or innovation playwright or company might attempt. Somewhat contaminated by sophistication and convention, it finally failed to control the appetite which had been so richly fed by the excitements and levities of the stage, and the Elizabethan audience in the end died of a surfeit of plays. Its monument is among the greatest that any public has ever received. For while the Elizabethan drama is far more than a record of the spacious time that produced it, there can be no doubt that it does embody with a completeness and vividness hardly known elsewhere the daily habit and custom, the external activities, the emotional storm and stress, the faiths and aspirations, dreams and fancies, of the audience for whom it was created.

APPENDIX I

This list is intended to include only stage directions that indicate unmistakably
the use of the inner stage. A few cases are debatable, but on the other hand large
groups of directions that seem to me to imply the curtain have been omitted. (1)
Where the reference may be to bed curtains or other special curtains. Some of these
are, I think, to the main curtain; special curtains being unnecessary. (2) Numerous references to arras or hangings used merely for the concealment of a single person, as Polonius in *Hamlet* or Falstaff in the *Merry Wives*. (3) References to caves,
studies, stops, temples, chambers, etc., when unsupported by mention of the curtain
or a discovery; usually omitted even when the direction reads "Enter as in the
tavern," "as in his study," etc. (4) Cases in which a tableau seems implied though
not explicitly a discovery, often at the beginning of scenes. (5) Cases in which properties are moved or set out or marked as "ready," which do not on their face indicate a discovery. I believe that a large number of these really were discoveries.
(6) Cases where the use of a curtain seems necessary though there is no direction;
e.g., *Pericles*, V. 1, or cases of a person sleeping on the stage through a change
of scene, as in *Endymion* and a *Midsummer Night's Dream*. I estimate that
these six groups would number as many plays as the following list. Of course no
mention has been made of the many instances in which the use of the curtain seems
probable though not supported by specific directions.

I fear the list is far from complete even with these restrictions, but it is more extensive than any list previously given and may serve to illustrate the nature of this
particular kind of evidence. I have marked a few directions with the name of the
modern editor, because I have not been able to verify these in the early editions. I
do not think there are many mistakes of this kind. The dates are those of publication, usually much later than the first presentation.

Albovine, 1629. V. 2. "A canopy is drawn, the King is discovered sleeping over papers." "He draws the arras and discovers Albovine, Rhodolinda, Valdaura, dead in chairs."

Alcazar, Battle of. Plat in Henslowe Papers, ed. Greg. II. "To
them (l)ying behind the Curtaines, 3 Furies," etc. See 2nd Dumb
Show.

All's Lost by Lust, 1633. "A bed discovered, on it Lazarillo at
[sic] Antonio."

Alphonsus of Arragon, 1599. "Let there be a Brazen Head set in the middle of the place behind the stage."

Amends for Ladies, 1618. V. 2. "A curtain drawn, a bed discovered; Ingen with his sword in his hand, and a pistol: the lady in her petticoat: the Parson."

Antonio's Revenge, 1602. V. 2. "The curtains being drawne, exit Andrugio." "The Curtains are drawne. Piero departeth." See also III. 4.

Anything for a Quiet Life, 1662. II. 2. "Water-Camlet, George and Ralph discovered" [a shop]. See V. 1. 123, where a change of scene takes place from street to interior. (Bullen.)

Atheist's Tragedy, 1611. V. 1. "A Clozet discover'd. A servant sleeping with lights and money before him."

Blurt, Master Constable, 1602. II. 2. "Good, draw the curtains, put out candles: and girls, to bed."

Bonduca, 1647. V. 1. "Enter Caratach upon a rock, and Hengo by him sleeping." See V. 3.

Brazen Age, 1613. II. 2. "Two fiery Buls are discovered, the Fleece hanging over them, and the dragon sleeping beneath them."

Brennoralt, 1646. III. 1. "Enter Francella as in a bed, asleep." *Hazlitt.*

Broken Heart, 1633. III. 2. "Ithocles discovered in a chair, and Penthea." V. 3. "An altar covered with white, two lights of virgin wax," etc.

Bussy D'Ambois, 1607. I. 1. "Table, Chesbord, & Tapers behind the Aarras." [In preparation for the next scene.]

Cæsar and Pompey, 1631. IV. 4. "Porcius discovers a bed, and a sword hanging by it which he takes down."

Captain Underwit. Ms. III. 1. *La.* "But prethe draw the Curtains close."

Careless Shepherd, 1658. II. 5. "A scene discovered etc. . . . scene closes up." V. 4. "Cleobulus draws the curtain and finds Coridon and Runius in a payre of stocks their hands tied and their mouths gagged."

Case is Altered, 1609. I. 1. "Iuniper a Cobbler is discovered sitting at worke in his shoppe and singing."

Catiline, 1611. I. 1. "The curtain draws, and Catiline is discovered in his study."

Chaste Maid in Cheapside, 1630. I. 1. Apparently a discovery, but see s. d. III. 2.

Christian Turn'd Turk, 1612. I. 1. "Enter Ward, Gismund, Albert, Ferd. Sailers rise from a Table."

City Madam, 1658. IV. 4. "Whilst the Act Plays, the Footstep, little Table, and Arras hung up for the Musicians."

City Match, 1639. III. 2. "Draws a curtain; behind it Timothy asleep like a strange fish" . . . "They draw the curtain before him." V. 7. "Draws the curtain; within are discovered Bright and Newcut."

City Night-Cap, 1661. II. 1. "A bed thrust out. Lodovico sleeping in his cloathes: Dorothea in bed: Enter Clown leading in Francisco." See II. 2; III. 2.

1 Contention between York and Lancaster, 1594. III. 2. "Exet Salisbury, Warwick drawes the curtains and showes Duke Humphrey in his bed."

Cromwell, Lord, 1602. III. 2. 126. "Goe draw the curtaines." II. 1. "Cromwell in his study." III. 2. "Hodge sits in the study."

Cupid's Revenge, 1615. II. 1. "Enter Hidaspes, Cleophila, and Hera. Hidaspes in a bed." See V. 3.

Cymbeline, 1623. II. 2. "Imogen in bed; a Lady." See also III. 3; V. 4.

David and Bethsabe, 1599. I. i. "He drawes a curtaine and discovers Bethsabe, with her Maid, bathing over a spring: she sings, and David sits above viewing her." l. 1910. "He goes to his pavilion and sits close a while." l. 1928. "He looks forth, and at the end sits close againe." l. 1934. "He unfolds the pavilion."

Death of Robert Earl of Huntingdon, 1601. I. "Draw the curtain: the King sits sleeping, his sword by his side."

Devil's Charter, 1607. I. 4. "Alexander in his study with books, coffers, his triple crowne upon a cushion before him." IV. 1. Study. IV. 4. Tent. V. 6. Curtain, study.

Devil's Law Case, 1623. "A table set forth with two tapers, a death's head, a book. Iolenta in mourning, Romelio sits by her." "Enter Crispiano like a judge with another judge, Cantelup, and another lawyer at one bar; Romelio, Ariosto, at another: Leonara with a black veil over her and Julio."

Dido, 1594. I. 1. "Here the curtains draw: there is discovered Jupiter dandling Ganymede upon his knee, and Mercury lying asleep." See III. 4.

Deserving Favourite, 1629. II. "Enter Clarinda and Lysander, (as in an Arbour), in the night."

Distresses, 1673. IV. i. Leonte "steps to the Arras softly, draws it. Claramente is discovered sleeping on her Book, her Glass by."

Double Marriage, 1647. II. 2. "He discovers Virolet and Ascanio in the bilboes."

Downfall of Robert, Earl of Huntingdon, 1601. I. 1. "they enfold each other and sit down within the curtains. . . . The curtains are again shut." III. 2. Curtains open: Robin Hood sleeps on a green bank, and Marian strewing flowers on him.

Duchess of Malfi, 1623. IV. 1. "Here is discover'd behind a travers, the artificial figures of Antonio and his children, appearing as if they were dead."

Eastward Hoe, 1605. I. 1. "At the middle dore, enter Golding, discovering a gold-smiths shoppe, and walking short turns before it." See also II. 1, III. 3, and IV. 1.

Edward I, 1593. Scene 10. "the Queen's tent opens. She is discovered in her bed, attended by Mary, Duchess of Lancaster, Joan of Acon her daughter; and the Queen dandles his young son." . . . "They close the tent." . . . "The Queen's tent opens; the king, his brother, the Earl of Glocester, enter." . . . "The Nurse closeth the tent." Sc. 25. "Elinor in child-bed with her daughter Ione and other Ladies." See Scenes 11 and 13.

2 Edward IV. II. Chorus. "Draw the curtain of our scene." See Albright, 56, 57, for cases of curtain in both Part I and Part II.

Fair Maid of the Inn, 1647. III. 2. "Enter Duke, Magistrate, Secretary, Baptista, Attendants, Mentivole (they sit). Mentivole stands by." IV. 1. "Enter Forobosco as in his study."

Fair Quarrel, 1617. IV. 2. A discovery. The colonel is lying wounded on a couch with friends about him.

Faithful Friends. Ms. 1. 2. [Four] "sitting around a table, every one pots in their hands." IV. 5. Altar.

Faithful Shepherdess, c. 1610. V. 1. "The Curtayne is drawne. Clorin appears sitting in the Cabin, Amoret sitting on one side of her. Allexis and Cloe on the other, the Satyre standing by."

Family of Love, 1608. III. 4. "Enter Maria and Gerardine out of the trunke." See III. 1, and III. 2.

Fatal Dowry, 1632. II. 2. "Draws a curtain" [special?]. IV. 1. "Enter Novall, junior, as newly dressed, a Taylor, Barber,

Perfumer, a looking glass. Liladam, Aymer, Page. Novall sits on
a chair. Barber orders his haire. Perfumer gives powder. Taylor
sets his clothes."

Faustus. (Later quartos) l. 1449. "Hell is discovered."

Fleire, 1607. "Enter Signior Albunio the Apothecarie in his
shop with wares about him."

Four Plays in One, 1647. Triumph of Love. IV. "Enter
Violante in a Bed; Angelina and Dorothea sitting by her."

Friar Bacon and Friar Bungay, 1594. IV. 1. "Enter Friar
Bacon drawing the courtaines, with a white sticke, a booke in his
hand, and a lampe lighted by him, and the brasen head and Miles,
with weapons by him."

Game at Chess, 1625. Induction. "Ignatius Loyola appearing.
Error at his feet as asleepe." V. 1. "An altar is discovered with
tapers and Images standing on each side."

Gentleman of Venice, 1655. III. 3. "opening the hangings."

Goblins, 1648. IV. p. 44, ed. Hazlitt. "Orsabrin discovered
in prison, bound." p. 62. "A curtain drawn; Prince, Philatel,
with others appear above." p. 37. Sabrina's chamber.

Golden Age, 1611. I. 1. "Enter Sibylla lying in child-bed with
her child lying by her."

Grim the Collier of Croydon, 1662. I. 1. "The curtains drawn
on a sudden; Pluto, Minos, Aeacus, Rhadamanthus set in counsel;
before them Malbecco's ghost guarded with furies."

Guardian, 1655. III. 9. "Enter Iolante (with a rich Banquet
and Tapers) in a Chair behind a Curtain."

Hector of Germany, c. 1613. I. 1. "A Bed Thrust out, the
Palsgrave lying sicke on it, the King of Bohemia, the Duke of
Savoy, the Marquisse Brandenburgh entring with him."

Henry VIII, 1623. II. 2. "Exit Lord Chamberlaine, and the
King drawes the Curtaine and sits reading pensively."

History of the Trial by Chivalry, 1605. II. 3. "Discover her
sitting in a chayre asleepe." See IV. 2. Three doors. V. "Enter
in the midst."

Histriomastix, 1610. II. 1. "Enter Countriman to them,
Clarke of the Market: hee wrings a bell and drawes a curtaine,
whereunder is a market set about a Crosse." See I. 3; V. 1.

Hoffman, 1631. I. 1. "Strikes ope a curtain where appears
a body." IV. 1. "Enter Ferdinand and Sarlois, open a curtain,
kneele Saxony, the hermit, and Mathias; tapers burning."

1 Honest Whore, 1604. Pearson ed., p. 12. *Duke*. "Uncurtain her." p. 17. "Enter Candidoes wife, George and two Prentises in the shop." See p. 39 and p. 61 for similar directions. p. 50. "Enter Bellafronte with Lute, Pen, inke, and paper being placed before her."

2 Honest Whore, 1630. III. 3. "Enter at one doore Lodovico and Carolo; at another Bots, and Mistris Horsleach; Candido and his wife appeare in the Shop."

Humorous Lieutenant, 1647. II. 3. " Enter Leucippe (reading) and two maids at a Table writing."

If It Be Not Good, the Devil is in It, 1612. I. "Narcisso stepping in before in the Scene, Enters here." V. "The play ending, as they goe off, from under the ground in severall places, rise up spirits, to them enter, leaping in great joy, Rufman, Shacklesoule, and Lurchall, discovering behind a curten, Ravillac, Guy Faulx, Bartervile, a Prodigall, standing in their torments." Later, "Curtaines are drawne over them."

1 If You Know not Me, You Know Nobody, 1605. "Enter Elizabeth in her bed."

2 If You Know not Me, You Know Nobody, 1606. "Enter in the shop two of Hobbins folks, and opening the shop" (Pearson, p. 283).

Imposture, 1653. II. 3. "Nuns discovered singing." (Dyce.)

Insatiate Countess, 1613. I. 1. "Isabella, Countess of Suevia, discovered sitting at a table covered with black on which stands two black tapers lighted, she in mourning."

1 Iron Age, 1632. IV. "Achilles discovered in his Tent, about him his bleeding Mermidons, himselfe wounded, and with him Ulisses."

2 Iron Age, 1632. II. "The Horse is discovered." III. "King Priam discovered kneeling at the Altar, with him Hecuba, Polixena, Andromache, Astianax: to them enter Pyrhus, and all the Greekes," etc.

Island Princess, 1647. II. 1. "The King appears laden with chains, his head and arms only above."

Jealous Lovers, 1632. V. vi. "Phronesium, Priests, and sacrifice, and Hymens statue discovered."

Jew of Malta, 1633. I. 1. "Enter Barabas in his Countinghouse, with heapes of gold before him." V. 4. "A charge, the cable cut, a caldron discovered into which Barabas falls."

Jovial Crew, 1641. I. "He opens the Scene; the Beggars are discovered in their postures; then they issue forth; and last the Patrico." II. "Randal opens the Scene. The beggars discovered at their Feast. After they have scrambled awhile at their Victuals: This Song."

King of Lombardy, 1673. V. 1. "A Canopy is drawn, the king is discover'd sleeping over Papers; Enter Paradine with his sword drawn."

Knight of Malta, 1647. V. 2. "An altar discovered, with Tapers and a book on it," etc. IV. 1, [near end] "discover Tombe."

Lady Errant, 1651. IV. 1. "Adraste, Lucasia, Malthora, Florina, Eumela, Cosmeta, Pendena, Rhodia, Machessa, sate as at Parliament." IV. 3. "She draws the hangings and shews 'em."

Looking Glass for London, 1594. II. 1. "Now ope ye foldes." "He drawes the Curtaines and finds her stroken with Thunder, blacke."

Lost Lady, 1639. I. 2. Tomb discovered. V. 1. "Enter the Moor on her bed, Hermione, Phillida, and Irene, the bed thrust out."

Lover's Melancholy, 1629. II. 2. "Draws the arras: Meleander discovered in a chair, sleeping."

Love's Mistress, 1636. III. 1. "Cupid discovered sleeping on a bed."

Love's Pilgrimage, 1647. I. 2. "Enter Theodosia and Phillipo on several Beds."

Lovers Progress, 1647. III. "Enter Clarinda with a Taper, and Lisander with a pistol, 2 chairs set out. Calista sitting behind a curtain."

Love's Sacrifice, 1633. II. 4. "Enter Bianca, her hair about her eares, in her night-mantle; she draws a curtain, and Fernando is discovered in bed sleeping; she sets down the candle before the bed, and goes to the bedside." V. 1. "A Curtain drawne, below are discovered Bianca in her night-attire, leaning on a cushion at a table, holding Fernando by the hand. Enter above Fiormonda." V. 3. "The tombe is discovered." See also II. 1.

Lust's Dominion, 1657. I. i. "Eleazer sitting on a chair suddenly draws the curtain." I. 3. "The Curtain being drawn, there appears in his bed King Philip, with his Lords, the Princess Isabella at the feet, Mendoza, Alvero, Hortenzo, Fernando, Roderigo; and to them enter the Queen in haste."

Mad Couple well Matched, 1653.   III. 1.   "The shop discover'd Alicia & Bellamy."   See IV. 3.

Mad Lover, 1647.   V. 1.   "Enter Nun, she opens the curtain to Calis.   Calis at the Oracle, Arras."   "Chilax and Priest, in the Oracle."

Mad World My Masters, 1608.   III. 2.   "viols, gallipots, plate, and an houre-glasse by her.   The Curtizen on a bed for her counterfeit fitt."   IV. 1.   "Enter in his chamber out of his studie, Master Penitent, Once Ill, a Booke in his hand reading."   See also II. 7.

Maid in the Mill, 1647.   V. 2.   "Florimel discovered."

Maid of Honour.   IV. 3.   "Bertoldo with a small booke in fetters, Jaylor."

Maid's Tragedy, 1619.   V. 1.   "King abed."

Martyred Soldier, 1638.   III. 2.   "Eugenius discovered sitting loaded with many Irons, a Lampe burning by him; then enter Clowne with a piece of browne bread and a Carret root."   See I. 1.

Massacre at Paris, n. d.   I. 5.   "Enter the Admirall in his bed."   I. 6.   "Enter into the Admiral's house and he in his bed."   I. 9. "Enter Ramus in his studie."

Match at Midnight, 1633.   II. 2.   "Enter in the Taverne, Alex, The Captaine, Lieutenant, Sue Shortheeles, a whore, Mistresse Cook, a Bawde."   See II. 1, and IV.

Match Me in London, 1631.   II.   "A shop opened.   Enter Bibbo and Lazarillo."

Mayor of Queensborough, 1661.   I. 2.   "Fortune discovered, in her hand a round ball full of lots," etc.

Merry Devil of Edmonton, 1608.   "Prologue draws curtain."

Michaelmas Term, 1607.   II. 1.   "Enter Rearage, Salewood, Lethe, Easy, and Shortyard, alias Blastfield, at dice."   III. 1.   "Enter Lethes pander, Helgill, the Countrie wench comming in with a new fashion gowne drest Gentlewoman like, the Taylor pointes it, and a Tyrewoman busie about her head."

Monsieur Thomas, 1639.   III. 1.   "Enter Frank sick, Physicians and an Apothecary."   V.   "A Bed discovered with a Blackmoore in it."

News from Plymouth, 1673.   IV. 2.   "A curtain drawn by Dash (his clerk) Trifle discover'd in his study.   Papers, taper, seal and wax before him, bell."

No Wit, no Help like a Woman's, 1657.   IV. 2.   "Several

servants discovered placing things in order, and Pickadill looking on." (Bullen.)

Old Fortunatus, 1600. III. 2. "A curtain being drawne, where Andelocia lies sleeping in Agripyne's lap."

Old Wives' Tale, 1595. Sc. 13. "He draweth a curtain and there Delia sitteth asleep."

Parson's Wedding, 1663. IV. 1. "They knock within, and the Parson discovered in his bed, and the Bawd with him." IV. 6. "The tiring room, curtains drawn, and they discourse. His chamber, two beds, two tables, looking glasses, night-clothes, waist-coats, sweet-bags, sweetmeats, and wine; Wanton dressed like a chambermaid. All above, if scene can be so ordered." V. 2. "The Fiddlers play in the tiring-room; and the stage curtains drawn, and discover a chamber. . . . The Music wakens the Widow. . . . She opens the curtain and calls her; she is under a canopy."

Picture, 1630. "They draw the curtaine."

Platonic Lovers, 1636. II. 1. "Draws a Canopy. Eurithea is found sleeping on a Couch, a Veil on, with her lute."

Politician, 1655. IV. 3. "Heraldus on a couch sick; Marpesa and Physicians."

Ram Alley, 1611. I. "Enter Throte the Lawyer from his study, bookes and bags of money on a Table, a chaire and cushion."

Rape of Lucrece, 1608. IV. 3. "Lucrece discovered in her bed." V. 1. "A table and chair covered with black; Lucrece and maid." V. 4. "A table and lights in a tent."

Rebellion of Naples, 1649. IV. 4. "The curtain drawn."

Renegado, 1630. I. 3. "A shop discovered, Gazet in it. Francisco and Vitelli walking by." See also II. 4, and II. 5.

Revenger's Tragedy, 1607. I. 4. "Enter Antonio . . . discovering her dead body to Hippolito, Piero, and Lords." V. 1. "The Duke's corpse, dressed in Vendice's disguise lying on a couch." See also II. 4.

Roaring Girl, 1611. I. "The three shops open in a rank: the first a Pothecary's shop, the next a fether Shop, the third a sempster's shop."

Romeo and Juliet, 1597. "She falls upon her bed, within the curtains." See IV. v.

St. Patrick for Ireland, 1640. II. 2. "The Temple. Ferochus and Enderius representing two Idols, before them an altar, at which stand Archimagus and Majicians; Rodamant is arranging lights and preparing incense." (Dyce.)

Sapho and Phao, 1584. "She falleth asleepe. The Curtaines drawne."

Satiromastix, 1602. I. 2. "Horace sitting in a study behinde a curtain, a candle by him burning, books lying confusedly."

Shoemaker's Holiday, 1600. IV. 1. "Enter Jane in a sempster's shop working, and Hammon muffled at another door; he stands aloof." IV. 2. "Enter Hodge at his shop board, Rafe, Firk, Hans, and a boy at work."

Siege (Cartwright), 1651. III. 1. "Misander discover'd asleep." III. 3. "Misander on a couch." III. 5. "Leucasia discover'd in a chair, and Euthalpe by her." V. 3. "Leucasia discover'd sleeping." V. 8. "They being all set, a Curtain being drawn discovers five valiant Generals, standing in Severall Postures, with fix'd Eyes like Statues . . . the Curtain in the mean time shutting . . . the curtain flies aside," etc.

Sir Giles Goosecap, 1606. V. 1. "He draws the curtains and sits within them."

Sir John Oldcastle, 1600. V. 1. "Enter Cambridge, Scroope, and Grey as in a chamber, and set down at a table, consulting about their treason: King Henry and Suffolke, listening at the door."

Sir John van Olden Barnaveldt. Ms. III. 6. "Son abed."

Sir Thomas More. Ms. I. 2. "An Arras is drawne and behind it (as in Sessions) sit the L. Maior, Justice Suresbie, and other Justices, Sheriffe Moore and the other Sherife sitting by. Smart is the Plaintife, Lifter the prisoner at the barre."

Sir Thomas Wyat, 1607. "Enter Winchester, Arundell, and other Lords, the Lord Treasurer kneeling at the Counsell Table."

Sophonisba, 1606. IV (end). "Syphax hasteneth within the canopy, as to Sophonisba's bed." V. 1. Syphax draws the curtains, and discovers Erichtho lying with him." See I. 2.

Spanish Tragedy, 1594. IV. 3. "Enter Hieronimo; he knocks up the curtaine." See IV. 4.

Tale of a Tub, 1640. V. 5. "Medley appears above the curtain."

2. Tamburlaine, 1590. II. 3. "The arras is drawen, and Zenocrate lies in her bed of State, Tamburlaine sitting beside her; three Phisitians about her bed tempering potions," etc. See IV. 1, and IV. 2.

Tancred and Gismunda, 1591. *Epi.* "Now draw the curtaines for our scene is done."

Tempest, 1623. V. 1. "Here Prospero discovers Ferdinand and Miranda playing at chess."

'Tis Pity She's a Whore, 1633. III. 6. "Enter the fryar sitting in a chayre; Annabella kneeling and whispering to him; a table before them and wax lights." V. 5. "Enter Giovanni and Annabella lying on a bed."

Traitor, 1635. V. 3. "The body of Amidea discovered on a bed, prepared by two Gentlewomen." See III. 1; III. 3; IV. 1.

Trick to Catch the Old One, 1608. IV. 5. "Dampit the Usurer in his bed, Audrey spinning by."

Two Merry Milkmaids, 1620. III. 2. "Enter the Duke, Iudges, Raymond, with others, the forme of a Court. Enter Dorigen plac'd at the Barre." See IV. 3.

Unfortunate Lovers, 1643. V. "Draws the hangings" . . . "Draws the hangings further."

Valentinian, 1647. II. 1. "Enter the Emperor, Maximus, Licinius, Proculus, Chilax, as at Dice." II. 4. Lucina says: "ha, ye may draw the curtain; I have seen em."

Virgin Martyr, 1622. V. 1. "Enter Theophilus in his study, books about him."

Volpone, 1607. V. 3. Volpone peeps from behind a traverse. See V. 10.

Westward Ho, 1607. IV. 2. "Earle draws a curtain, and sets forth a banquet."

What You Will, 1607. For full stage directions and discussion, see p. 119 ff.

White Devil, 1612. V. 4. "Cornelia, the Moore and 3 other Ladies discovered, winding Marcello's coarse. A song."

Whore of Babylon, 1607. *Prol.* "He draws a curtain discovering Truth in sad habiliments uncrowned, her hair discheveled, and sleeping on a rock," etc. p. 243. Pearson ed. "A cave suddenly breaks open, and out of it comes Falsehood," etc.

Wife for a Month, 1647, lic. 1624. II. 1. "A curtain drawn. The King, Queen, Valerio, Evanthe, Ladies, Attendants, Camillo, Cleanthes, Sorano, Menallo, A Mask." III. 1. "Rugio and Frier Marco, discover the Tomb and a chair."

Winter's Tale, 1623. V. 1. Paulina draws a curtain discovering Hermione. No. s. d.

Wisdom of Doctor Dodypoll, 1600. "A Curtaine drawne. Earle Lassingberg is discovered (like a Painter) painting Lucilia, who sits working on a piece of cushion work."

Wise Woman of Hogsdon, 1638. I. 2. "Enter Luce in a Sempster's shop."

Witch, Ms. 1778. "the Duke discovered on a couch."

Witty Fair One, 1633. III. 1. "Brains is discovered with a paper in his hand." III. 4. "Fowler, as if sick, upon a couch; and Manly disguised as a Physician attending him; phials, etc. on table."

Woman Hater, 1607. V. 1. "Secretary draws the curtain."

Woman in the Moon, 1597. I. 1. "They draw the Curtins from before Nature's shop, where stands an Image clad and some unclad, they bring forth the cloathed image."

Woman is a Weathercock, 1612. III. 2. "Scudmore passeth one door and entereth the other, when Bellafront sits asleep in a chair, under a taffeta canopy."

Women Pleased, 1647. I. 2. "Enter Lopez at a Table with Jewels and money upon it an egg roasting by a candle." See IV. 3.

Woman's Prize, 1647. V. "Enter Livia discovered abed and Morose by her."

Wonder of a Kingdom, 1636. III. "A bed discovered, Fiametta upon it. Enter 2 dukes, Piers, Gallants, Nurse, ladies, Angelo, Baptista ut antea Fyametta."

Yorkshire Tragedy, 1608. For stage directions and discussion, see p. 115ff.

Your Five Gallants, n. d. I. 1. Frippery discovered summing up his pawns. (Dyce.) See I. 3.

Wits, 1636. II. 4. "Leads him to look in 'tween the hangings." *Eld. Pal.* "A bed and canopy!"

APPENDIX II

BIBLIOGRAPHICAL NOTES

It is the purpose of these Notes to indicate the books and articles that have been of assistance in the preparation of this volume, and to furnish the student with a guide to the more important or more recent literature in the various fields. No effort has been made to supply an exhaustive list of the books consulted. Good general bibliographies can be found in Chambers' Medieval Stage, Greg's edition of Henslowe's Diary, vol. ii, Schelling's Elizabethan Drama, and the Cambridge History of English Literature, vols. v and vi, especially that for vol. vi, chap. x. Special bibliographies are noted in the following lists.

CHAPTER I

THE PLACE OF SHAKESPEARE'S THEATER IN THE HISTORY OF THE ENGLISH STAGE

Since the matter of this chapter is covered by the specific bibliographies for the later chapters, a list is given here of the more important authorities and collections of documents on the Shakespearian Theater. In footnotes to the text the author's name is used for reference, except in cases where there are more than one volume by the same author, when use is made of the abbreviations indicated below.

The titles of a few important books on the continental theater are included. Works on the Elizabethan Drama or Shakespeare are not included unless they are closely connected with the scope of this book.

Acts of the Privy Council of England. See Dasent.

Albright, V. E. The Shakespearian Stage. 1909. Chapter III was published separately as A Typical Shakespearian Stage, 1908.

Bapst, G. Essai sur l'histoire du Théâtre. Paris, 1893.

Boswell, J.   See Malone.

Calendar of Letters and Papers, Foreign and Domestic, of the Reign of Henry VIII.   Ed. Brewer, J. S., et al.   1862–.

Calendar of the Patent Rolls.   1891–1908.

Calendar of State Papers, Domestic Series, of the reigns of Edward VI, Mary, Elizabeth, and James I, preserved in the Public Record Office.   1856–72.   Ed. Lemon, M., and Green, M. A. E. 1856–72.   Of Charles I.   1858–97.

Chambers, E. K.   The Medieval Stage.   2 vols.   Oxford, 1903. Authoritative, with a valuable bibliography and appendixes.

Chalmers, G.   An Apology for the Believers in the Shakespeare Papers, which were exhibited in Norfolk Street.   1797.

——— A Supplemental Apology.   1799.

Collier, J. P.   The History of English Dramatic Poetry to the time of Shakespeare : and the Annals of the Stage to the Restoration.   1831.   3 vols.   *H. E. D. P.*   References are to this edition, except when the second edition of 1879 is specified.

——— For other works, see later bibliographies.   His edition of Henslowe's Diary has been entirely superseded by that of Greg.

Creizenach, W.   Die Geschichte des neueren Dramas.   Halle, 1893–.   Four vols. published; an English translation promised. Vol. iv deals with the English drama.

Dasent, J. R., ed.   Acts of the Privy Council of England.   New Series.   1890, etc.   *Acts.*

Cunningham, P.   Extracts from the Accounts of the Revels at Court in the Reigns of Queen Elizabeth and King James I. Shakespeare Society.   1842.   See Feuillerat, whose editions of the Revels Accounts now supersede Cunningham's.

Dictionary of National Biography.   1885–1900.   63 vols.

Downes.   Roscius Anglicanus, or An Historical Review of the Stage from 1660 to 1706.   Facsimile of ed. of 1708.   1886.

Feuillerat, A.   Documents relating to the Office of the Revels in the time of Queen Elizabeth.   Materialien zur Kunde des alteren Englischen Dramas.   Louvain, 1908.

——— Documents relating to the Revels at Court in the time of King Edward VI and Queen Mary.   Materialien.   Louvain, 1914.

Fleay, F. G.   A Biographical Chronicle of the English Drama, 1559–1642.   1891.   2 vols.   *Chronicle.*

——— A Chronicle History of the London Stage, 1559–1642. 1890.   *Stage.*

Gildersleeve, V. Government Regulation of the Elizabethan Theater. 1908.

Greg, W. W., ed. Henslowe's Diary. 1904-8. 2 vols. *H. D.* Invaluable both as a document and a commentary on the stage history.

—— Henslowe Papers: being Documents supplementary to Henslowe's Diary. 1907.

—— A List of English Plays written before 1643 and printed before 1700. Bibliographical Society. 1900. The title pages are reprinted.

—— A List of Masques, Pageants, etc., supplementary to A List of English Plays. Bibliographical Society. 1902.

Haigh, A. E. The Attic Theatre. 3d ed., 1907.

Halliwell-Phillipps, J. O. Illustrations of the Life of Shakespeare. 1874. Documents, reprinted in the *Outlines*, q.v.

Outlines of the Life of Shakespeare. 2 vols. 7th ed., 1887. All references are to this edition; later editions are reprints. *Outlines.*

Hastings, C. Le Théâtre Français et Anglais, ses origines Grecques et Latines. Paris, 1900. English trans. by F. A. Welby. 1901.

Hazlitt, W. C. The English Drama and Stage under the Tudor and Stuart Princes, 1543-1664. Roxburghe library. 1869. Prints important documents.

Historical Mss. Commission Reports, 1871-.

Kelly, W. Notices illustrative of the drama, etc., extracted from the Chamberlain's accounts and other manuscripts of the borough of Leicester. 1865.

Lawrence, W. J. The Elizabethan Playhouse and other Studies. Stratford, 1912.

—— The Elizabethan Playhouse. Second Series. Stratford, 1913.

Lee, S. A Life of William Shakespeare. New ed., 1915.

Loseley Mss., ed. A. J. Kempe. 1835.

Maas, H. Äussere Geschichte der Englischen Theatertruppen. 1559-1642. Materialien. 1907.

Malone, E. The Plays and Poems of William Shakespeare, edited by the late E. Malone [ed. by J. Boswell]. 21 vols. 1821. Includes Malone's History of the Stage. *Variorum.*

Malone Society, Publications of, especially Collections. Vol. I contains, among other matter, the Remembrancia, Dramatic Records from the Landsdowne Mss., Dramatic Records from the Patent Rolls,

Licenses, and Dramatic Records from the Privy Council Register, 1603–42. These documents are edited by E. K. Chambers and W. W. Greg. Vol. II, Part I, contains Blackfriar Records, ed. A. Feuillerat. *Malone Soc. Coll.*

Mantzius, K. A History of Theatrical Art in Ancient and Modern Times. Trans. by L. von Cossel. 4 vols. Vol. 3 deals with the Shakespearian period. 1904.

Matthews, B. Shakespeare as a Playwright. 1913.

—— Development of the Drama. 1906.

—— A Study of the Drama. 1910.

Murray, J. T. English Dramatic Companies. 1558–1642. 2 vols. 1910. Especially valuable for the provincial records printed in vol. ii.

Neilson, W. A., and Thorndike, A. H. The Facts about Shakespeare. 1913.

Remembrancia. Analytical Index to the Series of Records known as the Remembrancia. Preserved among the Archives of the City of London. 1579–1664. Ed. by W. H. and H. C. Overall. 1878. References in the text to *Remembrancia* are always to the Index, but accompanying references are given to the *Malone Soc. Coll.*, which print the literal text from the Records.

Rennert, H. A. The Spanish Stage in the time of Lope de Vega. 1909.

Rigal, A. Le Théâtre Français avant la periode classique. Paris, 1901.

—— Alexandre Hardy, et le Théâtre Français. Paris, 1889.

Schelling, F. E. Elizabethan Drama. 2 vols. 1908. The List of Plays in vol. ii serves as a general directory to both early and modern editions.

Smith, W. The Commedia dell' Arte. 1912.

Stuart, D. C. Stage Decoration in France in the Middle Ages. 1910.

Wright, J. Historia Histrionica. 1699. Repr. in Hazlitt's Dodsley. XV.

CHAPTER II

SHAKESPEARE'S LONDON

See bibliographies in the Cambridge Modern History, vol. iii, chap. x, and the Cambridge History of English Literature, vol. v, chap. xiv.   The two most accessible and important works on the subject are: William Harrison's *Description of Britaine and England*, in Holinshed's Chronicle, 1577, reprinted in the Shaks. Soc. Publ. 1877–8; and John Stow's Survey of London, 1st ed., 1598. The following list includes only more important and more recent books.

Aiken, L.   Memoirs of the Court of James I.   2d ed., 1822.

Ashton, J.   Humour, Wit, and Society in the Seventeenth Century.   1883.

Besant, Sir W.   London.   1892.

—— London in the Times of the Tudors.   1908.

Creighton, M.   The Age of Elizabeth.   1892.

Creizenach, W.   Geschichte des neueren Dramas.   Halle, 1893–.   See vol. iv, part i, book iii, Religios-sittliche und politisch-soziale Anschauungen der Theaterdichter.

Douce, F.   Illustrations of Shakespeare and of Ancient Manners. 1839.

Froude, J. A.   History of England from the Fall of Wolsey to the Defeat of the Armada.   1856–70.

Gardiner, S. R.   History of England from the Accession of James I to the Outbreak of the Civil War.   4 vols.   1893–97.

Hall, H.   Society in the Elizabethan Age.   4th ed., 1901.

Jusserand, J. J.   Histoire littéraire du peuple Anglais.   Paris, 1904.   English trans., 1909.   See especially vol. ii, book v, chap. i.

Lee, S.   Stratford-on-Avon from the earliest times to the death of Shakespeare.   1907.

—— An Account of Shakespeare's England, a survey of social life and conditions in the Elizabethan age (in preparation).

Nicholls, J.   The Progresses and Processions of Queen Elizabeth.   New ed.   3 vols.   1823.

—— The Progresses, Processions, and Festivities of King James I. 4 vols.   1828.

Rye, W. B.   England as seen by Foreigners in the Days of Elizabeth and James the First.   1865.

Stephenson, H. T.   Shakespeare's London.   1905.

—— The Elizabethan People.   1910.

Strutt, J.   Sports and Pastimes of the People of England.   1801. New ed., 1903.

Thompson, E. N. S.   The Controversy between the Puritans and the Stage.   Yale Studies in English, vol. xx.   New York, 1903.

Thornbury, G. W. Shakespeare's England. 2 vols. 1856.

Traill, H. D. Social England. 3d. ed., 1904. See vols. iii and iv.

Wakeman, H. O. The Church and the Puritans. 1570–1660. New ed., 1902.

Wheatley, H. B. London Past and Present. 3 vols. London, 1891.

Wilson, J. D. Life in Shakespeare's England. Cambridge, 1911. A good anthology.

CHAPTER III

THE PLAYHOUSES

Malone's *Variorum*, Collier's *H. E. D. P.*, Fleay's *Stage*, Halliwell-Phillipp's *Outlines*, and Greg's *H. D.*, and *Henslowe Papers*, all noted in the bibliography for Chap. I, are important here. Footnotes to the text call attention to the special value of recent investigations when they supersede earlier authorities, especially to documents published by Wallace and Feuillerat. A list of law suits dealing with theaters and companies is given with the Bibliographical Notes for Chaps. IX, X, XI.

Of the early maps and views showing bear rings or playhouses, the following notes may be useful to students. Three views agree in showing two bear or bull rings on the Bankside, presumably on the future locations of the Hope and the Globe. These are: (1) the Agas map of about 1570, in Civitas Londinum, issued ed. W. H. Overall, 1874. (2) The map attributed to Hoefnagel in the Brown and Hogenberg Atlas, 1572. (3) View of London about 1588 in Ms. of William Smith, printed in Baker's Development of Shakespeare as a Dramatist. The Newcourt-Faithorne map shows only one ring, labeled the Bear Garden. The earliest map to show a playhouse is that engraved by Van den Keere, published in Norden's Speculum Britanniæ, 1583, showing two buildings on the Bankside, one labeled 'The Beare howse,' the other 'The play howse,' presumably the Rose. Ryther's map of 1604 shows one theater on the Bankside, and two to the north, perhaps the Theatre and the Fortune. The Hondius view in Speed's Theatre of the Empire of Great Britaine, 1611, shows two theaters on the Bankside. Visscher's Panorama, 1616, reproduced by the London Topographical Society, is the earliest to show three theaters on the Bankside, and they are in the correct positions for the Globe, Hope, and Swan. An engraving after Delarum of an equestrian figure of James I also

shows three theaters on the Bankside. Merian's view in the Archon-
tologia of Gottfried, 1638, also has three theaters. The Porter
map (c. 1660) in the Crace collection shows a single theater. The
Hollar panorama of 1647 shows two theaters on the Bankside,
labeled 'Beerebayting' and the 'Globe.' The Hollar view in
Londinopolis, 1657, is the only one to represent four theaters on the
Bankside presumably the Globe, Hope, Rose, and Swan. Various
later maps show theaters on the Bankside. One in Hughson's
London (1805) vol. i, p. 140, shows a bear and a bull ring, and on
the north of the city two theaters in positions corresponding to
those on Ryther's map.

Adams, J. Q. The Four Pictorial Representations of the Elizabethan Stage. Journal Eng. and Germ. Phil. April, 1911.

Baines, W. W. Holywell Priory and the Site of the Theatre,
Shoreditch, London County Council — Indications of Houses of
Historical Interest in London. Part xliii. 1915.

Baker, G. P. The Development of Shakespeare as a Dramatist.
1907.

Crace, F. A Catalogue of Maps, Plans and Views of London.
1878.

Feuillerat, A. Origins of Shakespeare's Blackfriars Theater.
Shaks. Jahrbuch. 1912.

—— Blackfriars Records. *Malone Soc. Coll.*, II. i. 1913.

Graves, T. S. The Court and the London Theaters during the
Reign of Elizabeth. Menasha, Wis., 1913.

—— A Note on the Swan Theatre. Modern Philology. Jan.,
1912.

Hubbard, G. On the Exact Site of the Globe Playhouse of
Shakespeare. Trans. of the London and Middlesex Archeological
Society. New Series. Vol. II, part iii. 1912.

Greenstreet, J. The Blackfriars Playhouse: its Antecedents.
Athenæum. July 17, 1886, Jan. 7, 1888.

—— The Blackfriars Theater in the Time of Shakespeare.
Athenæum. April 7, 1888, April 21, 1888.

Martin, W. The Site of the Globe Playhouse of Shakespeare.
Reprinted from Surrey Archæological Collections, v. xxiii. 1910.

Ordish, T. F. Early London Theaters. 1894.

Rendle, W. The Bankside, Southwark, and the Globe Playhouse. Appendix I to Harrison's Description of England. Shaks.
Soc. Publ. Part II, 1878.

—— Old Southwark and its People. 1878.

Rendle, W., and Newman, P. The Inns of Old Southwark and their Associations. 1888.

Stopes, C. C. Burbage's Theatre. Fortnightly Review, July, 1909.

Wallace, C. W. The Children of the Chapel at Blackfriars. 1597–1603. Univ. of Nebraska Studies, 1908.

—— Shakespeare in London. Four Documents on the Poet and his Theaters. The Globe and the Blackfriars. London Times, Oct. 2, and Oct. 4, 1909.

—— Three London Theaters. Univ. of Nebraska Studies, 1909.

—— Evolution of the English Drama up to Shakespeare : with a history of the first Blackfriars Theatre. Berlin, 1912.

—— The Swan Theater and the Earl of Pembroke's Servants. Englische Studien, 1911.

—— The First London Theater. Univ. of Nebraska Studies, 1913.

—— New Light on Shakespeare (two articles concerning documents bearing on the Bankside locations). London Times, April 30, May 1, 1914.

Wheatley, H. B. On a Contemporary drawing of the interior of the Swan Theatre, 1596. Trans. New Shaks. Society. 1888.

Wilkinson, R. Londina Illustrata. 2 vols. 1819.

CHAPTERS IV AND V

THE PHYSICAL STAGE.   STAGE PRESENTATION

Older authorities as Malone, *Variorum*, and Collier, *H. E. D. P.*, are out of date but must be consulted on some matters.   Creizenach, Greg, *H. D.*, vol. ii, and *Henslowe Papers*, and Lawrence's two volumes on the *Elizabethan Playhouse* are important.

In Chap. IV, the conclusions presented are in general accord with Archer's article in the Quarterly Review and Albright's *Shakespearian Stage*, to which the chapter is greatly indebted.

In Chap. V, my conclusions differ in many particulars from those of preceding investigators.   I am indebted again to Albright's *Shakespearian Stage*, and also to many investigators holding views opposed to his, especially to Reynolds, Neuendorff, Graves, and Lawrence.

Albright, V. E. The Shakespearian Stage. 1909.

—— Percy's Plays as Proof of the Elizabethan Stage. Mod. Phil., Oct., 1913.

Archer, W. The Elizabethan Stage. The Quarterly Review, April, 1908.

—— A Sixteenth Century Playhouse. The Universal Review, August, 1888.

—— The Fortune Theater. London Tribune, Oct. 12, 1907. Repr. Shaks. Jahrbuch, 1908.

Baker, G. P. The Development of Shakespeare as a Dramatist. 1907.

—— Hamlet on an Elizabethan Stage. Shaks. Jahrbuch, xli. 296.

Bang, W. Zur Bühne Shakespeares. Jahrbuch. xl. 223.

Bell, H. Contributions to the History of the English Playhouse. Architectural Record, 1913. 262–267, 359–368.

Brandl, A. Quellen des weltlichen Dramas in England vor Shakespeare. Strassburg, 1898. See Einleitung.

—— A Review of Albright's Shakespearian Stage. Jahrbuch, 1910.

—— Eine Neue Art Shakespeare zu spielen. Deutsche Rundschau, April, 1905.

Brodmeier, C. Die Shakespeare-Bühne nach den alten Bühne-anweisungen. Weimar, 1904.

Chambers, E. K. The Stage of the Globe. In Works of William Shakespeare, vol. x. Stratford, 1907.

Child, H. The Elizabethan Theatre. In Cambridge History. Eng. Lit. vol. VI, chap. X. 1910.

Corbin, J. Shakespeare and the Plastic Stage. Atlantic Monthly, March, 1906.

—— Shakespeare his own Stage Manager. Century Magazine, Dec., 1911.

Flechsig, E. Dekoration der Modernen Bühne in Italien (to 1600). 1894.

Gaedertz, K. T. Zur Kenntnis der altenglischen Bühne, nebst andern Beitragen zur Shakespeare-Litteratur (with the picture of the Swan). Bremen, 1888.

Genée, R. Ueber die scenischen Formen Shakespeare's in ihrem Verhältniss zur Bühne seiner Zeit. Shaks. Jahrbuch, 1891.

Godfrey, W. H. See Archer, W., London Tribune, Oct. 12, 1907.

Grabau, C. Zur Englischen Bühne um 1600. Shaks. Jahrbuch, 1902.

Graves, T. S. The Court and the London Theaters during the Reign of Elizabeth. Menasha, Wis., 1913.

Kirkman, F. The Wits, or Sport upon Sport. 1673. Contains the so-called Red Bull picture.

Hale, E. E., Jr. Influence of Theatrical Conditions on Shakespeare. Mod. Phil., vol. i.

Lawrence, W. J. The Elizabethan Playhouse and Other Studies. Stratford, 1912. These essays had first appeared in Englische Studien and other publications.

—— The Elizabethan Playhouse. Second Series. 1913.

Logeman, H. Johannes de Witt's Visit to the Swan Theater. Anglia, 1897.

Monkemeyer, P. Prolegomena zu eines Darstellung der englischen Volksbühne zur Elizabeth- und Stuart-zeit. Leipzig, 1905.

Neuendorff, B. Die Englische Volksbühne im Zeitalter Shakespeares nach den Bühnenweisungen. Literarhistorische Forschungen. 1910.

Prölsz, R. Alt englisches Theater. (Meyer's Klassiker-Ausgaben.) 2 vols. 1904.

—— Von den ältesten Drucken der Dramen Shakespeares, etc. Leipzig, 1905.

Reynolds, G. F. Some Principles of Elizabethan Staging. Reprinted from Modern Philology. Chicago, 1905.

—— Trees on the Stage of Shakespeare. Modern Philology, 1907-8.

—— What we know of the Elizabethan stage. Modern Philology, July, 1911. With bibliography of recent discussions.

—— William Percy and His Plays. Mod. Phil., Oct., 1914.

Roy, E. Études sur le théâtre français du XIVe au XVIe siècles. Paris, 1906.

Spencer, M. L. Corpus Christi Pageants in England. 1911.

Stopes, C. C. Elizabethan Stage Scenery. Fortnightly Review, June, 1907.

Wallace, C. W. Shakspere and the Blackfriars. Century Magazine, Sept., 1910.

Wegener, R. Die Bühneneinrichtung des Shakespeareschen Theaters nach der zeitgenössischen Dramen. Halle, 1907.

CHAPTERS VI AND VII

THE COURT THEATER IN THE REIGN OF ELIZABETH. IN THE REIGNS
OF JAMES I AND CHARLES I

There is incidental discussion of the Court Theater in many of the books referred to in the bibliographies for earlier chapters. Malone, *Variorum*, Collier, *H. E. D. P*, Fleay, *Stage*, Chambers, Feuillerat, *Revels Accounts*, and Wallace, *Evolution*, are important. Documents are supplied in all of these books and in the Calendars of State Papers for the various reigns.

There is no good account of the court theater in the reign of Elizabeth, and Chapter VI is virtually the first effort at a systematic survey of the relations between the court and public theaters of this period.

For the performances of the Court Masques in the reigns of James I and Charles I, Brotanek and Reyher are the main authorities. To Reyher, in particular, I am much indebted. The influence of the classical theater on the modern, and the development of moving scenes, are topics deserving more detailed investigation than has yet been given to them.

The following list includes documents, volumes, and articles especially concerned with court performances.

Baker, G. P., ed. Endymion by John Lyly, with Introduction. Boston, 1894.

Boas, F. S. University Drama in the Tudor Age. Oxford, 1914.

Bond, R. W. The Complete Works of John Lyly. 3 vols. Oxford, 1902.

Blomfield, R. T. Inigo Jones. Portfolio, 1889.

Brotanek, R. Die Englischen Maskenspiele. Vienna and Leipzig, 1902.

Chamberlain, John. Letters written by J. C. Camden Soc. 1861.

Chambers, E. K. Notes on the History of the Revels Office under the Tudors. 1906.

Cunningham, P. Extracts from the Accounts of the Revels at Court. Shaks. Soc. Publ., 1842.

Durand, W. Y. Notes on Richard Edwards. Journal Germ. Phil. IV. 3, 1902.

—— Palæmon and Arcyte, Progne, Marcus Geminus, and the Theatre in which they were acted, as described by John Bereblock, (1596). Publ. Mod. Lang. Assn., 1905.

Evans, H. A. English Masques. Warwick Library. 1897.

Fairholt, F. W. History of Lord Mayor's Pageants. Percy Soc. Publ., 1843.

Feuillerat, A. *Revels Accounts.* See Bibliography, Chap. I.

—— Le Bureau des Menus-Plaisirs (office of the Revels) et la Mise en Scène à la cour d'Elizabeth. Louvain, 1910.

Graves, T. S. The Court and the London Theatres during the Reign of Elizabeth. Menasha, Wis., 1913.

Greg, W. W. Pastoral Poetry and Pastoral Drama. 1906.

Helmholtz-Phelan, A. A. The Staging of the Court Drama to 1595. Publ. Mod. Lang. Ass'n, 1909.

Kempe, A. J. The Loseley Manuscripts. 1835.

Laneham, R., Robert Laneham's Letter; Describing a part of the entertainment unto Queen Elizabeth at the Castle of Kenilworth in 1875. Ed. F. J. Furnivall, 1907.

Lanson, G. Note sur un Passage de Vitruve. Revue de la Renaissance, v. 72. 1904.

Marks, Jeanette. English Pastoral Drama. 1908.

Marsan, J. La Pastorale Dramatique en France, etc. Paris, 1905.

Maas, H. Die Kindertruppen. Göttingen, 1901.

Matthews, B. Evolution of Scene Painting. Scribner's Magazine, July, 1913.

Nicholls, J. The Progresses and Public Processions of Queen Elizabeth. New ed., 4 vols. 1823.

—— The Progresses, Processions, and Magnificent Festivities of King James the First. 4 vols. 1828.

Rimbault, E. F., ed. The Old Cheque Book of the Chapel Royal. Camden Soc. 1872.

Reyher, P. Les Masques Anglais — Étude sur les Ballets et la vie du cour en Angleterre. Paris, 1909. With full bibliography.

Sabbatini, N. Practica di fabricar Scene e Machine ne' Teatri. Ravenna, 1638.

Schelling, F. E. The Queen's Progress. 1904.

Small, R. A. The Stage-Quarrel between Ben Jonson and the So-called Poetasters. Breslau, 1899.

Soergel, A. Die Englischen Maskenspiele. Halle, 1882.

Stopes, C. C.   William Hunnis.   Jahrbuch, xxvii. 200.

—— William Hunnis and the Revels of the Chapel Royal. Materialien. 1910.

Sullivan, Mary.   Court Masques of James I.   1913.

Wallace, C. W.   Evolution of the English Drama up to Shakespeare.   Berlin, 1912.

—— The Children of the Chapel at Blackfriars.   1597–1603. Lincoln, Neb., 1908.

Winwood's Memorials.   Memorials of Affairs of State . . . from the Original Papers of Sir Ralph Winwood. 3 vols. 1725.

CHAPTER VIII

GOVERNMENTAL REGULATION

This chapter has been based largely on Dean Gildersleeve's *Government Regulation of the Elizabethan Drama*, and often follows it closely. The bibliography in that volume is ample. The collection of documents cited as Dasent, Brewer, Remembrancia, have been noted in the bibliography to Chapter I. When possible, references have been given to the reprints of documents in the *Malone Society Collections*, rather than to earlier publications. Murray, *Dramatic Companies*, Wallace, in various volumes of the *University of Nebraska Studies*, and E. K. Chambers have published documents and information since Dean Gildersleeve's volume appeared.

The subject of the Puritan opposition to the theater, touched on in this chapter, is treated from another point of view by E. N. S. Thompson, *Controversy between the Puritans and the Stage*. A full bibliography is supplied in the Cambridge History of English Literature, VI. xii.

CHAPTERS IX, X, XI

THE DRAMATIC COMPANIES.   THE LEADING COMPANIES IN THE REIGN OF ELIZABETH.   IN THE REIGNS OF JAMES I AND CHARLES I

The earlier authorities, Malone, *Variorum*, Chalmers, *Apology*, and Collier, *H. E. D. P.*, must be consulted for documents and other evidence although they have been mainly superseded. Fleay's *Stage* is still useful. Murray has corrected some of Fleay's errors, retained others, and added very valuable lists of provincial performances. Murray, *Dramatic Companies*, and Greg, *H. D.*, *vol. ii*, are now the main authorities but they require frequent correction in the light of more recent information. Chambers' papers in the Modern Language Review, and the documents of the various lawsuits published by Wallace and others, as listed below, are very important.

A satisfactory history of the companies is yet to be written, and may perhaps wait for the discovery of additional documents. In these chapters I have attempted only a brief outline, but I believe that it takes account of all the information now available.

LAWSUITS CONCERNING BLACKFRIARS. Fleay, *Stage*, 127–132; 210–251 : Clifton *v.* Robinson, Evans, et al., 1601. Evans *v.* Kirkham, 1612. Kirkham *v.* Painton, 1612. Wallace, *Univ. of Nebraska Studies*, 1910: Keysar *v.* Hemings, Condell, et al., 1608. Halliwell-Phillipps, *Outlines*, I. 312–9. Blackfriars Share Papers, 1635. This lawsuit also deals with the Globe.

LAWSUITS CONCERNING THE GLOBE. Wallace, *London Times*, Oct. 2, 4, 1909 (reprinted privately) : Mrs. Osteler *v.* Heminges (her father), 1614. *Century Magazine*, August, 1910: Witter *v.* Hemings and Condell, 1619. *Shakespeare Jahrbuch*, 1910: Hemings *v.* Taylor, 1610. See also documents in articles in the *London Times*, April 30, May 1, 1914.

LAWSUITS CONCERNING OTHER THEATERS. Wallace, *Univ. of Nebraska Studies*, 1913; *The First London Theater:* records of various lawsuits about the Theater in most of which James Burbage was a party. Some of these records are printed by Mrs. C. C. Stopes, *Burbage and Shakespeare's Stage*, 1913. Greenstreet, *New. Shaks. Soc. Trans.*, 1887–92 : Androwes *v.* Slater, 1609. (Whitefriars.) Fleay, *Stage*, 194–9, 270–97 : Woodford *v.* Holland, 1613. (Red Bull.) Green and Queen's company, 1623–6. Wallace, *Univ. of Nebraska Studies*, 1909, reprints these documents with some additions, especially of the Smith *v.* Beeston case. Mrs. C. C. Stopes, *Burbage and Shakespeare's Stage*, 1913, and Wallace, *Englische Studien*, 1911, 340–395 : Shaw et al. *v.* Langley, 1597–8. (Swan.)

The following list adds some volumes of importance in special fields, as notably that of foreign tours.

Bolte, J. Englische Komödianten in Dänemark und Scheweden. Shaks. Jahrbuch, 1888.

—— Englische Komödianten in Münster und Ulm. Shaks. Jahrbuch, 1900.

Chambers, E. K. Court Performances before Queen Elizabeth. Mod. Lang. Review, Oct. 1906.

—— Court Performances under James the First. Mod. Lang. Review, Jan., 1909.

Cohn, A. Shakespeare in Germany in the Sixteenth and Seventeenth Centuries. 1865.

—— Englische Komödianten in Köln (1592–1656). Shaks. Jahrbuch, 1886.

Creizenach, W. Schauspiele der englischen Komödianten. Kürschner's Deutsche National-Litt. Band 118. 1889. Most of this material reappears in Herz, q.v.

Harris, C. The English Comedians in Germany before the Thirty Years' War: the Financial Side. Publ. Mod. Lang. Assn. of America, Sept., 1907.

Herz, E. Englische Schauspieler und englisches Schauspiel zur Zeit Shakespeares in Deutschland. Theatergeschichtliche Forschungen. Leipzig, 1903.

Small, R. A. The Stage Quarrel between Ben Jonson and the So-called Poetasters. Breslau, 1899.

Thorndike, A. H. Influence of Beaumont and Fletcher on Shakspere. 1901. See Chap. II.

CHAPTERS XII, XIII, AND XIV

THE DRAMATISTS. ACTORS AND ACTING. THE AUDIENCE

Chapter XII draws on too varied material to permit of a bibliography. Fleay, *Stage* and *Chronicle*, Greg, *H. D.*, and the many biographical and critical accounts of Elizabethan dramatists are useful. Chapter XIII on Actors and Acting deals with a subject on which there is no general work of authority. Collier's *Actors*, Greg's *H. D.*, and the lives of actors in the *Dictionary of National Biography* are useful. Chapter XIV deals with a subject often discussed but on which there is little specific information.

Armin, R. Fools and Jesters: with a reprint of Robert Armin's Nest of Ninnies. Shaks. Soc. Publ. 1842.

Collier, J. P. Memoirs of the Principal Actors in the Plays of Shakespeare. 1846. *Actors*.

—— Memoirs of Edward Alleyn. Founder of Dulwich College. 1841.

—— Alleyn Papers, 1843.

Bolte, J. Die Singspiele der Englischen Komödianten in Deutschland. Hamburg, 1893.

Dekker, T. The Gull's Horn Book, 1609. Repeatedly reprinted.

Freeburg, V. E. Disguise plots in the Elizabethan Drama. 1915.

Fuller, T. The History of the Worthies of England. 1662.

Heywood, T. Dramatic Works. 6 vols. 1874.

Kemp's Nine Daies Wonder: performed in a daunce from London to Norwich. Camden Soc. Publ. 1840. Ed. E. Arber. 1883.

Bradley, A. C. "Shakespeare's Theater and Audience" in Oxford Lectures on Poetry. 1909.

Jusserand, J. J. A Literary History of the English People. 3 vols. 1910. See II, Book 5.

Lee, S. Shakespeare and the Modern Stage. 1906. See essay, Shakespeare and the Elizabethan Playgoer.

Matthews, Brander. Shakespere as a Playwright. 1913. See especially chaps. ix, x, and xvi.

Rothschild, J. A. de. Shakespeare and his Day. 1901.

Stopes, C. C. Burbage and Shakespeare's Stage. 1913.

Tarleton's Jests and News out of Purgatory. Ed. J. O. Halliwell. Shaks. Soc. Publ. 1844.

Warner, G. F. Catalogue of Manuscripts and Muniments of Alleyn's College of God's Gift at Dulwich. 1881.

Wood, A. Athenæ Oxonienses. Ed. P. Bliss. 1725.

Young, W. History of Dulwich College, with a life of the Founder, Edward Alleyn, and an accurate transcript of his Diary, 1617–1622. 2 vols. 1889.

INDEX

The Index is confined to the text, and records the titles of works and the names of companies, playhouses, authors, actors, and other persons of importance in connection with the drama. Names occurring only in lists of plays or actors are not indexed. References of importance are indicated by heavy-faced type.

461

THE following pages contain advertisements of a
few of the Macmillan books on kindred subjects

Master Will of Stratford : A Midwinter Night's Dream

By LOUISE AYRES GARNETT

Boards, 12mo, $0.50

Shakespeare's mother, Queen Elizabeth, Oberon, and Titania appear together on the stage in this charming new play for children. The scene is set in Stratford, on a New Year's Eve, and the story is of the midwinter dream of the boy Shakespeare — a delightful story of elves and enchantment and faeries' tricks and pranks, that ends when Master Will awakes. He remembers only that the faery people told him to seek his destiny in the fireplace — he looks, and finds a pen. The play is in three acts, with prologue and epilogue, and is a conspicuous addition to the interesting field of drama for young people.

What Is Shakespeare ?

By L. A. SHERMAN
Professor of Literature in the University of Nebraska

Standard Library Edition, $0.50. Cloth, 12mo, $1.00

"Emphatically a work without which the library of the Shakespeare student will be incomplete." — *Daily Telegraph*.

Professor Sherman has analyzed the literary construction and stage-craft of the greatest of the plays, to enable the student to realize the actual nature of Shakespeare's dramatic genius. An appendix provides a list of outline questions on the discussion.

An Introduction to Shakespeare

By H. N. MacCRACKEN, Ph.D., F. E. PIERCE, Ph.D., AND W. H. DURHAM, Ph.D.

Cloth, 12mo, $0.90

The book presents what is necessary for the majority of school and college classes as an introduction to the study of Shakespeare's works. The new and revised edition embodies the latest discoveries in the field.

THE MACMILLAN COMPANY

Publishers   64-66 Fifth Avenue   New York

Shakespearean Tragedy   Second Edition

Lectures on Hamlet, Othello, King Lear, and Macbeth

By A. C. BRADLEY, LL.D., Litt.D.

Professor of Poetry in the University of Oxford

Cloth, 8vo, xii+498 pp., $2.50

The Times, London: —

" Nothing has been written for many years that has done so much as these lectures will do to advance the understanding and the appreciation of the greatest things in Shakespeare's greatest plays. . . . One may well doubt whether in the whole field of English literary criticism anything has been written in the last twenty years more luminous, more masterly, more penetrating to the very centre of its subject."

Shakespeare: *A Critical Study*

By GEORGE BRANDES

Author of " Main Currents of Nineteenth Century Literature," etc.

Cloth, 8vo, 690 pp. and index, $2.60

The Athenæum, London: —

" On these volumes as a whole we can bestow hearty praise and commendation. No other single work on Shakespeare includes so much, and so much that is valuable. Dr. Brandes is a good, a first-rate ' all-round man.' There is no side of his subject which he neglects. He is both an antiquary and a critic, interested in the smallest details of biography, and also taking broad and comprehensive views of Shakespeare's thought and style. His book is in its way encyclopædic, and we venture to say that there are few people — few scholars — who would not find themselves the better informed and the wiser for its perusal. He has equipped himself for his task by wide study and research; and on all the materials he has amassed he has brought to bear a judgment well balanced and vigorous, and a mind liberal and independent. It is many years since there has been any contribution to Shakespearean literature of such importance as this. These two volumes are of solid worth, and deserve a place in every Shakespearean student's library."

THE MACMILLAN COMPANY

Publishers   64-66 Fifth Avenue   New York